Tech High - 4:30 -

ECONOMICS

By
IRA B. CROSS, Ph.D.
*Professor of Economics on the Flood Foundation,
University of California*

American Institute of Banking
Section American Bankers Association
22 East 40 Street   New York City

Copyright 1931
by
American Institute of Banking

First Printing, August 1931
Second Printing, August 1932

PREFACE

IN view of the fact that the courses in Economics and Money and Banking bear a certain relationship to each other, it was thought wise, in developing the Institute program, to ask one author to prepare both manuscripts.

Dr. Ira B. Cross of the University of California has taught both Economics and Money and Banking in the university and also in Institute classes. Therefore, he recognizes the difference between the two types of student bodies and the consequent necessity of a different interpretation for each student group. In developing the material for this text in Economics, Dr. Cross has employed a direct and vigorous style. While some economists may differ with him on the matter of interpretation, they will find that the basic facts as presented are in accord with generally accepted principles of economics.

In submitting this manuscript to his reviewers, Dr. Cross wrote, "The manuscript has not been written for the purpose of having the volume used in classes of college or university character. It has been prepared solely for the use of adult students in the American Institute of Banking. Long involved tables of figures and complicated diagrams have been omitted. Every effort has been made to use examples from the banking field in order to make the volume appeal to bankers and to bring the subject home to them as it relates to things with which they come in contact in their everyday business life.

"The volume contains a minimum of economic theorizing and the amount of theory that has been included is necessarily most general in character. The book has been written solely from the standpoint of the clashing of the groups of income receivers. In our economic life of today, as has always been the case, we have various groups that are eager for income in the form of wages, rents, interest, and profits. Throughout the volume, an attempt has been made to analyze the desires and activities of these different groups in such a way as to present to the reader a picture of what actually exists in the economic field.

"I have seen fit to throw aside the old idea of the functional distribution of wealth, involving the distribution of income among what economists have usually designated as the four factors of production—that is, land, labor, capital, and the entrepreneur. I have used another approach which is not found in textbooks, so far as I know; that approach is concerned with the personal distribution of income. The factors of production, as such, do not receive income; income is paid to individuals—both to those who render services and to those who own property.

"I have also seen fit to throw aside the old idea that there are four factors of production; namely, land, labor, capital, and the entrepreneur. It does not seem to me that this old approach is applicable to conditions as they exist in our economic life at the present time.

"The reviewers will undoubtedly notice that there is quite a bit of repetition in the volume. This policy has been followed for a purpose. Merely stating a thing once and expecting a student to remember it, as a rule, brings very unsatisfactory results. Consequently, I have referred to particular ideas time and time again, for the purpose of having these ideas soak into the minds of the students.

"From these comments, it can be seen that every effort has been made to prepare a volume that will appeal to Institute students as being of a practical character, based upon their everyday experiences, and written simply and with the sincere desire of getting the material over to the members of the class."

The Institute is indebted to the following men who have reviewed and criticized the manuscript:

Willard E. Atkins, Chairman of the Department of Economics, New York University, New York, N. Y.
Willis J. Ballinger, Professor of Economics, Goucher College, Baltimore, Maryland
Jesse H. Binford, Assistant Superintendent, Richmond Public Schools, Richmond, Virginia

HAROLD STONIER
National Educational Director

THE CURRICULUM OF THE INSTITUTE

COURSES IN BANK OPERATION

BANKING I: *Bank Organization and Operation*—This course deals with the problems of bank organization and describes the practical operation of the bank as a going concern.

LAW I: *Commercial Law*—This course is designed to familiarize the banker with those principles of business law involved in many of the bank's transactions.

LAW II: *Negotiable Instruments*—So far as the banker is concerned, this is the most important phase of commercial law, and an entire course is given to this one subject. The banker should be thoroughly familiar with the law surrounding the negotiable instruments that he handles from day to day.

COURSES IN BANKING THEORY

Economics—Unfortunately, generations ago some one dubbed economics as the dismal science. Students often approach this subject with a feeling that economics is removed from their daily life in the bank. The Institute has attempted to build this course so that it will not only be interesting but also stimulating to further and deeper thought on the current problems of modern business.

BANKING II: *Money and Banking*—The banker should have a knowledge of the history and theory which help to form the background of many of the present day problems in money, credit, and banking. Foreign banking systems are reviewed and the newer forms of bank organization are studied. The Federal Reserve System is treated to show its action and interaction on our banking structure.

COURSES IN MANAGEMENT

CREDITS I: *Credit Management*—The Institute believes that proper credit management is one of the most essential factors in successful banking. This course surveys the organization, operation, and management of the credit department in its various ramifications.

CREDITS II: *Analyzing Financial Statements*—In recent years the financial statement has assumed great importance in the problem of credit management. For that reason, the Institute has given an entire course to this one subject. Nearly one-half of the course is devoted to an understanding of accounting forms and nomenclature. The second half is designed to give the student a picture of how the financial statement is built and the methods used in analyzing it.

BANKING III: *Bank Management*—In recent years this subject has been emphasized by various banking associations throughout the United States. The course is the last one in our curriculum leading to the Standard Certificate. The Institute believes that after the student has studied the history, organization, and operation of the modern system of banking, he will be in a position to appreciate some of the problems of management discussed in this course.

The above courses lead to the Standard Certificate of the American Institute of Banking. In addition to these courses, the Institute offers special work in the fields of trusts, investments, and commercial banking leading to Special Graduate Certificates.

A Successful Banker is composed of about one-fifth accountant, two-fifths lawyer, three-fifths political economist, and four-fifths gentleman and scholar—total ten-fifths—double size. Any smaller person may be a pawnbroker or a promoter, but not a banker.

—George E. Allen

Contents

CHAPTER	Page
I. METHOD AND SCOPE OF ECONOMICS	13

Wealth Getting and Wealth Using—Sources of Income—Definition of Economics—Wealth—Social Phenomena—Economics Deals with Man—Relation of Economics to Other Subjects—Task of the Economist—Economics as a Social Science—Economics Not an Exact Science—Laboratory Experiments Not Possible—Economics Becoming More Exact—Popular Ideas of Economics—Necessity for Thought—Economists Differ—Inevitability of Change—Divisions of Economics—Consumption—Production—Exchange—Distribution—Government and Its Income—Why Bankers Should Have a Knowledge of Economics—Economics and Citizenship—Suggested Reading

II. CHARACTERISTICS OF PRESENT ECONOMIC SOCIETY 35
Economic Stages—Modified Capitalism—Dominance of the Machine—Collection of Raw Materials—Production for a Market and for a Profit—Increased Area of the Market—Employers versus Employees—Large Scale Production—Standardization—Government in Economic Life—Laissez Faire versus Social Control—Social Rights versus Natural Rights—Private Property—Contracts—Freedom of Competition—Monopoly and Combinations—Cooperation—Private Business Enterprise

III. FUNDAMENTAL CONCEPTS 55
Economic Motives—Goods and Utility Defined—Economic and Free Goods—Human and Non-Human Goods—Personal Services versus Personal Qualities—Consumption Goods and Production Goods—Wealth—Private and Public Wealth—Goodwill—Claim Goods as Wealth—Social Wealth—Wealth versus Income—Sources of Income—Income and Ethical Standards—Gross versus Net Income—Money Income versus Real Income—Expenditures and Personal Income—Wealth and Welfare

IV. CONSUMPTION 69
Exchange—Distribution—Consumption Given Increased Attention—Consumption Defined—Relation of Consumption to Pro-

7

CHAPTER IV—(Continued)   Page

duction—Consumption and Capital—Consumption and Distribution—Factors Affecting Human Wants—Two Characteristics of Human Wants—Law of Diminishing Utility—Kinds of Consumption — Necessities; Comforts; Luxuries — Consumption Standards of Business—Is Extravagant Expenditure Beneficial to Society—Social Waste—Control of Consumption—Family Expenditures at Different Income Levels

V. PRODUCTION 87

Nature of Production—Different Classes of Producers—Roundabout Production—Production for a Market—Physical Product versus Value Product—Factors of Production—Nature—Labor—Capital—Capital and Capital Goods—The Entrepreneur—Source of Capital—Wealth versus Capital—Use of Capital by Individual Proprietorship—Use of Capital by a Partnership—Use of Capital by a Corporation—Kinds of Capital Ownership—Production and Income—Three Factors of Production

VI. FACTORS OF PRODUCTION.. 111

Land—Physical Conditions of the United States—Agricultural Land—Extensive and Intensive Cultivation—Location—Agricultural Resources of the United States—Building Sites—Labor or Labor Power—Nature of Labor—Importance of Labor—Proper Care of Factors of Production—Supply of Labor Power—Birth and Death Rates—Immigration and Emigration—Age—Sex—Productivity of Labor—Standardization—Division of Labor—Factors Affecting Localization of Industry—Raw Materials—Markets—Power—Labor Supply—Momentum of an Early Start—Advantages of Division of Labor—Disadvantages of Division of Labor — Scientific Management — Other Factors Affecting Productivity of Laborers—Social Status of Labor—Mobility of Labor—Conservation of Labor Power—Capital Goods—Definition—Depreciation of Capital Goods—Obsolescence of Capital Goods—Depreciation and Obsolescence of Labor—Factors Affecting Business Returns—Returns on Capital—Law of Diminishing Productivity—Constant Productivity—Application of the Law of Diminishing Productivity—The Effect of Costs on Returns—Enterprises with Diminishing Returns—Enterprises with Increasing Returns—Enterprises with Constant Returns—Importance of Costs to Business Men

VII. MARKETING 149

Importance of the Market—Definition of a Market—Marketing

CHAPTER VII—(Continued)

a Phase of Production—Necessity for Marketing—Domestic Trade—Marketing Agents—The Wholesaler—The Retailer—Education of Retailers—Chain Stores—Advertising—Cooperative Marketing—Produce Markets—Stock Markets—Employment Exchanges—Our Marketing System Is Changing—Foreign Trade—Reasons for Foreign Trade—Content of Foreign Trade—Significance of Our Foreign Trade—Selling Necessitates Buying—Character of Our Foreign Trade—Basic Principle of Foreign Trade—Foreign Trade Policy—Tariffs—Purpose of Import Duties—Specific versus Ad Valorem Duties

VIII. TRANSPORTATION 177

Benefits of Transportation—Importance of Railroads—Brief Historical Sketch—Economic Characteristics of Railways—Railway Rates—Railways and the Shipper—Regulation of Railroads—Transportation Act of 1920—The Future of the Railroads—Water Transportation

IX. FORMS OF BUSINESS ORGANIZATION 193

The Individual Proprietorship—The Partnership—Advantages of the Partnership—Disadvantages of the Partnership—The Corporation—Structure of the Corporation—Stock Ownership—Kinds of Stock—Bonds—Rights of Bondholders—Bonds Supply Capital — Capital versus Capitalization — Overcapitalization—Regulation of Stock Watering—Advantages of the Corporation—Disadvantages of the Corporation—Stock Markets

X. LARGE SCALE PRODUCTION, COMBINATION, AND MONOPOLY 215

Large Scale Production—Two Phases of Big Business—Causes of the Development of Big Business—Disadvantages of Large Scale Production—Limitations on Large Scale Production—Limitation Due to Scarcity of Raw Materials — Limitation Due to Market Conditions—Limitation Due to Human Nature—Cumbersomeness of Big Business—Nature of the Business—Law of Diminishing Productivity—Large Scale Farming—Combination—Large Scale Production and Combination—Causes of Combination—Types of Combinations—Forms of Combination—Informal Associations—Pools—Trustee Trusts—Trustee Trust versus Voting Trust—Holding Companies—Interlocking Directorates—The Single Large Corporation—Advantages of Combination—Disadvantages of Combination—Monopoly—Definition of Monopoly—Classification of Monopolies

CHAPTER		Page
XI.	MONEY, BANKING, AND FOREIGN EXCHANGE	243

Money—Barter—Money Defined—Primitive Money—Superiority of Gold and Silver—Government Control of Money—Paper Money—Functions of Money—Money of the United States—Banking—Evolution of Credit and Credit Institutions—Basis of Credit—Bank Credit—Kinds of Banks—Foreign Exchange—Banks Aid in Financing Foreign Trade

XII.	DISTRIBUTION OF WEALTH	257

Distribution in Terms of Money—What Income Is—Income Classes—Chance Gains—Functional Distribution versus Personal Distribution of Wealth—Distribution of Wealth versus Distribution of Income—Distribution of Wealth in the United States—Income of the People of the United States—Poverty—Suggested Methods of Obtaining More Equal Division

XIII.	DIVISION OF INCOME	277

Contestants for Income—Classes of Income—Marginal Productivity Theory—Objections to the Marginal Productivity Theory—Why Distributive Shares Are Paid—How Distributive Shares Can Be Paid—Influences Affecting Distributive Shares

XIV.	WAGES	289

Classes of Laborers—Rates of Wages versus Wages Received—Money Wage versus Real Wage—Wage Theories—Subsistence Theory—Iron Law of Wages—Malthusian Theory of Population—Objections to the Malthusian Theory—Wages Fund Theory—Marginal Productivity Theory—Standard of Living Theory—Bargaining Theory of Wages—Demand for Labor—Supply of Labor—Bargaining and the Rate of Wages—Basis of Bargaining—Customary and Legal Rates of Wages—Salaries versus Wages—Effect of Certain Conditions on Wages—Bargaining Power and Fees—High Wages in the United States

XV.	LABOR PROBLEMS	311

Justification of Unions—Types of Unions—Affiliations of Organized Labor—Demands of Organized Labor—Wages—Hours—The Closed Union Shop—Restriction of Output—Methods of Enforcing Demands—Strikes—Boycott—Picketing—Union Label—Employers' Associations—Yellow Dog Contracts—Blacklist and Lockout—Industrial Peace—Conciliation—Arbitration—Compulsory Investigations—Railroad Labor Board

CONTENTS

CHAPTER XV—(Continued)   Page
—Profit Sharing—Employment Management—Labor Legislation—Factory Acts—Minimum Wage Laws—Workmen's Compensation

XVI. RENT 339
Nature of Rent—Rent versus Interest—Why Rent Is Paid—Justification of Rent—Agricultural Rents—Advantages and Disadvantages of Tenancy—Factors Affecting Agricultural Rent—Urban Rents—Extent of Urban Renters—Other Rentals—Fixation of Rents—Combinations among Rent Receivers—Conclusion

XVII. INTEREST 355
Nature of Interest—Money versus Credit—Interest Rates—Discount versus Loan—Objections to Interest—How Interest Can Be Paid—Why Interest Must Be Paid—Abstinence Theory—Time Preference Theory—Risk Theory—Scarcity Theory—Interest Rates—Productivity and the Interest Rate—Bargaining Theory—Supply of Funds—Demand for Funds

XVIII. PROFITS 373
Gains—How Profits Are Possible—Profits as Compensation for Managerial Ability—Profits as Compensation for Risk Taking—Risk Not a Cause of Profits—Social Approval of Profits and Gains—Profits Not Guaranteed—Who Receive Profits—Profits as a Residual Share—Factors Affecting Profits—Managerial Ability—Chance Gains—The Supply of Business Enterprises—Marginal Firms—Extent of Risk in Business—Gains from Unearned Increment—Regulation of Profits

XIX. BUSINESS CYCLES 399
Capitalism and the Business Cycle—Nature of the Business Cycle—Panics—Seasonal Variations—The Typical Business Cycle—Accident Theories—Weather and the Cycle—Psychology and the Cycle—Politics and the Cycle—Economic Causes of the Business Cycle—Savings and the Cycle—Overproduction and the Cycle—Mitchell's Theory of the Cycle—The Cycle—Conditions during a Depression—Psychological Change—Price Changes—Mistakes Made—Increase in Costs—Labor in Prosperity—Decline in Profits—Panic—Depression—Banking Policy in a Crisis—Value of Depression—Federal Reserve System and Panics—Business Barometers—Future of the Business Cycle—Control of the Business Cycle

CHAPTER

XX. PUBLIC RECEIPTS AND EXPENDITURES.................... 423

Public versus Private Enterprise—The Increase of Public Expenditures—The Expenditures of Cities—Theories of Expenditures for Public Good—Sources of Government Income—Classification of Public Revenues—Gratuitous Revenues—Contractual Revenues—Compulsory Revenues—The Benefit Theory of Taxation—The Ability to Pay Theory—Different Forms of the Taxing Power—The Importance of Taxation as a Source of Revenue—Equality in Taxation—Universality in Taxation—Single Tax versus Multiple Tax—Sources of Federal Revenues—Retention of the Income Tax—Sources of State Revenue—Revenue from Taxes—Revenue from Sources Other than Taxes—Exemptions under the General Property Tax—The Method of Apportionment—The Defects of the Property Tax—State Inheritance Taxes—Corporation Taxes—Franchise Taxes—Incorporation Fee—Taxation of the Right to Exist—Taxation of Public Utilities—Tax on Gross Earnings—Tax on Net Earnings—Necessary Reforms in Corporation Taxes—Taxation of Banks—Taxation of Insurance Companies—Taxes on Motors—Sources of Municipal Revenues—Municipal Revenues

XXI. VALUE AND PRICE.. 467

Price Economy—Problem of Prices—Demand and Supply—The Market—Scarcity and Prices—Factors Affecting Demand—Law of Diminishing Utility—Supply—Fixation of Price—Value versus Price—Intrinsic Value—Effect of Price on Demand—Inelastic and Elastic Demand—Effect of Price on Supply—Price of Land—Price and Cost of Production—Rent and Prices—Prices and Wages, Rent, and Interest—Joint Costs—Customary Prices—Public Authority—Monopoly Prices—Summary and Conclusions on Price Determination—Class Price—The General Price Level—Quantity Theory of Money—Supply of Dollars—Demand for Dollars—Application of the Quantity Theory

XXII. SUGGESTED METHODS OF REFORM........................ 509

Groups Advocating a Change—Social Reformers—Radicals—The Indictment of Capitalism—Groups of Radicals—Utopian Socialists—Christian Socialists—Fabian Socialists—State Socialists—Guild Socialists—Scientific or Marxian Socialists—Characteristics of a Socialist State—Socialist Methods of Obtaining Possession—Single Taxers—Anarchists—Syndicalists—Communists—Objections Offered to Radical Programs—Strength of Capitalism—Efficiency and Radical Programs

ECONOMICS

CHAPTER I

Method and Scope of Economics

PRACTICALLY all of us lead a very busy life. As bankers, we get up in the morning when the alarm clock rattles us out of our sleep, take a bath, dress, comb our hair, and hurry down to breakfast. When we have finished gulping down the last swallow of coffee, we dash for a street car, auto bus, or train, which carries us to our work at the bank. At noon we take a half hour or an hour for lunch at the cafeteria, automat, or restaurant and then go back for more hours at the bank. On our way home after quitting time, we stop to buy food, clothing, or other needed articles. After dinner, we have a game of bridge, drop into a movie or a theatre, or attend a class at the American Institute of Banking—then home and to bed. On Saturday afternoon, we may have a date with the doctor, lawyer, or dentist. When Sunday comes, we go to church, play golf, visit friends, or go fishing or for a drive in the country.

Wealth Getting and Wealth Using—In connection with these and other activities of our daily life, the things that concern us most are the necessity of getting the wherewithal to obtain the things that we desire for the purpose of satisfying our wants and the means that we employ in doing so. In other words, we are interested in wealth getting and wealth using, or, as we might say, in getting and in spending. Of course, a few things are given to us free of charge, but for the most part we have to pay for what we get, by means of money, credit, or barter or by rendering services to others.

We have to pay for the food that we eat, the clothes that we wear, the water in which we bathe, the towel, soap, comb, and razor that help us make our morning toilet, the chewing gum, lipstick, and face powder that we use, and so on through a long list of those things of a personal character which play a part in our daily life. The street car, auto bus, and railroad companies will not carry us unless we pay our fares. The church asks for subscriptions and contributions with which to meet the payments on its building, to provide a salary for its clergyman, and to care for its other activities. Our fishing and golfing outfits cost money. Automobiles have to be paid for and supplied with gas, oil, and tires. Our driver's license costs us more dollars, and so do the services of the doctor, lawyer, and dentist, as well as those of policemen, judges, and other officials of the government. Rent for our lodgings, interest on money borrowed, taxes to support schools, parks, highways, and county hospitals—all have to be paid by you and by me.

Sources of Income—Of equal importance is the problem of obtaining the means with which we pay for the things that we desire. For those of us who are members of the American Institute of Banking, the wages which we receive from the bank usually constitute our only source of income. A few of us may have stocks, bonds, mortgages, houses, and farms which yield additional returns. Some of us live at home and do not have to pay for board and room, and possibly not for clothing; but these things have to be paid for by our parents, who, in order to pay for them, must have an income from some source.

The farmer owns or rents land on which he raises various crops and cattle to be sold for the purpose of obtaining funds with which to pay for what he purchases. The shop keeper rents a store, buys supplies, advertises, hires clerks, and sells goods in order to obtain an income. The owner of stocks, bonds, land, and houses derives his income therefrom. The widow may receive the returns from a life insurance policy paid for by her deceased husband. The railroad charges for carrying freight and passengers, the telegraph company for sending messages, the electric company for the light and power which it supplies to the community, and the factory for its products. The national, state, county, or city government derives its income largely from taxes, out of which it pays for buildings, roads, schools, supplies, and the salaries of its employees.

Definition of Economics—It should be evident, therefore, that our life today is concerned primarily with the tasks of getting wealth and of using that wealth for the purpose of satisfying our wants. This, in short, constitutes the field of human activities with which the subject of economics is concerned. A more formal definition would be that economics deals with *those social phenomena which arise out of the wealth getting and wealth using activities of man.*

Wealth—What is wealth? and what are social phenomena? For present purposes it will be sufficient to define wealth as consisting of those things for which we are willing to give something in order to obtain them. This matter will be discussed at greater length in later pages.

Social Phenomena—The term "social phenomena" relates to those matters which affect the interests of society as well as those of the individual. If, as an amateur gardener, I spend my spare hours in raising flowers for my living room table, society is not concerned with how or when I plant my seed, what I plant, or how many days a year I work in my garden. It is, however, interested when I purchase seed, fertilizer, and tools or when the value of my land is increased by the beauty of my garden. When my activities affect others, they then become social in character, and when they affect others in a pecuniary or dollars and cents manner, they become of economic significance.

Economics Deals with Man—The science of economics deals with man. It is not concerned with whether fish swim or fly, whether bees have a king or a queen, or whether wild ducks are black or brown.

But if men go out to sea to fish in order to make a living, or if bees are kept by a farmer so as to enable him to sell us a jar of honey for our pantry shelves, or if wild ducks eat the rice that the farmer has planted and upon which he depends for a part of his income, such matters are of importance to the student of economics, because they affect man's wealth getting and wealth using activities. The horse that grazes wild on the range or the lion that roams the African jungle is of no concern to those who are studying economics. But if the horse is kept in a barn and if the lion is fed by its keeper in a Hollywood movie studio, then the cost of the food, the value of the barn and of the lion's cage, the wages of the keeper, and all such matters lie within the realm of our study, because they affect in a number of different ways man's wealth getting and wealth using activities.

Relation of Economics to Other Subjects—There is no field of human activity or thought that is unrelated to the subject of economics. When human beings devote practically all of their waking hours to making a living and to spending what they make, is it too much to expect that their activities in so doing will have a dominating influence in shaping their religious, social, and political institutions, their philosophy, and all other phases of their relationships? In the realm of religion, the student of economics is not concerned with such matters as whether our sacred books have been inspired or whether a belief in the hereafter is justified, but he is interested in ascertaining how economic conditions affect man's religious ideas. Why, for example, before the Civil War, did the churches in the southern states uphold slavery, while those in the northern states roundly condemned it? Such a situation was due to the fact that the economic life of the South was based upon large plantations which required slave labor, while that of the North was based upon small farms and a developing factory industry in connection with which slaves could not be used to advantage.

Political science or the study of government is closely related to economics, but the student of economics does not inquire as to how the President of the United States is chosen, what a city manager does as distinct from a city council, or why a state superintendent of banks is appointed instead of elected. These are questions for the political scientist to answer. What the economist tries to do is to get beneath the surface of things and to ascertain what the economic conditions are that make it possible for us to have a republican form of government instead of a monarchy, a city manager instead of a city council, and a state official who sees to it that the banks obey the law.

Economics and history are also closely related. History deals with the story of man's activities in the past. But of what use is a knowledge of dates of battles, names of kings and queens, and the story of voyages of discovery, unless one understands the economic conditions out of which such things have arisen? Wars have been fought primarily for economic reasons—for new lands, for tribute, for the right to immigrate, for taxation, for control of trade routes, and the like. The reigns of kings and queens can be interpreted only if one is acquainted with the economic and social life of the people. Voyages of discovery, with the exception of the few that have lately been made for the purpose of adding to our scientific knowledge, have been carried on for the purpose of discovering shorter trade routes and of obtaining control of new lands and their natural and human resources.

Economics is also concerned with law, but not because the student of economics wants to find out why a man is sentenced to prison for one year instead of for ten years or why the United States Supreme Court exercises the right to declare laws to be constitutional or unconstitutional. The economist wants to ascertain the reasons for our present laws and also the reasons for their continued modification. He sees in the changing economic life of the people the reason therefor. The building of railroads, the formation of combinations in business, the organization of unions, the growing economic independence of women are but a few of the economic developments that have forced the adoption of new laws or the modification of old ones.

In studying economics, at times one also crosses over into the realm of ethics, which is concerned with our ideas of right and wrong. The economist sets up no moral standards from which to judge economic activities. He does not condemn branch banking as being morally wrong, nor does he favor the protective tariff as being morally right. He inquires as to why our ethical ideals are modified with the passing of time and again finds the reason in our ever changing economic conditions. During medieval times, for example, the taking of interest was condemned by the church as sinful, but today it is generally approved. Business, as it grew in size and importance, demanded capital, and in order to obtain the use of the necessary funds, interest had to be paid, with the result that, in time, the doctrine of the church was accordingly modified to countenance this practice.

Task of the Economist—The task of the economist is really twofold in character. First, he attempts to understand and explain the working of our present complicated system of society, which we call *capitalism*. He wants to see how the economic scheme of things functions in its various parts, not to justify it. In this regard, he is like the physiologist, who studies the human body in order to see how and why it functions, not to justify it in any particular. Second, he is concerned with the desire to make recommendations for the improvement of our economic life, so as to provide more comfort and well-being for the various classes of society. He is not willing to admit that all things which we have today are for our best interests. He may condemn certain economic arrangements as being objectionable or undesirable, but he never classes them as being morally wrong. He may urge the adoption of various economic reforms for the purpose of removing certain defects in our economic scheme of things, so as to increase our economic welfare, but he does not do so on the basis of moral standards. In this regard, he is again like the physiologist, who knows of the harmful effects of liquor and drugs upon the organs of the human body, but who objects to their use not on the grounds of morality but because their consumption interferes with the proper and efficient functioning of the human organs.

Economics as a Social Science—Economics is commonly designated as a social science. As such, it is part of the larger subject of sociology, which concerns itself with the study of all phases of man's relations to other men and includes political science, history, geography, economics, anthropology, and psychology. These subjects are classed as social sciences just as chemistry and physics are classed as physical sciences.

Economics Not an Exact Science—The question has been raised as to whether or not economics should really be called a science. It may be admitted that it is not an exact science, such as physics or chemistry. We know, for example, that if in the physics laboratory we drop a lead ball and a feather in a vacuum, both will fall at the same rate of speed. We know that if in the chemistry laboratory we combine two volumes of hydrogen and one of oxygen, we obtain H_2O, or water. We can always be sure of our results, no matter how many times we conduct the same experiment.

Economics, however, deals with man, and he is a most uncertain creature. We never know just how he is going to react to any particular set of circumstances. If we offer two men who are employed as clerks in a bank at $100 a month a chance to accept positions with another institution in a nearby city at $150 a month, only one of them may accept. Under the same circumstances one man succeeds in business and another fails. One stock speculator makes a fortune, while another working beside him becomes bankrupt. Some bank clerks take the courses offered by the American Institute of Banking to prepare themselves for a better career, but others with the same opportunities do not do so.

Human beings are not like chemical elements or physical quantities. We can never be sure which way "they are going to jump." Consequently, with the subject of economics built around the activities of such an uncertain quantity as man, we have been unable to formulate a large number of laws, such as are found in the natural sciences.

Laboratory Experiments Not Possible—Furthermore, students of economics are handicapped because they cannot carry on economic experiments in a laboratory, as the natural scientist is able to do with the materials of the exact sciences. We cannot, for example, set up a Federal Reserve System or a branch banking system in the laboratory and see how it functions before trying it out on the public. We have to formulate our economic policies most cautiously, throwing various safeguards around them, forecasting possible effects as accurately as we can on the basis of the available data, and investigating the results of similar measures as tried out elsewhere or in the past, and then we have to put them into effect, hoping for their successful functioning but never being sure of the results. Sometimes they succeed and sometimes they fail. The failures are due partly to the uncertainties of the human element, partly to the nature of the policies themselves, and partly to the character of the surrounding economic, political, and religious conditions. The gold standard may work in England but fail in Brazil. Government ownership of railroads may succeed in Germany but fail in the United States. Cooperative marketing may work wonders for the farmers of Denmark yet bring only losses to the farmers of California. In our own field of banking, we know that certain banking practices which work wonderfully well in some banks bring only dismal failure when tried by other banks. It is because of these facts that economics is an interesting but confusing study for beginners, who are accustomed to accept broad and dogmatic generalizations in most fields of thought.

Economics Becoming More Exact—Although economics is not now and never can be made into an exact science, it may nevertheless be called a science. Economists have gathered a vast amount of data relating to various economic phenomena and their causes and results, and from these data they have been able to draw some very definite conclusions. Some of these conclusions have been formulated into laws, such as the law of diminishing utility, the law of diminishing productivity, and Gresham's law, while others are known only as theories, because the conclusions which they represent are not capable of being proved. Economists have gathered information relative to the length of man's life. They know that, as a rule, a certain number of persons out of any given number will die before reaching the age of forty-five and that a still larger number will die before reaching the age of sixty. Upon these data, known as mortality tables, are based our life insurance rates. Other kinds of risks have been studied for the same purpose. Economists also know that an over-issue of unsecured irredeemable paper money will raise prices, upset business, and result in disaster for the country concerned. Many other instances could be cited to show that each year the subject of economics, because of the continued collection and careful analysis of economic information, becomes a more exact science.

Popular Ideas of Economics—One difficulty that the economist has to face is that almost every person has his or her own ideas relative to the functioning of our economic organization and to how our various economic problems should be met and solved. Most of these popular ideas, however, are based upon bias or prejudice, early education or training, parental or employer influence, religious beliefs, insufficient evidence, or "hunches." The people as a whole have not been willing to give attention to the study of economics, because it involves serious and sustained thought. The result is that the economic beliefs of the general public are for the most part out of harmony with facts.

Necessity for Thought—As we study the many things that lie within the realm of economics we may be forced to abandon some of the beliefs which we have held since childhood, but this should not worry us. One of the joys of life should be to learn new things, to get new points of view, to keep our ideas up to date. We should never hesitate to abandon beliefs that are no longer tenable. The student's safest motto, no matter what his field of interest, is, "Question everything." Any belief that cannot stand being challenged, whether it concerns politics, science, religion, economics, or what not, is not worthy of being retained. Not only should we know what we believe, but we should also know why we believe as we do.

Economists Differ—Another matter which makes the study of economics difficult for those who approach it for the first time is the fact that the opinions of the economists differ on many important issues. For example, some advocate a high protective tariff, others urge the adoption of a free trade policy. Some favor branch banking, others oppose it. But this is only what is to be expected, because those who work in any field that is controversial in character are bound to reach conflicting conclusions. In the practical realm of engineering, for example, engineers differ as to the kind of bridge that should be built. Doctors disagree in diagnosing the ailment of a patient. One judge declares the defendant guilty, and upon appeal another judge holds him not guilty.

We must expect differences of opinion in all fields of thought. Human beings are not all made in the same mold and cannot, therefore, look at all matters from the same point of view. Every question has two sides.

No set of economic principles should be accepted or taught dogmatically as being the only right ones in existence. Controversy in any subject is bound to make for the progress of ideas.

Inevitability of Change—The student should also recognize the fact that in many fields of human endeavor there is always the certainty of change. Few things remain fixed. In nature, rivers shift their courses, mountains are worn down by the erosion of wind and water, the ocean shore is built up or torn down by the ever pounding waves. With human beings, our social, political, religious, and economic life is constantly changing. The things that we have today will be gone tomorrow, just as the things of yesterday passed away when they had outlived their usefulness. Those economic ideas and institutions which were suited to the past and which then satisfied the needs of the people were in turn outgrown and replaced by others with which you and I are now acquainted. Consequently, it is not advisable for us to discuss the economic problems of the twentieth century from the point of view of the economist of the eighteenth or the early nineteenth century, who lived and wrote in an entirely different economic environment.

We live surrounded by branch banks, big business, chain stores, radios, automobiles, flying machines, electric appliances, skyscrapers, and other similar indicators of a civilization vastly different from that of the past. Consequently, our economic ideas must be based upon an analysis of our present methods of getting a living and of spending what we make, not upon an analysis of what men did in the past. The fact that an economic policy worked most successfully during the Middle Ages or failed during the eighteenth century is little reason for our concluding that of necessity it must succeed or fail if put into effect at the present time. Changing economic conditions must always be taken into consideration. The fact that many people have no knowledge of history and consequently feel that what we now have has always been and therefore must always remain makes it difficult for many needed economic reforms or changes to be effected.

Divisions of Economics—The subject of economics covers such a vast range of human activities that it is impossible for us to discuss its manifold phases as an entity. We are compelled, therefore, to break it up into various subdivisions so as to enable us to grasp or understand its subject matter more readily. In mathematics, for example, we never study the field as a whole but devote our attention to arithmetic, algebra, geometry, trigonometry, calculus, and so on, while in history we are concerned with ancient history, medieval history, modern history, English history, American history, and other parts of the subject. In studying economics, we have to pursue the same policy.

Consumption—In analyzing the economic activities of society, the first thing that impresses us is the wants or desires of human beings. What do they want? How much do they want? Why do they have certain wants?

How much of their income do they spend for clothing, fuel, light, rent, insurance, personal services, and such things? A study of these matters involves what is technically known as the field of *consumption,* which relates to what people want and how they use commodities, including both tangible and intangible things, as well as personal services to satisfy those wants.

Production—With people wanting things, the next problem is to find ways and means of supplying them with what they want, and that causes us to discuss how goods are made and how personal services are rendered. When goods have been made, they have to be placed on the market. Likewise, individuals such as doctors, dentists, lawyers, and laborers who render personal services have to market their wares; that is, they have to find customers and employers. Therefore, marketing, which includes the practices and principles involved in domestic and foreign trade, transportation, and advertising, has to take place. These economic activities constitute the field of *production,* which deals with the creation and the marketing of goods and personal services for the purpose of satisfying human wants.

Exchange—How are these goods and services paid for? How are they exchanged for other goods? By what means do we buy and sell them? These questions necessitate our dealing with such topics as money, banking, and domestic and foreign exchange, all of which lie in the field of *exchange.* Exchange is really a part of production, as much, in fact, as is marketing, and is so classed by a few economists. Briefly, the reason for such classification is that money, banking, and foreign exchange make our present capitalistic production possible. Without their aid, the business activities of today could not be carried on. They are as necessary to the proper functioning of our present economic life as are machines, buildings, raw materials, and similar things. However, no harm is done if we treat exchange as a separate division of economics, for after all the real reason for classification of any sort is to permit a clear presentation of the subject in order that the reader may see the relationships existing between its various parts.

Distribution—Finally, we have to raise the issue as to what it is that induces people to produce goods and to render personal services. Why do we have farmers, manufacturers, bankers, professional men, laborers, foreign traders, and transporters, all engaged in productive activities of one kind or another? It is, as we have said before, because they are concerned with making a living—with getting an income. But where do they get that income? They get it by selling their goods or their personal services for money or its equivalent. But what are their goods and services worth? What is their value, their price? and what determines their value and price? A price is paid to the farmer for his crops, to the factory owner for his products, to the banker for the money which he lends to borrowers, to the professional man and the laborer for their services, to the railroad owner for carrying passengers and commodities. The products of society, therefore, are divided or distributed among the people as the result of prices that are charged for goods and services. The laborer gets wages, the professional man fees, the banker interest, the owner of a business dividends or profits, the landlord rent, and so on through the list of all those who receive a share of society's products or wealth. A study of these matters involves what is known as *distribution*. Distribution, therefore, deals with the payment of income in one form or another both to those who own property and to those who render personal services. The word distribution as used here should not be confused with the marketing or distribution of merchandise, in which sense it is sometimes employed.

Human beings have always struggled for a larger share of the products of society and have pursued various practices in doing so. Sometimes the measures adopted have taken the form of economic organizations, such as unions among laborers, cooperative marketing associations among farmers, and local and national defensive or aggressive associations among employers, foreign traders, and shop keepers. Sometimes these classes have attempted to attain their ends by engaging in political movements, as, for example, through the organization of labor or farmer parties, through the use of influence upon the party in power to enact desired legislation, and so forth. At times they have stood either for or against the extensive modification of our economic organization as demanded by the proponents of socialism, anarchism, the single tax, and other philosophies. Consequently, in presenting the practices, principles, and theories relating to the field of distribution, it is necessary not only to discuss such matters as value, price, rent, interest, wages, and profits but also to discuss those problems that arise out of the distribution of wealth, such as poverty, organized labor, labor and factory legislation, and the demands of socialists, anarchists, communists, and other radical groups.

Government and Its Income—The various forms of government—local, state, national—are also actively interested in economic matters, as is evidenced by the fact that they do many things for us that satisfy our wants. But where does a government get its income? Sometimes it sells its services or its products for a price, as when it charges for its publications, for railroad accommodations if it happens to own the railroads, for admission to national parks, or for the collection of garbage. Much of its income, however, is obtained by the imposition and collection of taxes. It, too, is as directly concerned with getting its share of society's income as is any professional man, laborer, factory owner, or agriculturist. The manner in which this income is collected and the objects for which it is spent are covered by the subject of taxation and public finance, although logically a discussion of the collection of the income lies in the domain of distribution, and a discussion of the things for which it is spent lies in the field of consumption.

Why Bankers Should Have a Knowledge of Economics—Many members of the American Institute of Banking fail to appreciate the importance of including the subject of economics in the list of courses required for the Institute Standard Certificate. They are eager to study Commercial Law, Negotiable Instruments, Investments, Trust Functions, and similar subjects, because they believe that they can make use of the information thus obtained in connection with their everyday duties at the bank. The subject of economics, however, seems to make a less urgent appeal, because on the surface it appears to possess no practical value so far as the banker is concerned.

Economics is not a bread and butter subject in the same sense as are typing, stenography, and bookkeeping; neither, for that matter, are Commercial Law, Negotiable Instruments, Investments, and Trust Functions. A course in any of the latter subjects may not of itself entitle a student of the American Institute of Banking to a better job in a bank or to a higher salary. All of the required courses contain material that makes it possible for the student to add to his knowledge of the affairs and practices of the banking world, but they are all based upon the economic activities of man. It is, therefore, advisable that the student have a knowledge of that field of human relations which forms the basis of all the courses presented by the American Institute of Banking.

Bankers are daily faced with various economic problems and hence should be acquainted with the material presented by this volume and by others concerned with the principles of economics. Bankers are actively engaged in operating a business. They have to know why it is better for them and for the public to have the bank function as a corporation than as a partnership. They have to employ clerks, and this requires a knowledge of labor problems and wages. They loan money and credit, which necessitates acquaintanceship with interest rates and the forces that affect them. They pay rent and possibly collect rents from those who occupy space in their bank building.

Advice has to be given to customers relative to the establishment of business enterprises and the organization of corporations. Many bankers serve as members of boards of directors of corporations engaged in manufacturing, merchandising, foreign trade, and railroad or airplane transportation, and therefore they should be versed in the economic principles affecting those fields. Plans for developing the economic resources of a district have to be formulated, and in this connection bankers, as members of the local chamber of commerce, have to discuss the advisability of more favorable railroad, telephone, gas, and electric rates.

The nation sometimes suffers from a business depression. Bankers should study its causes, as well as the probable means that should be adopted to bring it to an end. They should be interested in the formulation of sound policies for agricultural relief and also for the proper management of any business. Bankers act as advisers to their clients in connection with investments. The problems of the tariff, mergers, combinations, chain stores, instalment buying, insurance and radicalism are but a few of the many matters of economic significance which must be faced by the members of the banking fraternity.

Economics and Citizenship—Then, too, there is the matter of citizenship. All members of the American Institute of Banking either are now voters or soon will be. Practically all of the political issues upon which American voters are called to express an opinion are economic in character and involve in one manner or another the getting and spending of wealth. In order to vote intelligently, one must understand the economic principles involved in the issues before the public. Furthermore, the training that one gets from a course in economics makes for a better understanding of the information presented by daily newspapers and weekly and monthly magazines.

George E. Allen, formerly educational director of the American Institute of Banking, stressed the importance of economics as a preparatory subject when he said,

> A successful banker is composed of about one-fifth accountant, two-fifths lawyer, three-fifths political economist, and four-fifths gentleman and scholar—total ten-fifths—double size. Any smaller person may be a pawnbroker or a promoter, but not a banker.

Suggested Reading—Economics covers a large number of subjects. This text is only a brief summary of those subjects which are usually considered to be the most important in the field. The student may possibly wish to pursue further the study of some particular economic question. In the hope that this may be true of most of the members of the American Institute of Banking, a short list of books on economic subjects has been included in the manual for Institute instructors.

CHAPTER II

Characteristics of Present Economic Society

IN order to obtain a setting for an analysis of our present economic life, it is necessary to have an appreciation of some of its more outstanding characteristics. As already noted, man's wealth getting and wealth using activities have been continually modified with the passing of time; they have affected and have been affected by his political, social, and religious institutions.

Economic Stages—At first man made his living in simple ways, but with the progress of the centuries, the means which he has adopted have become increasingly complex. In looking over the past, we are able to distinguish several different general methods by means of which man has made his living.

The simplest method of getting a living is by hunting and fishing. A little higher in the scale is the keeping of herds of cattle and flocks of sheep. This method requires pasturage and the domestication and breeding of animals. Agriculture is still a little more advanced, for it necessitates the establishment of a more settled and fixed life for the people, the clearing of land, the collection, saving, and planting of seed, the harvesting of crops, and in time the search for markets, thus bringing about a slight development of commerce. As a result of the growth of population come cities and the increased importance of handicrafts, that is, the making of commodities for a customer by hand or by the use of tools. This stage, also, calls for the stressing of commercial activities, the growth of domestic and foreign trade, and the search for wider markets. In time there arises a demand for more goods, followed by the invention and use of power driven machinery. This last stage characterizes the present era, which is commonly known as the capitalistic or the machine age and dates roughly from the last half of the eighteenth century.

The use of large amounts of funds, or capital, in commerce through the fitting out of huge fleets or caravans and the hiring of many handicraftsmen or employees to work in one plant was not unknown prior to the latter half of the eighteenth century. That fact has caused some writers to claim that capitalism existed several centuries before the introduction of the steam engine and power driven machinery. For our purpose, however, we may continue to use the word capitalism as describing the outstanding characteristic of the present era, in which goods are manufactured primarily by private interests with the aid of hired workers who use machinery, the goods being produced for a market and for a profit. Private ownership and private property and all that those terms imply are the outstanding marks of capitalism—not the use of power driven machinery nor the existence of factories, shipyards, railroads, and the like. If, for example, the tools of production were owned by the public, with articles of consumption still remaining private property, we should have socialism; and if there were no private property at all, we should then have communism.

Modified Capitalism—We must not conclude that we are at present in an era of Simon-pure capitalism, for we have some government ownership, as exemplified by our post office system, navy yards, arsenals, schools, and so forth; and we also have some business enterprises that are cooperatively owned. Moreover, we must not conclude that production is carried on solely by power driven machinery, for we still have some people in the United States who live by hunting and fishing (note our numerous fishing fleets), some by tending herds and flocks (especially in the western and southwestern portions of our country), some by means of agriculture (in 1920 a little more than one-quarter of all persons ten years of age and over and engaged in gainful occupations were classified in the agriculture, forestry, and animal husbandry group), and some by the handicrafts (dentists, cobblers, carpenters, plasterers, and many other craftsmen who use hand tools, either solely or to a considerable extent, in acquiring an income). Nevertheless, capitalistic principles and practices dominate the field, and in discussing human relationships in any connection we are forced to pay most attention to those matters that are of a dominant character.

Man's methods of getting a living are always changing; in the past few centuries they have changed much more rapidly than formerly and will undoubtedly continue to change as the years come and go in endless succession.

Dominance of the Machine—In this volume, we are

not so much concerned with economic history—that is, the story of the wealth getting and wealth using activities of man in the past—as we are with the analysis of our present economic arrangements. As we look about us, we are impressed with two matters of outstanding importance: (1) the dominance of the machine and of the machine industry and (2) the overpowering and all pervasive influence of the idea of getting an income, not in goods but in terms of money. Seldom do we stop to appreciate how both of these factors color every phase of our lives.

In the past, goods were made by hand tools, but today in nearly every possible connection we make use of machinery driven by water, steam, gasoline, oil, or electrical power. So intricate and so wonderful in their workings as to appear to be almost human in their operations, machines enable us to produce goods at greater speed, in larger quantities, with greater accuracy, and much more cheaply than ever before.

Marvelous as our machines are, we are never content to "let well enough alone." Improvements and changes in all phases of our life, economic and otherwise, are continually being made and should continually be made, for a nation that does not advance is bound to retrograde and to pass the palm of leadership on to its more progressive competitors. The ox cart in time gave way to the horse and wagon, the railroad, the automobile, and the airplane. The grinding of wheat by hand was replaced by the use of wind, water, steam, and electrical power. Factories built and equipped today with the most up-to-date apparatus become obsolete in relatively few years through the advances made in productive methods. Wherever we can substitute machinery for hand labor we do so, regardless of whether it does the work of the unskilled laborer or of the skilled craftsman.

Collection of Raw Materials—Success and profit in manufacturing depend on an adequate supply of raw materials, and industrial nations are compelled to search throughout the world for the products of nature with which to keep their machinery busy. Rubber, ore, cotton, wool, lumber, and various other commodities are collected from all parts of the globe by those who live in a machine civilization and are fabricated by them into goods needed to satisfy human wants. The United States has been especially fortunate in its possession of bountiful supplies of raw materials, but with our progress as an industrial or manufacturing nation, we have had to depend to an increasing extent on raw materials imported from less economically advanced countries.

Production for a Market and for a Profit—Another outstanding characteristic of the age in which we live is the production of goods primarily for a market and for a profit or income. The homes of the early American frontiersmen were to a great extent self-sufficing in that these frontiersmen depended but little upon outside sources for the things that they desired. Soap, clothes, harness, farm tools, all were for the most part made in the home for the use of their producer. In the

Middle Ages, there were some handicraftsmen who produced yarn, clothes, and similar commodities for customers but not for the general market as such.

Today, however, very few things are made in the home or for the use of those who produce them. Less and less is being made at the order of the customer. The household industries have been shifted to the factory. Even our bread, jellies, salad dressing, preserved foods, and a long list of similar articles have, as a rule, ceased to be produced in the home. Goods are raised or made for sale in the market, and if possible for a profit. The men who make Lincoln and Cadillac automobiles seldom ride in them; the women who work on Parisian creations in New York dress factories never wear them. We are in a profit making era. Men do not engage in business, financiers do not operate banks, and farmers do not cultivate lands for the sole purpose of enjoying their activities or because they wish to give employment to blue-eyed girls or red-headed boys. They are engaged in productive activities because they hope to make a profit from their ventures.

Increased Area of the Market—Another element in the economic life of the people is the fact that the area of the market has continually expanded. At first markets were purely local, then regional, then national, but in recent years they have become truly international in character. Through trade development, business has reached into every nook and cranny of the earth to find buyers for its goods. Distance is no barrier to trade extension. Machinery enables us to produce so much that we are forced to go in search of foreign markets in order to dispose of our products. Capitalism is no respecter of the customary consumption standards of backward peoples. All must be taught to purchase and to use machine made goods. Improved means of transportation and communication have linked the various parts of the world more and more closely together, until today the markets in the interior of China are closer to us than were the markets of England a century ago.

These matters affect the producers of all nations who compete in the world's markets. The farmer of the United States is concerned with the failure or success of the wheat crop of Argentina, the olive and citrus fruit crops of Italy, the cotton crop of Egypt, and the wool output of Australia. A depression in Germany curtails trade and industry throughout Europe and the United States. The producers of manufactured goods in the United States are interested in the activities of their English, French, and German competitors, in the taxation and tariff measures of other nations, and, in fact, in all phases of the economic life of the world. Bankers are likewise affected by these matters, for it is bankers who supply most of the funds with which the economic activities of mankind are carried on. Today we are actually citizens of the world, concerned with world problems and world conditions, especially with economic conditions; therefore, our economic policies should be shaped accordingly.

Employers versus Employees—Modern industry

gives us a type of labor problem different from that which prevailed in past ages. Our workers are no longer slaves and serfs, but free men, empowered to vote, to hold office, to move about from place to place, to organize unions, and to strike for higher wages, shorter hours, and improved working conditions. In short, they possess the legal right to participate to a certain degree in dictating the policies not only of government but also of modern business. Offsetting them, we have the employers, who also in many cases have their associations, organized for the purpose of combating the demands of the laborers. The machine industry has, therefore, given us our problem of capital versus labor.

Large Scale Production—We have many small stores, mines, and factories, but far more dominant in shaping our economic life is the factor of "big business." The use of machinery has made large scale production advisable and inevitable. Machinery and the buildings to house machinery are costly. Plants must be used to the best advantage so as to yield the greatest return on the invested capital. Large numbers of men must be employed. A slight gain obtained from each of many employees may yield a larger net gain than does a larger return from each of a small number of employees. Many economies that are impossible for small concerns may be effected by big business. These economies are for the most part due to what are known as *division of labor* and *standardization*. Without at present discussing division of labor extensively, for we shall later devote more space to this subject, we may say that industry can be conducted more efficiently if each employee spends his time on one particular set of operations rather than on a large number. This specialization makes not only advisable but really necessary the employment of a large number of men to produce the finished article.

Standardization—Standardization is a practice that is prevalent throughout the business world, but the greater part of the general public is unacquainted with it or with its significance. It serves as a foundation for big business. Standardization merely means the production of a commodity in large quantities, each integral part having the same weight, size, color, and form as all the others of its kind—in short, mass or volume production.

An outstanding example of the practice of standardization arose during the World War in connection with the manufacture of airplanes. Before we entered upon that memorable conflict, the Allies were unable to obtain an adequate supply of airplane engines. Each engine had been built as a unit, the parts of one not fitting another. When we entered the World War in 1917, we designed the liberty motor and had its parts manufactured in various sections of the United States according to accurate specifications. When these parts were brought together at various assembling centers, they fitted together into an engine without the need of grinding or adjustment. They had been accurately made and were interchangeable.

Another example is found in the Burroughs adding

machine. Today, if a part of the adding machine upon which you are working breaks and needs to be repaired, the repair man appears and puts in a new part without having to make it and alter it to fit into the place where it belongs.

Our suits of clothes and our dresses are usually not made for each of us individually by custom tailors and dressmakers respectively, but are produced in lots of thousands and according to standardized measurements, needing at best only a slight amount of tailoring to make them fit our needs. Shoes, hats, automobiles, watches, bolts, nuts, canned goods, and practically all the things that we are accustomed to purchase are likewise standardized. If each of them had to be made to meet our individual requirements, they could not be produced as cheaply or as rapidly as is possible under the methods of standardization, nor should we have big business with its attendant benefits and problems.

Government in Economic Life—Although all of us are voters or prospective voters and although we are alive to the fact that we have various kinds of government (national, state, county, and city), few of us ever stop to appreciate the fact that the government plays an important part in our economic life. It affects in many ways our methods of getting and spending and in turn is affected by them. In the first place, the government maintains order, without which agriculture, manufacturing, banking, and commerce could not satisfactorily function. In order to realize the force of this statement, one merely needs to compare conditions in the United States with those existing in the interior of China or in certain sections of Mexico where organized government at times has completely broken down and where banditry, disorder, and violence sometimes reign supreme.

The government protects us in the possession of property and in the retention of our legal rights; it provides us with highways, with post offices, and with some government owned industries; it promotes health, safety, and education, enacts many laws governing the organization and practice of business, and lays down the general rules of the game, to which we must conform in carrying on our economic activities. In short, it is concerned primarily with those matters that relate to wealth, to wealth getting, and to wealth using.

At times, the government induces the establishment or promotes the success of certain kinds of business enterprises by such means as levying high protective tariff duties, as in the case of the beet sugar and chemical industries; by paying bounties, as in the case of the merchant marine in Japan and Germany; by reducing taxes, as in the case of many cities which adopt that practice for the purpose of inducing industries to locate with them; by building and financing irrigation and reclamation projects; and by other means.

Sometimes the acts of the government tend to hinder the growth of business. For example, a city may pass an ordinance which proves burdensome or detrimental to industry, such as one prohibiting spur railroad tracks on the city streets. A state legislature may enact a law increasing the taxes or imposing costly and annoying regulations upon business. The United States Government may eliminate an industry completely by taxing its products, as in the case of the law of 1912 which taxed the white phosphorus match industry out of existence because of its detrimental effect upon the health of the workers.

Frequently, business men attempt to prevent the enactment of progressive economic legislation, fearing that its effect will be injurious to their pecuniary interests. Usually, but not always, such fears prove to be groundless, and the new conditions which are imposed by such legislation often prove to be beneficial to business men as well as to the general public. Some bankers, for example, opposed the establishment of the Federal Reserve System, but now very few of them would consent to its abandonment. They bitterly fought the enactment of stricter banking requirements, which were necessary if excessive losses to the public were to be prevented. The new banking legislation, however, increased the confidence of the public, protected the conservative and intelligent banker, and in various other ways redounded to the benefit of those who had opposed it.

Laissez Faire versus Social Control—During the latter years of the eighteenth century and down through the first half of the nineteenth century, the ideal which a government was supposed to approximate was that of being merely a policeman, protecting property and persons against acts of violence. The philosophy of the time was based upon the principle of *laissez faire* (let alone), or the non-interference of government with economic activities. During the preceding two or three hundred years, the industries of the more progressive countries of Europe had experienced much intensive regulation by the central governments, through the fixation of prices and wages, the imposition of apprenticeship rules, and the control over domestic and foreign trade. This regulatory scheme of things was known as the mercantile system.

With the invention and adoption of power driven machinery, the establishment of factories, the opening of mines, and the building of canals and railroads—in short, with the growth of the influence of the capitalistic class—there came a reaction against these restrictive regulations. The new owners of industry wished to be free to do as they pleased, to run their establishments as they desired. This changed attitude on the part of the employing class provided the basis for an agitation demanding that the government keep its hands off business. It was claimed that every individual was endowed by nature with certain inalienable rights, among which were life, liberty, and property, and that if every one were free to enjoy those rights, to pursue his own interests without the interference of the government, the results would benefit society as a whole.

In line with this philosophy of individualism, or *laissez faire,* the owners of property were given practically a free hand in its use, with a resultant disregard for the welfare of the great mass of humanity. Unsanitary and unsafe buildings were erected; dangerous machinery was installed; long hours of labor and low wages were the accepted conditions; children and women were employed underground in mines and in unhealthy places; and many other serious abuses prevailed.

In time it became apparent that if the government was to conserve its own interests and those of the great mass of its citizens, it could not afford to continue keeping its hands off business. Consequently, it gradually began to impose restrictions on owners of private property and especially on the employing class. Child labor was prohibited under certain ages and in certain trades. Women were restrained from working long hours or in dangerous and unsanitary occupations. Factories, stores, and other buildings had to be constructed with due regard to the requirements of health and safety. Railroads and public utilities had to charge reasonable rates. Goods had to be properly labeled. Unions of workers were legalized so that they might protect the interests of their members. In some cases wage rates were fixed by law or by government boards. A large number of other similar regulatory measures were put into effect. By thus restricting the rights and privileges of property owners, primarily through the instrumentality of the government, society made it possible for the great mass of the people to enjoy many more of the good things of life than formerly. This is the policy of social control.

Social Rights versus Natural Rights—Out of this new state of affairs developed the philosophy of social rights, which maintains that a person does not possess political, economic, and other rights merely by having been born (that is, from nature) but by virtue of the customs and laws of the society in which he finds himself. Man's rights to life, liberty, and property are therefore social in character. We are permitted to live in a civilized country just so long as we do not commit certain acts which may cause the government to take away our right to live there. If cast up on the shore of an island inhabited by cannibals, we would not be given the right to live, even though by sign language or otherwise we expressed our willingness to behave according to the highest known code of morals. The government gives us our right to own and transfer property, to vote, to hold office, to worship according to the dictates of our conscience, to claim trial by jury. The government also has the power to control or to modify these rights at any time.

We also have certain rights or privileges given us by the group, or groups, with which we associate. As a member of the American Institute of Banking you are entitled to take certain courses of instruction, to work for and to receive the Institute Standard Certificate, to use the club rooms and to participate in other Institute activities. These rights are denied to your associates in the bank who do not belong to our organization. If you are a Mason or a Knight of Columbus, your organization accords you certain privileges which are not granted to non-members. Thus, it should be evident that our rights are social in character and not the gift of nature or a result of the fact that we are born into this life of human beings.

Private Property—The government grants us the right to own, to use, and to transfer property, but only under certain conditions, and those conditions are imposed for the purpose of conserving the general welfare of the people. Because of that fact, the owner of property is not permitted to erect a slaughter house in the residential section of the city, or to throw garbage into his back yard, or to keep cows, horses, pigs, or chickens within the limits of our large centers of population. Certain oil lands are withdrawn from private ownership so as to protect the interests of future citizens. Regulations are placed upon the operations of banks and upon the activities of bankers. When it comes to passing on property to one's heirs, the government again steps in and exercises control. It takes away a portion of the estate of the deceased by means of an inheritance tax and forces a division of the property in accordance with the provisions of the law.

Contracts—With the developing complexities of our economic life, the contract has become increasingly important. In former times, when most business transactions involved only small amounts of money, the contract was of slight significance, for if it was broken, neither party lost to any great degree. Today, however, when millions of dollars are frequently involved in a business transaction, it can readily be seen that the business world depends upon the rigid enforcement of all contracts. Unless such were the case, our economic world could not function properly. Business depends upon the fulfilment of contracts, and here again the government, through its courts and its laws, proves to be of great assistance in our economic life.

Freedom of Competition—During the dominance of the so-called mercantile system, it was customary for the king or queen to grant to favorites monopolies of some lines of trade, such as the sale of playing cards, tobacco, and other articles of consumption, as well as monopolies of trading rights with certain parts of the kingdom. The introduction of machine industry and the accompanying dominance of the philosophy of *laissez faire,* however, caused the pendulum to swing in the opposite direction and to bring in the widespread acceptance of the idea that "competition is the life of trade." Freedom of competition became the ideal of the times. The race belonged to the swift, and the devil was supposed to take the hindmost. It was felt that only by giving all business men an opportunity to compete freely with one another could the interests of society be conserved. The most heartless and what we today would call the most unfair methods of competition were freely indulged in, but the results were soon felt to be unsatisfactory, both by the people and by the business men themselves.

Monopoly and Combinations—In order to save themselves from extinction, those competitors who remained in the field found it advisable to get together in combinations of different sorts. Competition thus killed itself. During the past forty or fifty years, American industry has been significantly concerned with the growth of trusts, holding companies, mergers, and amalgamations, all looking toward the attainment of monopoly.

Not only does the public seemingly accept and approve the ideal of monopoly, to which earlier in the history of capitalism men were bitterly opposed, but even the government at times sanctions it and also makes it possible for monopoly to become a reality. Practically all of our cities have but one street car system, one telephone company, one electric and gas company. State governments, through their boards and commissions, have lately, in a number of cases, prohibited the establishment of competing lines in these public utility fields. The Interstate Commerce Commission and various state railroad commissions have prohibited the building of competing railroad lines. In Germany, before the World War, the government forced certain transatlantic steamship companies to combine and also actively aided in the formation of many monopolies among that country's industries. During the World War, our own National Government combined the express companies into one concern and, at the conclusion of the conflict, permitted that monopoly to be continued as a privately owned business. The progress of branch, group, and chain banking has made for a monopolization of the credit facilities of many communities. Thus, we see that society has again swung back to an era of monopoly in business, which was prominent during the period when the mercantile system prevailed.

Cooperation—Coincident with this growth of combinations has come a widespread adoption of the ideal of cooperation among business men and the consequent abandonment of the old practices of secrecy and cut-throat competition. Conventions are held, magazines are published, luncheon clubs meet, all for the purpose of enabling business leaders to get together and exchange ideas as to how best to carry on their affairs. To a great extent, the cards are now laid on the table. Business men are inclined to disclose to each other their methods of buying, selling, advertising, cost accounting, financing, preventing labor troubles, and similar practices of importance to the trade. This tendency toward cooperation is evidenced among the banking fraternity by the establishment of clearing houses, by the exchange of credit information, by the formation of group, state, and national associations, at meetings of which various banking problems and methods of solving them are most intimately and freely discussed, and so on. Competition is now "above board." The contestants for your dollar and for mine are playing the game under a much higher code of ethics than formerly. True, much still remains to be desired, but the progress that has already been made is most gratifying.

From what has been said, one must not conclude that at present we have no competition among our various business enterprises. Even a casual acquaintance with what is going on in one's own community will be sufficient to show that much competition still remains; but it is a different kind of competition from that which dominated the business world of the past. It now stands upon a much higher ethical plane than formerly. It is carried on in accordance with rules and regulations laid down to a great extent by the government and conforms to the standards adopted by the trade associations to which the competitors belong. Competition as the dominating factor in the business world has passed; cooperation and monopoly have supplanted it to a very marked degree.

Private Business Enterprise—Important as the influence and activities of the government appear to be, we must remember that we are living in an era of private business enterprise. Almost all business is privately owned and is administered by individuals who are concerned with deriving an income therefrom. They willingly assume the risk of making a gain or of taking a loss. They attempt to meet the public's taste, to give the public what it wants, not necessarily what it ideally should have. They invent new processes, try out new policies, and produce new commodities. Some succeed and many fail, frequently in either case through no ability or fault of their own. Sometimes the public, through being financially interested as stockholders and bondholders in corporations concerning which they know nothing or as depositors in banks, suffer heavy losses through business failures. Periods of business depression succeed periods of prosperity and cause much suffering to all classes of society, employer and employee, rich and poor, farmer and industrialist, storekeeper and banker.

CHAPTER III

Fundamental Concepts

PRACTICALLY all of us go through life without knowing or caring very much about why we do the things that constitute our daily activities. We get a job at the bank, usually more or less by accident; some one tells us of an opening or we happen to know some one on the staff who speaks a good word for us to the boss. We receive a certain wage and never question the means by which the bank arrives at its decision to pay us only a certain sum each month. We spend our salary and never inquire of ourselves as to why we spend it for certain things and not for others. With most of us, life is at best a sort of unthinking affair. The real object in studying economics is to raise questions as to the *what* and the *why* of our daily life and to attempt to answer those questions, at least to our individual satisfaction. You may be content with one answer, while I am content only with another. Differences of opinion are bound to arise.

Economic Motives—One of the first questions that we must answer, and in this connection no doubt all of us will be able to agree as to the answer, is: "Why do we engage in various kinds of economic activities?" We work for wages; we loan money at interest; we establish banks, factories, and stores; we dig mines; we engage in agricultural pursuits; we rent buildings and land to others. But why? Is it not in order that we may obtain an income? But why do we want an income? Is it not in order that we may be able to have the means with which to satisfy our wants? The reason why we have certain wants will be discussed in subsequent chapters.

Goods and Utility Defined—The satisfaction of human wants, therefore, is the motive of our economic activities. It matters not whether we desire to satisfy our want for religion, politics, education, fame, art, clothes, food, or what not, an income, large or small, is necessary. Those things that satisfy our wants we call *goods*. They have a want satisfying quality which we call *utility;* they are useful.

Of course, all things are not useful to all people. A coin counting machine is useful to a bank but not to a farmer. A lipstick satisfies the wants of many women but not of men. The services of a doctor are useful to a sick person but not to one who does not require medical attention. We realize, therefore, that the term useful is relative in character, as are so many of the terms that we employ in our daily conversation.

One must also keep in mind the fact that in using the word good or goods to refer to those things that satisfy our wants, we are not concerned with the question of whether or not such goods are beneficial to the user or of whether society approves of their use. Opium is a "good" to a drug addict; so is a jimmy to a burglar, a revolver to an assassin, and a supply of whiskey to a drunkard. All possess utility or want satisfying qualities so far as the respective individual consumers are concerned.

Economic and Free Goods—We are willing to give something for most of the goods that we want—in other words, to pay for them. That is because they exist in too limited a quantity to satisfy completely man's desire for them. We call these goods *economic goods*. But there are a few things, such as air, sunshine, climate, and water in the ocean, which we are not willing to pay for because they exist in a quantity more than sufficient to satisfy all of our wants. We call them *free goods*.

Sometimes, however, we do pay for air, for sunshine, and for other things that ordinarily are free goods, and they then become economic goods. For example, when you go to a moving picture theatre which has to spend a large sum of money yearly on its ventilating plant so as to provide the patrons with fresh air, your admission fee goes in part to pay for the expense involved in getting that air into the theatre. Air, then, becomes an economic good. Sometimes the owner of a building in New York City will pay the owner of an adjoining lot a yearly sum if the latter will agree not to build so as to cut off light and air from the upper floors of the former's building. Free goods thus become economic goods when people are willing to pay for them.

In this connection the question arises as to whether or not an economic good, such as apples, can become a free good through the existence of what is known as an oversupply. At times in many farming communities it does not pay to harvest the apple crop because of the low price being paid for apples. This does not make apples a free good, however, for you and I are still in want of apples. The desire of human beings for apples is not by any means completely satisfied, but the low price which they command in a market makes it unprofitable for the farmer to harvest them. Therefore, they continue to remain an economic good, even though an oversupply exists.

Human and Non-Human Goods—The things that satisfy our wants are composed of (1) those things that are non-human in character and (2) personal services, which are human in character. Typewriters, adding machines, bank buildings, suits of clothes, automobiles, houses, railroads, factories, stocks, bonds, mortgages— all these are examples of *commodities,* or *non-human* things, while the services of bank employees, unskilled and skilled laborers, doctors, lawyers, clergymen, teachers, policemen, and judges and other government officials are examples of *personal services,* or things that are *human* in character.

Personal Services versus Personal Qualities—A pianist may have a worldwide reputation, but it is not his ability to play or his reputation that we pay for when we attend one of his concerts. We cannot buy any of his technique or ability. He satisfies our wants only when he plays for us. It is his personal services, not his personal qualities, for which we pay. Personal qualities, therefore, are not goods, but personal services are goods.

Consumption Goods and Production Goods —

Goods satisfy our wants in two different ways, directly and indirectly. Those that satisfy our wants directly we call *consumption goods;* those that satisfy our wants indirectly we call *production goods.* A slice of bread, a picture, clothing, a cup of coffee, the singing of an opera star, an apartment house, all satisfy our wants immediately or directly and are, therefore, consumption goods. However, when a factory owner buys raw materials, machinery, or the services of laborers, he does so for the purpose of producing goods which will be sold to the public for the satisfaction of its wants. The raw materials, the machinery, and the services of employees are all considered production goods, because they indirectly satisfy the wants of the public through producing goods later to be consumed by it.

Wealth—The question next arises as to whether or not all goods are to be classed as wealth. Such a thing, of course, cannot validly be done. No one would think of classifying a gorgeous sunset, an ocean wave, or the air of a balmy spring day as wealth. It is not possible to sell them; no one can lay claim to them. They are free goods. But what about economic goods? Are they wealth? Yes, for besides having utility, as do both free and economic goods, they are scarce, and somebody has a title or claim to them. The title may rest with an individual, with an impersonal business enterprise, such as a partnership or a corporation, or with a governmental unit, such as a nation, state, or city. They have a monetary value even though they may not be for sale. I may possess an old Roman coin which I do not care to dispose of, yet I class it as part of my wealth, for it may be listed in the coin catalogue as being worth $500. A city hall, the Capitol at Washington, and public roads are also instances of goods that are not for sale, but which we classify as wealth.

Private and Public Wealth—All wealth may be grouped into two classes, *public* and *private*. Public wealth is that which is owned by the various branches of our government and includes our public highways, parks, buildings, war vessels, arsenals, forts, and similar things. Private wealth includes all other economic goods, such as privately owned buildings, business enterprises, farms, steamboats, patents, franchises, automobiles, clothes, stocks, bonds, money, mortgages, bank accounts, and many other things. For example, if I am the owner of a professional baseball team and Babe Ruth has signed a year's contract with me, that contract is part of my wealth. I can sell it to another baseball team manager for a large sum of money. But I can sell only the services of Babe Ruth as a ball player; I cannot sell the man himself as a slave was sold in former days. When slavery flourished, and even today it exists in many places, the slaves constituted part of their owner's wealth. Free persons, however, cannot under any circumstances be classed as private wealth.

Goodwill—Goodwill is another interesting kind of wealth. If I sell my cigar store to you, I will charge not only for the actual value of the stock on hand, the cash register, and the show cases, but also for the trade or *goodwill* which I have built up among the smokers who pass my store. I cannot be sure that they will still stay with you and continue to purchase smoking supplies from you, but I sell that goodwill to you together with my store and its equipment, and I may be able to charge you a large sum for it. I count it as part of my private property. There is much private wealth wrapped up in such trade names as Ivory Soap, Kodak, Piggly Wiggly, and First National.

Claim Goods as Wealth—As the owner of a 5% $5,000 United States Steel Company bond, I hold merely a claim to the payment of the principal of $5,000 and to 5% interest on the funds which I have loaned to that company. My bond is a claim to wealth, as are also stocks, mortgages, promissory notes, commercial paper, and franchises. Claims are intangible things, but they are wealth to the individual who owns them. Economic goods include tangible and intangible goods.

Social Wealth—If we were to make a compilation of the wealth of our country, should we not include all public and all private wealth? Obviously not, for if we should do so, we would have some double counting or duplications in our results. That part of private wealth which consists of all claim goods would have to be eliminated, because these goods merely represent claims to wealth. If we should count the claims to wealth and the wealth itself, we should have duplication. For example, if I borrow $10,000 from your bank, giving it a mortgage on my $50,000 farm as security for the loan, no new wealth is created at the time that the loan is made. I have a $50,000 farm and a $10,000 loan, and your bank has a $10,000 mortgage. Your bank counts the mortgage as part of its wealth, and I count the farm and the funds that I get from the bank as part of my wealth. But when we consider the matter from the standpoint of the nation, no new wealth has been brought into existence. After the loan has been made, the country still has $60,000 of wealth (the $50,000 farm and the $10,000 in money), not $70,000. Therefore, to obtain a correct figure showing how much wealth a country has, it is necessary to deduct from the total of public and private wealth the amount that is represented by all claim goods, such as mortgages, stocks, bonds, promissory notes, and commercial paper.

Wealth versus Income—We have seen that wealth is anything that can be privately or publicly owned. The possession of a large amount of wealth, however, does not of necessity imply that its owner has a large income. I may have $50,000 in money buried in my back yard. I have wealth but no income. You may own a farm valued at $50,000, which yields a much smaller return than it takes to operate it. You are what is called "land poor," since you possess wealth but receive only a small income. A bank may own a magnificent building, furnished with elegant equipment, yet find that its expenses are so large and its income is so small that it is forced to close its doors. On the other hand, a bank executive may receive a salary of $25,000 a year and yet possess no wealth other than his own personal belongings, such as clothes and an automobile. He may live in a hotel and not even own the rugs on the floor. These examples serve to illustrate the importance of using the receipt of income as an economic yardstick, as contrasted with using the ownership of wealth for that purpose.

All wealth yields an income, either monetary or psychological in character. We receive satisfactions or psychic income from the use or possession of all wealth. A cup of coffee which we drink, a dress which we wear, a picture which we have in our home, all satisfy our desires. They give us a psychic income. Yet, on the other hand, they yield us no income in terms of money. A restaurant, however, sells coffee, a store sells dresses, and an artist sells pictures, but in each case for money or in terms of money. You work for $100 a month; I work for my board and room; a money lender receives interest; a landowner or apartment house owner receives rent; the stockholder receives dividends; and the government receives taxes. These are all instances of monetary income, or income in terms of money. *Income, therefore, represents not wealth that is owned privately or publicly, but wealth that is received by private or public parties from others for the use or from the sale of economic goods* (property and personal services). This definition differs somewhat from those which are customarily found in income tax laws and in court decisions relating thereto. In the latter instances the definitions which are given relate to that portion of the income which is subject to taxation, that is, to the taxable income, and not to the total or gross income. In this part of our discussion of economic activities, we are concerned only with total income. In later pages we shall define income for taxation purposes.

Income is usually, though not always, measured in terms of money. When I work for $30 a month and board, if the board is worth $35 a month, my income is really at the rate of $65 a month. If you are hired by a factory and receive a salary of $5,000 a year and, in addition, the free rental of a house which would ordinarily rent for $1,200 a year, both items must be included as parts of your income.

Sources of Income—Income is received from only two sources—from the ownership of property and from the rendering of services to others. If you loan money, if you own a business or a part of it, if you lease a farm, building, or any other tangible property such as an automobile or a dress suit, if you loan stocks and bonds to others (as is commonly done in financial circles), then the income which you receive is derived from the property that you own. On the other hand, if you are a bank employee, a ditch digger, a skilled laborer, the superintendent of a factory, the general manager of a railroad, a member of a state bank commission, the President of the United States, a doctor, a lawyer, a professor, or a clergyman, the income which you receive in the form of wages, salary, or fees is in return for the rendering of services.

The taxes which the government collects from you and from me are exacted in return for the services which it renders to us in maintaining order, in providing fire protection, in guarding us against foreign enemies, in furnishing schools and roads.

Income consists of those payments which are received from others. Thus, when you cook a meal for yourself, or work in your garden, or sweep the floor of your apartment, even though you are performing tasks which you might hire others to do for you, you receive no wages therefor and, consequently, no monetary income. When a farmer raises cotton, he receives no income unless he sells his crop to others. Income is obtained from others because they buy your goods, use your property, or employ your services. Gifts from the living and inheritances from the estates of the dead are not included in income, since they are not received as payments, either for services or for the use of property.

Income and Ethical Standards—No moral standards are employed in deciding whether or not certain payments are to be designated as income. The money received by a bootlegger for his wares, the payments made by gullible citizens to the dispensers of fake medical cures, the sums received by peddlers of opium, cocaine, and morphine are all to be classed as income. Funds obtained by burglars, safe crackers, and pickpockets are not to be so considered, however, for they are not payments for services or for use of property.

Gross versus Net Income—In using the term income, a distinction must be made between *gross income* and *net income*. A bank may be doing a big business, making many loans, discounting much commercial paper, investing skilfully and profitably in bonds, and, as a consequence, obtain a large income. This is what is called a *gross income*. But expenses have to be met. Clerks and executive officers have to be paid salaries, supplies and equipment have to be purchased, the building has to be kept in repair, taxes must be met, and other items of expense must be discharged. That which remains after such expenditures have been made is called *net income,* and out of it dividends are paid and a surplus is accumulated. If expenses are very great as compared with gross income, the bank may have only a small net income resulting from its year's operation, or it may even have to eat into its surplus in order to meet part of its expenses.

The term net income is never used in connection with the receipts of an employee in the sense of payment for services rendered less his expenses. It does not apply to the amount that he saves annually. It is a term applied only to the receipts of a business, such as those of a farm, store, mine, bank, or railroad.

Money Income versus Real Income—A distinction must also be made between *money income* and *real income*. The former term applies to the number of dollars in money or in credit that is received from others; the latter applies to what those dollars will buy. An unmarried bank clerk may be able to care for his needs on $200 a month, but if prices rise to twice what they were before, his real income, or what his salary will buy, is cut in half, and his $200 will buy only what $100 purchased before the rise in prices. This is the reason why, in periods of rising prices, those who work for wages and salaries always demand higher compensation. It is also one of the reasons why rent and interest rates tend to rise at such times.

Expenditures and Personal Income—In connection with the discussion of matters relating to income, we come in contact with an interesting phenomenon which is common to most of humanity, namely, that as our money income increases, we usually increase our expenditures correspondingly. When we are receiving $2,500 a year, we day dream about how happy we would be if we only had $5,000. After we obtain $5,000 a year, we find that it is not enough, because we have increased our expenditures, and hence we long for $10,000. Another matter commonly overlooked is that living costs vary as between communities. A bank executive receiving $3,000 in a small town feels complimented at being offered $6,000 by a New York institution, but, after having accepted the latter position, he finds that $6,000 does not go as far in buying things in New York City as $3,000 did in his home town.

Wealth and Welfare—Although we are interested in studying wealth and income and the host of problems, principles, and practices relating to how they are obtained and used, we must not forget that the most important matter always to be kept in mind in studying economics is man and man's welfare. In the past many ways of obtaining wealth and income have resulted in the enrichment of a few at the expense of many. This state of affairs was true, for example, in the days of slavery and serfdom and in the early years of capitalism. The interests of the common people were overlooked or neglected. A nation might be considered wealthy, even though the mass of its people eked out only a miserable existence.

Today, however, we find the situation greatly changed. It is no longer wealth and the interests of wealth that are dominant in our thought and discussion; it is the importance of conserving the welfare of the general public. Wealth must be so obtained and so used and business of all kinds must be so conducted as to redound to the interests of society as a whole and not to the interests of any particular class of people. It is the public, primarily through the various branches of its government, that sets up the standards which must be followed in most of our wealth getting and in many of our wealth using activities. The ideal sought is that of genuinely good living, comfort, health, and happiness for the greatest number of our citizens. There is much difference of opinion as to the details of that ideal and as to how it should be attained, but much progress has already been made in the direction of its attainment. No one can deny that today all of us enjoy comforts that formerly were the privilege of only the rich and the politically powerful. Long hours of labor, low wages, unsanitary homes, unsatisfactory conditions of employment, ignorance, questionable business practices—these and many other objectionable features of the business world are giving way to higher economic ideals and practices.

CHAPTER IV

Consumption

DURING the countless centuries that preceded the use of power driven machinery, man's most pressing economic problem was that of providing enough goods, especially food, to satisfy his wants. History is replete with stories of ever recurring famines and with tales of the dire poverty of the human race. How to increase production, therefore, was a question of first importance. The invention of machinery and its continued improvement, the use of water, steam, and electric power, and the introduction of new business practices have given to the capitalistic countries a more than adequate supply of manufactured goods. The use of commercial fertilizers and agricultural machinery, the production of new grains, fruits, vegetables, and better breeds of stock, the development of irrigation and reclamation projects, the application of refrigeration processes, the growth in rapid transportation, all have increased the output of our farms to such an extent that agricultural products are sometimes a drug on the market and the farmer is unable to sell his crops at prices sufficiently high to cover his expenses. Today the problem of the producer is not how to produce enough commodities, but how to find consumers for the goods that he manufactures or raises for the market. Mass production demands mass consumption, and because consumption does not keep pace with production, our economic machinery often gets out of order.

Exchange—Coincident with this growth in the productivity of our farms, mines, railroads, and factories came the necessity for better facilities for making exchanges of commodities and services. Consequently, much thought was given to devising new monetary and banking systems and new domestic and foreign exchange practices, so as to meet successfully the changed and changing needs of the business world.

Distribution—To a considerable degree, we have solved the problems arising from production and exchange. Our efforts are now directed primarily toward meeting those problems that arise from distribution, or toward the division of the wealth and income of society. As previously stated, these problems involve questions of wages, interest, rent, profits, riches, poverty, suggested methods of reforming our present economic society so as to bring about a more equitable division of wealth and income, and similar perplexing issues.

Consumption Given Increased Attention—The subject of consumption, which is concerned with man's wants and the manner in which he satisfies them, has been practically neglected by the economists, yet it provides the foundation for man's economic activity. Man works to satisfy his wants. His economic institutions are shaped with that end and with that end only in view.

It was during the years of the World War that economists, who had previously studied and written much on production, exchange, and distribution, began to turn their attention to consumption. Prices were rapidly rising, and wage earners and salaried employees were demanding higher rates of compensation. Questions were then raised as to how high the wages or salaries of employees should be raised, as to how laborers spent their incomes, and as to how much was required to provide them with a comfortable standard of living. Many worth-while investigations were made by the United States Government and by private parties; a number of volumes, pamphlets, and articles were written on the subject; but much still remains to be done before we shall have as wide a knowledge of the field of consumption as we have of production, exchange, and distribution.

Consumption Defined — The term consumption refers to the using up or the destruction of a want satisfying good, as when a boy eats an apple, a stove burns wood, or an automobile uses up oil, gas, and tires. It also relates to the use made of other goods that are not destroyed when used to satisfy human wants, such as pictures that never wear out, houses that depreciate slowly, diamonds that never lose their brilliancy, and heirlooms that become more valuable as they get older.

Relation of Consumption to Production—Consumption is a tremendously important phase of our economic life. It plays a much more significant rôle in our individual and social affairs than is generally recognized. If people want things, those things must be produced in one form or another. On the other hand, the consumer cannot be forced to purchase things that he does not want, unless, of course, he is compelled to do so by law, and even then great difficulty is experienced in making him change his desires. Man wants food, clothing, shelter, amusement, comfort, means of satisfying his aesthetic tastes and religious impulses, transportation, and similar everyday necessities. Man also wants the means of providing or of creating the commodities and services with which these desires can be satisfied. Thus, a desire for food may create bread, while the production of bread, in turn, calls for the manufacture of farm machinery, the cultivation of land, the building of grain elevators, the construction of railroads, the erection of bakeries, the establishment of stores, the use of delivery wagons, the manufacture of twine, paper, and cash registers, and the creation of money and banks.

The demands of consumption, therefore, result in production and to a surprising degree control it. If a sufficient number of people want white bread, it will be produced. If they want high heeled shoes, closed automobiles, short skirts, and lipsticks, producers will always be found ready to supply those wants. Many a firm has become either prosperous or bankrupt because of the changing desires of the consuming public. Miniature golf courses became popular over night and just about as rapidly disappeared from the scene. The public is a fickle customer.

Advertising and high pressure salesmanship are frequently able to turn us from one kind of breakfast food or soap to another, but no amount of advertising can induce us to abandon the automobile for the horse and buggy. Producers may create new kinds of commodities, but they can never be sure that by advertising or by any other means will they be able to induce the customer to purchase them. Consumption, therefore, has a determining influence upon the channels into which producers will throw their capital and efforts.

Consumption and Capital—Consumption ideals also affect production in still another manner. As we shall see later, we would have no capital were it not for the savings that are made by individuals and by business firms. If all individuals and if all firms saved nothing and spent their entire income for goods that were not to be used in producing more goods, our supply of capital would not increase and productive activities would be greatly curtailed.

Consumption and Distribution—Consumption also affects distribution. If a laborer, a money lender, or a land owner has high ideals as to how he wants to live, he will demand higher returns for his labor, his money, and his farm products, respectively; in other words, he will demand more of the wealth or income of society because of that fact. Whether or not he will be able to obtain it is, of course, another matter.

In passing, it is advisable to point out that while we have stressed the importance of consumption, yet all of the four fields of economic activity—consumption, production, exchange, and distribution—mutually affect one another. Many instances of this fact will appear in subsequent pages.

Factors Affecting Human Wants—An interesting matter, which we can touch upon only slightly in this text, is the question of why we have certain wants and why we satisfy them in the manner in which we do. In the first place, there are our fundamental desires, which it will be sufficient merely to list, since they are self-explanatory in character. They consist of our desire to exist (food, shelter, clothing), to escape discomfort, to have a change or variety (that is, to get away from the sameness of things), to live in groups (instinct of the herd), to imitate (follow the leader), to have power and prestige (to keep up with or surpass others), to save for a rainy day or for some future expenditure, to move about (transportation), to satisfy our aesthetic and religious impulses, to have things in the present rather than in the future.

Then, too, our wants to a surprising degree are fixed by custom and tradition. The Frenchman likes his wine; the German, his beer; the Englishman, his mutton and cabbage; the American, a varied diet. Pies are practically unknown to the English. Chewing gum is a late innovation in Europe. Custom may decree formal evening dress for the wealthy at their social functions but not for the working class. These few examples disclose the fact that consumption ideals are standardized on national and class lines rather than on lines of individual choice.

The methods employed in the production and distribution of wealth affect our wants and the manner in which we satisfy them. As man has invented or designed new products and has made outstanding progress in manufacturing them, the application of machine methods of mass production, or standardization, has tended to bring about lower prices and has enabled the people in our more advanced countries to enjoy a greater variety of goods and a greater quantity of them than is the case with less progressive people. Moreover, mass production has standardized the goods consumed and this has promoted a standardization of consuming habits over the entire area of industrial populations. The United States stands as the foremost exponent of machine or mass production. Its people, with their radios, automobiles, washing machines, electric lights, bathtubs, and all the other accompaniments of modern American life, today live as do those of no other nation. High wages have also played their part, for if the worker is paid much, he can buy much. When wages fall, consumption decreases, and the consumption ideals of the workers are accordingly lowered.

Advertising has a significant influence on our wants. It may not be able to persuade me to change my desire for a house to a desire for an automobile. However, it intensifies my desires. Advertising defines my desires in terms of trademarks, packages, color schemes, and slogans and thus tends to subordinate my judgment of the technical qualities of the goods.

Some of the present tendencies in consumption appear to be the development of the habit of eating out in public kitchens and dining rooms and the habit of spending leisure time outside the home in theatre going, joy riding, and golf playing. All of these factors seem to point to the declining importance of the home and the family as a center of consuming behavior and to the increasing commercialization of living. Leisure time activities call increasingly for spending money and take the place of such activities as visiting with neighbors. These changes, of course, increase the pressure to make money.

Two Characteristics of Human Wants—Human wants, no matter how varied, have two outstanding characteristics. First, *human wants are capable of unlimited expansion*. We are never completely satisfied with what we have; we always want more. If we receive a salary of $200 a month, we want $300. If we have last year's model of an automobile, we want this year's model, or possibly a more expensive make of car. More and better food, clothing, shelter, and other want satisfying goods are continually being demanded by every one of us, no matter whether we are ignorant or intelligent, rich or poor, barbaric or civilized. It is well that such is the case, for contentment with what one has does not make for progress.

Second, *our desire for a particular thing at a particular time can be completely satisfied, or satiated*. When the dentist puts a filling in our tooth, our want in that regard is satisfied for the time being, although later we may want him to fill another tooth for us. Our desire for coffee for breakfast may be satisfied with the consumption of two cups, although at lunch and dinner we may again take coffee instead of milk or tea. Possibly ten pieces of candy at one sitting will be sufficient to satisfy our desire for candy at that time, although a few hours later we may desire to have more candy. Thus, our wants for a particular thing at a particular time can be fully met, or satiated.

Law of Diminishing Utility—In connection with a discussion of the satisfaction of wants, we meet with an interesting phenomenon, one of the very few economic laws, known as the law of *diminishing utility*. Stated briefly, it is to the effect that *each want tends to diminish in intensity as it is progressively satisfied*. This law applies both when a person increases his store of want satisfying goods and when he uses up portions of his supply.

For example, if you are a stamp collector and have long wanted to have in your collection a certain rare stamp, the first copy that you obtain means a very great deal to you; you prize it highly. If, perchance, you are able to purchase another, neither of the two copies means quite so much to you as the first did when you had just one copy of your greatly desired stamp. Each successive copy has less want satisfying power, or utility, than its predecessor had. *The utility of a thing is its power to satisfy human wants*. Of course, you value both of the stamps together more than you did the first one that you obtained, but when you have two of them, each is just a little less important in your estimation than was the first one when you obtained it.

To use another illustration of this law of diminishing

utility, let us say that you come to town with only one dollar in your pocket. That one dollar means much to you, because it will have to buy a night's lodging and the next morning's breakfast. But if you have $1,000 in your wallet, what then does one dollar mean to you? Obviously, it means far less than when you had only one dollar.

If we look at consumption from the point of view of using up goods rather than from that of obtaining a supply or store of them, we find that here also the law of diminishing utility applies. For example, if, hot and thirsty after a long walk, you stop at a soda fountain, the first drink of lemonade "hits the spot." It is what you have been wanting during the past hour or so. The second glass of lemonade means a little less, and the third gives an even smaller amount of satisfaction or utility than did either the first or the second glass. Although you have to pay the same amount of money for each glass of lemonade, your desire for glasses of lemonade diminishes in intensity as it becomes progressively satisfied.

The law of diminishing utility applies to all want satisfying goods and under all circumstances, whether we look at the matter from the standpoint of either using up goods or of increasing our store or supply of them. The more we have of any one particular thing, the less we value each unit of our supply. The more we use a want satisfying good at any one time, the less each unit of that good satisfies our desire for it.

Kinds of Consumption—Consumption may be final,

productive, harmful, or destructive in character. Coal burned in a stove for the purpose of heating our living room is an instance of final consumption. When it is burned under a boiler for the purpose of making steam to operate an engine that runs machinery used in manufacturing cloth, bolts, or some other commodity, then we have an example of productive consumption. The use of drugs, intoxicating liquor, and other articles injurious to health or morals is classed as harmful consumption. When a child tears apart a toy to satisfy its wants, or a feeble minded person sets fire to a building for the same reason, such consumption is said to be destructive.

Necessities; Comforts; Luxuries—Human wants may be divided into three classes on the basis of their necessity. Are they concerned with providing (1) the necessities, (2) the comforts, or (3) the luxuries of life? These terms are difficult to define accurately, for what is a necessity to one person may be a luxury to another. An automobile, for example, is a necessity to a doctor and to many middle class and wealthy families, yet it may be an extreme luxury to the family of a coal miner or of a textile factory worker. Therefore, we cannot classify wants for goods on the basis of the goods themselves, but only on the basis of an individual's personal point of view. The time element must also be taken into consideration, as is evident when we remember that many goods which were luxuries to the American frontiersmen one hundred years ago are now considered necessities by all classes of our people.

The term "necessities" may be applied to those goods that a person considers imperative and essential to his plane of living. "Plane of living" is here used to refer to the level at which a person actually lives. The term "standard of living" refers to the level at which a person would like to live.

Luxuries are those goods which satisfy the wants that are less urgent or essential, while comforts lie in between the extremes of luxuries and necessities. They may tend to increase the efficiency of those who enjoy them. Sometimes luxuries also tend to increase efficiency, as is the case with art treasures, travel, and so forth, although frequently luxuries diminish efficiency, as is the case with too rich food and easy living. Luxuries are often considered as involving wasteful or conspicuous expenditure and as yielding returns of far less value or worth than they cost. They also comprise many things that some people are prevented from purchasing because of their high price.

Consumption Standards of Business—Every business is faced with the problem of purchasing only necessities or of indulging in comforts and luxuries. A plain, pine top desk and a straight back chair may suffice for many a business office. An oak desk and a revolving chair may make for comfort, while a carved mahogany desk and a chair to match may represent luxury. In some business offices, however, the mahogany equipment may even be considered a necessity, because to have anything else would prevent the institution from maintaining the proper standing in its field.

Is Extravagant Expenditure Beneficial to Society?
—Extravagant or wasteful expenditure is often justified on the grounds that it puts money into circulation, that it makes trade good, and that it provides employment. For instance, Mrs. Jones gives a fancy dress ball, involving the expenditure of $50,000. The ball room has to be rented, musicians, waiters, and decorators have to be employed, flowers and refreshments have to be purchased. Is such an extravagance beneficial to society? Is it to be sanctioned, while countless thousands are unable to obtain even the necessities of life? Would it not be better that the $50,000 be spent, not for one night's pleasure but for more lasting contributions to the welfare of society? Should it not be spent in opening stores, establishing factories, digging mines, or planting more acreage to farm crops, in connection with which employment might be provided for many people, not merely for the night but for many years thereafter? Should it not be spent in giving employment to people who would produce goods of more permanent character than flowers, music, refreshments, and entertainment?

On the other hand, it is urged that we already have too many stores, factories, mines, and farms, many of which have found it impossible to operate at a profit. It has been estimated that during the period from 1925 to 1930 over 13,000,000 acres of land were withdrawn from cultivation in the United States because of the overproduction of agricultural goods. It is said that American shoe factories are equipped to produce 900,000,000 pairs of shoes a year for a market that can absorb only 300,000,000 pairs. Our coal mines can produce at least 750,000,000 tons a year, but the market can take only two-thirds of that amount. Woolen mills are able to make $1,750,000,000 worth of goods and yet are able to sell but $656,000,000 worth of their products. Our oil refineries have operated to but approximately 76% of their capacity for the past ten years, gas plants to about 66%, the machine tool industry to about 65%, sugar refineries to about 50%, and flour mills to only about 40%. Therefore, it is argued, wherein lies the need for more production with the market already unable to absorb what is being offered to it at present?

Then, too, it is claimed that if musicians, waiters, decorators, gardeners, and caterers are not employed in connection with luxurious parties, they will swell the army of those already searching for work and thus further intensify our unemployment problem. Another matter that is frequently overlooked is that those who receive the $50,000 in turn spend it for necessities, comforts, and luxuries. In time, this money finds its way, at least for the most part, into the banks, where it is or can be loaned out to those who desire to start or to carry on stores, factories, mines, and farming operations.

As can be readily appreciated, the question has many angles, all of which should be taken into consideration before you and I decide whether we should condemn or approve extravagant expenditures. However, there is one result that without question can be condemned, and that is the effect that such extravagant expenditures have on those who are in no position to participate in them and who look upon them merely as the flaunting of the wealth of those who "have" in the faces of those who "have not." So long as poverty and misery persist, such wanton use and display of wealth will continue to arouse bitterness and discontent among the masses.

To many people, luxury represents a waste which adds nothing to the comfort, health, or efficiency of the consumer, but it cannot be denied that at least it does provide satisfaction to those who enjoy it. It supplies the need for a certain psychological something which all of us desire. When a working man buys a kewpie doll at Coney Island (a luxury to him), or when Mrs. Jones, the millionaire's wife, buys a $16,000 automobile (a luxury to her), each gets an immeasurable amount of satisfaction out of having done so.

Social Waste—It cannot be denied that unquestionably there is a large amount of waste in our present economic system. The failure to select the proper foods for the family, the purchase of needless and expensive commodities, the loss in fuel due to poorly designed stoves, and the waste of food in its preparation are but a few instances of waste which affect the operation of the household. The money spent for our large military establishments, harmful drugs, commercialized vice, adulterated foodstuffs, quack medicines and appliances, stock swindling projects, fads of fashion, public graft, and other similar matters represent, so it is estimated by Stuart Chase, the annual expenditure of the labor power of more than 10,000,000 persons. Naturally, this figure is nothing but a guess; yet if it were reduced to a third or a fourth, it would still represent an appalling waste of money and effort.

Control of Consumption—From time immemorial, man has been hampered by social, religious, or legal restrictions in satisfying his wants according to his desires. These restrictions have been and usually are justified as being necessary to protect the health and morals of the people, although sometimes they are also justified on the ground of economic advisability. Savage tribes impose certain regulations upon their members as to what may or may not be eaten, worn, or drunk. Religion also plays its part in regulating consumption, as is shown by the fact that the members of some faiths are forbidden to eat pork, or to read certain books, or to eat meat on Friday. An indirect method of discouraging the use of certain articles is to levy an import duty or an internal revenue tax upon them so as to make them more expensive or to prevent their production or use. The latter method is exemplified by the federal tax of two cents a hundred levied by the United States Government on matches made with white phosphorus and by the federal tax of 10% imposed in 1866 upon state bank note issues. The laws proved to be most effective in prohibiting the production of white phosphorus matches and the use of state bank notes.

At times governments have resorted to the enactment of sumptuary laws for the purpose of restricting or controlling consumption practices. Laws directed against gambling, against the sale and use of habit-forming drugs, against the sale of obscene or radical literature, of wild fish, wild fowl, and the meat of wild game, against the manufacture and sale of intoxicating liquors (as in the United States under the Eighteenth Amendment to the Constitution), laws providing for the censorship of moving pictures, laws regulating the length and character of bathing suits, laws fixing or determining the specifications of buildings—all are evidences of sumptuary legislation.

At times, sumptuary legislation is of an affirmative rather than of a negative character, compelling rather than prohibiting the consumption of certain commodities. In the fourteenth century, England prescribed the various kinds of clothing that the different classes should wear. To build up its merchant marine and to encourage the growth of the fishing fleet, England passed a law in 1549 requiring that the people should eat fish on Saturday, the Ember days, Vigils, and during Lent, as well as on Friday.

Family Expenditures at Different Income Levels—Studies that have been made of family expenditures disclose some interesting facts. As a family doubles its income, it does not double the amounts spent for food, clothing, rent, and so forth. Universally, as income increases, the percentage of outlay for sundries (those things which are not necessities) increases greatly, and as a rule the percentage of outlay for food decreases. In other words, if a family with a small income is spending 40% of it for food and 20% for sundries, then as the amount of the family income is doubled, it will possibly spend 30% of the larger income for sundries and possibly 30% for food. After the family has the larger income, it will, of course, spend more dollars for food than it did when it had the smaller income, but it will not spend a proportionally greater sum (a higher percentage) for food than before. In the United States, investigations have shown that for families with incomes under $2,500 a year the percentage outlay for food increases with an increase in income and the percentage outlay for rent decreases. From the available but insufficient data based upon families having an income of more than $5,000 a year, the reverse appears to be the case.

Government Aids in Consumption—In discussing the subject of consumption, we must not overlook the fact that our local, state, and national governments also spend considerable sums of money annually to care for their needs. With the passing of time, they have greatly extended their operations and now reach out to do things for us that formerly were not deemed to be within the scope of their functions. The money collected by taxation and by other means is spent on parks, schools, highways, insane asylums, prisons, the police department, courts, regulatory commissions, agricultural research and relief, development of domestic and foreign markets, and many other things that affect our consumption standards in one manner or another. Although a discussion of these matters logically falls in the field of consumption, we shall nevertheless postpone our treatment of them to Chapter XX, which deals with the subject of Public Receipts and Expenditures.

CHAPTER V

Production

ALL of the wants of man, except those for rain, sunshine, air, and other forms of free goods, can be satisfied only by means of productive activity. A discussion of production, therefore, logically follows that of consumption, for we are interested in learning how man goes about obtaining or creating those things that he uses to satisfy his wants.

Nature of Production—We have seen that anything that satisfies a human want has utility. Free goods, such as air and sunshine, have utility, as also do economic goods, which, as already noted, include both personal services and property. Man's wants, therefore, are satisfied by things that possess utility, and it is such things that he is interested in producing.

Man cannot create raw materials, such as wood, ore, water, and land. These things are produced only by nature. All that man can do is to take nature's resources, mold or shape them into the form that is desired, at the time when they are desired, and put them in the place where they are desired. Consequently, he is concerned with the creation of what we call *form utility, time utility,* and *place utility.* To satisfy wants, all goods must possess these three kinds of utility. Bathing suits at the North Pole have no utility to the Eskimos, nor do furs have any utility to the native tribes at the equator. However, wheat raised by the farmer is in the form desired and is raised because there is a demand for it at the time when and in the place where it is raised. The Ford Motor Company takes metal, cloth, glass, wood, and rubber and fashions them into an automobile, which it sells in the market at the time when and in the place where it is desired. However, an automobile would have neither form, time, nor place utility in the territory of the headwaters of the Amazon, for it would be of no use to the inhabitants of that region.

Different Classes of Producers—Many persons fail to see that producers, such as farmers, machinists, blacksmiths, and so forth, who are concerned with the production of concrete, physical goods, are not the only creative group. The rendering of personal services by the doctor, the lawyer, the dentist, the teacher, the policeman, and the President of the United States is equally productive in character. As is true in the case of concrete, physical goods, personal services must possess form, time, and place utility. They must be in the form desired and must be available at the time when and in the place where desired. You and I have no need for the services of an Indian medicine man, yet those services possess utility to the Indian tribesmen. The lawyer sits in his office and gives advice when people ask for it in the form of a written or an oral statement. The manager of a factory gives orders to his subordinates at the time when and in the place where they are needed in carrying on the operations of the plant.

Many individuals fail to consider storekeepers, advertisers, railroads, and steamship companies as being engaged in productive activity, because they do not create the form of things that man wants. However, any one who satisfies human wants by creating form, time, or place utilities is a producer. The storekeeper has his goods on hand in the place where and at the time when you want them. The advertiser aids in creating a demand for a commodity or service which, if we had no advertising, might not be produced. He aids in its marketing by giving it time and place utility. Railroads and steamboats likewise are busy bringing things to us when we want them and putting them in places where we want them. A banker renders services by providing the public with funds in the form and in the place and at the time desired. Similarly, the actor, the poet, and the musician are producers of things that satisfy our wants. It matters not how depraved our wants may be, whether they call for drugs, obscene literature, bootleg whiskey, or other objectionable commodities, any person engaged in satisfying those wants is a producer.

Roundabout Production — Production today is greatly changed from what it was in the past. The frontiersmen of our country were accustomed to produce things for the direct satisfaction of their wants. They raised sheep, clipped the wool, carded and spun it into yarn, made it into cloth, and fashioned their own clothing. Cattle were raised to supply the home with milk, meat, and leather. Today, however, sheep are raised in the western sections of the United States, and the wool is clipped and sent east where it is made into cloth and clothing. The latter is then sent to all parts of the country, and the sheep raiser buys his suits of clothes from the local store. For example, cattle are raised in Texas and sold to a Chicago packing house. The hides are tanned and sold to a shoe factory in Massachusetts. A rancher in Texas may perchance purchase from his local store a pair of shoes made from the hides of the cattle that he raised.

Although it can be seen that this is a roundabout process of producing goods, it appears even more so when we consider the many intervening steps that are necessary before the final product comes into existence. There are, for example, the machines and the plants that are required to build machines; the mines that supply the ore and the forests that provide the lumber used in making the machines; the railroads and the steamships required to transport the goods; the telegraph, telephone, and mail service that carry the messages; the advertisers, wholesalers, jobbers, and retailers who place the goods on the market; and so on through a long list of similar requirements, made necessary by our present roundabout system of production.

Production for a Market—Production in the past was also characterized by the fact that it was carried on primarily for the purpose of directly satisfying the wants of the producer. Grain, cattle, and chickens were raised for home consumption. Bread, pies, and clothing were made for the use of the immediate members of the family. Today, however, goods are produced for the market, in which it is hoped they can be sold at a profit. The farmer now raises grain, cattle, and chickens primarily for sale. Bread, pies, and clothing are made in shops for sale to the public. Those laborers who are engaged in manufacturing high priced watches will usually be found carrying low priced time pieces. Those who are busy in steel mills never have need for any of their products. Workers in a plow factory never use the plow in the field. Today, the requirements or possibilities of the local, national, or international market are the primary concern of the producer.

Physical Product versus Value Product—In the past, the frontiersman was interested in producing as large a crop of grain and as many cattle, chickens, and sheep as possible, because thus he and his family could live better, having more to eat and more money with which to buy things to enjoy. Today, however, the amount of the *physical* product is not the essential thing. The producer is interested in what his goods will sell for, or, in other words, in the *value* product. It may be that a farmer will get a larger financial return from his crops if he raises less, that a manufacturer will sell his products for more if he curtails his production, and that a laborer will be able to have more employment if he "lies down on the job" and draws it out for a longer time. Instances are numerous where farmers have reduced their planting or have destroyed their crops, where manufacturers have curtailed their production, and where laborers have restricted their output with this idea in mind. Present-day production, therefore, is concerned primarily with the dollars and cents return, or the value product, rather than with the amount of the physical product.

The quality of the product should also be of interest to the producer, but under our present scheme of things it is of concern to him only in so far as it is required to yield a dollars and cents return. Rarely does one find a producer who would rather lose money than sacrifice the quality of his output. We occasionally find a wealthy farmer who, for the joy of it or for the reputation derived, spends huge sums of money in raising fine horses or cattle with no idea of making money out of his venture; but such instances are so unusual as not to invalidate the foregoing statement.

Factors of Production—By what means are productive activities carried on? What are the factors or elements involved that make them possible? Practically all economists agree that there are four factors of production; namely, nature (sometimes called land), labor, capital, and the entrepreneur. Let us first consider the generally accepted ideas of the economists and then later see if it is not possible for us to arrive at a more logical and workable classification, one which is more in accord with our present economic arrangements. As we have so frequently stated in this volume, our ideas of things should change with changing economic conditions, but economists, like most of the rest of us, sometimes continue to believe in and to write about ideas that have long since become out of date.

Nature—The term "nature" is used to include all

gifts of nature, such as soil, the contents of the earth, climate, air, rivers, oceans, fish in the sea, wild birds, wild beasts, and all other natural resources. In the first place, man must have standing room in which to live, to walk, and to erect his buildings and factories, and he must have soil in which to plant his seeds, vines, and trees. As already noted, man cannot create raw materials; these things are provided for him by nature. Man cannot increase the gifts of nature, but he can decrease them, change their form, and improve upon them. He can fertilize, drain, and irrigate land; he can dig and refine ore, and use the metals thus obtained to manufacture goods; he can cut down trees and make lumber; he can harness water power and use the electricity thus provided; but he cannot create any natural resources.

Most economists use the word land interchangeably with the word nature; but for our purpose it is best to have the term land applied merely to the solid portion of the earth, including its surface and contents, to which title of possession can be obtained. Not all of nature's gifts are used for productive purposes. Much mountain and desert land lies idle, and many rivers, creeks, and waterfalls are not utilized. Many farmers allow a portion of their land to lie idle. In cities, much but not all of the land is used for home sites or for consumption purposes, not for production. The air that we ordinarily breathe (excluding that which is furnished us in theatres and office buildings by ventilating apparatus), sunshine, rainfall, and other free goods cannot be owned as property; they are the means of keeping us alive as individuals, not as producers. They should not, therefore, be included as production agents. In subsequent pages, we shall use the term land to refer to those gifts of nature that are owned by man and are used either for consumption or for production purposes. In designating land as a factor of production, we are concerned with only those parts of nature that are owned and used to create want satisfying goods that have a money value.

Labor—Labor or labor power, as a productive factor, is defined as *human effort, physical or mental, expended not as an end in itself but in the creation of commodities or in the rendering of services for an economic purpose.* There are three parts to this definition that should be carefully noted.

First, we speak only of human effort. We are not concerned with the efforts of horses, oxen, or other beasts of burden.

Second, we include both physical and mental effort. Many persons seem to think of labor as embodying only the services of those engaged in putting forth physical effort—carpenters, printers, ditch diggers, and machine workers, for example. The term labor, however, includes the services of stenographers, office employees, bank cashiers, factory managers, teachers, and all of our political office holders—in fact, all of those who receive or expect to receive payment for their efforts. In order to be laborers, they do not necessarily have to be hired by others, although as a rule they are so hired. The farmer who does his own plowing is as much a laborer as is the farm hand whom he employs. This matter should be kept clearly in mind, because usually the word laborer is popularly, although incorrectly, applied only to hired workers.

Third, it should be noted that, in order to be labor, human effort must be expended for an economic purpose; it must be expended in making something that is demanded by others or in doing something that satisfies the desires of others; it must be put forth in the hope of receiving payment or of having others receive payment, the payment being made in money or in other things of value, such as meals, room rent, and house rent. If this statement is kept clearly in mind, no trouble will be experienced in differentiating between play and labor. Babe Ruth, who is paid a large sum per year for his services, is a laborer when he plays professional baseball. If, however, you can induce him to come out in the pasture lot and play a game of ball with your team without his being paid for it, he is then not classed as a laborer but as one who is engaged in play.

Capital—Practically all economists agree in their definitions of land and labor but differ in their definitions of capital and the entrepreneur. It is difficult to harmonize their many points of view. Let us first consider the generally accepted ideas of these economists and later frame definitions for ourselves that appear to be more in harmony with the practices of the business world.

Capital is usually defined by economists as being anything that has been produced and is used in further production. Man cannot exist without nature. He can live in his wild state without expending very much effort; he can pick berries and fruit and catch certain insects, birds, and animals with his hands. If he makes a crude spear, a bow and an arrow, a trap, or a fish hook, he can then supply his simple needs a little more easily. But what shall we call those things that he has produced and has used to produce or obtain food for himself? Economists generally call them capital. If man plants seeds with his hands, he does the work very inefficiently and obtains only a small crop, because he can plant only a limited area. However, if he makes a crude plow out of a bent limb of a tree and pulls it across the ground, or if he hitches his wife or some animal to it, then a larger crop can be produced. His crude plow, which he has made and used to produce more goods, is classified as capital. If part of the seed that he has raised is saved and planted next year, that also is an instance of the use of capital in primitive economic life.

Capital and Capital Goods—When the economists find it necessary or advisable to differentiate between the value of the produced things that are used in further production and the concrete, physical things themselves that have been produced and are used in further production, they call the former *capital* and the latter *capital goods*. For example, they would say that if a printing office has $50,000 worth of linotypes, presses, furniture, and supplies, the $50,000 is the amount of the capital represented and the linotypes, presses, furniture, and supplies are the capital goods.

We shall later see that capital represents funds invested in a productive enterprise and that capital goods are the concrete physical things which have been produced and are used for further production.

The Entrepreneur—Now, what about the entrepreneur? It is doubtful if any other term in economics has been dignified by so many different definitions. It is usually declared that land, labor, and capital cannot of themselves engage in any productive activity. Farm land may exist in an abundant supply, there may be many efficient farm laborers available, and capital also may be plentiful; but unless some one brings that land, labor, and capital together and sets them to producing, there can be no production. In other words, economists usually describe the entrepreneur as being the one who gets land, labor, and capital to function in a productive manner. He is sometimes called the enterpriser, the captain of industry, or the manager.

If the enterpriser performs the function we have described, is he not putting forth mental effort for an economic purpose? He cannot manage or organize a business unless he uses mental energy; and would not that, therefore, make him a laborer under our preceding definition? If so, is it not best for us to classify him as a laborer, in so far as his organizing and managing efforts are concerned? If he is a professional organizer or promoter of business enterprises, he is paid a salary or a fee or a part of the capital stock of the company in return for his organizing or promotional activities, and this we should and can call wages that are paid for his labor.

Other economists state that the entrepreneur is the one upon whom rests the responsibility of making ultimate decisions in connection with the conduct of a business. Regardless of whether the entrepreneur may be said to be the individual owner of a business or a partner or a stockholder (a stockholder being a part owner of a business), any decisions that may be made by the owners of a business or by others delegated by them to make such decisions (as in the case of the board of directors of a corporation) are the result of mental effort expended for an economic purpose and should, therefore, be classed as labor or labor power.

We also find some economists defining the entrepreneur as the owner or part owner of the business. When we have a partnership or a corporation, the term entrepreneur is used by this group of economists in a collective sense to designate the owners thereof. They claim that the entrepreneur puts his capital into the business and also, at times, borrows additional capital from banks, bondholders, or others for the business. As the owner of the business, he takes the risk of making a profit or of suffering a loss. He is thus said to be a "risk taker" and is supposed to be paid a return in the form of profits for such risk taking.

Let us now analyze the ideas of those who claim that the entrepreneur is a risk taker. In the first place, in addition to the owners, there are others who are concerned with production and who take risks arising out of the business. The bankers and bondholders who lend it funds take the risk of not being paid interest and principal. The laborers take risks of injury and death arising out of the nature of their employment. If land is rented to the business enterprise, the owner of the land, that is, the landlord, takes the risk of not receiving his rentals. Consequently, the risk taking function of the so-called entrepreneur does not set him off as a factor separate and distinct from other factors.

Now, what about the entrepreneur as the owner of the business unit? Does mere ownership constitute a sufficient basis for giving him a separate classification? If he is to be defined as the owner of the business, it is self-evident that he must have capital invested in it. If he is the owner of capital, should he not then be classified as a capitalist, since he is the owner of funds productively employed?

Thus, we have broken up the functions of the so-called entrepreneur into two parts: (1) his managing or personal service activities and (2) his ownership activities. As a manager, a promoter, or an individual who renders services, he must be classified as a laborer. As the owner of a business or as a risk taker, he must be classified as the owner of capital, or a capitalist. In subsequent pages, therefore, we shall omit all mention of the entrepreneur as a separate factor in production, for in reality he does not exist.

Let us pursue our discussion further and see if it is not possible for us to analyze our capitalistic, or present-day, productive activity from the standpoint of what is actually going on around us. We are interested in the things of today, in the ideas and practices of today.

Source of Capital—We have already noted the part

that capital plays in the modern business world. Where does capital come from? What is its source? Capital arises from savings. It results from the existence of a surplus of production over consumption. If we used up or made away with all that we produced, we should have nothing remaining to be employed in further production. If we spent all of our income for clothing, food, and other consumption goods, we should not be able to lay aside any funds for the use of ourselves or others in carrying on productive activities. This is one of the reasons why business firms lay aside a surplus from their earnings. By saving a portion of their earnings and using this portion to build up a surplus, they increase the amount of funds that can be devoted as capital to the development of their business. Saving takes place because we expect to receive in the future a larger return than we could receive if we spent or used all our income in the present. To become capital, however, our savings must be used for a productive purpose, either by ourselves or by others.

Wealth versus Capital—*Capital represents funds that have been saved and are used for purposes of production,* that is, to create or to provide want satisfying goods (including services) which have a money value and from which, usually, a money income is expected. The word funds is used to designate both money and credit. We are compelled to employ the word "usually" in the latter part of our definition of capital because sometimes, although very seldom, production is carried on with no hope or expectation of a monetary return, as when the United States Government produces its own war supplies.

How does capital differ from wealth and money? Wealth consists of economic goods, that is, those things which satisfy human wants but which are limited in quantity. It excludes free goods, such as free air and sunshine, things for which we are not willing to give anything or to make any sacrifice to obtain. Capital is a part of wealth, being funds that are used for productive purposes. Household furniture, pleasure automobiles, and grass on our lawns are but a few of many things that are wealth but not capital, owing to the fact that they satisfy our wants directly. As we have noted earlier, the goods in which capital is invested satisfy our wants indirectly by being used to produce goods, including personal services, that we desire. Money of all kinds, whether it be paper or metallic, is wealth, but only that portion of money becomes capital which is used to make productive activities possible. If I buy an ice cream soda for ten cents, that money is wealth to me; but if the soda fountain dealer uses the ten cents to pay wages or to expand his business, it then becomes capital to him.

If I put $5,000 in a bank, that money is my wealth. I do not invest it in my business or in the business of of the bank. It is merely left with the bank as a deposit. It is my property. I may receive from 3% to 4% interest on it, not as a return upon capital, but as a return upon my wealth or property. The bank, however, counts my deposit as part of the funds which it uses in the hope of obtaining an income. It lends my deposit out to others or uses it to pay part of its operating expenses. The bank considers my deposit as part of its working capital. If it loans $5,000 to you to enable you to buy a home, that $5,000 is not capital to you; it is wealth. Your house is not going to be used to produce goods for sale in the market for the purpose of obtaining an income. If, however, a factory owner borrows $5,000 from the bank and uses it in his business activities, he considers that $5,000 as part of his working capital. Thus, it can be seen that funds which are only wealth in the hands of one person may become capital in the hands of another, this classification depending entirely on the use to which the funds are put.

Use of Capital by Individual Proprietorship—As stated, there are only three types of business organization—the individual proprietorship, the partnership, and the corporation. When an individual prepares to start a business—a store, for example—he has to have some funds with which to begin. Let us say that he has $10,000, either in money or in his account at the bank. With this $10,000 he rents a store, buys goods, hires clerks, and opens his establishment to the public. He has turned his $10,000 of wealth into capital. Let us say that he deems it necessary to borrow $3,000 from the bank. He now has $13,000 of capital, or working funds, from which he expects to obtain a monetary return. At the end of the year, he finds that he has made $2,000 over and above all expenses, or, in other words, he has received a 20%

return on his $10,000. Although he used $13,000 of capital to obtain an income of $2,000, nevertheless he figures the percentage of return upon the $10,000 of his own capital. Possibly he may turn that $2,000 back into his business. If so, he would then have $12,000 of his own capital in the business and, at the end of the second year, would figure the percentage of his income on the basis of $12,000, not on that of $10,000.

Use of Capital by a Partnership—The description given in the preceding paragraph still holds good if you substitute two or three partners for the individual owner. Therefore, it is unnecessary for us to give separate treatment to the use of capital by a partnership, for nothing would be added to the discussion by our doing so.

Use of Capital by a Corporation—When we consider the corporation as a business concern, we have a slightly different situation from that which we have just described. We now have to distinguish between *capital* and *capitalization*. When a corporation is organized, it has to have what is called capital stock. In other words, it has to be capitalized at a certain sum of money.

Let us consider a simple example; all other instances will vary merely in degree, no matter how complicated they may be. Let us say that our friend John Jones and you and I decide to open a store and deem it best to organize a corporation to be known as the City Grocery Company. We agree that our corporation is to have a capital stock of $20,000. (As we have seen, capital stock is not issued in the case of an individual proprietorship or a partnership.) We incorporate and issue stock to the amount of $20,000, the three of us purchasing all of the stock at its full face value. The corporation thus starts out with $20,000 in the treasury. This sum represents both the amount of the capital of the business and the extent of the capitalization of the corporation. Let us then issue $5,000 worth of bonds, which we sell to others, thus adding $5,000 to our capital. Our capital stock or capitalization remains at $20,000, although our capital has been increased to $25,000. We then purchase machinery and supplies, hire the necessary laborers, and start the corporation upon its career as a grocery company.

At the end of the first year, we find that we have been very prosperous and are able to set aside $2,000 as a surplus. This amount constitutes additional working capital for our corporation. Let us then borrow $1,000 from the bank. At the end of the second year, we still have $20,000 of capital stock, or capitalization, but we also have $5,000 which has been received from the sale of bonds, $1,000 as a loan from the bank, and $2,000 which has been added as surplus out of earnings, or a total working capital of $28,000, which we have used in our business for the purpose of obtaining an income. In calculating our net earnings at the end of the second year, however, we use as a basis the $20,000 capital stock or capitalization and not the $28,000 capital which we have been using.

In the case of a bank, a similar, although not an identical, situation exists. A bank starts out with a certain amount of money on hand which it has received from the sale of its capital stock. It accepts deposits from the public and accumulates a surplus from its earnings. It cannot issue bonds, but it may obtain additional funds by borrowing from other banks or by rediscounting commercial paper with them. Its capital stock represents its capitalization, upon which dividends are paid. Its working capital, however, includes not only the funds received from the sale of its capital stock but also those which it has available from its deposits and surplus and from its borrowing and rediscounting operations.

Kinds of Capital Ownership—In our present state of capitalistic society, capital is owned primarily by individuals or by other private parties such as partnerships and corporations. This predominance of private ownership of capital has led many persons to overlook other types of capital ownership. The various branches of our government also own and use capital. For example, the National Government may own and operate arsenals, railways, canals, and so forth; states may operate printing plants; and cities may invest their funds in garbage incinerators. Such ownership may and does exist, even under our present state of capitalism, and is known as *government ownership* or *public ownership*. If at any time we should abolish capitalism and introduce socialism or guild socialism, the productive enterprises of the country would be publicly owned, but a state of society different from that which we now have would be brought into existence as a consequence of the change in the character of the ownership of capital. Finally, we have productive enterprises owned completely by those who work in them. This system is known as *cooperative ownership,* and it is the type of ownership that is championed by the advocates of syndicalism, anarchism, and communism. There are relatively few cooperatively owned establishments in the United States, but there are many such establishments in European countries.

In this chapter, we are concerned with an analysis of the ideals and practices of capitalism, but in Chapter XXII we shall discuss the demands of those who wish to abolish the private ownership of capital and substitute therefor either public ownership or cooperative ownership. In passing, it may be well to remind the student that those who desire radically to change our present state of society, which is based on the private ownership of capital, do not seek to abolish capital but wish only to change its private ownership to public ownership or cooperative ownership.

Production and Income—With this preliminary survey behind us, let us analyze the situation as it exists at present in the field of capitalistic production. Production is carried on for the purpose of gaining an income in terms of money. When a person starts any kind of business enterprise, he is interested in obtaining a money return therefrom. We must remember, however, that there are also money returns available from non-productive activities, such as renting houses, hiring automobiles, and the like. In this chapter, we are concerned only with those things that yield an income as a result of productive activity, because we are discussing production and not the sources from which incomes arise.

Three Factors of Production—When we started the grocery store mentioned in preceding paragraphs, we invested our funds (which then became capital) in land (not capable of being produced by man) and in a building, a cash register, groceries, and counters (all of which are capable of being produced by man). Let us use the term capital goods to apply to the latter class of goods—to the concrete, physical things that have been produced and are used in further production. We also used our capital to hire laborers to perform personal services for us. In other words, we purchased the labor power of clerks, delivery boys, and so forth.

As the days and weeks passed, we received money from the sale of our groceries. We used this money in paying wages to our employees, in purchasing groceries to replace those that had been sold, and in meeting our taxes, fire insurance premiums, and so forth. Such funds or income were also a part of our working capital. We borrowed funds from the bank, and they too became part of our working capital.

Thus, in our productive enterprise we did as all business men do—we employed funds (which then became capital) to obtain the use of land, labor or labor power, and capital goods, the three factors of production. Capital itself does no producing. Capital is merely the funds which are invested in the business and upon which a monetary return is expected as a result of the production and sale of goods, made possible by the application of labor power to capital goods and land.

Human and Non-Human Elements—Land and capital goods are non-human in character. They are capable of being divorced or separated from their owners, which statement is not true of labor power. When you sell your business, the person who buys it purchases it as a going concern. You sell him not only the land and the capital goods but also the goodwill which you have built up among your customers. He may not be able to retain this goodwill, but nevertheless he has to pay for it. Another interesting thing is that your business is valuable partly because of the services of the laborers whom you have employed. You may have in your employ an especially skilful advertising expert, who has been of great service in making your business a profitable concern; yet the person who buys your enterprise cannot be sure that your labor staff will remain when he takes it over. Thus, when you sell your business, you can guarantee that the purchaser will be able definitely to command the use of the material or non-human side of it, but you cannot guarantee that he will be certain of commanding or retaining the goodwill and the personal services of your laborers, or the human side of it.

Capital Goods and Labor Power Not Limited—The total amount of land that can be used for productive purposes is limited in amount. Man cannot increase its quantity by any means, although he can change the purposes for which it is used. There is, however, practically no limit to the amount of capital and capital goods that can be produced. Both are continually being consciously and intentionally created in huge amounts. Human beings increase in number, and their productive power can be greatly expanded by various means which have already been mentioned, thus bringing about an increase in the amount of labor power in a country. Human beings, unlike capital and capital goods, are not intentionally brought into the world for the purpose of increasing the productive capacity of society. It takes years for a child to grow up and become a laborer. The gifts of nature and produced goods, however, can be turned into productive channels in a very short time.

Conclusion—From the above analysis, we have seen that production involves the use of three factors—the human element of *labor* and the non-human elements of *land* (which cannot be produced) and *capital goods* (which have been and can be produced in varying amounts). Capital may, therefore, be re-defined as being the funds (money and credit) employed to obtain the use of both human and non-human elements for a productive purpose.

In later chapters, we shall see that when it comes to the division or distribution of the income of society, we have a twofold classification, corresponding closely, although not exactly, to the classification here given, for we shall then have to deal with the division of income among (1) those who render personal services and (2) those who own property. The latter group will, however, include both those who obtain an income from productive enterprises and those who obtain an income from the leasing or renting of property used not for productive purposes but for the satisfaction of consumption demands.

CHAPTER VI

Factors of Production

NATURE is not only the source of our standing room; it is also the source of all raw materials that are used in production. Any country that is blessed with bountiful natural resources inevitably takes a leading part in the economic affairs of the world when it has learned how best to utilize those resources. Such a country is our own United States, which is endowed and blessed with wonderful physical conditions.

Land

Physical Conditions of the United States—Advantageous location is a dominating factor in the industrial and commercial progress of a nation. We are fortunate in being a neighbor of Europe, South America, and Asia. Our country ranks in area with Russia, Brazil, China, and Australia. Its extensive seacoast and excellent harbors, the Great Lakes, and numerous internal waterways facilitate entrance into and exit from a vast empire. A temperate climate, and adequate rainfall, great fertile valleys, supplies of lumber and minerals, numerous water power sites, expansive grazing areas, and the excellent surface features of our land that make for ease in building railways, locating industries, and distributing population, all have been instrumental in enabling the United States to play a dominant part in the economic development of the world during the past century.

Agricultural Land—All land, or the solid portion of the earth's surface, may be classified, according to the purpose which it serves, as (1) land of value because of natural resources—agricultural land, forest land, and power site land, for example—and (2) land of value because of population density, such as building sites.

The value of agricultural land depends on the value of the crops that can be raised thereon, and this in turn depends on the fertility and location of the land and on the price level in the market. The fertility of the soil varies greatly in different tracts, even on a small farm.

Extensive and Intensive Cultivation — Farmers tend to cultivate their better grades of land more intensively than their poorer land. Intensive cultivation is effected by the use of a large number of laborers and by the investment of more capital in equipment, orchards, vineyards, gardens, and the like. The use of a small amount of capital per acre for seed, equipment, labor, and so forth is called extensive cultivation. Typical of the latter type is a farm devoted to grain raising. With the growth in population, resulting in an increased demand for foodstuffs, the tendency toward an increased intensive cultivation has been very noticeable.

Land that is considered to be worthless for some

crops will occasionally be found to be extremely productive when used for others. For example, in California great areas of sticky, gummy soil lay idle for many years and were considered to be of slight value until it was discovered that they could be used most profitably for rice planting, whereupon their price was greatly increased.

Location—Location also affects the value of agricultural land. Nearness to markets or cities and to cheap and efficient means of transportation, such as railways, rivers, canals, and automobile highways, makes land of slight fertility frequently much more valuable than land of much greater fertility which is not so advantageously located.

Agricultural Resources of the United States—It is impossible to make accurate comparisons between the agricultural resources of the United States and those of other countries, but no matter from what angle the matter is approached, it is admitted that we stand in a preferred position. Over one-half of our total area is adapted to the production of crops, although by no means is all of that amount being so used at present. A large part of the remainder is suitable for grazing. An important factor favoring agriculture is the sparseness of the population in agricultural areas; only about one-quarter of our total population was designated by the census of 1920 as being "agricultural population." The proportion of land at present providing agricultural products is three acres to each inhabitant. Compare this with one and six-tenths acres for each inhabitant of Poland and Hungary, four-fifths of an acre per unit of population in Germany and Italy, and one-third of an acre per unit of population in Japan. In no part of the world do agriculturists use so much machinery as in the United States. Is it any wonder, therefore, that we have our problem of farm relief, caused primarily by our ability to produce such large quantities of foodstuffs and animal products?

The United States is also blessed because of the great variety of crops that can be raised within its borders. We can produce practically all kinds of grains, fruits, and vegetables. Bananas, tea, and coffee are the three outstanding exceptions that we must note cannot be raised here.

Building Sites—Fertility plays no part in determining the extent of the productivity of land used for building sites. City land is more valuable than farm land because of the presence of a more congested population; hence, location is the only factor that is considered. Location, however, varies with the use for which buildings are intended. For residential purposes, the advent of the automobile has made it possible to reside at a great distance from the place of work. Restricted residential districts have higher values than do unrestricted districts. In unrestricted areas, the tendency is for the higher priced dwellings to be turned into rooming houses, which, in turn, give way to various kinds of business establishments. The character of any economic area within a city is constantly changing, although at times the change is impeded by regulatory laws.

In locating retail stores, one factor that was considered important in the past was the number of people daily passing the proposed site, which, in turn, was usually dependent upon the location of railway stations, street car lines, theatres, and the post office. However, the use of the automobile to bring passengers to buy and of trucks to transport merchandise has tended to bring about the decentralization of retail trade. In the wholesale trade, location in close proximity to others engaged in similar lines of activity is regarded as an advantage to purchasers. For manufacturing sites, natural conditions, such as climate, harbors, rivers, elevation, and proximity to productive soils and mines, originally made one manufacturing site more valuable than another, but at present the development of transportation, the localization of capital and labor, and other artificial or man-made conditions are of increasing importance in determining the location of factories.

Labor or Labor Power

Nature of Labor—The term labor has a variety of meanings. It is quite commonly employed to refer only to the "horny-handed sons of toil," to those who are engaged in hard manual labor. Sometimes it is used in such a way as to include the white-collared employees, such as clerks, stenographers, and floor walkers. Again, it may refer to the working class in general, or more specifically only to the organized labor movement. It is also used to designate human effort expended for an economic purpose. In this text, however, we shall use the word labor in two different senses—one as referring to laborers as a class and the other to the efforts which they put forth. The sense in which the word is used will be clear from the context in which it appears. More frequently, however, the term labor power will be employed to designate productive effort. It will be remembered that in earlier pages we defined labor or labor power as consisting of any physical or mental effort of man put forth for an economic purpose or in the hope of an economic reward. Therefore, it includes the economic efforts of all who are paid or who expect to be paid for their services, regardless of whether they receive wages, salaries, or fees, or whether they are superintendents, foremen, employees, or self-employed workers (as dentists, lawyers, doctors, and farmers who do their own work).

Importance of Labor—Some individuals hold that the laboring class is the most important class in society and that labor power is the most important factor of production. In analyzing our present economic society, however, we find that no one class or factor is any more important than any other. The capitalist class depends upon the laboring class for labor power, and the laboring class depends upon the capitalist class for employment. Labor power cannot be expended without the aid of land and capital goods, nor can land

and capital goods be used in production without the aid of labor power. Therefore, in considering our present productive processes, it should be evident that no one factor is more important than any other.

Labor power is tied up with the human element, while land and capital goods are not. Labor power cannot be separated from the laborer; he has to be present when it is expended. The owner of land and capital goods, however, does not have to be present when these factors are used. This state of affairs has to be taken into consideration in all productive activities. It is one reason why laborers are more difficult to handle in production than are land and capital goods. The latter are non-human in character—they do not think; they do not vote; they cannot organize unions and strike against their owners; they may be abused without protest, although not without producing decreased returns. Capital (funds invested in a productive enterprise) is also non-human in character, but its owners are as human as are those who sell their labor power.

Labor power is perishable, much more so than are capital goods and land. Land and capital goods may wear out, but if not used today, they can be used tomorrow. Land, if allowed to lie idle, will actually regain a part of its former fertility. Labor power, however, if not expended today, because the laborer is not at work, is lost. It cannot be stored up and sold, as can nuts or bolts or yards of cloth. Moreover, the quality of the labor power of the worker (his skill) is reduced if he is not regularly employed.

Proper Care of Factors of Production—Inasmuch as labor power cannot be separated from the laborer, the employer cannot disregard the conditions under which the laborer works. The health, safety, and happiness of the latter must be conserved if the best results are to be obtained. A similar situation exists, to a certain extent, in connection with the non-human things in which capital is invested. Land must be drained, irrigated, and fertilized; crops must be rotated; and care must be used in determining what crops are to be planted. The right kind of machinery must be installed in a factory; it must be kept greased, oiled, and repaired; and it must be operated at the proper speed. The most satisfactory conditions under which every phase of production is carried on must be provided, so as to obtain the greatest possible return from the use of land, labor power, and capital goods.

Supply of Labor Power—What are the factors that affect or determine the amount of the labor power of a community, nation, or society? They are (1) the number of laborers available and (2) the productivity of the laborers.

Birth and Death Rates—The number of laborers is dependent upon population, and population in turn is dependent upon various factors. First of all, population depends upon the excess of births over deaths. The birth and death rates of the countries of the world are determined by certain biological, social, religious, and economic conditions. In India and China the birth rate is high; so also is the death rate. In France the birth rate is so low as to give great concern to some French statesmen, who are more worried, however, about man power for use on the field of battle than they are about man power for use in the field of production. In the United States both the birth rate and the death rate have steadily declined. The decline in the birth rate has been due to the desire of parents to have fewer children and to give them more advantages than would otherwise be possible. The high costs of medical care at childbirth, the desire of married women to work rather than to remain at home and care for children, and the bother of raising children in our present-day apartment house life are also factors that have affected the birth rate. The decreased death rate has been brought about by the progress of medical science, the increased intelligence of our people, and our raised economic status with its high plane of living and improved working conditions.

Immigration and Emigration—The number of laborers in a country is also affected by the extent of its immigration and emigration. Immigration into the United States has been greater than into any other country. It has been estimated that during the past century about 30,000,000 people have come to our shores from other lands. Prior to the outbreak of the World War, immigrants were arriving at the rate of about 1,000,000 per year. They formerly came primarily from the northern and northeastern countries of Europe, but beginning with the last decade of the nineteenth century, those arriving from southern and southeastern Europe have greatly outnumbered all others.

Immigration has played an important rôle in our political, social, and economic life. This great influx of people assisted in settling the West, in developing agriculture, mining, and lumbering, in operating manufacturing plants, and in carrying on many other lines of productive activity. As a rule, immigrants have a lower plane of living, a higher birth rate, and a higher death rate than do native born families. In certain lines of work, immigrants have often displaced American laborers, but more frequently they have stimulated the American to enter the more skilled trades, leaving the rough, unskilled work to be taken care of by the immigrants.

Some countries, such as Ireland and Italy, have lost a considerable number of their laborers through emigration. There has always been some emigration from the United States, a number of our immigrants returning to their home lands and many Americans emigrating to Canada, attracted by the availability of cheaper farm land in that country.

Age—Age also affects the supply of laborers in a community. A very old or a very young person cannot be employed productively. Most of our immigrants have been of working age. Sometimes it happens that the young men of a country migrate to other lands and thus decrease the local labor supply. Many successful farmers and business men retire to spend their declining years in Florida or Southern California, thus greatly increasing the population of those sections of the United States, but adding nothing to their labor supply.

Sex—In the past, sex played a much more important part in affecting the number of laborers than it does today. Formerly, woman's place was in the home, but we now find her in practically every type of occupation and profession, thus swelling the available labor power of the country.

Productivity of Labor—To consider only the number of laborers as the index of the supply of labor power is not sufficient. The productivity of the laborers must also be taken into consideration. China has many laborers, but it cannot produce as much as could the United States with the same number, because our labor force is much more productive. This difference is due to our having so greatly developed or improved our industrial technique, that is, the processes which we employ in our productive activities.

Standardization—An outstanding characteristic of our industrial technique is the fact that we are interested in mass production or *standardization*. We produce thousands or millions of units of an article, all exactly alike as to color, weight, and measurements. If one part of a machine breaks, we purchase a new part which fits without having to be filed or adjusted to its place. We use machinery which never tires and which produces uniform articles in endless amounts. If each product were made to satisfy a special customer or to suit a particular situation, production would be slowed up, costs would mount to higher levels, and the opportunity of our people to enjoy a wide variety of goods, machine-made though they are, would be sacrificed.

Division of Labor—Another characteristic of our industrial technique is the fact that we practise in every possible connection what is known as *division of labor*. Briefly, it amounts to specialization and is made more easily possible because of our machine industry. We have four kinds of division of labor.

1. Occupational division of labor. Today, we have relatively few "Jacks of all trades." A worker is usually employed at one occupation. He is a carpenter or a molder or a printer or a lawyer or a teacher or a banker—in other words, a specialist. A banker, for example, does not do his own plastering, plumbing, or bricklaying. He is busy with the tasks of a banker. He is a specialist, as are most of our workers.

2. Technical division of labor. Many laborers specialize within their crafts. Frequently a machinist works only on a lathe, a doctor works only on skin diseases, a lawyer handles only patent cases. Many factory employees work only on machines that produce but a small part of the finished article, such as nuts or bolts or screws. In a bank, some clerks list checks, others act only as messengers, tellers, or bookkeepers. These are all instances of the technical division of

labor, or specialization, within an occupation or craft.

3. Industrial division of labor. As a consequence of developments within our machine industry, we have many factories that produce only a portion of the finished product. For example, one plant may make only the chassis of an automobile, another may make only tires, others may make only roller bearings or headlights or horns, for example. In the banking field, we find the same sort of specialization, for some institutions act only as savings banks, others only as commercial banks, and still others only as trust companies.

4. Geographical and territorial division of labor. Many communities find it more profitable to specialize in the production of a certain kind of commodity than to produce many different kinds. Although this is really a type of localization of industry, it is commonly called geographical or territorial division of labor. Florida and California, for example, are known for their fruits and vegetables, the middle western states for their corn and wheat, Massachusetts for its shoes, Pennsylvania for its coal, Michigan for its automobiles, Pittsburgh for its steel, Chicago and Kansas City for meat products, Troy, New York for collars, cuffs, and shirts, and Akron, Ohio for all sorts of rubber products.

Factors Affecting Localization of Industry—What are the factors that influence the localization of industries, or, in other words, the geographical division of labor? They may be briefly summarized as being a proximity to raw materials, markets, and cheap power, the existence of a satisfactory labor supply, and the momentum of an early start.

Raw Materials—An enterprise should be located near the source of the needed raw materials. This does not necessarily mean that the industry must be near mines or forests, but rather that it should be so situated that the materials for its use can be secured at a satisfactory cost. This cost is partly but not entirely a matter of transportation charges.

Markets—With most goods, the distance from the market is not so important as the cost of transportation. With perishable products, the time factor must also be taken into consideration. Producers tend so to relate themselves to the market that they can place their products in the hands of the consumers at a cost no higher than that of the most favorably situated competitor. This fact partly accounts for the establishment of branch factories in centers of population far distant from the home office. Industries that are concerned with servicing and repairing must of necessity be close to the consumers who constitute their principal markets.

Power—The importance of power as a factor affecting the localization of industry varies considerably with the nature of the industry. In the early days of the United States, industries requiring power were forced to locate near available water power sites. Later, the discovery of coal, gas, and oil decreased the importance of the water power resources of the northeastern states and made it possible for industries to be established in the middle western and southern states. During the past decade the outstanding development of hydro-electric power and the improvement of the gasoline engine have been influential in spreading industries over the country to places where markets, labor power, and raw materials can be obtained at the most satisfactory rates.

Perhaps the greatest advantage to industry in locating in a district where power is cheap and abundant lies in the fact that large public service corporations stand ready to furnish light, heat, and power in any desired quantity at reasonable rates. Under such circumstances, the necessity of a large capital investment in a power plant which may have to stand idle during periods of depression and which will probably have to be maintained at a capacity in excess of the requirements of daily use is avoided.

Labor Supply—For the most part, unskilled laborers are employed in mining and agriculture. They are highly mobile and usually go where there is a demand for their services. In the more highly developed forms of industry, however, the existence of an adequate supply of laborers is a most important factor affecting the location of a manufacturing plant. Factories must have laborers, and at times laborers are difficult to move to new locations. Even within cities, factories tend to gravitate to those districts where they can be easily reached by the workers.

Momentum of an Early Start—There is no reason why Akron, Ohio should have become the center of the rubber manufacturing industry of the United States, except that the production of rubber goods was first begun in that city. Skilled laborers were developed for the industry and they thus were available to others interested in establishing rubber goods factories in the same community. The fur market of the United States is at St. Louis because the trappers of the early days brought their skins to that city from the northwest territory to be graded, prepared, and sold at auction to the buyers who came from other parts of the country. Many other instances could be cited to show that the momentum of an early start has much to do with explaining why some of our industries are located in certain parts of the United States.

Advantages of Division of Labor—Much can be said both for and against the division of labor. Undoubtedly its greatest advantage lies in the fact that it increases the productivity of the worker. When a man devotes his time and energy to doing but one thing, whether it be working at one occupation or at only one small part of it, he soon develops a high degree of skill because of the constant repetition that is involved. When a farmer raises only oranges, or a doctor gives his attention only to eye diseases, or a vice president of a bank devotes his time only to foreign exchange transactions, he is bound to become more proficient than if he were to spread his efforts and attention over a large number of fields. Much time is also saved by having a worker stay at one machine or on one job instead of moving from one machine or one job to another.

Inventions also are encouraged by division of labor. If a man, working alone, makes a complete typewriter, the process is most complicated. It would be impossible to invent a machine that could produce a typewriter. However, if the process is broken up into a number of minute operations, it becomes a relatively simple matter to invent a machine that will make the case, another that will make the frame, and still another that will make the levers. Thus, division of labor provides the opportunity for inventions which, in turn, usually involve the use of more machinery. The substitution of machinery for hand labor not only greatly increases the amount of goods that a worker can produce but also makes it possible for the goods to be sold at lower prices and to be of better quality and of more uniform character than if made by hand.

With industry characterized by the division of labor, the worker can more easily find the type of employment for which he is best suited. The more skilled workers will be used on the more difficult tasks, the less skilled on those that are more simple. Workers who are physically or mentally weak can likewise be placed on jobs for which they are adapted. Thus, through specialization each person's strength and ability can be employed to the best advantage.

Through division of labor the best results are obtained from the employment of capital. When a laborer works on a number of different machines, part of the equipment must necessarily lie idle, and when a machine lies idle it earns nothing on the capital that has been invested in it. When a man works constantly on one machine, there is no such waste of capital resources. If every farmer owned a well digging machine, it would be used for only a few days to dig a well; but if one farmer in the district purchases such a machine and goes from farm to farm digging wells for others, such division of labor enables the capital that is invested in the machine to be used to the best advantage.

Disadvantages of Division of Labor—As is true of all things, there are certain disadvantages, as well as advantages, that result from the division of labor. It is evident that it has destroyed the demand for certain types of skilled laborers. To operate many of our machines, one merely has to push a button or to pull a lever. However, there are many complicated machines that require greater skill and knowledge than were formerly possessed by the clever handicraftsmen of long ago. Today, many professional men are far more skilled in their profession, because they have specialized in some one branch of it, than were the general practitioners of the past, who covered the entire field of their profession and thus failed to become proficient in any one phase of it. It is true, however, that the average factory worker no longer needs to learn a trade. His job is less educational in character than was the case before the practice of division of labor became so widely adopted.

Many claim that for the factory worker division of labor has resulted in deadly monotony. If you and I were to go through a factory and stand beside a machine where all day long the employee merely fed the machine with material and stepped on a lever, we would undoubtedly say that such employment was most monotonous and fatiguing to the worker. Possibly it would be for you and me, but if you were to ask the man who operates the machine as to how it affected him, he would probably surprise you by saying that he liked the job as well as any he had ever had and that he did not consider it monotonous in character. Usually, we are eager to generalize from our own experience and point of view, forgetting that others do not feel the same way about all things as we do. Most machine workers enjoy and prefer to be employed at jobs that you and I would find most deadening and monotonous. Jobs that involve repetition soon become more or less routine to most workers, a matter of habit, involving automatic or subconscious movements and necessitating little or no mental effort. A high strung, nervous, temperamental individual would probably balk at a repetitive task; but that is not true of the majority of machine workers, many of whom prefer to do the same sort of task day in and day out, because they find it less fatiguing and monotonous than having to adjust themselves to changing tasks that require different body movements and mental attitudes.

It is also claimed that division of labor has made the hired worker more dependent on the employer than in the past, but many of us forget that a hired laborer always has had to depend on an employer for his job. Also, we usually overlook the fact that when a man is a skilled craftsman, he is restricted for employment to his particular craft. The hired worker, whether skilled or unskilled, is dependent upon the employer for a job, as he always has been, but he now has many employers in many industries to whom he can apply for work. This opportunity of shifting from one boss to another has given the worker an increased bargaining power in demanding higher wages, shorter hours, and better conditions of employment.

Scientific Management—A third outstanding characteristic of our industrial technique is the application of the principles and practices of scientific management. Our industries have undoubtedly gone farther in this regard than have those of any other country. In brief, scientific management may be defined as the arrangement of productive processes in such a manner as to bring about increased production with a minimum of effort and fatigue on the part of the worker and with minimum costs for the employer.

Many of our factories are poorly arranged or poorly laid out, and this defect in structure gives rise to needless expense, wasted effort, and loss of time, because the materials are sent back and forth across the plant on their way to becoming finished products. Many factories are poorly lighted and poorly ventilated; they are equipped with antiquated machinery and use out of date processes. The workers themselves seldom give thought to how they could perform their tasks more efficiently. Like their employers, too frequently they are dominated by the old practices of the trade.

Many of the factories or plants that have adopted the fundamental principles of scientific management have a staff of men whose duty it is to see that all things are done efficiently. These men are commonly known as efficiency experts. They watch the workers at their tasks, study their movements, and teach them how to eliminate wasted effort. They re-route the materials through the factory so that there is a steady procession from the beginning of the process to the end, with no waste of time, effort, or material. They devise new methods and introduce new machinery, so that costs may be reduced, time saved, and the body movements of the workers decreased in number. They map out just how each job is to be done so as to have it completed in the most efficient manner. They improve the lighting and ventilating systems.

Scientific management does not mean "rushing" the worker. Its aim is to enable the employee to produce more with less effort and fatigue. It does not imply the cutting of wages, for with more product more wages are possible, because, as we shall see in later chapters, wages depend on the amount of the product turned out. Scientific management also tends to increase the purchasing power of the workers, because cheaper production tends to result in lower prices.

In the field of banking, to bring the discussion home to our own occupation, how many times have you ever given thought to devising easier and more efficient methods of doing your work? In listing checks, for example, have you ever attempted to work out a method of your own which would enable you to do the work more quickly and easily? Are you working at a desk that is too high or sitting before a desk on a chair that is too low? In some banks, the lighting and ventilation are inadequate, with the result that the best results cannot be obtained from the employees. The banking room may be poorly arranged and may require a great deal of needless walking on the part of the members of the staff. In some banks, however, much progress has been made toward introducing efficient methods. Adding machines, coin and paper money wrapping machines, comptometers, and calculators have been installed and have greatly increased the efficiency of the staff. The principles of scientific management can thus be applied to banking as well as to other lines of business.

Other Factors Affecting Productivity of Laborers—There are many other factors on which the productivity of the labor force depends, such as physical strength, native ingenuity, general education, technical training, and temperament. The people of various nations differ in the degree to which they are characterized by these qualities. The Chinese have great physical endurance, yet they possess scanty technical training. The East Indian or Hindu is faithful and is willing to work long hours, but he is physically weak. English laborers are well informed and highly trained in factory methods, but they are conservative and reluctant to adopt new practices. In the United States and Germany, the workers are highly productive and possibly are the most competent of all laborers because of educational facilities, native ingenuity, progressive attitude, and general training.

Social Status of Labor—The social status of the laboring class also has much to do with its productivity. Those who first worked for others were slaves; they possessed no economic privileges and had nothing to look forward to as a result of their efforts. Such labor proved to be most inefficient, and in time slavery was replaced by serfdom. The serfs were compelled to work on the land of their lord for a certain number of days each week; in return they received a small plot of ground which they cultivated for themselves but which they could never own. They were not permitted to leave the estate of their lord, nor were they permitted to work into higher positions. Serf labor was more efficient than slave labor and satisfied the requirements of the times, but still it was far from being as efficient as the labor which we have today.

Capitalism is based upon the use of free labor, with the hired workers possessing many social, economic, and political privileges, among which is their ability to improve their status by their own efforts. It provides greater incentives to the workers than did either slavery or serfdom.

Mobility of Labor—In contrast with conditions in many foreign countries, in the United States laborers are permitted to work at any kind of employment that is available. With educational facilities either free or at reasonable cost, there is an opportunity for a laborer to advance from one position to another. A lad who starts out as an office boy may in time become the head of a large banking institution. A machinist may work up to become the head of a large automobile manufacturing company. The possibility of such advancement has a tendency to increase the efficiency of our laborers. This is what is known in economics as the *vertical mobility of labor*.

Workers also may pass from one kind of employment to another of the same grade. This is called the *horizontal mobility of labor*. Except for some reason external to industry, an unskilled laborer is not compelled to spend his life at a blast furnace. Generally he has the opportunity of obtaining employment as an unskilled worker in a steel and iron mill, a ship yard, a railroad round house, or a cannery, to cite but a few examples. This ability to shift from one industry to another plays a very important part in influencing the average worker's employment, because during periods of normal business activity he need not ordinarily be out of work for a long period of time.

Finally, laborers possess what is known as *geographical mobility;* that is, they may go about from place to place in search of employment. The worker is not compelled to remain in one place during his lifetime but may, if he so desires, travel through the country or through several countries. Some of the factors that restrict the geographical mobility of labor are love of home, lack of funds, absence of that pioneering spirit which is willing to take a chance, and lack of knowledge as to the places where labor is most in demand.

Conservation of Labor Power—During the early years of capitalism, little attention was paid to conserving the labor power of a country. The laborers had come up through centuries of slavery and serfdom without the right to vote or to wield political influence. However, as we look back upon the past, we can appreciate what has been done to conserve the interests of the laboring class. Much has been accomplished in eliminating the wastage of human beings in industry. Safety campaigns have been carried on and many devices have been introduced to protect the workers from the hazards of their daily occupations. Laws have been passed with the intent of abolishing the abuses of child and woman labor. Efforts, to a certain extent successful, have been made to eliminate the horrors of the sweated trades. Steps have been taken to prepare workers for their occupations by compulsory education and by training in trade and technical schools. Much yet remains to be done, and one must remember that society will never be without its economic problems. The most we can do under the circumstances is to appreciate what these problems are and to give constructive thought and effort toward their solution.

Capital Goods

Definition—Capital goods, as we have seen, are the produced, concrete physical goods which are used for further production. They include such things as factory buildings, machinery, typewriters, desks, plows, tools, ships, docks, warehouses, store buildings, adding machines, record books, railway engines, coaches, freight cars, commercial trucks, equipment used for transmitting messages (telephone and telegraph instruments, pneumatic tubes, and so forth)—in fact all articles of wealth, other than land and labor power, that are used to create more goods.

Depreciation of Capital Goods—In the course of production, capital goods ordinarily wear out. The machine in the factory, the typewriter in the bank, the plow on the farm, all depreciate with use and have to be repaired from time to time. Not only is this true, but sometimes the depreciation is so great that repairs are impossible, and a new machine, typewriter, or plow has to be purchased. Land or soil also wears out as it is cultivated. Some crops, especially tobacco, rapidly destroy the fertility of the soil. Therefore, farmers annually spend large sums of money for natural and commercial fertilizers.

Every productive enterprise should keep in first class condition those things in which it has invested its capital and should also replace those that cannot be repaired to advantage. To take care of repairs and replacements, it should set aside a depreciation fund out of its income and in this way maintain the worth of its capital investment.

Obsolescence of Capital Goods—With our rapidly developing and changing methods of production, our capital goods (machinery, factory buildings, office equipment, and so forth) rapidly become obsolete or out of date. When the visible typewriter was invented, the old style typewriters were discarded. In banks, the old fashioned counters, desks, and filing cases are being replaced by others of improved design. Farmers likewise are affected by changes in consumption ideals; they may have to uproot one kind of orchard or vineyard and plant another that will yield crops to satisfy the changed tastes of the public. Thus, capital goods become obsolete, and to maintain the value of the business enterprise, it is necessary that a fund known as an obsolescence fund be set aside from the earnings of the business. This fund is usually merged with the depreciation fund; rarely is it kept separately. Depreciation and obsolescence must be provided for; otherwise the productive strength and efficiency of the enterprise will in time become impaired.

Depreciation and Obsolescence of Labor—We have seen that land and capital goods depreciate and that capital goods may become obsolete. But what about depreciation and obsolescence in the case of laborers? They grow old; they become incapacitated by sickness and accident; sometimes they are killed, just as machines are sometimes destroyed in the productive process. The invention of machinery and the changing styles of the market place force many skilled laborers out of their jobs and compel them to take up other kinds of occupations, which are usually less skilled in character and pay lower wages. Thus laborers, as well as land and capital goods, suffer from depreciation and obsolescence.

In this connection, should not the business enterprise care for its laborers as it does for land and capital goods? This is actually being done today to an ever increasing extent. In the United States, all but a few of our commonwealths now provide for the payment of workmen's compensation to employees who are injured, and death benefits to the dependents of those who are killed in the course of their employment. A few states also provide old age pensions. Some of our larger business concerns carry sickness insurance for their workers and grant old age pensions to their employees. It is doubtful if anything ever will or can be done to provide for the losses sustained by those whose skill is made obsolete by the changing methods of production, but the problem of providing insurance or wages for the unemployed is one that we shall have to face in the future. Some large corporations (the General Electric Company, for example) are now protecting their workers in this regard by means of unemployment insurance.

Factors Affecting Business Returns

Returns on Capital—Every productive enterprise is concerned with the monetary returns obtained on the capital that is invested in the business, that is, in the factors of production. The student should remember that the amount of the capital on which returns are paid is not the same as the amount of the capital that is actually used in the business. You may have $10,000 invested in your grocery business, yet during the year, out of the income which you receive from the sale of your groceries and from bank loans, you may spend an amount of capital equaling $50,000 for groceries so as to keep your shelves filled, for wages of laborers, and for taxes, insurance, and other expenses of doing business. However, you will calculate your returns from the business only on the basis of the $10,000 of capital which you have invested.

The monetary returns which you receive will depend on a number of different factors, such as the prosperity of your community, the effect of your advertising campaigns, your skill at buying groceries and in hiring and managing employees, the goodwill of your customers, competition, fires, accidents to your employees, accidents to other people caused by your employees, and many other matters of similar character. Equally important is the internal arrangement of your business enterprise.

You may invest too much or too little capital in your store equipment. You may purchase too expensive a delivery wagon. You may hire too many or too few employees. You may spread your store out over too large a land area. In other words, you may not be using your factors of production in the right proportions to obtain the best results. This matter of proportionality is a most important element in every business enterprise, regardless of whether it is engaged in farming, in store keeping, in operating a factory or a bank or in carrying on a railroad or a telephone business. It is concerned with the physical output as well as with the financial returns from the business—in other words, with both the physical and the value productivity of the land, labor power, and capital goods used by the business enterprise.

Law of Diminishing Productivity—Every productive enterprise sooner or later comes face to face with what is known as the *law of diminishing productivity*. Briefly stated, it is to the effect that as more units of land or labor power or capital goods are added in production, a point will eventually be reached where the physical product per unit of land, labor power, or capital goods, respectively, will decrease. In presenting a theoretical discussion of this law, it should be remembered that each unit of land, labor power, or capital goods is considered as being the exact equivalent of every other unit of land, labor power, or capital goods, respectively. In the actual business world, however, allowance is made for the fact that the units of land, labor power, and capital goods that are used vary greatly in quality; but, even so, the law of diminishing productivity still holds good in practice.

Considering first the working of the law in the field of agriculture, let us start with one unit of land (an acre), one unit of capital goods (represented by hoes, spades, rakes, and so forth, valued at $100), and one unit of labor power (a laborer). We get a certain product from such a combination of the factors of production. If we add another acre of the same kind of land (that is, if we cultivate more extensively), we have to spread our small amount of capital and the efforts of our one laborer over a much larger area; therefore, we obtain a decreased product per acre of land cultivated. The effect is the same as when we put a tablespoonful of vanilla extract into a gallon of ice cream, which proportion gives us the right flavor, as contrasted with putting the same amount of vanilla extract into five gallons of ice cream, which proportion gives us only the faintest evidence of flavor. Our vanilla has been spread out through too large a mass, and we therefore get decreased results from it.

If we cultivate our one acre of land *intensively* by adding more laborers possessed of the same skill or more capital goods of the same kind, we get an increased product per acre up to a certain point, beyond which diminishing productivity appears. The following table presents the idea more clearly than the simple statement of fact and illustrates what may occur by varying the number of units of labor. Similar results can be obtained by varying the number of units of capital goods.

DIMINISHING RETURNS IN PRODUCTION OF CORN

Amount of land cultivated, 100 acres

Laborers Employed	Total Yield	Yield per Acre	Yield per Laborer
10	2,000	20	200
11	2,300	23	209
12	2,350	23½	196
13	2,400	24	170

In this example, a diminished physical product per laborer is reached with the twelfth laborer, and it is even more noticeable with the thirteenth laborer, although the total yield for the 100 acres is greater with thirteen laborers than with ten, eleven, or twelve laborers.

Constant Productivity—In some kinds of business, we have constant productivity up to a certain point, beyond which diminishing productivity sets in. A plant that is engaged in the manufacture of cigars or clothing by hand is typical of this type of enterprise. Extra laborers can be added, or extra benches can be placed in the shop up to a certain point, without either increasing or decreasing the physical output per man. After a while, however, too many laborers may be employed and too many benches may be added, thus causing congestion and the interference of one laborer with another and resulting in a decreased physical output per employee or per unit of capital goods.

Application of the Law of Diminishing Productivity—If there were no law of diminishing productivity, it would be possible for a farmer to keep on adding laborers and capital goods to an acre of land and thus produce enough crops to feed the entire nation; or it would be possible for a clothing manufacturer to add more benches, laborers, and machinery to his factory until he could produce enough clothing to satisfy the needs of all the people of the world. Every productive enterprise has to watch most carefully the various proportions of land, labor power, and capital goods that are consumed. If it does not do so, it will find that it is obtaining too small a physical product in comparison with the costs of the land, labor power, and capital goods that are being used. At times, when the physical productivity of an enterprise is decreasing, the addition of more land or labor power or capital goods, or a combination of them, may result in an increased physical output; but if too much of any one or of all of the factors of production is added, productivity will again decrease.

It should be noted that the point at which diminishing physical productivity begins to operate does not coincide with the point at which a financial loss will be incurred by the business. Even after diminishing physical productivity has set in, the price received for the product is always high enough to permit production to be pushed further by the addition of more land or labor power or capital goods. The point at which the producer should stop, at least theoretically, is where the cost of adding another unit of land or labor power or capital goods will just equal the value of the goods that are added to the product of the enterprise. By no means do producers always stop, even at that point. Of course, many do not know when that point has been reached; hence they continue to expand their business, finally making no profits whatsoever, or possibly even becoming bankrupt. Certain factors other than the physical productivity of land, labor power, and capital goods bring about business failures, and those other elements will be discussed at length in subsequent pages of this text.

The Effect of Costs on Returns—Not only is the owner of a business enterprise interested in the fact that the productivity of the land, labor power, and capital goods, when measured in terms of physical quantities of goods produced, tends to decrease after a certain point has been reached, but he is also vitally concerned with the equally important matters of the costs of the product per unit of output and the price that he gets for his goods or products when he sells them. To state the proposition in another manner, we may say that the producer is interested not only in the physical output of his enterprise but also in the value of his output, that is, in the money return he receives per unit of product. If the costs per unit increase as more is produced, we have a business of increasing costs or of decreasing financial returns per unit of product. If the costs decrease per unit as more is produced, we then have a business of decreasing costs or increasing financial returns per unit of product. Some kinds of business have constant costs up to a certain point and therefore constant financial returns per unit of product; but after that point has been reached, if the enterprise is further expanded, its costs increase and its financial returns per unit of product decrease. It should be evident that as costs increase (if other conditions, such as price, remain the same), the returns that business receives will decrease, and conversely. Consequently, increasing costs mean decreasing financial returns and decreasing costs mean increasing financial returns.

Enterprises with Diminishing Returns—Some enterprises are characterized by decreasing financial returns per unit from the outset. This is true in the case of extensive agriculture. It is also true of the telephone business. The cheapest message which a telephone company can handle is one that is cared for by a small country exchange, employing only one operator. As business expands and more switchboards and more operators are required, the cost per message increases, and the financial returns per unit of land, labor power, and capital goods used decrease. With the further expansion in the number of calls, an exchange of several floors has to be built, necessitating the use of much more expensive equipment. Where several exchanges have to be erected to serve the telephone needs of a large city, calls have to be relayed across the city and from floor to floor in the exchanges, with still greater costs than before; therefore, the cost per call increases with the number of calls handled, and a smaller financial return is obtained from each call. However, so many more calls are taken care of that the company does not become bankrupt as a result of its expanding business and increasing costs. It is merely a case of many sales and a small profit on each sale, rather than a few sales and a large profit on each sale.

Enterprises with Increasing Returns—Some enterprises are characterized by increasing returns up to a certain point, which, of course, varies with each business; but beyond this point decreased financial returns set in. A small business may be very successful, and its owners may feel that greater profits can be secured if it is expanded. More space is taken, more laborers are hired, and more goods are purchased. The profits or financial gains may increase at a greater rate than before. Where they were 5% they may become 6%. Further expansion may be decided upon, but the returns may then, much to the surprise of the owners of the business, decrease to 5% and with still further expansion may drop to 4%. Too much capital has been invested in the business for increased amounts of land, labor power, and capital goods. Costs have risen, while sales have not increased as expected. This is the story of many a firm that has attempted to increase its profits by expanding beyond the requirements of the market.

Enterprises with Constant Returns—In the case of those enterprises that are characterized by constant costs, if too many laborers, too much land, or too great an amount of capital goods is added, costs will increase and the financial returns per unit of product will concurrently diminish.

Importance of Costs to Business Men—The matters which have just been discussed are of importance to every person engaged in a business enterprise. The costs per unit of output must be carefully watched and must be considered in relation to the price that is obtained for the goods or the services when sold in the market. When the costs per unit of output increase, the financial return per unit must necessarily decrease.

Banks have to watch their costs just as carefully as does any other kind of business. For example, today as never before banks are giving serious attention to the cost of handling depositors' accounts. Many institutions now levy a service charge of fifty cents or one dollar per month to defray the cost of handling small checking accounts. They are beginning to appreciate the fact that, because of the element of increasing costs, a large amount of business may be less profitable than a small amount. Some banks are housed in banking quarters that are most ostentatious and entail great expense. Some suffer from having to carry a heavy overhead of too many high salaried officials. Others do not skilfully invest their funds so as to obtain the maximum return. Many give an excess of free service to their depositors at an expense that is far greater than the monetary return that is indirectly received therefrom.

An interesting statement of how the costs of carrying on certain phases of the banking business actually increase with the amount of business transacted is contained in the January 1931 issue of The Burroughs Clearing House, a banking magazine. In discussing the costs of making small personal loans through the Morris Plan banks, this article makes the following statement:

"The percentage of cost of doing business on a volume of $200,000 in personal loans rises as the volume increases up to $10,000,000. In Morris Plan banks the lowest overhead per one dollar loaned exists, on the average, in the smaller institutions. The largest banks do not have the lowest operating costs. . . . More specifically, the actual cost of lending money in the smaller industrial banks—those lending usually less than

$500,000—is six and one-half cents per dollar loaned, or $12.60 per loan made; and in the larger banks, as the amount annually loaned increases to $10,000,000 and more, the cost per dollar loaned increases to seven and one-third cents and the cost per loan made to $19.88."

CHAPTER VII

Marketing

PRODUCTION today is carried on primarily for sale in the market place and not for the personal use of the producers themselves. The farmer raises wheat, corn, and cotton for sale to others in order to obtain a money income with which to buy clothes, food, farm machinery, and other commodities that he desires. A mining company has no need of the ores which it digs from the earth, except to sell them to others. The manufacturer of cloth, metal, and wooden products is likewise interested in finding a market for his goods. Those who have money to lend must find borrowers, and those who have stocks and bonds to sell must find parties willing to buy. Storekeepers must have customers. Those who stand ready to render personal services to others, such as lawyers, dentists, teachers, and skilled and unskilled laborers, must find clients, patients, and employers, respectively, before they can engage in productive activities.

The market, therefore constitutes an important phase of our economic life. If we cannot sell our goods, we will not raise or make them, and if there is no one willing to purchase our personal services, we cannot render them. It may be that there is a market for our goods and services already in existence; if not, we may have to create one by resorting to advertising. Modern production could not continue without a market.

Definition of a Market—We may define a market as the combination of those conditions which make it possible for a buyer and a seller or many buyers and many sellers to come into contact with one another for the purpose of making an exchange. The subject of marketing covers the functions and activities of all those who are engaged in buying and selling goods. More technically, the term *marketing* is sometimes used to refer only to the selling of commodities in wholesale lots, while the term *merchandising* is used ordinarily to refer to the selling of commodities at retail.

Marketing a Phase of Production—Production is concerned with the creation of commodities and the rendering of personal services; in other words, with the creation of form, time, and place utilities. Those who make or raise commodities and those who render services are primarily interested in the matter of form utility, while those who are engaged in the marketing processes are concerned primarily with time and place utilities. The wholesaler, the jobber, the storekeeper, the foreign trader, and the railroad, steamship, and airplane carriers do not change the form of the product. They merely assist in putting the commodity in the place where the public wants it at the time when it is wanted, but all of them are as much engaged in productive activity as are those persons who raise farm products, dig ore, or manufacture goods out of cloth, metal, and wood, and society is willing to compensate them for their efforts.

Necessity for Marketing—Marketing is trading. Men have always traded the things that they have for those things that others have. No man has ever been completely self-sufficient in his economic activities. Even among the members of the most barbaric tribes there exists a considerable amount of trading or barter. No nation, not even the United States with all of its great and varied resources and its modern and efficient methods of exploiting them, can produce all the things that are demanded by its people. Tea, coffee, bananas, rubber, nitrates, and hundreds of other products must be obtained by us from various countries, in return for which we export our own products. It is this demand for the goods of other countries that brings about foreign trade with its many interesting and perplexing problems.

Domestic Trade

Marketing Agents—There are two general classes of marketing agents, wholesalers and retailers. The wholesaler deals in large lots and seldom makes an effort to reach the ultimate consumer. The retailer, on the other hand, is concerned with selling goods to the ultimate consumer, and he sells those goods in small quantities.

The Wholesaler—Very few manufacturers sell to the retailer, and still fewer attempt to sell directly to the consumer. This is so, not because they do not wish to make the effort, but because they cannot build up an organization that will enable them to carry on that phase of the business on a scale sufficiently large to permit them to dispose of their products, or else because they are certain that the wholesaler-retailer plan is more efficient than any which they themselves could develop.

Likewise, very few farmers sell directly to the retailer or to the consumer. They usually sell to wholesalers, either private or cooperative in character, because they thus have a ready market established for their goods without any effort on their part and because they feel that they obtain better monetary results by doing so.

The wholesaler performs a number of different functions. Frequently he purchases goods in small amounts from farmers or manufacturers and, by assembling them in large enough quantities to supply the trade, renders a valuable economic service. He also frequently stores the goods from the time they have been made or raised until they can be passed on to the retailer.

For instance, when the walnut crop has been harvested in the fall of the year, it cannot be sold in its entirety in a week or two. It has to be stored while being gradually passed on to the retailers. The wholesaler assumes a great risk in buying goods at current prices and holding them for sale in the future, because during the interval between purchase and sale prices may fall to lower levels. He frequently grades, sorts, and packs the products that he buys. Wheat, coffee, wool, and other farm products have to be cleaned and graded before being passed on to other purchasers. At times, also, the wholesaler packs the products under his own labels and, by advertising their qualities, creates a demand for them. The wholesaler not infrequently finances the retailer by extending him credit for goods purchased.

The Retailer—The retailers constitute by far the largest group of traders. They are the storekeepers of the land. The old fashioned general country store, in which practically every sort of commodity could be purchased, is rapidly passing from the scene. Even our large department stores have not noticeably increased in number during the past two decades. Retail establishments have become increasingly specialized, not infrequently handling a single kind of article. Thus it is that we have shoe stores, grocery stores, meat markets, haberdasheries, shirt shops, cigar stores, and even necktie stores.

The retailer has to carry so many different brands of goods or so many different grades of the same goods in stock that it is usually impossible for him to buy directly from the manufacturer. It is far better for him to have only one or two wholesalers from whom to purchase his supplies than to be compelled to buy from many different producers the various kinds of articles that he carries. He saves time by doing so, and he is also able to obtain the kind of credit cooperation that he needs, which would not be available if he attempted to purchase his supplies from forty or fifty manufacturers.

Education of Retailers—Too many people believe that it requires no skill or ability to set oneself up in business as a storekeeper. This belief accounts for the very high mortality rate among the country's retail establishments. During periods of depression, the number of such concerns that fail is surprisingly large. The duty of educating the retailer falls upon the wholesaler and the banker. The wholesaler can advise him as to how large a stock of goods to carry, how to dress his window and arrange the interior of his shop, how to keep his accounts, and how to follow the fundamental principles of good salesmanship. Every storekeeper who goes into bankruptcy and fails to pay his bills merely increases the cost of buying for the public. This is so because the wholesaler has to treat bad debts as a cost of doing business and, wherever possible, adds such cost to the price that he charges other retailers, who in their turn attempt, sometimes successfully, to pass the increase in price on to the general buying public.

The banker can advise the retailer as to the amount of credit that should be extended to his customers, for usually in a small or medium sized town the local banker is intimately acquainted with a large proportion of the population. Bankers can also aid in establishing retail credit associations for the purpose of remedying or improving local credit conditions. They should, moreover, educate the retailer as to the importance of taking his discounts. If the wholesaler sells to the retailer on the basis of 1%—10 days or 30 days net, it means that the retailer obtains a discount of 1% on the face value of his bill by paying cash within ten days, but that if he does not do so, he then has to pay the full amount of the bill at the conclusion of thirty days. If he pays the bill within ten days, he gains 1%, or 18% per year. Even though a retailer has to borrow money at 7% or 8% in order to take a discount, it really pays him to do so. He not only gains his discount, less interest on the loan if he has to borrow to take the discount, but he also obtains a better credit standing with his wholesaler and with his banker as well.

Chain Stores—One of the most significant developments in the retail field has been the rapid growth in the chain store movement. The Piggly Wiggly stores are found all over the world. There is no good sized city in the United States that lacks a cigar store, a grocery store, a five and ten cent store, or a drug store that is owned by a chain company. Chains also operate department stores, gasoline stations, upstairs clothing stores, dental offices, and so forth. Independent dealers are faced with vigorous competition from the chain companies and, in many cases, have been forced into bankruptcy because of it. Chain stores operate on a standardized basis as to prices, equipment, advertising, and sales policies. The head office purchases in large quantities and at low prices, advantages which are in part passed on to the consumer. In practically all cases they do a "cash and carry" business, thereby eliminating the costs due to delivery expenses and to the extension of credit with its accompanying unpaid bills.

They operate with large amounts of capital and are thus placed in a financial position better than that of the small independent dealer, who may be handicapped by lack of working capital.

Another interesting development during the past decade has been the entrance into the retail field by the large mail order houses. Sears Roebuck and Company, Montgomery Ward & Company, and other similar concerns have established retail stores in advantageous locations, and as a result they have greatly increased the total amounts of their sales, thereby cutting deeply into the trade of the local independent dealers.

Advertising—In order to market goods or services, advertising in various forms is resorted to. The brands of goods that are for sale must be kept constantly before the consuming public. Slogans of various kinds, striking words and phrases, pictures, and other devices are employed, sometimes truthfully and sometimes not, for the purpose of inducing the buyer, who knows nothing whatsoever about the real worth of the advertised goods, to buy one particular kind of product or service rather than another. Our annual expenditures for advertising exceed $1,500,000,000, and much of this huge sum is spent in coaxing people to purchase goods that they do not want or do not need. Advertising gives the buyer information (sometimes misleading) as to the desirable qualities of the goods advertised, their prices, and the stores where they may be purchased. Advertising is helpful in production, because it tends to build up sales, and without sales, production as it is carried on today in this country could not exist.

Cooperative Marketing—We have a few cooperative stores in the United States, but for the most part they have not been successful. They have usually been poorly managed, inadequately supplied with capital, and handicapped by the refusal of many wholesalers to sell to them because of the opposition of independent retailers. Our experience with agricultural cooperative marketing associations has been a little more satisfactory in character; some of them have been in existence for many years and have proved to be profitable to their members. Farmers who belong to the cooperative marketing associations can turn their crops over to the associations to be marketed in a much more systematic manner than would be possible if each of the farmers attempted individually to market his own crops.

Produce Markets—Mention must also be made of our large organized markets, known as produce exchanges, in which agricultural products are sold. The Chicago Board of Trade is the most outstanding example of this type of exchange in the United States, although there are others not quite so important, such as the New York Cotton Exchange and the New York Coffee Exchange. These exchanges afford an organized market for trading in large amounts of coffee, cotton, wheat, and other agricultural crops, similar to that afforded the financial world by the stock and bond exchanges. They are associations of the more important dealers, who meet daily at certain hours to buy and sell the farm products that are in the market or are later to come into it. The exchanges function under rigid rules, settle disputes between their members, establish grades for the goods dealt in, and supply information as to crops and markets throughout the world, thus facilitating the purchase and sale of such products. By their transactions, they set the prices of the important agricultural commodities, and these prices form the basis for those paid elsewhere throughout the country.

Stock Markets—Stocks and bonds also must be marketed. Every large center of population has a stock exchange, the most important in the United States being that of New York City. The members of a stock exchange are the only persons who have the privilege of buying and selling securities on its floor. Securities are also bought and sold by stock and bond houses and by brokers who have no connection whatsoever with any stock exchange. The prices at which most stocks and bonds are sold to the public are those that are quoted daily on the stock exchanges of the larger cities.

Employment Exchanges—Laborers also have to find buyers or employers who are willing to purchase their services. Lawyers, doctors, and dentists must obtain clients or patients; sometimes they advertise their services and sometimes they do not. To a considerable extent, teachers and both skilled and unskilled manual laborers obtain their positions through employment agencies. These agencies usually charge a fee for their services. As a rule, they are owned and operated privately, although in some instances they are owned and managed by a municipality or by the state.

Our Marketing System Is Changing—Among the most interesting developments that have occurred in the past generation are those concerned with our marketing processes. We have learned how to make goods at low cost and how to raise farm products cheaply, but their marketing has involved excessive expenditures of money. The practices which we have been accustomed to follow have been clumsy, inefficient, and costly. Much progress has recently been made in eliminating waste of effort and of money, but much yet remains to be done before we can claim to have an efficient marketing system. New practices and policies must be devised and applied, economies must be effected, and marketing methods must be systematized. It may be that in time big business will dominate the field of marketing, as it already dominates the field of production, and thus will bring to the public the benefits of large scale operations in the elimination of waste products, wasted effort, and wasted capital.

Foreign Trade

Reasons for Foreign Trade—Foreign trade has

always been and still is a realm filled with romance for the human race. The tales of adventure of those who sail the high seas or follow the caravans over the sandy deserts or through the mountain passes have always carried a thrill for all of us. But as students of economics, we must concern ourselves with the more practical and less romantic aspects of the subject. The human race engages in foreign trade for two reasons: (1) in order that people may obtain from other countries goods which they themselves cannot produce, and (2) in order that they may obtain goods more cheaply than they themselves can produce those goods. The United States, for example, cannot produce tea, coffee, tin, and many other products which it needs, and it therefore imports them from abroad. We do produce olive oil, watches, wheat, wool, shoes, and thousands of other commodities, but even so we import many of these products also, because other countries are able to lay them down on our shores and in our markets at prices which induce us to purchase them. We, in turn, export goods to other countries, and these countries buy them from us for the reasons that have just been enumerated.

Content of Foreign Trade—Most of us think of foreign trade as involving only the importation or exportation of raw materials, gold, and manufactured goods—in other words, the tangible or visible items of trade. Therefore, we commonly speak of a *favorable balance of trade* when we export more of such goods than we import and of an *unfavorable balance of trade* when we import a greater quantity of such goods than we export.

Such tangible or visible items, however, constitute only a part of the content of foreign trade. There are many other items involved, which we designate as "invisible items." At present, the invisible items comprise about one-third of the value of the total foreign trade of the United States. They consist of credits and services of one kind or another, involving payments by us to foreigners and payments by them to us. Foreign ships carry much of our ocean freight, as well as many of our tourists, and we have to pay the owners of these foreign ships large sums of money each year for such services. Our tourists annually take abroad funds approximating $300,000,000. Foreign insurance companies write marine, life, accident, and other kinds of policies for our citizens, and we have to pay millions of dollars annually for them. Foreigners residing in the United States annually send abroad about $250,-000,000 to friends and relatives. Loans are made by our government and by our financial institutions to foreign governments. Americans purchase foreign securities, invest billions of dollars abroad, pay motion picture royalties, subscribe for foreign magazines, contribute to missionary and charitable activities, and pay out sums of money for foreign advertising. All of these transactions involve the making of payments to the people of foreign countries, and they, in turn, make payments to us for similar kinds of credit accommodation and service.

Realizing, therefore, that foreign trade is made up

of both visible and invisible items, we can appreciate why it is that authors in this field now speak of a *balance of international payments* instead, as formerly, of a balance of trade. Over a period of years, a nation's total imports and exports must balance, or an adjustment is necessary. The goods and services that we sell to other countries must be paid for by them in terms of goods and services. If a balance remains unpaid, they must extend us credit or pay us in gold, gold being the international medium of exchange. On the other hand, if we purchase more from other countries than we sell to them, it is obvious that we are forced to pay the balance by extending them credit or by shipping gold.

Significance of Our Foreign Trade—The interest of Americans in foreign trade became increasingly active after the Spanish-American War, but it was not until the period of the World War that foreign trade began to make a significant appeal to the American business man. During that period, many exporting and importing firms were established to exploit the foreign markets which had been abandoned by the European nations that were forced to concern themselves with a life and death struggle at home. Another circumstance that gave us prominence in the realm of foreign trade was the fact that the United States remained upon a gold basis while the countries of Europe adopted a depreciated paper money standard, with accompanying disastrous results for themselves both at home and abroad. The worldwide post-war depression of 1920-1921 seriously curtailed our foreign trade activities, causing many importing and exporting firms to fail and much money to be lost. Since that time we have had to rebuild slowly upon a more solid and certain foundation.

For the fiscal year ending June 30, 1929, both our exports and our imports expanded to the highest points since the World War. Merchandise exports (not including re-exports) amounted to $5,157,083,000, and merchandise imports exceeded $4,756,000,000. The totals of our exports and our imports (both visible and invisible) were each about $10,000,000,000. It is interesting to note that the value of our exports of merchandise is estimated to be approximately 11% of the value of our total production of goods. This fact has led many persons to claim that we are spending too much energy and money in developing our foreign trade and that it would be better for us to confine our efforts to exploiting the home markets more thoroughly. The advocates of this latter policy, however, overlook the important fact that foreign trade enables many of our producers to make a profitable return on the remaining percentage of the goods which they sell at home. If all of our products had to be thrown onto the home market, prices might be so greatly depressed that there would be no profit for the producer. When he can sell a portion of his goods in a foreign market, he is able to operate on a much broader basis than if he were producing only for domestic markets, and thus he can secure the economies arising from large scale operations.

Selling Necessitates Buying—Many of those who are interested in developing foreign trade look upon it only as the exportation of goods. The average American fails to appreciate the fact that foreign trade involves both imports and exports and necessitates reciprocal relations. If we desire to sell to foreign countries, we must buy from them. If a local merchant wishes to sell to his fellow citizens, he can do so only if they have money, goods, or services to give him in exchange for his goods. They must work for him or for others, or they must sell to him or to others, in order to get the funds with which to make their purchases. He cannot continue to sell to them indefinitely unless they have the means with which to buy. The same principle is involved in connection with our foreign trade activities. If we wish to sell to European countries, they must have the means with which to buy. They may pay us in merchandise, services, credit, or gold. So far as gold is concerned, however, there is not enough gold in the world to enable them to use it indefinitely in paying us for what they purchase. At present, we have no desire to borrow from them, because we are amply supplied with gold and credit, while they have no spare funds to lend. Our tourist expenditures in Europe, amounting to about $300,000,000 a year, help out the situation to a certain extent, as do those charges which are made for services of various kinds rendered to our citizens by Europeans. The fundamental basis for our foreign trade activities must, therefore, remain an exchange of our raw materials, manufactured goods, and services for the raw materials, manufactured goods, and services that are produced by foreign countries.

Character of Our Foreign Trade—In the early history of the foreign trade of our country, we imported large amounts of manufactured goods and exported quantities of raw materials. Later, however, the tide turned, and we are now importing increasingly greater quantities of raw materials and exporting larger and larger amounts of manufactured goods. We are no longer predominantly an agricultural people. The sources of certain of our raw materials are being rapidly exhausted, and this situation is forcing us to look to other countries for the needed supplies. Our manufacturing industries are expanding and have already reached a point where our own people cannot consume all that they produce, thus making it necessary for us to go in search of foreign markets and to cultivate a demand among foreigners for American made goods. This tendency will unquestionably become stronger with the passing of time and will lead to the further expansion of our foreign trade activities.

Not only is the character of our foreign trade changing, but the relative importance of our trade with various portions of the world is also undergoing a transformation. Europe is still our best customer, but the percentage of our total exports to South America has been showing an upward trend, while the percentage of our total exports to Europe has been showing a downward trend. The undeveloped sections of the globe may prove to be our best markets in the future, and they are also likely to be the sources from which we shall have to draw our largest supplies of foodstuffs and raw materials.

Basic Principle of Foreign Trade—As already noted, trade between nations develops because the various countries cannot produce all of the commodities they desire and because some countries can produce certain commodities more cheaply than others. China can produce tea, but the United States cannot. Therefore, we say that in this regard China has an *absolute* advantage over the United States. If the United States can produce both steel rails and cutlery more cheaply than England, it is said to have an absolute advantage over England in the production of those two commodities. But let us say that the United States can produce steel rails more cheaply than cutlery and that England can produce cutlery more cheaply than steel rails; then from the standpoint of the comparative advantage of both countries, it is better for the United States to specialize on steel rails and for England to specialize on cutlery, for by so doing each country will be using its productive agencies to the best advantage. The United States would probably make more profit by specializing on rails and exchanging them for English cutlery than by trying to produce both commodities.

This is an illustration of what is known as the principle of comparative costs. Briefly defined, it is to the effect that a country should specialize in producing those commodities which it can produce the most cheaply or in which it enjoys a comparative advantage. To illustrate this principle further in a crude sort of way, let us say that a lawyer is also an expert stenographer; in fact, he is a better stenographer than any one in his employ. But even though that is the case, it is better for him to give his entire attention to his law practice and to hire others to carry on his stenographic work, for by so doing he can obtain a much larger income.

Nations also are interested in obtaining larger incomes, and it is urged that they, too, should follow the principle of comparative costs in connection with their productive and trading activities. In practice, however, while theoretically sound, this principle is not widely adopted. Each nation desires to make itself as self-sufficient as possible and hence tries to develop within its boundaries industries which are not by any means the most profitable it could pursue and which frequently are not able to compete with similar industries elsewhere. Satisfactory cost of production figures as between various countries cannot be obtained, and as a consequence it is not possible to secure a basis for an estimate of the comparative advantages of the several industries of those countries. Also, the owners of capital do not concern themselves with the principle of comparative costs; they are interested only in the return upon their invested capital. Even though the United States has a comparative advantage over England in the production of steel rails, our capitalists will invest their funds in the production of cutlery, provided they can make a fair return upon their investment in that field. The imposition of a protective tariff, as we shall see later, precludes the application of this principle of comparative costs.

Foreign Trade Policy—The foreign trade policy of a government is a subject of many phases. To discuss it thoroughly would require a consideration of the attitude of the government toward its merchant marine, the granting of bounties or subsidies to ship owners, the enactment of legislation regulating registry under the country's flag, the creation and support of a satisfactory consular and commercial attaché service, the drafting of commercial treaties, the policy of the government in encouraging or discouraging foreign investments, as well as a number of other similar topics. In this brief textbook we can consider only the matter of tariff policy.

Tariffs—The Articles of Confederation adopted at the conclusion of the Revolutionary War did not prohibit the various states from levying duties upon goods crossing their boundaries, even though the goods came from other states, and as a consequence, much difficulty was experienced by merchants and traders. Interstate tariffs constituted one of the reasons for the adoption of the Constitution of the United States. Our Constitution prohibits the individual states of the Union from levying tariffs. Congress alone has that privilege, although it is prohibited from levying duties on exports. From 1789 down to date, the United States has been primarily a high tariff or protective tariff country. The tariff issue has always been with us and has provided us with a considerable amount of controversial literature.

Purpose of Import Duties—Duties on imports are levied for one or both of two reasons. If a tariff is imposed only for the purpose of raising a revenue for the government, it is called a *tariff for revenue only*. It is more frequently referred to as embodying a free trade policy. When such a tariff is in effect, duties are levied only on goods that are not produced within the country concerned and no effort is made to prevent their importation. If duties are imposed for the purpose of preventing certain foreign made goods from entering the country or of making it more difficult for them to enter, so as to protect the products of the country concerned, it is then known as a *protective tariff*. A tariff, however, is usually framed both for the purpose of providing revenue for the government and for the purpose of protecting home products.

Specific versus Ad Valorem Duties—The duties of a tariff measure may be specific or *ad valorem* in character. A specific duty is one that is levied at so much per yard, per pound, per quart, or per article, while an *ad valorem* duty is a percentage of the value of the goods.

Arguments for and against a Protective Tariff— Many arguments have been advanced both for and against the protective tariff. Only a few of the more important of those arguments can be considered in this text.

It is urged that a protective tariff is desirable because it assists our infant industries to become more firmly established and thus enables them to meet foreign competition in a satisfactory manner. When a new industry is being started, it is in a weak condition competitively. It has to face the attacks of foreign firms which have long been in the field. It must force its way into new markets. Just as parents protect their children while they are growing up, so it is claimed that the government should protect its young industries until they attain maturity and are able to stand alone. There is one difficulty about such tariff protection, however, and that is the fact that the infant industries are never willing to admit that they have grown up. Once protected by the tariff, they insist upon continued protection, no matter how strong and dominating a factor in the home or foreign markets they may have become.

Another argument for protection is based upon the claims of those who are interested in military preparedness. It is urged that a country should encourage and develop its industries so as to become self-sufficient in time of war. The protective tariff is urged as a means to that end. During the World War, for example, the importation of dyestuffs from Germany was suspended and our textile industries were greatly handicapped because of the lack of satisfactory dyes. Therefore, it is claimed that a protective tariff upon dyestuffs should be imposed so as to enable our chemical industries to perfect the manufacture of dyes and thus free us from having to depend upon Germany or any other country in the future. On the other hand, it is argued that the protective tariff has frequently been one of the causes of war and that its abolition would do much toward bringing about world peace. The assassination of the heir to the throne of Austria-Hungary in 1914, which let loose the dogs of the World War, was caused in part by the intense hatred aroused in the Serbians by a discriminatory tariff on Serbian pigs imposed by Austria-Hungary. During the discussion of the Hawley-Smoot Tariff Act of 1930, a number of nations protested to the United States against the enactment of its provisions, and some threatened and actually put into effect retaliatory tariff measures. The result was increased tension and hard feeling between those nations and our own country.

An affirmative argument that is very commonly resorted to, especially in connection with the political aspects of the protective tariff, is the wage argument. The American workers and voters are told that the protective tariff is responsible for the high level of wages in the United States. Protection, it is claimed, brings prosperity to American industries by eliminating foreign competition and thereby makes for employment, high prices, and high wages. Another phase of the argument is that the protective tariff guards the high wages and the high plane of living of the American workers by keeping out the cheap products of the foreign workers who have low wages and a low plane of living. In reply, it is maintained that our wage scale has always been higher than that of Europe because of the greater productivity of American workers. Wages are paid out of product, and the greater the product, the greater the wage. If, for example, the Chinese government should absolutely prohibit the importation of any foreign made goods into China, would the Chinese laborers, with their inefficient methods of production and their low productive power, be able to command a wage equal to that paid the American workers?

At election time, candidates for political office inform their constituents that the American workingman is the most efficient and productive worker in the world; yet, in the next breath, they announce that the efficient American workingman cannot compete with the inefficient foreign worker. In golf, as in many other athletic contests, the stronger player is never given a handicap over the weaker player, because it is known that the comparatively strong player can take care of his own interests. The weaker player is the one who is usually protected. Why, then, should the efficient workingman be protected against the inefficient workingman by the means of a protective tariff? It is interesting to note that in some of the European countries the above argument has been given a peculiar twist, resulting in the advocacy of a protective tariff for the purpose of protecting the inefficient European worker against the competition of the highly efficient American worker.

It is also pointed out by the opponents of the protective tariff that protected industries do not pay a higher wage than do those that are not protected, and also that there are many millions of workers in the United States who are not employed in any protected industry, such as those who work on railroads, in offices, in banks, and in the building industries, and who yet receive a high wage.

Another argument for the protective tariff concerns the advisability of cultivating the home market. It is claimed that under a protective tariff home industries will be encouraged. Factories in many different lines will spring up, using the country's raw materials and providing employment for our citizens. The home market is the sure, certain market, where no difficulties arise because of changes in the monetary or banking systems or in the tariff, or because of war. This line of reasoning is a phase of the "trade at home" theory. On the other hand, no country can live by itself alone. We must trade with other countries; our people cannot consume all that we produce; our producers of raw materials and manufactured goods must have foreign markets in which to sell their wares. The larger the number of countries dealt with, the more diversified are the risks entailed and the less serious are the results of any local disturbance.

The opponents of the protective tariff inquire why, if a protective tariff is a good thing for a nation, it should not be equally beneficial to a city or a state. In the United States, for example, shoes made in Massachusetts compete in California with shoes manufactured in that state, and Minnesota wheat competes with wheat raised in Illinois. Yet among our people there is no demand for a protective tariff as between the various political divisions of our government. Trade, either domestic or foreign, profits from lack of restriction in its movement between markets. Free trade has worked out satisfactorily within the United States. Why, one might ask, would it not be advisable to put it into effect between all the nations of the world?

The advocates of free trade maintain that a protective tariff leads to inefficiency in production. Basing their arguments upon the principle of comparative costs, they claim that every country should produce those things which it can produce the most efficiently, and then exchange those goods for the goods of other countries, which likewise should produce commodities that they can produce the most efficiently. They argue that when a country protects an industry, it is keeping alive an industry that cannot stand upon its own feet and that the consumers have to pay the costs thereof in the form of higher prices. If, for example, the lemon growers of the United States cannot compete with those of Italy, why should a tariff be levied upon lemons, thereby forcing the American people to pay high prices for them? Why not abolish the tariff and lower the price of lemons? Then if the lemon growers cannot meet the Italian competition, they will be forced to transfer their capital and efforts to some other form of agricultural crop that can exist without the aid of a protective tariff.

The opponents of the protective tariff maintain that it is the consumer who foots the bills by being forced to pay higher prices for protected goods. They claim that on imported goods the duty is added to the original price and that on domestic articles the producer keeps his price at a high level because of the existence of the protective tariff. It is true that the duty is often passed on to the consumer, but this is by no means always possible.

Conclusion—The question of the protective tariff is still a live political issue. It is interesting to note that in England, where since the middle of the nineteenth century a policy of tariff for revenue only has been consistently followed, a widespread campaign is now being waged for the adoption of a protective tariff. In the United States, on the other hand, there appears to be a growing sentiment in favor of a lower tariff policy. During the discussion of the Hawley-Smoot Tariff of 1930 many of our leading financiers, industrialists, and foreign traders, as well as some of our most conservative periodicals, protested against the upward revision of the tariff. The claim was made that our manufacturers needed to obtain raw materials from abroad as cheaply as possible in order to have low costs of production so as to compete successfully in foreign markets. Foreign traders urged that the ill will engendered abroad by the imposition of a higher tariff would greatly hamper their efforts in disposing of American made goods to the people of foreign countries. With the increased importance of our manufacturing interests and their demand for cheap supplies of raw materials, with a larger share of our population residing in cities and being employed in manufacturing, transportation, and allied industries, and with a smaller proportion of our people engaged in agriculture and in the extractive industries, we shall undoubtedly soon find a changed attitude among Americans as to the advisability and necessity of a high protective tariff.

CHAPTER VIII

Transportation

IN order that those who have commodities and services to sell may have access to markets, transportation facilities of various kinds are required. In primitive times goods were carried on the backs of men and beasts of burden, or, where possible, in crudely designed water crafts. The invention of the wheel brought about the introduction of the wheelbarrow, the cart, and the wagon. Still greater progress was made when the steam engine was adapted to both land and water transportation, giving us the railroad train and the steamboat. It is difficult to appreciate fully the results that have come about in transportation methods from the development of the steam engine.

In discussing the transportation system of a country today, we must include not only the facilities afforded by the steam railroads and the water carriers but also those supplied by electric railways, pipelines, airplanes, motor cars, and motor busses. Only within the past decade or two has motor transportation appeared as an effective competitor of both rail and water carriers. Even more lately has the airplane attracted attention as a potential factor in the field of transportation.

Benefits of Transportation—Transportation has made possible a great expansion in the area of the market. In early days trade was confined primarily to the local community; today it is worldwide in character.

Transportation methods have become increasingly efficient. Speed and ease in moving freight and passengers have been attained as a result of continued improvements. The costs of transporting both goods and persons have been decreased. This is especially true in the case of goods, because low freight rates stimulate traffic to a greater extent than do low passenger rates. These changes have had many far reaching effects. The prices of commodities have been decreased. Backward or undeveloped districts have been opened up, providing the people with an outlet for their products as well as an opportunity of more easily and more cheaply purchasing the products of other communities. In some areas rents have been held down to reasonable levels, while rents in other areas have been increased. Large scale production has been made possible, because raw materials can be cheaply and speedily assembled and products can be sent to distant markets in an effective manner. Localization of industry has been assisted by making it easier for each community to specialize in the production of those goods which are the most profitable and to exchange them for the goods of other communities. Modern transportation methods have also made it possible more effectively to weld the various parts of our country into a national unit.

Importance of Railroads—The railroad map of the United States shows a veritable network of lines in the territory lying to the east of the Rocky Mountains, with only a few railroads to the west of the mountains. This is accounted for by the fact that the eastern section of our country contains the greater proportion of our population and also provides the greater number of business opportunities for the railroads. In 1928 the railroad system of the United States represented an investment of approximately $24,900,000,000, with a funded debt of about $12,300,000,000 and various classes of capital stock amounting to approximately $9,700,000,000; about 1,700,000 persons were employed. In 1928 the railroads operated more than 400,000 miles of tracks, including, first, second, third, fourth, and other main tracks, yard tracks, and sidings; they owned more than 2,370,000 freight cars; they had some 63,000 locomotives in service and about 55,000 passenger cars. They transported about 436,087 tons of revenue freight per mile and 31,718 passengers per mile.

Brief Historical Sketch—During colonial times, the transportation facilities of our country were exceedingly crude. There were a few wagon roads, which at certain times of the year were impassable. Sailing vessels plied up and down the coasts and entered the navigable streams and harbors. With the urge of population to move westward, there came an increased demand for better wagon roads, with the result that both the federal and the various state governments, as well as private parties, expended huge sums of money in constructing a network of wagon roads covering the eastern section of the United States. Later came the use of the stern wheel steamboat on the navigable streams, followed by the development of a system of canals which united many of the inland waterways. The Erie Canal, completed by the State of New York in 1825, joined Lake Erie with New York by way of the Hudson River; the Ohio River was connected with Lake Erie in 1832. Numerous other artificial waterways were constructed during that period, most of which were financed either partly or entirely by public funds.

In 1827 the Baltimore & Ohio Railroad was chartered, first using sails and horses as means of locomotion, but later resorting to the steam locomotive. During the next twenty-five years many other railroads were built, all short lines, totaling slightly more than 9,000 miles of track. During this period the canals were easily able to hold their own in competition with rail transportation, but after the Civil War, with the rapid improvement of railroad service and the very great increase in railroad mileage, the canals were gradually forced from the field. During the formative period of the railroads, both federal and state governments invested heavily in railroad securities. It is estimated that at one time their investments exceeded $700,000,000.

The phenomenal growth of the American railway system occurred during the period from 1850 to 1880, and by the close of that period more than 93,000 miles of track were in operation. It was during that time that the first transcontinental line was completed, San Francisco being joined with the East in 1869. Many of the small local lines were merged into larger systems, such as the New York Central, the Pennsylvania, the Erie, and others. From 1880 to 1890, some 63,000 additional miles of track were operated and from 1890 to 1910 approximately 84,000 more miles. Since 1910 the rate of expansion has been greatly retarded. During the decade from 1920 to 1930 there was no appreciable addition to the railway mileage of the United States, practically every section of the country apparently being adequately supplied with rail facilities. As to future developments, it is safe to predict that there will undoubtedly be some construction of feeder lines, although most of the untapped territory will have its needs cared for by motor busses. In fact, a number of the railroad companies have lately entered the field of motor transportation for the handling of both freight and passenger traffic.

Economic Characteristics of Railways—Railways have certain outstanding economic characteristics which set them apart from the usual run of business enterprises. First, there is the large size of the plant. Rails stretch for miles and miles across the country, requiring an enormous investment of capital and giving employment to thousands of workers. Most of the plant cannot be moved, nor as a rule can it be abandoned, as can be done in the case of almost every other type of business enterprise. Even though a railroad is bankrupt, it must continue in operation, unless permitted by the proper government authorities to do otherwise, because the freight and the passengers of the nation must be moved. The needs of the public are paramount to the needs of those who own railroad stocks and bonds. Such a situation does not exist in the case of stores, factories, or farms, because the public is not so dependent upon the continued operation of any one store, factory, or farm as it is upon the continued operation of a railroad. If railroad lines could be indiscriminately abandoned just because it did not pay to operate them, the entire business of the nation would quickly become demoralized. At times, a railroad is permitted by government authorities to abandon short branch lines, but only because the traffic is being satisfactorily cared for by other means. When a railroad becomes bankrupt, a receiver is appointed, and he usually directs its operations until it has been financially reorganized or until it has been restored to a paying position.

In the second place, a railroad is subject to very great overhead expense. Regardless of whether a railroad does a large or a small amount of business, it has to pay taxes, interest on its bonds, and salaries to a large staff of employees; it has to maintain its right of way in a satisfactory condition and to keep its stations and its telegraph system in a state of repair. Although the statement is not strictly correct, it is rather commonly remarked that it costs very nearly as much to let a railroad stand idle as it does to operate it. Less than half of the expenses of a railroad vary with the amount of traffic that it carries.

A third characteristic of the railway system is that it represents a business of increasing returns or of decreasing costs. With such heavy fixed charges as it is forced to meet, a railroad is eager to increase the amount of traffic which it carries, because the greater the amount of traffic, the greater will be the return upon each unit carried until, of course, a certain point has been reached where the expenditure of additional capital is required. Few passenger trains are completely filled, and few freight trains are loaded to capacity. No railroad system is so crowded that more traffic could not be carried. The situation, therefore, is such that, although increased traffic would lead to a slight increase in the expenses of the railroad, the increased outlay would be small in comparison with the extent of the returns received from the additional traffic. It is agreed that operating expenses tend to increase about one-half as rapidly as the amount of the traffic carried; therefore, if the traffic increases 20%, operating expenses increase by about 10%. Thus, an increase in the traffic of a railroad yields a return proportionately higher than its costs.

A fourth characteristic is that in its operation a railroad is subject to joint expenses. The costs of caring for any single part of its business cannot be accurately allocated among the various units of the road. Both passenger and freight trains use the same tracks, stations, and telegraph system and operate under the same executive or administrative officials. Sometimes a locomotive pulls both freight and passenger cars simultaneously. Some passenger trains move rapidly; others operate on slower schedules. Some travel long distances, others short distances. In agriculture, when a farmer raises a cow, he cannot tell how much it costs to raise the hoofs, the horns, the porterhouse steak, the liver, or the heart of the animal. He may know how much it costs him to raise the cow, but he cannot know how great was the expense of raising any one of its parts. The same is true of many of the costs involved in handling freight and passenger traffic. The apportionment cannot be made except on a somewhat arbitrary basis.

Railway Rates—About the most difficult and most delicate problem that arises in connection with the operation of a railway is the fixation of freight and passenger rates. Justice requires that the interests of the shipper, the public, and the company itself must be conserved. During the early years of railroad transportation in the United States, no attempt was made by the government to regulate the rates that were charged the public. At present, however, railway rates for interstate traffic are fixed by a federal body known as the Interstate Commerce Commission, while rates for intrastate traffic are fixed by the various state railroad commissions.

A railroad rate is the price which is charged by the railroad for its service in transporting freight and passengers. Freight of all kinds and descriptions, in large and small quantities, must be hauled for various distances, and passengers must be carried for long and short hauls and provided with different kinds of accommodations. How, then, or upon what basis, should railroad rates be fixed? No discrimination is permitted as to shippers, localities, or passengers receiving the same type of service. Rebates also are prohibited. Those who ship in trainload lots receive no lower rates than those who ship in carload lots.

Many theories have been advanced as to the basis upon which rates should be fixed, but we shall have space in this volume for a consideration of only two of them. The one that makes the widest public appeal is that rates should be established on the basis of the *cost of the service rendered*. The Interstate Commerce Commission has forced all railroads in the United States to adopt a uniform system of accounting and has thus made it possible to ascertain more closely the costs of operation. Even so, since railroad operations are characterized by joint costs, it is impossible to determine the cost of any service accurately enough to provide a basis for rate making. The total cost of operation, however, can be determined; therefore, it is claimed by some that the rate for each kind of accommodation should be fixed at such a level as to make it possible for the railroad to meet its total cost and still have remaining a large enough income to pay a satisfactory dividend to its stockholders, or owners.

On what basis should these individual rates be fixed? It is equitable to charge the same fare to all passengers receiving the same kind of service. But is it equitable or advisable to charge the same rate per pound or per ton for each kind of commodity carried? Should hay, bricks, and ore pay the same rates as jewelry, automobiles, cloth, and machinery. They may take up the same space as, or even a greater space than, the latter group of articles, and they may be shipped in equal weights. But will they be moved if they have to pay the same railroad rates? High priced articles can afford to pay more freight than low priced articles. Bricks, hay, and ore will not and cannot be moved if they have to pay high freight rates. Therefore, in order to obtain a greater amount of traffic than would otherwise be possible and thereby reduce its expenses per unit of traffic moved, the railroad charges less for carrying bulky, cheap commodities than for carrying goods of high value in small bulk. This principle of rate fixation involves what is called *charging what the traffic will bear*. By this means, the total expenses of the railroad are met by a variety of commodities in proportion to their ability to bear the burden.

Railroad rates should be fixed so as to yield an adequate return to the owners of the enterprise. But what basis should be taken in calculating the rate of such return? Should rates be fixed so as to yield a return (1) upon the value of the original investment in the road or (2) upon the present value or cost of reproducing the road? There is a marked difference of opinion on this matter, the tendency appearing to be the acceptance of the original investment idea with various modifications.

Railways and the Shipper—Complaints have always been made about the rates charged by the railroads. Today, as was true in the past, shippers demand lower rates because they desire to move their goods to the market at the lowest possible cost. It is interesting to note that freight charges amount to about 10% of the value of the product at its point of final destination. In considering the matter of the demand for lower rates, it should be remembered that railroads are going concerns which have to pay their way. They are not guaranteed a return by the government; therefore, they cannot be asked to operate at a financial loss, especially when their rates are determined by government commissions. If a shipper cannot carry on his business successfully when paying a freight rate that yields only a fair return to the railroad, then it is advisable for him to abandon his enterprise or to move to a more desirable location.

On the other hand, there has lately been much discussion relative to the efficiency of railroad management. It is claimed that millions of dollars could be saved by the introduction of various economies. Of course, waste can never be justified, and the public should not be called upon to pay rates that permit the railroads to be wasteful.

Another matter that has aroused considerable debate is the fair valuation of the railroads upon which the net yield of operations is calculated. If the valuation is placed at too high a figure, then the public may be asked to pay excessive rates. However, efforts have been made by the various government commissions to fix a fair valuation, and many economies have lately been introduced by the railroads resulting in improved and more efficient service for the public. Each year freight cars are being moved in greater numbers and with greater speed and dispatch, and the requests of shippers for cars are being adequately met. Damages on freight shipments have been greatly lessened.

Regulation of Railroads—With the growth of the American railway systems, many serious abuses arose. Intense cut-throat competition developed, usually taking the form of rate wars, the objective being to force competitors from the field. Then came the urge to get together, to combine in order to survive, with the result that pooling was resorted to. The pools that were organized took various forms. Sometimes the competing railroads divided the territory among themselves, agreeing not to extend their lines into the districts served by other roads. At times they pooled their incomes, placing all of the proceeds in a common treasury. Each road then received its share in accordance with the terms of a prearranged plan. Sometimes they divided the traffic among themselves, each road in the pool having a share in the freight or the passenger traffic. At other times they made agreements as to the rates that were to be charged the public. It is evident that the intent behind such pooling arrangements was the restraint of trade and the elimination of competition.

Another abuse that arose was discrimination in rates as between shippers and as between localities. Certain cities were favored with low rates to the disadvantage of others, thus making it possible for the favored cities to build up their industries and destroying or handicapping the industries in the less favored cities. Some shippers were accorded lower rates than others or were granted rebates on their shipments and were thus placed in a favored competitive position in the market. At times, discrimination took the form of supplying one shipper promptly with all the cars that he required or speedily granting his claims for damages or favoring him in other ways, while at the same time tardily providing his competitors with cars, holding up their damage claims, or in other ways handicapping them in shipping their goods. The situation ultimately became so unbearable that the public demanded protection, with the result that in 1887 Congress passed the Interstate Commerce Act, primarily with the object of preventing such discrimination. Pooling was declared to be illegal, and efforts were made to enforce competition among the railroads.

Transportation Act of 1920—The Interstate Commerce Act has been frequently and considerably amended since its adoption in 1887. The present law, the Transportation Act of 1920, provides for an Interstate Commerce Commission of eleven members, The regulatory clauses of the act cover the operation of railroads, pipelines, sleeping car companies, and telegraph, telephone, and certain other kinds of public utilities. Authority is granted to the commission to fix rates that will be fair and reasonable. Discrimination of every type is prohibited. An individual is not permitted to serve as a director of competing railroad companies without the consent of the commission. The commission is given the power completely to control the issue of securities by the companies under its jurisdiction. Railways may not be constructed, extended, or abandoned without its permission. With certain exceptions, free passes for interstate travel cannot be granted. Railroads are not allowed to charge more for a short haul than for a long haul without the consent of the commission. Rates must be so fixed as to enable the railroads to earn a net operating income of 6% upon the value of the railway property held for and used by them in the service of transportation. If the earnings exceed that percentage, one-half of the excess must be paid to the Federal Government and goes into a fund which may be used by the government to extend loans to interstate carriers or to purchase equipment for lease to such carriers. Strangely enough, the law permits pooling, but only under the supervision of the commission. The clause concerning this provision, however, is a dead letter, because the railroads have learned how to accomplish their ends by other and more satisfactory means.

Other sections of the Transportation Act of 1920 indicate that our lawmakers have at last come to appreciate the evils of railroad competition. Under these sections, the Interstate Commerce Commission is empowered to approve the consolidation of competing railway lines. When the act was passed, the commission was formally instructed to work out a plan of nationwide consolidation, and it has since done so, recommending that all railroads be grouped into nineteen systems. Some consolidations have already been effected, although others that have been requested by the railroads themselves have been denied. It appears evident that the future will see a nationwide movement toward railway consolidation, resulting in the formation of a few large railroad systems, which may possibly serve the needs of the public more effectively than does the present competitive scheme of things.

The Future of the Railroads—What the future has in store for the railroads of the United States cannot be forecast. The competition of motor transportation has very seriously eaten into both the freight and the passenger traffic of the railroads, especially for short hauls. (Thus far the airplane has been of slight consequence as a competitor.) Many of the railroads are in a much better financial condition than heretofore, but there remains always the necessity of keeping progressively up to date the services that they offer the public. That the public seemingly is more content than formerly with the accommodations provided by the railroads appears to be evidenced by the fact that the demand for government ownership has practically died out.

Water Transportation—Since the Civil War but little attention has been given by our citizens to the matter of inland water transportation. However, the Federal Government has lately attempted to encourage the development of our domestic waterways, especially through the use of steam-towed barges upon the Ohio and Mississippi rivers. During the World War we were compelled to "bridge the ocean" with our ships in order to carry troops and supplies to Europe. For some years after the conclusion of that conflict, we proudly talked of the return of the American merchant marine as an important factor in ocean traffic, but the results obtained up to the present time have been far from encouraging. Foreign countries can build and operate steel vessels more cheaply than can we in the United States. As long as American capital can earn a greater return by staying at home and investing in domestic enterprises, it will not venture out upon the high seas for a smaller return.

Advantages of Water Transportation—Generally speaking, water transportation is cheaper than any other form of transportation. It takes less power to pull or to push a boat over the water than to pull or to push the same load on land, the reason being that water buoys up the load and only motive power is required. The average ocean haul is longer than the average land haul. Less fixed capital is necessary in water transportation, because a right of way does not have to be purchased and maintained in repair, stations do not have to be built every few miles, and telegraph systems are unnecessary. Ocean vessels, especially tramp steamers, can go from one port to another, unrestricted by schedules and seeking trade wherever it is to be found. Railroads, however, must confine themselves to their right of way and must run according to schedule. An individual may engage in or retire from a water transportation enterprise whenever he wishes to do so, because no government regulations compel the maintenance of the service and because it is relatively easy to sell a vessel.

Consolidation Movement—There has been a concentration or consolidation movement in progress among shipping interests as well as among the railroads. Ships have become more costly, competition more severe, the demands of the shipper more exacting, and the business risks greater. There has also grown up a widespread network of agreements and conferences among water carriers with the object of eliminating some of the unsatisfactory features of competition.

CHAPTER IX

Forms of Business Organization

WHEN land, labor, and capital goods are brought together into a productive enterprise, the resulting form of business organization may be an individual proprietorship, a partnership, or a corporation. Each form of organization has its advantages and disadvantages, but no one form is adapted to fit the requirements of all kinds of business. The individual proprietorship is suited to the needs of small business and local markets, the partnership to larger undertakings and wider markets, while the corporation is a reflection of the necessity for the accumulation of vast sums of capital in order that large scale production may be carried on with a proper degree of safety for those who have invested their funds therein and in order that wider markets may be exploited. The forms arose in the order mentioned and grew out of the requirements of a developing economic world.

The Individual Proprietorship—In the individual proprietorship form of organization, the business is owned by an individual who furnishes all or a large part of the capital and either performs all of the labor himself or hires others to assist him. Ownership and management are vested in one person, who takes all the gains and assumes all the losses. The individual proprietorship is easily organized and abandoned. The owner is his own boss and is free to carry out his plans without asking the consent of others. His reward is in direct proportion to his effort, skill, and luck. Our very small business enterprises, as well as many farming enterprises, are usually representative of the individual proprietorship.

The Partnership—The partnership is based upon an agreement, generally but not necessarily written, between two or more parties, by the terms of which the partners bind themselves jointly and severally to conduct a business. The agreement covers the relations existing between the partners, but it cannot control the relations between the partnership and its customers. The partnership requires no formality in organization and but little in dissolution.

Advantages of the Partnership—The partnership has two advantages over the individual proprietorship. First, it makes larger undertakings possible through the greater accumulation of capital; second, it enables the man who has money but no business experience, or who does not want to assume the responsibility of carrying on a business, to advance his funds against the skill and experience of another. There are many such "silent partners" in the business field. The partnership makes possible the benefits to be obtained from the consultation and combined judgment of the partners. It also is an elastic form of organization—its policies can easily be changed, and there is scarcely any form of business which it cannot undertake. Two exceptions to this latter statement are banking and insurance. Our laws usually require that these two kinds of enterprises be carried on only by corporations.

Disadvantages of the Partnership—The partnership, however, has certain serious disadvantages. It is not adapted to the needs of large scale production, because it cannot accumulate capital in sufficient amounts. For example, no partnership could get together enough funds to meet the requirements of the United States Steel Corporation. Then, too, the partnership is not a permanent form of business organization. It is automatically terminated by the death or withdrawal of any one of the partners. Unless the remaining partners are able to purchase the interest of the deceased or retiring partner, or unless they are able to find an outsider who will do so, the business must be closed out and its assets distributed. Our present business world could not function satisfactorily unless a more permanent form of organization were provided by the existence of the corporation. Another serious disadvantage is that any one of the partners may be held liable for all of the debts of the partnership. The partnership has no right to sue or to be sued as a legal entity. It is a group of individuals, any one of whom may be called upon to pay all of the obligations of the firm. In such an event, he in turn may sue the other partners in an effort to collect their share of the firm's debts. Finally, because of the possibility of differences of opinion among the partners as to what policies ought to be pursued, it may become difficult to secure uniformity of action in case of an emergency.

The Corporation—The changing needs of the business world in the course of time made possible and necessary the introduction of the corporate form of business organization. This form of organization is much older than many persons realize. The early trading and colonizing companies, such as the East India Company and the Hudson Bay Company, were organized as corporations. In the United States the corporate form of business organization became increasingly popular during the period of prosperity following the Civil War. Today, although the corporations of our country constitute in number only about 30% of all business enterprises (including the field of agriculture), their output exceeds 80% of the total product, and they hire more than 70% of our wage earners.

Structure of the Corporation—Whereas the partnership is based upon a consentual relationship among the partners and is created by mutual agreement, the corporation is brought into existence by a charter, which it obtains from the state or the Federal Government. It is a non-personal, legal being, or entity, separate and distinct from those who own or manage it.

Let us take a concrete example in order to make clear the nature of the corporation. Suppose five of us desire to organize a national bank in our home town. We fill out all the necessary blanks and send them, with an application for a charter, to the United States Comptroller of the Currency in Washington, D. C. If he is satisfied that there is need for a national bank in our community and that we are responsible parties, he will issue a charter for our institution when all the preliminaries have been complied with. The charter brings the national bank into existence. We are the owners of the bank, yet we, as individuals, are not the bank corporation. The bank can sue and be sued as a going concern, separate and distinct from us, its owners. In fact, we, as stockholders, can sue the bank, and it, in turn, can sue us. It can buy and sell property and carry on various business activities, just as though it were an individual.

The stockholders of a corporation number from a minimum of three up to many thousands. It is not possible for the stockholders combined to manage the business, even though they may wish to do so. Consequently, they elect a board of directors. This board consists of an uneven number of stockholders, usually three, five, or seven, although sometimes it consists of many times that number. The directors make decisions upon any important policies, such as the expenditure of large sums of money for buildings, the institution of advertising campaigns, the opening of additional branches of the business, and other major projects. They also elect the officers of the corporation, the usual officers being a president, a vice president, a cashier, a secretary-treasurer, and a superintendent or manager. The directors themselves do not really manage the business; they place that task in the hands of the officers of the corporation. Frequently the general manager selects the foreman and the heads of the various departments of the business, and they, in turn, hire the necessary help to carry out the general orders of the board of directors. Thus, the corporation is owned by the stockholders, who elect the board of directors, and the board of directors chooses the officers, who manage its affairs.

Stock Ownership—The extent of our individual ownership in the national bank which we have organized and in which we are stockholders is evidenced by the number of shares of stock that we own. If our bank is capitalized at $100,000 and its shares are in $100 amounts, then if we own ten shares, we own $1,000 worth of its stock. We may not have ten pieces of paper, one for each share of stock; we probably have only one piece of paper, which is called a stock certificate. This certificate states that we are the owner of ten shares of stock, with all the rights and privileges appertaining thereto.

The capital stock of our bank is in $100 shares. We call this its par (or face) value. Somewhat later this stock may sell for $200 in the market, because our bank in the meantime has become a very profitable institution and pays large dividends. What the stock actually sells for is called its market value. Some corporations, on the other hand, are organized on a no par stock basis. If such a corporation were established with a capital stock of $50,000 and you owned one-tenth of that amount, you would not hold a certificate saying that you owned $5,000 worth of stock. Your stock certificate would merely state that you owned one-tenth of the corporation's stock and were therefore entitled to one-tenth of the company's earnings and to one-tenth of the company's assets if later it should dissolve.

Kinds of Stock—There are only two general classes of capital stock, common and preferred. Many corporations have no preferred stock, in which case the shares are known merely as shares of stock. This is the case, for example, with all incorporated banks, regardless of whether they have a state or a national charter. On the other hand, many of our small, as well as our large, corporations have both common and preferred stock.

Preferred stock usually gives its owner a preferred or prior lien on the dividends and on the assets of the corporation if it should dissolve. The extent of preference or claim for dividends is commonly designated. For example, a corporation may have issued 6% preferred stock. In this case, before any dividends are paid to the holders of common stock, dividends at the rate of 6% must be paid to those who own the preferred stock. If the company dissolves or fails, the holders of the preferred stock usually have a claim on the assets of the corporation before anything can be paid to the holders of the common stock. Sometimes preferred stock is participating in character. This means that after its owners have received the fixed dividend and after the owners of common stock have received a dividend at the same rate, then the remainder of the earnings is shared among the owners of both kinds of stock upon a predetermined basis.

Preferred stock may be cumulative or non-cumulative. If it is cumulative, the unpaid dividends become a claim on the future earnings of the company. Thus, if only 5% out of a 6% dividend on preferred stock is paid this year, the 1% that remains unpaid is added to the 6% for next year, and the holders of the preferred stock then have a prior claim to 7% dividends. In the case of non-cumulative preferred stock, however, the dividends, if unpaid, do not accumulate.

Ordinarily, the holders of common stock get what is left of the corporation's earnings after the dividends have been paid upon preferred stock. This frequently means that common stock receives a much higher return than preferred stock and thus commands a much higher price in the market.

Seldom do the holders of preferred stock have the right to vote for members of the board of directors. The holders of common stock have the right to vote, the basis being one vote for one share, except in the case of some cooperative associations which grant only one vote to a stockholder regardless of how much stock he owns. Since the World War, a number of corporations have been reorganized and have so re-shaped their stock structure as to grant the right to vote to only a small amount of the common stock. In such cases the voting common stock is closely held by a small group of "insiders," who thus control the affairs of the corporation, the preferred stock and the non-voting stock merely carrying the privilege of receiving the dividends that are paid on such stock.

Corporations obtain a large share of their working funds or capital from the sale of capital stock. If a corporation is chartered with $500,000 of capital stock, this amount is its authorized capital stock. The corporation, however, may desire to sell only $250,000 of its authorized capital stock. In this event, the $250,000 is known as its issued capital stock. The shares may have a par value of $100 and yet may sell for only $75 each, thus netting the company only $187,500 of capital.

Bonds—Large corporations usually issue bonds, sometimes at the time of their organization, although frequently at later dates. Most of them have various issues of bonds outstanding at all times. Bonds are evidences of indebtedness, while stocks are evidences of ownership. A stockholder is a part owner of the corporation, but a bondholder is a creditor of the corporation.

Whenever a corporation issues bonds, it has to put up security for the loan. It may give a mortgage on all of its property, or only on a certain part, such as its buildings, right of way, equipment, rolling stock, income, and terminals, or on the stocks and bonds of other companies which it happens to have in its treasury. It is not possible for a corporation to give a separate mortgage to each of the bondholders; consequently, it places the mortgage with a trustee or a trust company, which holds the mortgage for the protection of the bondholders.

Bonds may run for a specific length of time, generally from five to fifty years, or longer; or they may be issued with no definite date of maturity. They usually call for the semi-annual payment of a fixed rate of interest, although in some cases the interest is payable quarterly or annually. Also, there are bonds which are not entitled to a fixed return, the interest being made dependent upon earnings. At the end of the time for which the bonds are to run—that is, at their maturity—the face value or the principal must be paid by the corporation to the owners of the bonds.

Rights of Bondholders—If the interest or principal is not paid when due, and when the mortgage indenture so provides, the bondholders have a legal right to have the mortgage foreclosed, so as to protect their claims to payment. Like preferred stockholders, bondholders usually lack the right to vote at the annual meetings of the corporation. In a general way, both groups are also alike in that they have a claim to a fixed return, although perhaps more frequently the preferred stockholders do not have the right to claim dividends unless earned; and if dividends are not earned or remain unpaid, the stockholders as a rule cannot throw the corporation into the hands of a receiver, as can be done by the bondholders if interest or principal is not paid. On the basis of preference of claims upon the earnings or assets of a corporation, the bondholders generally come first, then the preferred stockholders, and last the common stockholders.

Bonds Supply Capital—An issue of bonds provides an additional amount of capital for the corporation. The funds thus obtained are usually employed for permanent improvements, such as the purchase of rights of way, the erection of buildings, and the purchase of another business. Funds to care for the temporary needs of the corporation, as for the purchase of materials, the payment of wages, and the meeting of other operating expenses, are obtained by the corporation through bank loans or through the sale of commercial paper, in the open market or to its bank.

Capital versus Capitalization—The student should be careful to distinguish between the capital of a corporation and its capitalization. If a corporation is authorized to issue $500,000 in capital stock, that amount constitutes its *capitalization;* in other words, the corporation is capitalized at that amount. If the corporation sells only $250,000 of that sum and receives therefor only $187,500 because the stock is sold at $75 a share, the $187,500 constitutes its *capital*. If it then obtains $100,000 from the sale of bonds, its capital is increased to $287,500. Its capitalization, however, has not been changed. If it borrows $50,000 from the bank, its capital is further increased to $337,500. If, after a year's operations, it lays aside a surplus of $10,000 out of earnings, its capital then stands at $347,500, provided that, in the meantime, it has not repaid its loan at the bank. As previously stated, capital is the amount of funds invested in productive property of any kind from which a monetary return is expected.

Overcapitalization—From time to time there has been much public discussion of overcapitalization, but care is seldom taken to distinguish between the two meanings of this term. First, a firm may be overcapitalized because it has too much capital invested in proportion to the amount of business it can hope to transact. If you and I put $10,000 into a peanut and popcorn stand, we cannot expect to derive a large enough income from our business even to pay expenses, to say nothing of dividends or profits on such a large investment. This kind of overcapitalization causes the public no serious concern, except in cases in which losses arise from the failure of the companies that are thus overcapitalized.

A second kind of overcapitalization is known more commonly as "stock watering" and is of vital concern to stockholders and to the public in general, provided the practice is indulged in too freely. If you and I, together with our friends, organize a corporation with a capital stock of $500,000 although, as a matter of fact, there is only $200,000 of actual property value behind that large amount of capitalization, then our corporation has $300,000 of "water" in its stock. As can be readily appreciated, it is seldom possible for any corporation to have the amount of its capital stock at any time exactly equal to the value of its property, because the latter necessarily fluctuates from day to day. No complaint is ever made if the value of the property of a corporation is greater than the amount of its capital stock, but if the capital stock is greatly in excess of the value of its property, then there is just cause for complaint.

Stock is watered primarily for one or more of three

reasons. In the first place, the practice is resorted to for the purpose of concealing dividends. If a corporation has issued $500,000 worth of capital stock and is paying a 20% dividend, it will probably be subjected to condemnation by the press and by politicians, especially if it is selling a product which is widely consumed by the public. Consequently, to avoid criticism, the corporation may reorganize by increasing its capital stock to four times the previous amount—that is, to $2,000,000—thus giving each stockholder four shares where before he held but one. The corporation can then pay 5% on each share of stock, and the stockholders will receive on their four shares the same total amount of dividends as formerly. By this means the corporation is able to conceal the actual extent of its earnings.

In the second place, capital stock is watered when a corporation is formed with the expectation that, as the years pass and its business expands, the value of its property will accordingly increase and thus absorb the water in the stock. In the case of American railways, for example, the early years saw their stock greatly watered. As time passed, however, land values rose, population increased, cities sprang up along the right of way, and the expanding value of railway property squeezed the water out of the capital stock.

In the third place, many companies prefer to have their stock sell at about its par value. If the $100 shares of stock of a corporation are selling at $200, the granting of two shares for one—in other words, the declaration of a stock dividend—will force down the market price of the stock to about $100. If the market price of a stock is kept close to its par value, it is possible for the stock to be held more widely by the public.

At times stock is watered with the direct intention of defrauding the public. If I am one of the organizers of a corporation and turn over to it a piece of property valued at $50,000, for which I receive $100,000 worth of stock, the public has no way of knowing what has been done. It merely sees $100,000 of capital stock issued, and it notes that property valued on the books at $100,000 is in the possession of the corporation; hence it concludes that the values represented by the transaction are actually as stated. Only when the company finds it impossible to pay dividends on its capital stock because of the water which its stock contains does the public begin to surmise that all is not well with the stock and that watering has taken place.

Besides being assailed on the ground that it misleads the public as to earnings and investors as to the worth of the corporation's property, watered stock is condemned also on the ground that it leads or may lead to exorbitant charges or prices for the commodity or service sold by the corporation that is guilty of stock watering. In order that dividends may be paid on a capitalization larger than is justifiable, greater returns have to be earned, and it is claimed that in many cases this fact leads to the public's being compelled to pay higher prices than would be the case if there were no water in the corporation's stock.

Regulation of Stock Watering—In recent years

some progress has been made in the United States toward removing the abuses of watered stock, through the operation of what are known as blue sky laws. In those states that have enacted such legislation, the approval of a corporation commissioner, or of a security commissioner, must be obtained before stocks and bonds may be issued and sold to the public by home corporations, or before they may be advertised for sale and sold within the state by corporations organized in other states. Blue sky law officials apply different tests and impose various standards to which the issues of stocks and bonds must comply, the intent being to force the corporations to show that they are substantial going concerns, that their issues of securities are justifiable, and that there is no intention to perpetrate a fraud on the public.

Advantages of the Corporation—The corporation, as a form of business organization, is superior in many regards to both the individual proprietorship and the partnership. This fact accounts for its rapid growth in importance as the business unit has grown in size. First of all, it has *permanency*. Its continued existence is not dependent upon the death or withdrawal of a stockholder. Although formerly corporations were organized to last for only a fixed number of years, such as twenty or fifty, practically all states at present grant corporations the right to perpetual existence.

Second, the corporation is a *legal entity,* separate and distinct from its owners. It can sue and be sued as a legal person and has certain other legal rights.

Third, the stockholders have *limited liability*. In the case of the individual proprietorship and the partnership, on the other hand, the owners have unlimited liability. With society demanding larger business undertakings, it was realized that unless the liability of the owners of a business were limited in some manner, large undertakings would be impossible. There are three types of limited liability.

1. The stockholders of corporations chartered in all states other than California (except at times those of state chartered banks) have *ordinary limited liability*. This means that if the capital stock has been fully paid up—that is, if for a $100 share of stock the company itself has received $100—the owner of the stock can be held liable for no additional sum, regardless of the amount for which the company fails. If the company has received $50 for a $100 share of stock and if it then fails, the holder may be held liable for an additional $50, in order that his stock may be fully paid up. If the corporation has sold to me a $100 share of stock for $75, and I sell it to you several years later for $200, the company, of course, receives nothing out of this $200. However, $25 still remains unpaid on that share of stock, as is evidenced by the books of the corporation, and if the company fails, you will be held liable to pay $25 but no more.

2. At times a stockholder has what is called *double liability*. For example, suppose you hold a $100 share of fully paid-up stock in a national bank (all stock in a national bank must be fully paid up within six months after the bank opens its doors) and the bank fails. You

can then be held liable for an additional $100 but no more.

3. Finally, there is what is known as *proportional liability*—a type which, up to 1931, was found only in California. Previous to 1931, the stockholders of all corporations incorporated under the California laws (including state chartered banks) were proportionally liable for the debts of the corporation, the extent of their liability being based upon the proportion of the corporation's stock which they held. Thus, even though a person's stock were fully paid up, if he held one-tenth of the corporation's stock, he could be held liable for one-tenth of the company's debts in the event of its failure.

A fourth advantage of the corporate form of business organization is that it makes possible the *accumulation of large amounts of capital,* as needed, by present-day big business. The individual proprietorship and the partnership could at best gather together only a few thousand dollars of capital. In the case of the corporation, however, there is really no limit to the amount of funds that can be obtained. The corporation taps all classes of owners of funds. If you have only a few hundred dollars, it is possible for you to become a stockholder or a bondholder in a corporation, although with your small capital you could not start a business of your own or a partnership in company with your friends. Those with large sums of money at their disposal can also become stockholders or bondholders in a corporation. The corporation supplies so many different kinds of securities for speculative and investment purposes that practically every individual, no matter what his wishes or requirements, can find the type that suits his needs and desires.

Fifth, stockholders and bondholders of a corporation can *easily transfer their securities* to others. If I have $50,000 worth of stocks and $100,000 worth of bonds, I can sell all or a part of my holdings to others, usually experiencing little difficulty in doing so. To facilitate such transfers there are a number of stock exchanges and thousands of stock and bond houses, brokers, and agents.

Sixth, the corporate form of business organization *centralizes authority* over the business, placing it with the board of directors. In the case of the partnership, any one partner, as a rule, has the right to bind the partnership to buy or to sell in accordance with his wishes and orders, without consulting the other partners, although sometimes the partnership agreement limits the rights of a partner in that regard. Then, too, partners frequently disagree, and the enterprise suffers as a consequence. In the case of a corporation, however, a majority vote of the directors decides all questions involving corporate management and policies. Such a procedure results in certainty as to authority and responsibility.

Disadvantages of a Corporation—Several disadvantages are claimed for the corporate form of organization. First, it is held that the corporation, being a legal entity and not a human being, has no soul, no heart or feelings, and that it is organized solely for the purpose of making profits for its owners, without regard to any humanitarian ideal. In the past, the policies of many corporations and the manner in which those policies were carried out afforded abundant evidence that this contention was not without some basis. Today, however, the situation is greatly changed. The policies of many corporations are now shaped with due regard for the interests of their employees and of the public. The ideal of such organizations is that the public shall be served, the term service being more than a mere luncheon club slogan. Their attitude toward employees and even toward competitors has also undergone a decided change for the better.

Second, it is claimed that the corporation has brought about gambling and speculating. The public can now buy stocks and bonds, especially the former, not with any idea of holding them as long time investments but merely as a means of making speculative gains, through either a rise or a fall in their prices. Gambling, that is, betting on the rise or fall of security prices, is also prevalent.

Many persons fail to distinguish between gambling and speculating and urge that both practices should be prohibited by law. In either case, risks are taken voluntarily and in either the outcome is uncertain; in neither case is the outcome dependent to any very great extent (and generally to no extent whatsoever) upon the skill or the knowledge of the operator; yet gambling is illegal, while speculation is legal. Why the distinction? The answer is simply that gambling in no way serves the needs of the public, while speculation does.

The business world of today could easily get along if there were no gambling, but it could not function if speculation were not permitted. If I own a business, no matter of what kind it may be, I am engaged in a speculative enterprise—I do not know whether I am going to make or to lose money. If I sell my business to you, you then assume the risks. You engage in a speculative enterprise. If I own a share of stock, I own part of a business enterprise and I must have the right to sell that stock to some one else if I desire to do so, just as I must have the right to sell other kinds of property that I own. You likewise have the right to buy my share of stock if you wish to do so, and you may sell it to another person at a higher price if you can.

Speculation in stocks and bonds is concerned with the legal transfer of property rights. Society could not exist without such transfers being sanctioned. The loss suffered by the public when the stock market collapses is usually due to the fact that the public has been dabbling in a field of activity about which it knows little or nothing. If it did the same thing in other realms of business or finance, it would also suffer great losses.

Third, it is argued that the corporate form of business organization has made possible an undue concentration of ownership and control. Individual proprietors and partnerships seldom own more than one concern. By means of the corporation, however, it is possible for one organization to own stock in a number of others and thus to control their policies and activities. One person or a group of persons is similarly able to invest funds in a number of corporations so as to control them.

A very interesting development has arisen in this connection during recent years and has resulted in a much wider ownership or distribution of stocks than was formerly deemed possible. The United States Steel Corporation, for example, had only 20,075 stockholders in December 1906, but this number had increased to 189,900 by December 31, 1930. Many of our public service corporations, such as gas and electric companies, and street railways, and a number of the larger industrial concerns and department stores have sold considerable amounts of their stock to employees and to the consuming public. The stock of some of our banks is widely held by their employees. During and following the World War, the public purchased large amounts of liberty and victory bonds. As these bonds were paid off by the United States Government, the public, having become interested in holding securities, went into the market and absorbed large holdings of corporate stocks and bonds.

Stock Markets—With the development of the corporation, there naturally came a time when many people desired to buy and to sell securities in an easier and simpler manner than had before been possible, and thus there arose a need for an organized stock and bond market. Stock exchanges were established, the first in the United States being that of New York City, which dates from about 1792.

The stock exchange is an unincorporated association

of individuals, known as members, who purchase seats or memberships in the organization. The number of memberships is limited. Corporations cannot belong, but they pay for the membership of their representatives, in whose names the seats are held.

The stock exchange is a highly organized, complex body, the actions of whose members are hedged in and restricted by many exacting rules and regulations too detailed to be described in this brief text. One rule, however, which must be called to the attention of the student is that all sales made on the floor of the exchange are *bona fide* (actual) in character. There can be no fake or "wash" sales. Delivery of the securities sold must be made at the time agreed upon between the seller and the buyer.

Frequently a member will sell a certain stock *short;* that is, he will sell stock which he does not possess at the moment but which he must buy in time to make the delivery as agreed upon. If he is *long* on the market, he possesses a large number of shares of a security which he is eager to sell. If he is a *bear* on a certain stock, he has sold short and desires to depress its price so as to be able to purchase the stock at a lower figure than that at which he has agreed to sell. If he is a *bull* on a certain stock, he has a supply of it on hand and is eager to push up its price so as to make a gain by its sale. No person on the floor of a stock exchange is a bull on all stocks or a bear on all stocks. A member of the exchange is both a bull and a bear, being desirous of selling some stocks at high prices and of buying others at low prices.

CHAPTER X

Large Scale Production, Combination, and Monopoly

WHICHEVER way we turn, we are faced with evidence of the fact that we are at present living in an era where bigness appears as an outstanding characteristic of every phase of our economic life. Large factories, tall skyscrapers, apartment houses covering a block of land, railroads spanning the continent, ships so large that special docks have to be built to accommodate them, F. W. Woolworth Company and S. H. Kress & Company stores in all large cities, Sears, Roebuck and Company and Montgomery Ward & Company with their numerous retail stores, branch, chain, and group banking systems covering a state or even several states, universities with enrolments sometimes in excess of thirty thousand students, stadia seating one hundred thousand spectators—these are but a few of the many things that stamp the present economic world as different from that of fifty years ago.

Before the invention of power driven machinery, business was conducted on a small scale, because it was not profitable to engage in large scale production when only hand methods could be used. Since the advent of power driven machinery, however, big business has been the ideal of practically all producers wherever its methods could be employed. However, those articles that require a large amount of hand labor in their production are not amenable to the machine process, because they cannot be standardized. This is true of many of our luxuries. We still have a large number of small stores, repair shops, banks, and farms, but they by no means play a dominant part in our economic life, as they formerly did.

Large Scale Production

Two Phases of Big Business—In discussing big business, the student has in mind principally the large factory, the railroad, and the department store. He frequently overlooks one of the most interesting developments in the realm of big business during the past twenty years, and that is the control of a large number of smaller plants, stores, or banks by one firm or company. Henry Ford, for example, manufactures his cars at Detroit, but they are assembled in many plants located in different sections of the country. The F. W. Woolworth Company controls hundreds of small stores, as do S. H. Kress & Company, S. S. Kresge Company, the Great Atlantic & Pacific Tea Company, Piggly Wiggly, the United Cigar Stores Company, and others. Branch, chain, and group banking systems operate through many small banks advantageously situated but controlled by the head office. The economies of big business are thus obtained, regardless of whether we have the one big factory, bank, or store, or whether we have a large number of small factories, banks, or stores controlled by one central organization.

Causes of the Development of Big Business—The

growth in the size of the business unit has been brought about by many factors. First, there has been the growth in the extent or area of the market. The great increase in the population of the world and the creation of more efficient means of transportation have made possible the sale of a much larger output. Goods cannot be advantageously manufactured in quantity unless there is a market provided for their disposal. Improvements in transportation methods have also facilitated the obtaining of raw materials and have given the purchasing public access to the markets where goods are sold and services are rendered. Second, large scale production makes possible certain economies, which lower costs of production and hence tend to increase profits. These economies will be discussed in the paragraphs which follow.

1. Equipment. The plant and its equipment can be used to better advantage in large scale production. The type of machinery which increases the efficiency of production is expensive. A small plant cannot afford to purchase such machinery, because its output is so limited that the machinery cannot be employed profitably. A small bank, for example, has no use for a coin counting machine or for some of the more expensive bookkeeping machines that form a part of the equipment of our larger banking houses.

2. Utilization of by-products. In making almost any article of consumption, there is bound to be a certain amount of waste. In building a house, for instance, there are usually small quantities of sand, mortar, brick, lath, and lumber left over. In making a suit of clothes

or a dress, there are scraps of cloth remaining after the article has been finished. These examples are typical of the situation in almost all lines of production. In a small business no effort is made to use these left-over pieces, because there are not enough of them to make it worth while to attempt to do so. The situation is different in a large business, however. A country butcher throws away bones, scraps of meat, horns, and other waste materials, but the great packing houses of Chicago and Kansas City, with their huge supplies of such materials, manufacture many salable by-products, such as buttons, glue, fertilizer, gelatine, chemicals, and lard. The small woolen factory finds it difficult to dispose of the grease which it washes out of the wool, but the large factory manufactures perfumed cold cream from the great quantity of grease which it obtains, thus adding to its income. The sulphurous fumes of the small ore smelter poison the surrounding atmosphere and kill off the vegetation, but the large smelter reclaims the waste material from the fumes and either sells this by-product for bleaching purposes or manufactures sulphuric acid for commercial uses. The Ford Motor Company is said to have obtained more than $16,000,000 from its by-products in 1928. In most of our banks waste paper is burned, but in a few of our larger institutions it is baled and sold to junkmen, who dispose of it to paper manufacturers.

3. Better use of labor. A small plant is not able to take advantage of the benefits to be derived from the division of labor to the same extent as is a large plant. Where a great volume of output is maintained, each

worker may specialize and devote more time and attention to learning how to do one particular job efficiently. Thus, in making garments one man may become an expert in testing and selecting cloth, another in making patterns, another in pressing and shaping the completed garment. In a small tailor shop where only a few men are employed, such specialization, with its advantages of greater skill and better utilization of the labor staff, is not possible. In a small bank, an employee who is vitally interested in real estate loans is compelled to divide his attention among eight or ten different tasks, but in a large bank he has the opportunity of following out his desire to specialize in making real estate loans. Big business also makes possible the employment of high grade executives at high salaries. A small business enterprise cannot compete in the matter of salaries with the larger organizations and consequently loses most of its best men.

4. Encouragement of research. Practically all large manufacturing concerns employ a staff of inventors and research men, who are kept busy inventing new products and processes and perfecting old ones. The Burroughs Adding Machine Company, the Eastman Kodak Company, the various automobile companies, the General Electric Company, and the American Telephone & Telegraph Company are a few of the well known organizations that spend millions of dollars annually in support of research and invention. Such work, of course, is not possible in the small business enterprise.

5. Employment conditions. It is also interesting to note that, as a rule, the employment conditions main-

tained by big business are superior to those of the small concerns. A large scale enterprise has an established reputation. It has abundant funds. Not only can it afford the expense of providing better working conditions for its employees, but frequently its executives are progressive minded and appreciate the fact that superior employment conditions produce a better satisfied working group and hence lead to greater production and increased profits. Contrary to the commonly accepted belief, the head of a small business enterprise is a hard task master. If he is just starting in business and is eager to make his reputation as well as profits, he cannot afford to spend large sums of money on cafeterias, rest rooms, ventilating apparatus, safety devices, and vacations on pay; nor is he able to pay high wages, grant short hours, or supply his employees with group insurance and other benefits.

6. *Other economies.* Big business reduces its costs of production by buying supplies in large quantities, by advertising more effectively, and by shipping in carload and trainload lots rather than in broken lots. Large banks purchase their supplies in much larger quantities and therefore more cheaply than do small banks. Big business also obtains its funds at slightly lower interest rates than does the small business concern. This is primarily due to the fact that it usually keeps itself in much better financial condition. It maintains an adequate cost accounting system and can readily provide such information as is contained in balance sheets and profit and loss statements, which are required by the lenders of funds. The small business unit usually

borrows only from the local bank at the current rate for commercial loans, while the large organization is able to float bonds and to sell commercial paper (short term promissory notes, bank acceptances, and trade acceptances, for example), thus tapping a wider market and obtaining the needed funds at a lower rate.

Disadvantages of Large Scale Production—Big business, however, has not always adhered to the highest code of ethics in dealing with its competitors. Frequently, for the purpose of driving others from the field, it has employed certain practices which have amounted to cold and calculating ruthlessness. Big business has constantly been active in the legislative halls of the nation and has been roundly condemned for the methods which it has used to obtain the enactment of laws favorable to it or to kill measures to which it was opposed, many of the latter having been of a progressive character and designed to protect the interests of the general public. Big business has been concerned primarily with obtaining profits rather than with rendering service, although in recent years its attitude in this regard has changed to an outstanding extent.

Big business has made it increasingly difficult for new concerns to enter the field, not only because of its opposition but also because of the difficulty which beginners experience in obtaining the large amount of capital necessary to engage in mass production. Less and less is it possible for an individual to establish his own business in a small way in our main lines of manufacturing industry, in transportation, and in banking. More and more is big business making us into a nation of employees rather than permitting us to remain a nation of small independent business men.

Limitations on Large Scale Production—It is commonly believed that there are no limitations whatsoever upon large scale production and that in time each field of business will be controlled by one company, or at best by a few companies. The situation, however, is not quite so simple as the unthinking observer might surmise, for there are certain very evident limitations that are continually handicapping the growth and extension of big business.

Limitation Due to Scarcity of Raw Materials—Possibly the least important of the factors limiting large scale production, in some cases, is the quantity of material available. For example, we cannot expect those companies that are interested in mining diamonds, tin, nickel, and similar minerals to continue to expand indefinitely, because there are only a few places in the world in which such substances are found. Art treasures, antiques, and similar articles, because they exist in such small quantities, are goods which can never be handled on a large scale basis.

Limitation Due to Market Conditions—Unless there is a wide market for a product, that product cannot be handled advantageously on a large scale. No business executive would ever dream of gathering together into one large studio all of the artists of the United States for the purpose of producing paintings on a wholesale basis. There must be a wide market, either already in existence or capable of being created by advertising, in order that big business may exist. The development of transportation facilities has been a powerful factor in the growth of large scale production, because of its influence in expanding the area of the market.

Limitation Due to Human Nature—Business depends for its growth in size upon the ability of managers to manage effectively. First class executives are scarce, and they cannot be developed over night. In order to meet the demands of business in this regard, high schools, colleges of commerce, and graduate schools of business administration are now devoting considerable time and money to the training of business executives. But even so, it is still most difficult to find capable individuals who can efficiently care for the manifold and complex problems of large national and international concerns. Formerly, almost any person was equipped to become a banker or a bank employee. Little or no native ability or training was required. Big business, however, demands "big" bankers, and in order to train the bank employee of today for the greater responsibilities of tomorrow, the American Bankers Association, through the American Institute of Banking, has seen fit to provide a series of educational courses on banking and kindred subjects. Big business, whatever its form, is bound to be a failure unless enough good executives are developed to administer it effectively.

Cumbersomeness of Big Business—The cumbersomeness or awkwardness of big business must also be considered as a limitation upon its future development. Small bodies move or adjust themselves more readily than do large bodies. The same thing is true in the business world. For years the Ford Motor Company refused, in spite of public demand, to change from the Model T car to a more modernized mechanism. Finally, however, the new Model A was produced, but at an expense of millions of dollars, necessitating the complete rearrangement of the Ford plant and the invention and manufacture of much costly machinery. The entire automobile industry and many allied industries were paralyzed while this change was being made, because the country was waiting to see what Mr. Ford was going to do. A small plant could have been remodeled with much greater speed and ease and with no resulting disturbance to the general business world.

Because of the cumbersomeness of big business, there is a noticeable tendency for it to desire to remain fixed and unchanging, and to refuse, unless forced to do so, to modify its organization or its product in accordance with the requirements of new conditions. This is a most important characteristic of big business, which in the future, as business operations become even more extended than they are today, may produce serious defects in our economic system. The desire of big business to "stay put," to vegetate, must be vigorously guarded against; otherwise, our business methods and our products will fall behind those of more progressive countries.

Nature of the Business—Not every kind of business enterprise is adapted to the ideals and methods of large scale production. Where a great deal of hand labor is required, the advantages of mass production are not obtainable. One can hardly imagine a barber shop, or a ladies' beauty shop, or a shoe shining parlor covering an acre of ground and employing thousands of workers; nor can one picture a thousand-acre farm being devoted to the culture of poppies or chrysanthemums. There are certain kinds of business enterprise that, because of their very nature, will always remain relatively small in scale. Small specialty shops engaged in selling hats, dresses, shirts, and other commodities are frequently located close to large department stores and are able to compete successfully with them in the sale of special lines of goods.

Law of Diminishing Productivity—Large scale production is undertaken primarily because the numerous economies that can be effected result in lower costs. Although, as we have seen in preceding pages, lower costs may result as the size of the plant is increased, sooner or later in the case of every business enterprise a point is reached beyond which the return from added units of land or labor power or capital goods begins to diminish. To increase the size of a business, more land must be obtained, more laborers must be hired, or more capital goods must be purchased. Regardless of how precisely the quantity of each factor is gauged, after a certain point is reached, which of course varies with each enterprise, the cost per unit of land or labor power or capital goods begins to increase. Not only does the physical product decrease, but the money cost of each unit of product increases as the business expands beyond a certain point. If production is pushed too far, the cost will exceed the return obtained from the sale of the product, thus resulting in loss to the enterprise. The increased cost is due to many factors, such as the overcrowding of machines and workers, the necessity for more bookkeeping records, the hiring of too many high priced executives, the difficulty of inspiring loyalty among the employees of a large impersonal corporation, and so on.

Large Scale Farming—We must not overlook the fact that farming is a business, just as much as are manufacturing, mining, banking, and store keeping. How has the trend toward large scale production affected agriculture? Up to the present time, agriculture has been conducted primarily on a small scale basis. Today, two diverse tendencies are in evidence. In some districts, the size of the farm is noticeably increasing; in others, it is decreasing. The acreage of the average farm in the United States increased slightly up to the year 1920, but since then it has declined. Some writers prophesy that the growth of corporation farming and the increased use of agricultural machinery, especially the tractor, will bring about a rather decided trend toward large scale production in agriculture, just as in our cities the application of the machine process has produced big business in all of its various phases. One of the important results of the industrialization of agriculture has been the increased efficiency in farm management. During the past decade, although more than 13,000,000 acres of farm land have been withdrawn from production and although our farm population has decreased by 15%, there has been a decided increase in agricultural production. It will be interesting to watch the developments of the next decade.

Combination

Large Scale Production and Combination—To most people large scale production appears to be possible only as the result of a combination among a number of producers. While it is true that many large business enterprises have originated in this manner, yet there are many others that have never been a party to a combination. The Ford Motor Company, for example, began as a very small concern and has never combined with any other automobile manufacturing plant, yet today it is one of the world's largest producers of automobiles.

Causes of Combination—Combinations for the most part have come about as the direct result of the evil effects of competition among a number of companies in the same field. Frequently, it has been a case of "combine or fail," although at times two or more very successful competitive firms have combined in the hope of making larger profits and effecting greater economies. If given a free hand, competition usually kills itself by forcing competitors to combine. This is the main reason why it is so difficult and at the same time so economically unsound for the government to attempt to encourage or even to enforce competition in the business world.

Types of Combinations—Combinations may be classified as vertical or horizontal or a combination of both. A horizontal combination involves a number of stores, industries, or stages of production which are similar in character. For example, a horizontal combination results when ten banks are brought together in one organization. A vertical combination takes place when a number of concerns which are dependent upon each other for a part of the materials used in their productive operations come together to form one business unit. The United States Steel Corporation, for example, was formed by the combination of various organizations that were engaged in mining and transporting ore and in operating steel mills, tube works, tin plate factories, and other allied industries. The United States Steel Corporation wished to control the entire process of steel production from the raw material stage down to the marketing of the finished product.

The ideal of a vertical combination is the integration of industry, or the integration of the productive processes. This tendency to integrate is noticeable today in many lines of industry. It does not always result from or grow out of a combination. The Ford Motor Company, for example, which has never combined with any other concern, now operates its own mines, lumber mills, glass works, steel mills, and assembling plants and boats, and makes practically all of the articles that go into the construction of its cars. Integration is also evident in the case of department stores and mail order houses, which reach back in ownership to the factories that manufacture the goods sold in the stores. It is also found among certain manufacturing companies, which reach forward in the productive process for the purpose of owning a chain of stores or a series of marketing agencies.

Occasionally, we find a combination that is both horizontal and vertical in character. Such, for example, was the American Tobacco Company before it was dissolved by the United States Supreme Court in 1911. It had been formed out of companies that controlled the raw materials of tobacco and licorice, companies that were engaged in manufacturing cigars, cigarettes, plug tobacco, and snuff, and companies that were operating cigar stores throughout the United States.

Forms of Combination—The particular form in which combination has occurred in the United States has varied from time to time to meet changing economic conditions and changing legal requirements. As one form has been evolved and has later been banned by the courts as constituting an illegal restraint of trade, another form has been devised to take its place.

Informal Associations—An easy, although inefficient, method of getting business concerns together for the attainment of a certain object is to call a dinner meeting of the parties concerned, at which time matters of mutual interest are discussed, prices are fixed, territory is divided, and various other matters of mutual concern are agreed on. It is difficult to bring this type of combination before the courts, because it keeps no records and affords no tangible evidence as a basis for prosecution.

Pools—Pooling was formerly popular among competitive companies. There were many types of pooling arrangements, all of which were much more formal in character than the dinner meetings of competitors. Sometimes a pool required the posting of a bond, which would be forfeited by the party violating the terms of the agreement. Railroads were especially active in effecting pools. Two or more railroads might agree to pool their receipts. All of the income received would be put into a common fund, and each railroad would then share according to a prearranged plan. A railroad pool might divide the territory among the members, railroad A agreeing not to extend its lines into the territory of railroad B so long as railroad B did not extend its lines into the territory of railroad A. The pool might divide the traffic going out of a certain city among the members on a certain percentage basis.

When such pooling arrangements were brought before the courts, they were declared to be illegal, under the old common law of conspiracy, as constituting restraint of trade. Therefore, a new scheme or plan which might withstand the scrutiny of the courts was found imperative if competitors were to combine, and out of the needs of the situation there arose the trustee trust.

Trustee Trusts—In discussing corporation and business problems, most individuals employ the word "trust" to signify any large business. In this text, however, we shall use it as applying only to the trustee trust. The term "trustee trust" originated as a result of the practice of using a trustee to make a combination possible. Under the law, it is legal for me to turn over to you a certain sum of money or other property and authorize you to care for it as my interests may require. You are then acting as my trustee. In searching about for some means of evading the law, executives of competitive companies concluded that it ought to be legal for them to use the trustee principle in effecting a combination. Accordingly, each company interested in a proposed combination appointed one person to act as the trustee for its stockholders, who thereupon turned over to him all of their voting stock. In exchange for the stock, each stockholder received a trustee certificate, on which dividends were paid but which conferred no voting rights upon the holder. In this manner the right to vote the stock was placed in the hands of the trustee. Each trustee, therefore, completely controlled the affairs of the company which he represented. The trustees of the several companies then met and agreed upon the policies to be pursued by their respective companies as to prices, production, territory to be exploited, and other matters of mutual interest, thus bringing about unity of action and the abolition of competition.

The Standard Oil Company of 1882 was the first large combination to be brought together on this basis. In 1890, however, the trustee trust was declared illegal by the Supreme Court of New York in the Sugar Trust case.

Trustee Trust versus Voting Trust—The trustee trust must not be confused with the voting trust, which one frequently finds mentioned in newspapers and financial magazines. There has never been any question as to the legality of the voting trust. If, for example, several factions among the stockholders of a certain corporation are fighting each other, a situation that frequently results in the business going from bad to worse, it is not at all unusual for the stockholders to elect three or five or more persons to act as trustees, and to turn their stock over to these trustees, in order to place control of the business in their hands. A voting trust may last for a year or for a period of years and frequently results in the corporation's affairs being returned to a sound condition. A trustee trust represents a combination among competing companies. A voting trust, on the other hand, is not concerned with a combination of competing companies but arises from the desire of the stockholders of a company to increase the prosperity of their own enterprise.

Holding Companies—In 1890, Congress passed the Sherman Anti-Trust Act, which declared illegal any combination or contract in restraint of interstate trade. This law and the adverse decisions of the courts relative to the legality of the trustee trust forced business leaders to devise still another form of combination, which they hoped would meet the requirements of the law. The holding company was the result of their efforts. There was no law prohibiting an individual or a corporation from holding as much stock of any corporation as might be purchased. Therefore, the leaders of competing companies decided to employ this means of effecting combinations. Two types of holding companies were developed—the holding company formed for the sole purpose of holding stocks in other companies and the holding company which, in addition to holding stocks in other companies, was actively engaged in carrying on a business of its own.

A holding company attains its desired objective either by exchanging its stock for the stock of the companies which it wishes to combine or by purchasing the stock of the latter in the market. It is not necessary for a holding company to own a majority of the stock of a corporation in order to obtain control. The stock of a large corporation is usually very widely scattered. Then, too, friends can be depended upon to assist in securing a majority of the votes represented at the annual meeting of stockholders. Finally, very seldom is 100% of the company's stock voted at the annual meeting. These conditions render it possible at times for the ownership of from 25% to 35% of the company's stock to control its affairs. In this way a holding company may dominate a number of corporations possessing a larger combined capitalization than the holding company itself.

The holding company type of organization is very generally used today in connection with group banking systems. In such cases a corporation is formed, and the corporation then exchanges its stock for the stock of a number of banks. The banks that are thus controlled continue to function as independent institutions under their original titles, but under orders from the officers of the holding company.

The first pronounced combination movement in the United States, which occurred during the period from 1897 to 1904, was characterized by the organization of holding companies. For several years this type of combination remained unmolested, and many persons surmised that at last the requirements of the law had been successfully met. In 1911, however, the United States Supreme Court, in the American Tobacco Company and Standard Oil Company cases, held that both of these concerns were illegal as constituting an unreasonable restraint of trade. This decision has been severely condemned by jurists, lawyers, and economists—and, in fact, by the minority of the United States Supreme Court itself—not because these two combinations were held to be illegal, but because the court, by its decision, practically read into the Sherman Anti-Trust Act the word "unreasonable." This act, as we have seen, held as illegal all combinations that restrained interstate trade, and it did not distinguish between reasonable and unreasonable restraint. The United States Supreme Court, by a majority vote, justified its position in the two cases in question by maintaining that had it declared illegal all combinations that restrained interstate trade, the result would be the widespread disruption of business. This decision by the United States Supreme Court has long been known as "the rule of reason."

Interlocking Directorates—Still another method employed to stifle competition and to effect combination was the use of the interlocking directorate. This method is still used to some extent. Unity of action between two corporations can easily be obtained by having the same men serve on the board of directors of each corporation. The control of a majority, or at times of even a small number, of directors is sufficient to bring about the desired result. In states in which laws have been passed prohibiting a director of one company from serving on the boards of competing companies, the offending director merely resigns from all but one board and sees to it that a number of his friends are chosen to succeed him, one for each of the boards on which he has previously served. By this means, the provisions of the law are complied with, but the community of interest among the corporations concerned is not in any way affected. This evasion demonstrates the difficulty of framing laws, the intent of which cannot be nullified.

The Single Large Corporation—The decision of

the United States Supreme Court in the American Tobacco Company and Standard Oil Company cases had a most disturbing effect on the business world. It was felt that if the authority to decide whether or not a combination was in unreasonable restraint of trade resided solely in the courts, there was no way of determining the status of a combination until its case was passed upon by the courts. Consequently there gradually developed a tendency, which is still in evidence at the present time, to create a single large corporation by the merging of a number of individual concerns. By this means, the original companies are wiped out of existence as separate entities. They no longer retain their individuality; they are not held together by an agreement or by a holding company; in fact, they completely lose their identity as a result of being purchased by a single large corporation. This new form of organization, therefore, is not a combination because the companies that are brought together are owned outright by one company. Several cases have been brought before the courts, which have held that these single large corporations are not illegal merely because of their size or because of their monopolistic character.

We still have a large number of holding companies, which are operating legally because they do not restrain trade unreasonably and because they are not guilty of unfair competitive practices. However, because of the uncertainty of the attitude of the courts toward the principle of the holding company, the form of organization that has been most commonly adopted during the second period of the combination movement in the

United States, dating roughly from the year 1920, has been that of the single large corporation.

Advantages of Combination—The advantages of combination are primarily those of large scale production, which have already been discussed, and the elimination or curtailment of competition. There is another advantage, however, which arises in connection with earnings. A small business has only itself to depend upon for profits, but in the case of a combination one part may suffer heavy losses, while another may earn large profits, thus making possible more stable dividends for the enterprise as a whole.

Disadvantages of Combination—The disadvantages of combination are those of large scale production, and, in some cases, also those of monopoly. It has been shown that frequently the earnings of a combination have been less than those of the constituent companies before they were brought together into a combination, for at times, those in control of a combination are more vitally interested in the gains made through speculation in its securities than in the profits derived from the sale of its products to the public.

Definition of Monopoly—Many students confuse the terms monopoly and combination. There may be a combination which is yet not a monopoly. For example, a large branch banking system may be built up as the result of a combination of several hundred banks, without obtaining a monopoly of the banking field. Ten drug stores in a city may be merged into one company without obtaining a monopoly of the drug store business. On the other hand, we may have a monopoly without a combination having been effected. The owner of a patent has a monopoly, yet he is not a party to a combination.

A monopoly is defined as "that which gives exclusive control of some commodity or service, more particularly, though not solely, with respect to price." The owner of a patent, for example, has exclusive control over his article, yet he cannot always fix its price at the point he desires, because he has to face the competition of articles which are similar in character to his patented commodity. On the other hand, the United States Steel Corporation may control a little less than half of the production of iron and steel in the United States, yet, because of its dominating position, it may control the prices of iron and steel products, since other companies will follow its lead in raising or lowering prices.

Classification of Monopolies—Monopolies may be publicly owned, as is the postal service in the United States, or privately owned by individuals, firms, or corporations. They may be based upon the idea of promoting the general welfare, as in the case of patents, trademarks, and copyrights or in the case of what are termed public consumption monopolies and fiscal monopolies. A public consumption monopoly exists when the government itself manages a business, such as in the sale of liquor, or when it grants a monopoly to some company to do so, with the object of regulating the consumption of the article concerned. A fiscal monopoly exists when the government engages in a monopolistic business for the sole purpose of obtaining a financial return from its operation.

Monopolies may arise from either public or private favoritism. If the government frees a monopoly from foreign competition by levying a high protective tariff, the control exercised by the monopoly is based on public favoritism. If a monopoly derives its power from railroad rebates, manufacturers' rebates, or similar sources, it is then based on private favoritism.

Those monopolies that depend for their existence on natural resources, as distinguished from social arrangements, are known as natural monopolies. Mineral springs and the diamond mines of South Africa are examples of natural monopolies which result from the fact that the supply of raw materials is limited. There still exist some monopolies that are based on secret formulæ or secret processes, although with the rapid development of industrial chemistry and with the spread of the cooperative spirit among producers, secrecy is becoming less and less usual as a basis of monopoly. Those natural monopolies that arise from properties inherent in the business itself play an important part in our economic life. Such monopolies are railroads, canals, bridges, ferries, and public utilities.

Causes Promoting Combination and Monopoly —It is rather commonly claimed that the tariff is the mother of the trust. It is said that the protective tariff frees domestic concerns from the competition of foreign companies and thus makes possible combination and monopoly. As a matter of fact, however, the United States has been an adherent of the protective tariff policy from the first; yet it has been only since the latter part of the nineteenth century that we have had a "trust problem." Evidently something other than a protective tariff must have made it possible for monopolies and combinations to be formed. In England, which has no protective tariff, combinations and monopolies exist, as they do in all industrial nations. Monopolies and combinations, therefore, appear to be the natural, inevitable results of a developing economic society.

The means used to effect combinations and monopolies and to give them control of their respective fields of economic activity are, for the most part, to be classed under the general heading of unfair competition, which may take a variety of forms. It may be local price cutting—the cutting of prices in a competitor's territory to less than cost and the raising of prices elsewhere to offset the losses thus incurred. Railroads or manufacturers may be forced to grant rebates (or they may grant them voluntarily) to one concern and not to its competitors, thus giving the one concern an advantage. An agreement may be made by a manufacturer or a wholesaler with a retailer, whereby the latter promises to sell only the products of the former. This is known as a factor's agreement. Other forms of unfair competition have included the following: employment of spies to obtain details of competitors' business transactions, use of employees of competitors or use of shipping companies, through bribery, to secure the needed information, use of threats and other forms of intimidation, and even the use of subsidiary companies as bogus independent concerns.

Public Policies—The attitude of the public toward combinations and monopolies has changed greatly with the passing of time. At first the public was not at all interested in the matter. The government was expected to follow the policy of "hands off" and permit affairs in the business world to develop naturally and freely. The consequences of this *laissez faire,* or "let alone," policy so unfavorably affected the interests of the public that there arose a demand for the dissolution of all combinations. It was found, however, that the adoption and enforcement of this dissolution policy did not result in permanent benefits, for when one form of combination was declared to be illegal, another was immediately devised which came within the provisions of the law—at least, for the time being. The policy followed at present is that of government regulation, based upon the fundamental idea that, inasmuch as combinations are inevitable, it is advisable to remove or to prevent the more flagrant abuses and to retain for the benefit of the public the advantages which result from restricting freedom of competition.

Mention has already been made of the passage by Congress of the Sherman Anti-Trust Act, which declared illegal all contracts or combinations in restraint of interstate trade. This act remained practically a dead letter until 1911, when the United States Supreme Court declared the American Tobacco Company and the Standard Oil Company to be guilty of unreasonable restraint of trade and therefore illegal.

In 1914, Congress passed the Clayton Anti-Trust Act and the Federal Trade Commission Act. The former act amended the Sherman Anti-Trust Act in several particulars. It declared illegal the holding of stock by one corporation in other corporations for the purpose, substantially, of restraining competition or for the purpose of creating a monopoly. It also prohibited interlocking directorates, as well as certain unfair competitive practices. The Federal Trade Commission Act created the Federal Trade Commission, which is composed of five members appointed by the President of the United States, and is empowered to investigate complaints arising under federal anti-trust laws, to issue orders restraining the use of unfair competitive business practices, to recommend to the federal courts plans for reorganizing or dissolving offending combinations, and to follow up court decisions to see that the decrees are satisfactorily carried out.

Both of these measures, together with the Sherman Anti-Trust Act, have been helpful in removing some, though by no means all, of the abuses resulting from the everyday practices of big business. Because some of these abuses remain, the assertion has been made that the only possible method of obtaining complete and permanent reform is to have the government own and operate big business. Some persons go even farther in their demands and urge the complete reorganization of our economic world by the adoption of socialism, syndicalism, anarchism, or some other radical plan.

CHAPTER XI

Money, Banking, and Foreign Exchange

AFTER goods have been produced, the question naturally arises as to how title to them can be secured by others. In short, how can they be purchased? This question brings us to the next major division of economics—to the subject of exchange, which embodies a discussion of money, banking, and foreign exchange. Inasmuch as the Institute textbooks entitled Bank Organization and Operation (Banking I) and Money and Banking (Banking II) cover these subjects in a detailed and comprehensive manner, only a few of the more important aspects of exchange need be referred to in this chapter.

Money

Barter— In primitive times, goods were traded directly for goods—that is, they were bartered, because no other means were available whereby exchanges could be made. Barter functioned successfully in those early times, because goods did not differ greatly in value. However, in the highly complex economic civilization of today, barter would not suffice as a means of making exchanges. It would be exceedingly difficult for you to find some one who had exactly what you wanted and who wanted exactly what you wished to dispose of. If you wanted to trade a radio for a saxophone, you would be compelled to find some individual who had a saxophone which he desired to trade for a radio. Ordinarily, such an exchange would not be easy of accomplishment. Barter also has the disadvantage of not enabling one to save for the future. How, for example, could one store up fish or fruit for several years, thus providing for the proverbial rainy day? Barter would be entirely impossible today in handling our large sales and purchases.

Money Defined—With the passing of time and with the development of commerce, it was necessary that a more satisfactory method of making exchanges be devised, and, as a consequence, over a period of centuries money was evolved. Money may be defined as any medium of exchange that has general acceptability. By the term medium, we mean anything that is used as a go-between or as a means by which one commodity is exchanged for another. We have many different kinds of media of exchange (coins, paper money, checks, drafts, stocks and bonds, and so forth), yet only those that are generally acceptable—acceptable without question—are designated as being money.

Primitive Money—Many strange commodities have been used as money, such as cattle among early peoples, furs in the cold climates, tobacco in Maryland and Virginia, dates in Arabia, wampum and ammunition among the early colonists of our country, and the baser metals (iron, tin, and copper).

Superiority of Gold and Silver—In time, gold and

silver came to be the metals most commonly used for monetary purposes, because of the fact that they possess great value in proportion to their weight and bulk, a quality which makes it convenient to carry and to ship coins minted from them. Gold and silver are easily coined, or minted; they are readily distinguishable from other metals; they are extremely durable; and they are in great demand in the manufacture of jewelry, dental supplies, and works of art. They also exist in much more limited quantities than do other metals, a condition which makes it difficult to increase the amount in the market rapidly. This limitation aids in the maintenance of a more stable value than is possible with other metals. Only about one-half of the gold that is mined is used for monetary purposes, the remainder being absorbed by the arts. Coins of small value are usually made from copper and nickel, although aluminum has also been used for that purpose.

Government Control of Money—The government customarily retains the sole right to issue coins, although at times in the past coins have been minted and put into circulation by individuals. When it issues a coin, the government merely certifies to the weight and fineness, or purity, of the metal which the coin contains; it does not certify to the value, or purchasing power, of the coin. For example, when a silver dollar leaves the United States Mint, it has a weight of 412½ grains of silver, nine-tenths fine, or pure; the remaining one-tenth consists of copper, which is added for the purpose of hardening the silver and making it more durable. A full weight gold dollar contains 25.8 grains of gold, nine-tenths fine. It is not possible for the government to certify to the value of its coins, because their value, or purchasing power—in other words, what they will buy—varies from day to day with changes in the general price level.

Paper Money—The people of practically all countries use a considerable amount of paper money, which is frequently 100% secured by gold, silver, government bonds, or commercial paper. Paper money is more convenient to handle in large amounts than is metallic money. It is usually issued by the government and by banks, although at times in the past it has been issued by individuals.

Functions of Money—Not only does money serve as a medium of exchange, or as a means by which we conveniently make our purchases, but it also performs certain other functions. It serves as a standard of value, for it is in terms of money that we measure the value of everything else. The value of commodities, services, health, education, and at times even broken hearts is measured in terms of money. Money is the measuring rod by which we gauge the worth of all wealth. As a standard of value, money is important in connection with deferred or postponed payments. If I borrow $1,000 from you at 6% for one year, I pay you $1,060 at the end of the twelve months' period, regardless of how high or how low prices have become in the meantime. By means of money, also, values may be stored in convenient form. If I raise grapes, I cannot keep them for several years, but I can sell them and store up their value in money, which I can keep as long as I desire.

Money of the United States—In the United States, we have copper, nickel, silver, and gold coins, all issued by the National Government. At present, the value of the metal in our copper, nickel, and silver coins, even though they are of full weight, is not equal to the face value of the coins. The value of the metal in these coins varies with its price in the market. Only when silver is selling for a little more than $1.29 an ounce is there a dollar's worth of silver in a silver dollar. In February 1931, silver sold for as low as 26½ cents an ounce. Two halves or four quarters or ten dimes are 6.9% lighter in weight than a silver dollar; hence silver would have to rise to a price which is slightly more than 6.9% higher than $1.29 before these subsidiary silver coins would contain silver equal to their face value. For a very short time during the World War, the price of nickel was so high, because of the scarcity of the supply of that metal, that the five cent nickel piece was actually worth six cents. Our copper, nickel, and silver coins circulate at their face value because of the faith of the people in the solvency of the United States Government and also because, if at any time they should lack such faith, the Secretary of the Treasury would be compelled by law to redeem the coins in gold. In normal times, they are not directly redeemable in gold.

In the case of our gold coins, however, a different situation exists. The full weight gold coins always contain an amount of gold equal to their face value. The price of gold in the United States is fixed by the National Government at $18.60+ per ounce for gold that is nine-tenths pure. The price does not change from day to day. Therefore, 25.8 grains of gold is always worth $1.

We have seven different kinds of paper money in the United States. Four of these—gold certificates, silver certificates, greenbacks (or United States notes), and treasury notes of 1890—are issued by the United States Government. Gold certificates are 100% secured by gold coins and gold bars, while silver certificates are fully backed by silver dollars. The total amount of greenbacks outstanding can never exceed $346,681,016. Behind this amount the United States Treasury is compelled by law to keep a gold fund of approximately $150,000,000. The treasury notes, of which there is only about $1,000,000 in amount still outstanding, are secured 100% by coined silver dollars and gold funds of the United States Treasury.

National bank notes are issued by national banks, and Federal Reserve bank notes are issued by Federal Reserve banks. Both kinds of notes are backed 100% by deposits of United States bonds which can legally be used for note issue purposes. At present, only the 2% Panama Canal bonds of 1916-1936 and 1918-1938 and the United States 2% consols may be thus used. Federal Reserve notes are issued to the Federal Reserve banks by the Federal Reserve Board against a minimum security of 40% in gold and 60% in prescribed rediscounted commercial paper or against a maximum security of 100% in gold. The security is deposited by the Federal Reserve banks with the Federal Reserve agent, who represents the Federal Reserve Board. The Federal Reserve banks pay out the Federal Reserve notes to banks and to others when business demands more money; they retire the notes when the need of business for funds decreases. The Federal Reserve notes provide the only elastic element in our monetary system; and they were introduced in order that the supply of the country's money might expand and contract in accordance with the demands of business.

BANKING

Evolution of Credit and Credit Institutions—Barter met successfully the needs of people in primitive times. Money later did likewise for the period of small business and small financial transactions. But as business units increased in size and as the sums involved in transactions became greater, the need arose for a more satisfactory medium of exchange. Money in large amounts, even though it be paper money, is bulky and difficult to handle. It cannot be shipped without risk, because of the possibility of theft; in the case of paper money, there is the additional risk of destruction by fire. Then, too, the amount of money available gradually proved insufficient for the demands of business. The dollar, as money, can never be more than a dollar, and as long as it is used solely as money, there is no means by which it can be stretched into two or three or four dollars' worth of purchasing power. The expanding needs of business required some means whereby our dollar might be used as a basis for the creation of more dollars. As a consequence, credit gradually came into use. In time it made necessary the establishment of various kinds of credit instruments and credit institutions. Banks made it possible for credit to be created in almost unlimited amounts, and they also provided for its conversion into money, or cash, on demand.

It is difficult to bring to the student an appreciation of the long period of time and the many steps required to evolve a money economy out of a barter economy and our present credit economy out of a money economy. We still have some barter transactions in the United States, but they are insignificant in extent. Money also is used, of course, but primarily for purchases involving small sums. It is estimated that from 90% to 95% of all business today is carried on by means of various kinds of credit instruments—checks, drafts, and other bills of exchange.

Basis of Credit—Credit involves two basic elements —that of postponed payment and that of confidence. A credit transaction rests upon a promise to pay in the future. When you purchase goods on credit at the store, you agree to pay at some future date. When you give me a check on your bank account, that check represents a claim to funds in the bank, and I can obtain the funds only by cashing the check, which takes time. Credit also calls for confidence in the person who agrees to pay at some time in the future. Without confidence, credit could not exist.

There is a type of credit used today which does not arise in connection with the facilities provided by banks. Thus, you purchase goods on credit at the store, the retailer purchases on credit from the wholesaler, and the wholesaler purchases on credit from the jobber or manufacturer. In this discussion, however, we are interested only in those payments that are effected by means of credit instruments, most of which arise because of the existence and practices of banking institutions.

Bank Credit—Our credit structure of today, then, rests upon banking institutions, without which we should be unable to use checks, drafts, and other bills of exchange as we do at present. How do banks provide us with the means by which to carry on credit transactions? A bank is organized with a certain amount of money, which its owners pay for its capital stock. Let us say that it has obtained $200,000 in this manner. It then opens its doors for the transaction of business. The public deposits $750,000 with it. The bank then has $950,000 to use as it desires under the requirements laid down by the banking law. It cannot loan or invest all of this money, because it has to keep a certain amount on hand for the purpose of meeting the demands of its customers for money over the counter. It is also required to keep what is known as a legal reserve behind all its deposits. This reserve varies under the terms of the several banking laws. Let us say that our bank has to keep a legal reserve of 10%. This means that for every $100 of deposits, $10 has to be retained as a reserve. The remaining $90 may be used by the bank partly for counter or till money and partly for loans and investments of various types.

The bank would make no money if it kept the entire $950,000 on hand. Consequently, it invests a portion of this amount in government bonds and in various kinds of commercial paper, both of which really represent loans. It also loans large sums of money to its depositors and others. When a loan is made, the borrower seldom asks to be given the amount of his loan in cash. He customarily directs that the sum borrowed be deposited to his account. Let us say that he borrows $1,000 and has it deposited. Against this amount, the bank must keep a reserve of $100. It also has to keep on hand a certain amount to care for checks that will be drawn against the borrower's account. Let us say that the bank keeps $400, this amount plus the $100 reserve making $500 in all. Thus, on the basis of $500, the bank has created a credit that amounts to the sum of $1,000.

In a similar manner, credit institutions stretch our dollars of money into more dollars of credit and thus make them go farther in meeting the demands of business for additional funds. It is not unusual under our present banking structure for $1 to serve as a basis for $10 or more of credit. If this is done and if a $10 check passes through ten hands before being presented for payment at the bank upon which it has been drawn, that check will have paid $100 worth of debts, and yet only one dollar of actual money will have served as a basis for such payments.

Another interesting phenomenon arises in connection

with the use of credit and shows how credit expands the usefulness of money. If A draws a check for the purpose of paying B and if both have accounts with the same bank, the check will be deposited by B to his account, and no cash will be required to complete the transaction. If, perchance, the checking accounts of A and B are in different banks, practically the same result is obtained by our system of clearing checks through clearing houses. When we learn that we have only about $8,000,000,000 of money in the United States and that the total amount of checks cleared each year (the amount cleared is far less than the amount used) approximates $500,000,000,000, the economic importance of credit, by far the most common evidence of which is the check, can be easily appreciated. The check thus makes an extremely valuable contribution to our modern economic system.

Kinds of Banks—Two general classifications may be used in grouping banking institutions: (1) according to the type of charter issued, if any, and (2) according to the functions performed, or the type of banking that is engaged in. The first group includes private banks owned by individuals or by partnerships, which possess no charter, banks chartered by the state, and banks chartered by the National Government. Banks chartered by the National Government include national banks, which may conduct commercial, thrift, and trust company business; Federal Reserve banks, which, briefly, are bankers' banks; Federal Land banks and Joint Stock Land banks, which make loans to farmers on real estate for from five to forty years; Federal Intermediate Credit banks, which loan to farmers' cooperative marketing associations for from one to three years; and several other kinds of institutions which need not be mentioned in this brief discussion of our banking system. State chartered banks usually conduct savings, commercial, and trust company business, although some of them confine themselves to only one kind of business.

On the basis of the functions performed, we may classify banking institutions as saving banks, commercial banks, or trust companies. Frequently, one banking institution performs all of these functions. Savings banks pay interest to their depositors, encourage thrift, and invest a large part of their funds in long time loans up to five years. Commercial banks gather in the funds of business enterprises and individuals; they pay interest on these funds only when large balances are maintained. They usually confine their loans to a maximum duration of ninety days; thus they engage in carrying on a short time credit business. Their accounts are subject to withdrawal by depositors on demand. Savings banks, on the other hand, reserve the right to require thirty days' notice before permitting depositors to withdraw their funds.

Trust companies or the trust departments of banks act as agents or trustees for clients in performing almost any function of a financial character. They are usually authorized to act as executors or administrators of the estates of deceased persons; to serve as guardians of the estates of minors and as conservators of the property of adults who are feeble minded, insane, or otherwise incompetent; to float or underwrite issues of stocks and bonds; to act as treasurers or financial agents of churches, lodges, and corporations; and to perform many other functions of a financial character for customers. There is scarcely any task involving finance that a trust company or the trust department of a bank may not care for under the terms and provisions of its organization.

Banks perform a most necessary and indispensable service in our modern economic life, receiving deposits, making loans to individuals and to business firms, discounting commercial paper, and acting in a fiduciary or trustee capacity. National banks and Federal Reserve banks have the additional right to issue bank notes, and the latter institutions make possible the issue of Federal Reserve notes, which are more widely used at present than is any other kind of money.

Foreign Exchange

Banks Aid in Financing Foreign Trade—Not only do banks enable us to finance our domestic activities by means of loans and discounts, but they also provide the means whereby practically all of our foreign trade is financed. Foreign exchange is concerned with the methods employed in making payments between buyers and sellers, or debtors and creditors, residing in different countries. The details of the instruments used and the practices followed have been fully discussed in the Institute textbook entitled Bank Organization and

Operation and therefore need not be repeated in this text. It will be sufficient to recall to the mind of the student the fact that credit instruments known as foreign bills of exchange are customarily employed in making payments abroad, although under certain circumstances it may become necessary or profitable to import or export gold.

CHAPTER XII

Distribution of Wealth

THUS far in our study of economics, we have considered the nature of human wants and their satisfaction by means of goods, including personal services. We have seen that in order to satisfy man's wants, commodities must be produced and services must be rendered and that this involves the creation of form, time, and place utilities. We have also noted that after production has taken place, means must be provided in order that consumers may obtain possession and use of the commodities and services and that, therefore, various methods of making exchanges have been devised. In other words, we have covered the fields of consumption, production, and exchange. We now turn our attention to the field of distribution, the division of the subject of economics which is probably the most difficult of all to present.

Distribution in Terms of Money—Distribution is concerned with those theories, principles, practices, and problems that arise out of (1) the *division of wealth* among the people and (2) the *division of income* among those who own property or who render personal services. As has been so frequently stated in previous pages, we engage in some form of economic activity in order to obtain an income. We must have an income in order to live, and that income for the most part is received in the form of money or credit. We still have some laborers who are paid partly in terms of room and board, and there are some farmers who rent their farms to others in return for one-half or one-third of the crop produced by the tenants. But these instances are not typical of the practices that prevail at present in our capitalistic machine age of pecuniary economy. No matter whether we receive our income in the form of room and board or crops or checks or gold, it is always measured in terms of money.

What Income Is—Our income consists of payments made to us in return for our having rendered personal services at the request of others or in return for our having allowed others to use our property. However, not all payments that are made to us can be classed as income. For example, if I pay you $12,500 for 100 shares of bank stock, most assuredly you will not count that payment as part of your income; you will count it as wealth. If I give you $1,000 as a reward for being the best student in this year's class of the American Institute of Banking, or if, when I die, I bequeath you $10,000, again you will not count this payment as part of your income. In none of these cases will the payments have been made by me because you have rendered me service or because you have permitted me to use your property. In the last two cases, the payments are gifts, made to you voluntarily and without your having any claim upon me for the sums involved.

Income consists of payments received from others. Therefore, a housewife cannot count as income servants' wages which she does not have to pay if she does her own work; nor can the vegetables which a farmer raises and serves on his own table be classed as income. In either case, the family is saved an expenditure of money, but in neither case is payment made by others for services rendered or for property used.

An increase in the value of our possessions, such as an increase in the value of our farm, home, or stocks and bonds, is not to be classed as income. If we were to sell our property, we should not count the selling price as income; we should be concerned with the receipt of wealth, not with the receipt of income, which we have defined as payments made to us for services rendered or for the use of our property.

Income Classes—Those who receive an income from rendering personal services may be classified as (1) skilled and unskilled laborers of all sorts, including manual laborers, so-called white-collared employees, members of boards of directors, managers, foremen, and business executives in general, all of whom receive wages or salaries, as the case may be; and (2) professional workers, such as lawyers, doctors, and dentists, who receive fees from their clients.

The owners of property likewise fall into several classes. There are those who own and lease land, buildings, and other property, receiving their income in the form of rent. There are others who loan funds (money and credit) for interest. There are also the owners or part owners of farms, stores, banks, factories, railroads, mines, and other business enterprises, who in each case hope that the enterprise will yield a return large enough not only to pay expenses and to care for certain other needs of the business but also to reimburse them for having put their funds into the business. This last class, the owners of the country's business enterprises, receives its income in the form of profits, or dividends.

Although the various classes of income receivers fall into two main groups—the renderers of personal services and the owners of property—it does not follow that, in the scramble for income, the members of the one group directly oppose those of the other. In fact, we find all classes of income receivers continually demanding larger returns. The owners of land and buildings want higher rents; the lenders of funds are eager for higher interest rates; the owners of business enterprises seek greater profits; skilled and unskilled laborers clamor for more wages; the professional workers seek larger fees. Each class is eager to get more, because the wants of its members are capable of indefinite expansion and, for the most part, can be satisfied only by the receipt of bigger incomes. Although there is this clashing of interests, it is interesting to note that when it is necessary to act upon various economic and political issues, these income receiving groups at times form certain alliances. The people of the city oppose those of the country. The manufacturer opposes the farmer. The employing or business-owning class opposes the skilled and unskilled employees. The professional workers, the salaried employees (clerks, stenographers, teachers, and so forth), and the business executives (superintendents, managers, and foremen) usually ally themselves with the property-owning class in opposing the demands of the so-called "working class." Later we shall discuss the methods used by these classes in their efforts to obtain a larger share of the income of society.

Chance Gains—The fact that a person receives an income does not necessarily mean that he is personally doing anything to merit that income, either by adding to the wealth of society or by increasing its well-being. It merely shows that he is doing something that some one is willing to pay for or that he possesses property for the use of which some one is willing to pay. The purveyor of poisonous bootleg liquor that kills its consumers, the vendor of such harmful drugs as morphine, cocaine, and opium, and the publisher and seller of obscene or trashy literature are not conserving the welfare of society. The feeble-minded son who inherits a million dollar fortune in stocks and bonds has done nothing to merit the income which he receives. The banker who paid $25,000 for a home site on Signal Hill in Long Beach, California, upon which oil was later discovered, did nothing personally to merit the oil royalties which he still receives annually. In the last two cases, however, the wealth and well-being of society are incidentally enhanced. In the case of the feeble-minded son who inherits his father's fortune, the property undoubtedly consists of funds invested in factories, railroads, and other productive enterprises which benefit society. In the case of the lucky banker who became an oil magnate, society benefits from the oil that is being produced by the wells that were found on his estate.

Much of the income arising from both personal services and property ownership owes its existence to what we may call "fortuitous circumstances"; that is, to conditions over which the laborers and the property owners have no control. For example, let us suppose that war is declared. The laboring class has not brought on the war, yet immediately a demand arises for boiler makers and for other laborers to work in war industries. Wages rise to dizzy heights, and the workers gain accordingly. Suppose a flood or a conflagration wipes out a city. Here again, there is a demand for laborers, and employment opportunities are plentiful.

Let us consider a few cases in which property owners profit by chance gains. I discover a cave on my land and charge admission to the public. John Jones opens a restaurant, and the King of England, riding by in his automobile, stops to eat at Jones's restaurant. Trade immediately picks up and a rushing business is done, because the public clamors to eat at a place that has been host to a king. William Smith buys a building in Miami, Florida and opens a store. An era of land speculation sets in, and Smith's store grows into a huge establishment. Tom Andrews owns stock in a certain company, and one of the employees discovers a new process which increases the profits of the business many fold. These are typical instances of chance gains enjoyed by the owners of property through no particular effort on their part.

On the other hand, the reverse of this situation is all too frequently found. Incomes often decrease through no fault of the laborers or of the property owners. A business depression may occur. Millions of men who are eager to work are unable to find employment. Enterprises that have been most carefully and intelligently managed are forced to the wall or suffer greatly reduced incomes through no fault of their executives or owners. A land boom may subside, wiping out millions of dollars' worth of property values and incomes. Fashions may change, as in the case of hoop skirts, corsets, bicycles, and hairnets, and force some of the manufacturers into bankruptcy. These few examples serve to make clear the fact that the extent of the income received by those who render personal services and by those who own property is frequently affected by conditions that are entirely beyond their control.

Functional Distribution versus Personal Distribution of Wealth—Practically all economists discuss what is called the functional distribution of wealth. As we have already noted, they claim that there are four factors of production—land, labor, capital, and the entrepreneur. Accordingly, they maintain that the products of society, or its income, are divided among these four factors, land receiving rent, labor receiving wages, capital receiving interest, and the entrepreneur receiving what is left over, or profits. After discussing these matters, they pass on to what they call the personal distribution of wealth, or its division among individuals as distinct from its division among the factors of production.

It is well for us, however, to consider matters in the economic world as they actually exist. You and I are concerned with the cold facts of the world of reality, of business as it actually functions at present. Even you, who are just beginning the study of the subject of economics, know that we do not pay anything to land and to capital as such. Land may be exceedingly fertile, yet we do not take $1,000 a year in gold, for example, and give it to the land; nor do we pay a return to capital or to labor power in a similar manner. We pay a return to the individuals who are the owners of land, capital, and other forms of wealth that yield an income and to the laborers who perform labor power or personal services for us.

In short, when it comes to the division of the income of society, we are concerned with the distribution of income among individuals, some of whom are not at all concerned with producing utilities or goods. For example, suppose you inherit $500,000 and lend $1,000 to me. By no stretch of imagination can you be classed as a producer; yet I pay you 6% a year on the loan. Suppose I have a wonderful cave on my land and charge an admission fee of fifty cents. I have not produced form, time, or place utility, yet I receive an income from the admission fees which I collect. It ought to be evident, therefore, that in the economic world we are concerned only with the personal distribution of wealth—that is, with the division of the income of society among individuals who render services or who own property, regardless of whether or not that property is used for productive purposes.

In discussing the factors of production, we found that there is really a twofold classification: (1) the human element, or labor (labor power) and (2) the non-human element (land and capital goods). We also discovered that capital represents funds (money or credit) which are used to pay for those things that are used in a productive enterprise. We divided the usually assigned functions of the entrepreneur into two parts—that of managing, which we classed as a personal service, and that of owning a business enterprise or being a risk taker, which we classed as a function of the owner of capital. Therefore, we were able to rid ourselves of the necessity of considering the entrepreneur as a factor in production—in other words, as a separate party entitled to a claim upon the income of society.

In discussing the division of the income of society among its various members, we also have a twofold classification: (1) those who render personal services and (2) those who own property. Again it is necessary to point out that the latter group includes not only those who are engaged in productive enterprises as the owners of capital but also those who possess other forms of wealth that are used to satisfy consumption demands directly, such as, for example, the owners of buildings which may be leased and of automobiles which may be rented. Income, therefore, is paid not only to those who engage in productive activity but also, under certain circumstances, to those who do not.

Hence the theory of the functional distribution or division of income on the basis of payments to land, labor, capital, and the entrepreneur has to be abandoned for the more practical, reasonable theory of the distribution of income to individuals on the basis of returns arising from the rendering of personal services and from the owning of property. This latter theory is known as the theory of personal distribution. Although it is true that partnerships, corporations, and the estates of deceased persons own property and receive income therefrom, yet this fact in no way renders illogical or false our theory of personal distribution, for these impersonal partnerships, corporations, and estates are in their turn owned by individuals to whom the income is paid after the expenses and other charges have been deducted. Therefore, society is concerned with the distribution or division of income and of wealth among individuals, not with its distribution among the factors of production.

Distribution of Wealth versus Distribution of Income—In discussing personal distribution, we face two problems: (1) the distribution or division of *wealth* among individuals and (2) the distribution or division of *income* among individuals. A few examples will make clear the fact that these are not two statements of the same problem. I may own $100,000 worth of stock from which I receive no return. I have wealth but no income. On the other hand, you are a bank clerk receiving a salary of $100 a month, but you own no house, farm, or property of any kind other than a few personal belongings. You have an income, which, of course, is wealth, but only a small amount of property. Thus, while all income is wealth, not all wealth is income. It will be made clear in the succeeding pages that much of the wealth of our people has not been obtained as a result of their having earned it in the form of income.

Distribution of Wealth in the United States—Our problem concerning the division of wealth among individuals has to do (1) with the question of whether the wealth of the United States is widely held or whether it is in the hands of a few people and (2) with the question of whether there is a tendency for this wealth to fall into the hands of a few people or whether there is a tendency for it to be divided among an increasingly larger number of individuals. Many studies bearing on these matters have been made, but the information available for scrutiny is so incomplete and so unsatisfactory that the results thus far obtained represent mere estimates rather than dependable conclusions.

One of the outstanding investigations in this connection was made by Dr. W. I. King under the direction of the National Bureau of Economic Research, and dealt with conditions in the United States in the year 1921. Dr. King estimated that of our population of over 108,000,000 about two-thirds were not property owners. It is true that a large part of that fraction was made up of wives and children, but there were included many individuals who depended entirely upon their earnings for an income. Dr. King concluded that a little less than 1% of all the people in the United States owned about one-quarter of the wealth of the country, that a little more than 5% owned more than one-half, and that a little more than 20% owned more than three-fourths.

Many persons have contended that the wealth of our country is gradually being concentrated in the hands of fewer and fewer individuals and that the condition of the poorer element of our population is becoming increasingly distressing in character. There are, however, no data available which support such contentions. The statement has also been frequently made that the rich are getting richer and that, at the same time, the condition of the poorer class is improving. Some persons declare that the rich are getting richer much more rapidly than the condition of the poor is improving and that the breach is widening, while others contend that the poor are gaining on the rich and that the breach is narrowing. Again must we admit that there are no supporting data for such statements.

Undoubtedly the working class is better off today than at any time during the past. No one would be so foolish as to claim that the condition of the workingman of today is worse than that of the slave or serf of the past. Also it would require a vivid imagination and a disregard for facts to claim that the workingman of a hundred years ago was better off than the workingman of the present. A century ago the hours of labor frequently ranged from twelve to fifteen per day; the conditions of employment were extremely unsatisfactory in factories, mines, and stores; wages were low in comparison with prices; living conditions were inferior to those of today—there were no public schools, automobiles, bathtubs, washing machines, radios, and the thousand and one other things that tend to make life more satisfactory. Attention should also be called to the improved political and social position occupied by the workingman of today.

Income of the People of the United States—Mere lack of the possession of property by an individual does not necessarily mean that he is in a state of poverty. There are many people who have a fairly high standard of living yet are entirely dependent on their salaries or wages for a livelihood. However, in spite of our high plane of living in the United States, one is forced to admit that a very considerable amount of poverty exists. Many authorities have estimated that the number of our people who at all times live in a condition of poverty, "underfed, poorly clothed, and improperly housed," runs into the millions. This state of affairs results from an inadequate income or from lack of any income at all.

The information relative to the incomes of our people is very unsatisfactory. A detailed survey of the distribution of income in the United States, made by the National Bureau of Economic Research in 1918, disclosed some interesting contrasts. According to the results of that survey, it was estimated that about 12% of the national income was received by seven-tenths of 1% of the income receivers; that about 28% of the national income went to less than 6% of the income receivers;

and that over 50% went to 28% of the income receivers. Although this statement appears to be rather startling in character, it becomes less so when we realize that we have to go as low as $10,000 a year to include the seven-tenths of 1% of the income receivers and as low as $1,500 to include the 28% of the income receivers, and also that about 60% of the total income of the country went to those who received from $1,000 to $3,000 a year. In fact, 39% of the total income in 1918 went to those who received less than $1,000.

In 1915, two American economists, Lauck and Lydenstriker, after a very careful investigation of the actual incomes of workingmen in the United States, concluded that over 80% of the heads of working class families received less than $800 per year apiece.

The federal income tax statistics afford some basis for the contention that the incomes of the people of the United States are not as high as many persons have surmised to be the case. In 1928, returns were made by only 2,523,063 persons taxable under the federal income tax provisions. Incomes are taxable if in excess of $1,500 for a single person and if in excess of $3,500 for a married person or a head of a family, with an exemption of $400 for each child or other person dependent upon the taxpayer and also with an exemption for dividends received from a corporation subject to the income tax. In 1928, 511 persons reported incomes in excess of $1,000,000, representing an increase over previous years, as is evidenced by the fact that those reporting incomes in excess of $1,000,000 totaled 206 in 1916, 141 in 1917, 21 in 1921, 75 in 1924, and 209 in 1927.

Frequently, newspapers and magazines publish data regarding the per capita income of the people of the United States (the total money income of the country divided by the number of its inhabitants). Such information is misleading, because the public is not educated to understand the significance of such figures or to interpret them properly. The most reliable estimates of per capita income (which, however, are themselves nothing more than estimates made in as careful and exact a manner as possible) are those of the National Bureau of Economic Research. The data for the period from 1913 to 1926 are set forth in the following table:

PER CAPITA INCOME OF THE UNITED STATES
1913-1926

Year	Per Capita Income	Per Capita Income on Basis of 1913 Price Level
1913	$329	$329
1914	320	316
1915	326	319
1916	385	349
1917	470	361
1918	537	340
1919	640	358
1920	697	341
1921	579	334
1922	597	369
1923	689	421
1924	700	426
1925	752	445
1926	770	455

The figures shown in the second column do not indicate that every man, woman, and child in the United States received the sums mentioned. The total estimated income of the country has been divided by the total estimated population, which of course includes many millions of individuals who received no income.

Another matter which must be kept in mind is that the dollar income of the individual is not indicative of his real income. For example, suppose I have been receiving $100 per month and my salary is increased to $200 per month. If, at the same time, prices, or the costs of living, are doubled, my real income—what my money will buy—has remained unchanged. The third column in the table shows the effect of the changing price level, the dollar per capita income for each year having been adjusted to the price level of 1913. For example, if your income had risen from $329 in 1913 to $697 in 1920, although your money income had more than doubled, your $697 would have purchased only what could have been bought with $341 in 1913. Your real income, therefore, had increased by the difference between $329 and $341. This example shows how necessary it is, in discussing incomes arising from any source, whether they be received as wages, rent, interest, or profits, to take into consideration the changing price level, or what those incomes will actually buy.

Poverty—Poverty is caused by factors which tend to produce inequality in the distribution of wealth and income. These factors may be classified roughly into two groups, individual and social. Let us consider first the individual causes of poverty. It must be admitted that there are some people who are inherently lazy and inefficient. They could not acquire wealth if given every possible opportunity of doing so. Some are born mentally incompetent (insane or feeble-minded), while some who have normal mental equipment do not take advantage of their educational opportunities. Others are drug addicts or drunkards. Before the enactment of the prohibition law in the United States, it was commonly stated that drink was the most important cause of poverty. Many workers make no effort to obtain the necessary training to fit themselves for better jobs, just as many bankers lack sufficient ambition to take advantage of the courses offered by the American Institute of Banking. Success in securing a large income and great wealth is likely, although by no means certain, to come to those who are keen minded, alert, ambitious, and energetic. On the other hand, many who possess wealth do not possess these personal qualities.

The social causes of inequality in the distribution of wealth and income, which are by far the more important of the two groups of factors, are not personal shortcomings or deficiencies. First of all, there is the environment into which a person is born and in which he lives. Opportunities are by no means equal. Those who are born of well to do parents have many advantages over those who are born into poverty. Many of the latter are handicapped by lack of food, clothing, education, and social and economic opportunities. They have no one to place them in executive positions or to start them out in life in a business of their own. They inherit no fortunes. They begin, so to speak, with their bare hands in an effort to make a living. Sickness is more prevalent among them, and they lack the funds with which to obtain the proper medical care.

Sickness and death in the family are usually listed as the second greatest cause of poverty among those who apply for aid.

The members of the laboring class are also exposed to industrial accidents, which frequently result in disability or death. An injured worker or the family of a worker who is killed obtains no income unless protected by workmen's compensation laws (to be discussed in a later chapter). Before such laws were adopted by the individual states, industrial accidents were listed as the third greatest cause of poverty among those applying for charity. Other causes are wars, revolutions, earthquakes, floods, and business depressions, which wreck fortunes and bring poverty in their train.

As has been already stated, the accumulation of wealth has by no means always resulted from the efforts of an individual, unassisted by social arrangements and conditions. No one, with the exception of a few pugilists and motion picture actors, has ever become wealthy because of the wages that he has received. The same statement applies to those who receive large interest payments, for as a rule large interest payments arise from fortunes already accumulated. Great wealth is usually the result of inheritance, speculation in stocks and land, exploitation of natural resources, huge business profits, or sheer luck. Fortunes have been made and lost in the stock market and on the board of trade. They have arisen from land speculation and from the exploitation of our coal, oil, metal, and lumber resources. Many persons have become wealthy from monopoly gains, while others have obtained wealth by the lucky discovery of oil or mineral deposits. Not a few of our wealthy citizens have obtained their fortunes from business profits or from rents, made possible for the most part by the growth of their city's population. Some of the vast accumulations of wealth have been earned in that they have been obtained through the efforts of their owners, while others have been unearned, having resulted from lucky circumstances or from some act of society.

Suggested Methods of Obtaining More Equal Division—Many measures have been suggested for obtaining a greater diffusion of wealth among the members of society—not that it is deemed desirable to bring about an equal division of wealth, but it is thought that society would be better off if those that "have not" had a little more and if those that "have" had a little less. It has been urged by some that no one should be permitted to receive an income of more than $10,000 to $25,000 a year. Others have maintained that the wealthy should be heavily taxed on incomes and on inheritances. Both forms of taxation exist at present, and in some instances the rates are surprisingly high, the rate being graduated according to the size of the income or inheritance. It has also been suggested that when a wealthy person dies, he should not be permitted to leave his estate intact in a perpetual trust fund, from which his heirs are paid only the income, since this policy prevents the breaking up of large fortunes and their ultimate distribution among the heirs. At present, the laws of many states prohibit the creation of such perpetuities, thus insuring the division of estates into smaller portions.

Attention should be called to the fact that during the past twenty years, serious, and for the most part effective, efforts have been made by law to prevent the accumulation of wealth by such unfair business practices as characterized the acts of many of the founders of present-day fortunes. At the same time, much has also been done to insure greater equality of opportunity for our people by means of public education, improved industrial conditions, social legislation, and other devices. Finally, we have the proposals of the radical groups, the single-taxers, the socialists, the anarchists, and others, who are desirous of bringing about greater equality of wealth and income by changing either completely or in part our present social and economic arrangements. Their proposals will be considered in Chapter XXII.

CHAPTER XIII

Division of Income

IN our political world we have the ever present conflict between democrats and republicans. In the religious field we have the various large groups opposing one another—Christians, Buddhists, Mohammedans, and so on—and we also have the numerous Christian sects contending with one another for supremacy of faith. In all of its various aspects life represents a struggle. This is the story of the human race and civilization.

Contestants for Income—In the economic field, a contest is similarly waged over income. We find those who own property and receive an income therefrom contesting with those who have only personal services for sale. The landlord, the money lender, the wage earner, the professional man, and the business owner oppose one another in the struggle for a greater share of society's income. The employee opposes the employer, and the farmer opposes the business man. The big business concerns and the small business concerns compete with each other as well as among themselves. The railroads demand higher rates, but passengers and shippers demand lower rates. An electric power company asks for a greater return upon its investment, but the working people, storekeepers, manufacturers, and farmers join forces to obtain their supply of electricity at lower rates.

These cases of conflict are not all inclusive, but they are indicative of how our many groups and combinations of groups engage in the never ending struggle for a larger share of society's income. Mention should also be made of the efforts of the various branches of our government to obtain their share by means of taxation and also of the opposition of the public to the attempts of the government to increase the burden of taxation.

This chapter and subsequent chapters are devoted to a discussion of the means employed to obtain an income by some of the more important groups engaged in the struggle and also to the presentation of various ideas or theories that have been advanced relative to certain principles which are said to fix or determine the amounts that go to the contestants ultimately in the form of wages, rent, interest, and profits. Students would do well to give special attention to these matters.

Classes of Income—Wages are paid for personal services of all kinds; rent is received by those who lease property, such as grazing land, farms, buildings, automobiles, and dress suits; interest is paid to the lenders of funds (money or credit), regardless of whether those funds are used for production or for consumption purposes; and profits go to those who own business or productive enterprises. In the case of wages, payment is made for labor power (the human element), while in the case of rent, interest, and profits, payment is made for the use of property of one kind or another (the non-human element). The difference between these two groups of income should not, in and of itself, make it impossible for us to employ the same theory in ascertaining what determines or affects the amount of the return paid in each instance.

Marginal Productivity Theory—One of the most commonly accepted theories relating to the division of income is known as the *marginal productivity theory of distribution.* Briefly, it is to the effect that, in the long run, each factor of production tends to receive as its return an amount of society's income equal to what it adds to the product, the amount of the return being determined by the productivity of the marginal unit of the factor concerned. In other words, each factor of production tends to get what it produces. This statement of the marginal productivity theory means nothing to one who comes into contact with it for the first time; hence an explanation is advisable.

First, we must recall the law of diminishing productivity, because the marginal productivity theory of distribution is based upon it. In an earlier chapter we learned that, in the case of all productive enterprises, if the amount of land or labor power or capital goods is increased, sooner or later a point is reached where the returns per unit of land or labor power or capital goods begin to diminish. This is known as the point of diminishing productivity. We also learned that, theoretically, a business will not stop expanding at that point but will push on farther, adding more land or labor power or capital goods until a point is reached where the greatest net returns are obtained.

It is well for us to review the statement of the law of diminishing productivity in a rather detailed manner, in order to obtain a basis for understanding the marginal productivity theory of distribution. Let us say that Jones has an acre of land upon which he uses $100 worth of capital goods in the form of plows, seeds, fertilizer, and so forth and that he employs one laborer. Let us say that his product then equals an amount represented by the following figure which is in the shape of a rectangle:

He adds another laborer but does not increase the amount of land and capital goods. The total product received then equals the area represented by both of the following rectangles:

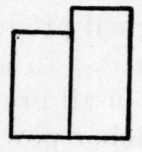

If he adds two more laborers, he finds that his product has further increased as follows:

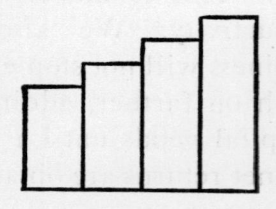

But when he adds another laborer, he discovers that the addition of the fifth laborer results in a reduced product and that this laborer adds less than did the fourth laborer. Hence, the point of diminishing productivity was reached with the addition of the fourth laborer, as is shown in the following diagram:

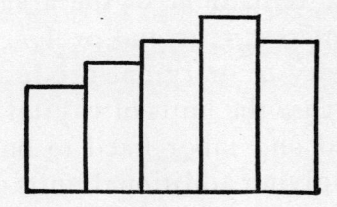

Jones, however, adds a sixth, a seventh, and an eighth laborer, with the result that the returns per laborer further decrease, as is shown in the diagram which follows:

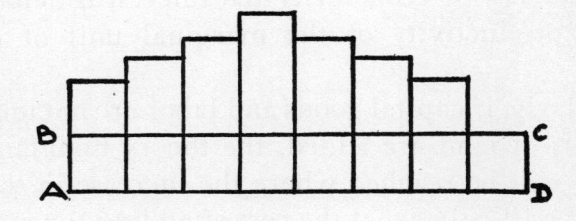

Jones finds that the addition of the eighth laborer increases the total product only by an amount equal to the wages which have to be paid to him. In other words, the product of the eighth laborer equals only his wages. Because of that fact, the eighth laborer in this case is known as the marginal laborer. Jones makes nothing out of hiring him, because the total product has been increased only by an amount equal to his wages. Inasmuch as all of the laborers in this particular instance receive the same wages, the advocates of the marginal productivity theory maintain that wages are determined by or are equal to the product of the marginal laborer. In the last diagram, the area ABCD represents the total wages, while the remainder of the area above the line BC represents interest, rent, and profits.

The same theory of marginal productivity is said to apply if we increase the units of capital goods but keep the units of land and labor fixed to one acre and one laborer. By applying additional units of capital goods a point will be reached where the addition of another unit will increase the total product only by an amount equal to the cost of using this extra unit—in other words, by an amount equal to the interest which must be paid for the marginal unit of capital goods. Therefore, it is said by economists that interest is determined by the productivity of the marginal unit of capital goods.

Similarly, if capital goods and labor are not increased but units of land are added, the theory maintains that a point will be reached where the increase in the total product will only equal the cost of adding the marginal unit of land, or its rent. Therefore, it is again said that rent is fixed by the productivity of the marginal unit of land.

Objections to the Marginal Productivity Theory— The marginal productivity theory is very generally employed by economists to explain the division of the income of society, yet it appears to have some very serious defects. In the first place, it is based on what is known as circular reasoning; in other words, it reasons in a circle and gets nowhere in explaining the factors that determine rent, wages, interest, and profits. It states, for example, that wages are determined by the product of the marginal laborer. But who is the marginal laborer? He is the man whose product equals his wage. But what fixes his wage? It is his product, the product of the marginal laborer. What makes him the marginal laborer? It is the fact that his product equals his wage. As can be seen, the theory reasons in a circle and does not really explain anything.

In the second place, the employer probably has never heard of the marginal laborer. If he were asked to explain what part the marginal laborer plays in the distribution of the income of society, he would not know. The cost accounting system of any business is not sufficiently accurate to disclose which laborer increases the product of the business by an amount equal to his wage.

In the third place, how can an employer fix the wage of his manager on the basis of marginal productivity when he hires only one manager? When an employer hires only two laborers, how can he know how many more will have to be hired before reaching the marginal laborer, whose product is the amount to be used in fixing the wages of the two men whom he actually hires?

We have seen that the dentist, the lawyer, or the physician is classed as a laborer because he renders personal services. How is a dentist to fix his fees (his wages) on the basis of the marginal productivity theory? Many other arguments could be and have been advanced to show that we must search elsewhere for theories or principles to explain what determines the wages, the salaries, and the fees that are paid to those who render personal services.

The marginal productivity theory, as we have observed, is also supposed to explain the amounts that are paid for rent, interest, and profits, but inasmuch as the defects of the theory have been made evident in the case of labor and wages, there is no need for us to devote further space to its consideration. The application of the theory in the case of rent, interest, and profits and the arguments against it would run along lines similar to those already stated.

There are, however, two general arguments against the theory that have not yet been mentioned. One is that there is no method by which the amount of the product contributed by the land itself or by the labor power itself or by the capital goods themselves can be ascertained. Fertile land that lies idle produces nothing but grass, weeds, and brush. If the owner simply places a plow, a tractor, seeds, and a harvester on that land but hires no laborers, the land and the capital goods will produce nothing. But let laborers be employed and products will begin to appear. Is one, therefore, justified in claiming that all of the product belongs to labor because without its aid no product could be obtained? If all of the product does not belong to labor, then how much of it belongs to labor, how much to land, and how much to capital goods? Is it possible to fix even roughly the amount of the product that is due to the use of each of these three factors of production? If such a distribution cannot be made, then is it not likewise impossible to allocate to each laborer, to each acre of land, or to each unit of capital goods the amount that each in turn produces as they are successively added until the so-called marginal unit in each case has been reached?

A final objection lies in the fact that the theory, as advanced by its advocates, applies only to that income which is received as a result of productive activities. We have already noted that many individuals receive an income although no production has taken place, as, for example, when I lend you money for consumption purposes (to buy a fur coat) or when I rent my house to you for $50 a month. A theory of distribution should cover all cases in which income is received, without any regard whatsoever to the source from which the income arises.

Economic theories are advanced for the purpose of explaining the facts of our present economic life. They must be tested and judged in the light of what we find about us. It is because the marginal productivity theory fails to stand up under such a test that we have to abandon it for a theory that is more practical and more in accord with the facts of the everyday world of business activity as we know and find them in our daily life.

Why Distributive Shares Are Paid—In explaining

the personal distribution of the income of society, we are concerned with three problems. First, we have to learn *why* rent, interest, wages, and profits must be paid under our capitalistic system of society. That question is very simply answered. We have to pay rent to landlords and to others because they lease or rent us property. We have to pay interest to those who lend us money or credit solely because they have something for the use of which we are willing to pay a price. We have to pay wages for personal services or for labor power because laborers will not work for us unless we pay them. They have to live, and they can live only by selling their labor power. Those who have funds will not invest them in a business unless they are given an opportunity of making a profit from the investment; they will not become the owners of a business enterprise unless they feel that they will be the recipients of an income from it, the income being paid to them on the basis of the extent of their ownership in the business enterprise.

How Distributive Shares Can Be Paid—Our second problem is concerned with *how* it is possible for us to pay rent, wages, interest, and profits. Rent can be paid for consumption goods, such as houses, automobiles, and dress suits, because we receive from other sources an income that permits us to spend money for these things. We receive no addition to our money income from the use of such consumption goods, but since they satisfy our wants directly, we are willing to pay for them. However, when we rent land or buildings from others and when we hire laborers and borrow money or credit and thus engage in a productive enterprise, we hope to be successful in our venture and to obtain an income sufficient to enable us to pay rent, wages, interest, and profits. Laborers cannot work efficiently without capital goods and land.

The three factors of production, land, labor power, and capital, all working together can produce considerably more than land and labor power could produce unaided by capital. Hence, the greater product that is obtainable under such circumstances makes it worth our while to use land, labor power, and capital goods, and this greater product makes it possible for us to pay rent, wages, and interest in connection with our productive activities. Anything remaining after those payments have been made constitutes profits, to which as a matter of course the owners of the business are entitled. Profits, therefore, can be paid if the enterprise is conducted with sufficient skill to take care of all the expenses or costs of production and leave a residue.

Influences Affecting Distributive Shares—Our third problem is concerned with a discussion of those factors or influences which determine, wholly or in part, *how much* we must pay in rent, wages, interest, and profits—in other words, a discussion of the means used by all income receivers to obtain what they consider to be their share in the income of society. We shall find that our analysis of the present situation forces us to accept a *bargaining theory of distribution,* in accordance with which the amounts of wages, rent, interest, and profits which are obtained by individuals are held to depend upon the bargaining power of those individuals.

CHAPTER XIV
Wages

THE division of the income of society is made between those who render personal services (labor power) and those who own property. There are no fixed rules in the game of scramble between these two groups, nor is there any way of deciding ethically or legally just how much each should receive as its share. It is a case of each getting all that it possibly can and using every socially justifiable and available legal means in doing so. The practices adopted by both groups have been modified with the passing of time and will continue to be modified in the future. Expediency and effectiveness are the two standards by which each group judges the means that are employed.

Classes of Laborers—Let us first consider the group that renders personal services and see of what members of society it consists and also what means these members employ in obtaining a share of society's income.

We broadly designate as laborers those who render personal services in the hope of an economic reward. This group includes those who work for wages, such as our skilled and unskilled laborers (whom we shall call wage earners), those who work for salaries, such as managers, foremen, clerks, teachers, business executives, and most of our governmental officials, and the professional class, which consists of doctors, lawyers, dentists, and others who work for fees.

When we use the term "wages" to designate the payments which are made to those who render personal services, we mean it to include salaries and fees as well as what we ordinarily call wages. Salaries, as such, are paid to those who are employed on a monthly or a yearly basis. They may work longer or shorter hours than the skilled and unskilled factory, mine, and building construction workers. Usually they are not members of unions. Their jobs are of a white-collared, soft-handed character. If they are temporarily incapacitated because of illness, their salaries, as a rule, are not affected. They work in a more congenial environment and have a higher social standing and more opportunity for promotion than does the wage earner.

Those who receive fees are usually self-employers, members of the professional class, although there are some governmental officials, such as justices of the peace and consular service employees, who, in some cases, receive fees. Professional workers may be associated with others as partners, but ordinarily they have their own offices and their own patients and clients.

The wage earner is an employee. He may be paid on the time basis of a certain amount per hour or day or week or on the piece basis of a certain amount per unit of product. If, for example, you receive five cents per hundred for listing items on depositors' statements, you are paid on a piece rate basis. If you receive $100 a month as a bank clerk, you are paid on a time rate basis. It is not unusual for wage earners who are employed on a time basis to be required to produce a certain amount of work each day in order to be retained on the payroll.

Wage earners usually prefer to be hired on the time basis, for when piece rates are paid, they fear the rate of pay will be so low that they will be compelled to work exceedingly fast in order to obtain a decent living wage.

Where it is at all feasible, employers usually prefer to pay on the piece rate basis, because they feel that, by so doing, they have greater assurance of getting what is commonly referred to as a "fair 'day's work" out of their employees. Some employers have installed various kinds of bonus or premium systems of wage payments, but these systems are too complicated to discuss in this elementary text. The principle involved is that of setting a minimum amount of output which the worker must produce in order to receive the customary wage; then if more is produced, he receives a bonus or premium on the excess amount.

Rates of Wages versus Wages Received—Many people base their estimate of the condition of the wage earner on what is known as the rate of wages. For example, the carpenter receives $12 a day, the bank cashier $3,000 a year. On the basis of 300 working days during the year, the carpenter apparently would receive an income of $3,600, which would be larger than the income of the cashier. But the carpenter's employment is intermittent; he may work but 200 days a year and thus receive only $2,400, or he may work even less than that number of days and receive a correspondingly smaller income. The same situation holds in the case of those who are paid in fees. A dentist, for example, may charge $15 an hour and still be unable to obtain enough patients to yield $200 a month.

The fallacy of judging the incomes of those who render personal services on the basis of the rate of the wages, salaries, or fees which they receive is evident. It is the yearly income that is important; yet, strangely enough, it is practically impossible to obtain statistics showing the annual incomes of our workers, especially incomes of the wage earners. This is one reason why we should hesitate to accept published statements concerning the yearly incomes of the members of the laboring class.

Money Wage versus Real Wage—In considering the return received by those who render personal services, we must revert to our earlier discussion of money income versus real income. The money wage is the amount of money that the laborer receives. His condition cannot be gauged solely from a study of his money wage. If you are receiving $100 a month and the cost of living doubles, the purchasing power of your salary (in other words, its value) has been cut in half. If your salary is now increased to $150 a month, it appears to be much larger than formerly, yet it will not buy as much as it did before the cost of living doubled. To keep pace with the increased cost of living, your wage would have to be raised to $200 a month, and even then you would have only the same purchasing power you had before prices rose. If you were to have a real advance over your previous salary, your income would have to be increased to more than $200 a month.

This, again, illustrates how necessary it is to consider what wages will purchase—in other words, what *real wages* are—before claiming that high money wages bring about better living on the part of those who render personal services. During the World War, there was considerable discussion in the newspapers and elsewhere relative to the high earnings of our wage earners. During that period prices more than doubled, but the rates of wages did not increase in the same proportion. The outstanding reason why the wage earning class was better off than before was that its members were more steadily employed and therefore were receiving larger annual incomes than formerly.

Wage Theories

Subsistence Theory—Various explanations have been offered regarding the factors or forces that determine or assist in determining the returns paid to those who render personal services. One of the oldest wage theories advanced by economists, one still believed in by many radical thinkers, is to the effect that wages tend to equal an amount of money that will barely enable the workers to keep "body and soul" together. This is known as the *subsistence wage theory*. As is true of theories in all other fields, the subsistence wage theory grew out of existing conditions. During the last quarter of the eighteenth century and the first quarter of the nineteenth, wages in England were extremely low. The workers were not permitted to organize unions and accordingly possessed but slight bargaining power in their efforts to obtain higher remuneration. The English law of the time required that if the worker could not maintain himself and family on his wage, he was entitled to receive public funds to make up the difference. This statute, as can be appreciated, was in itself a powerful influence in keeping wages at a very low level.

Iron Law of Wages—The subsistence theory was later modified into what was called the *iron law of wages*. This law asserted that wages would always remain at the subsistence level because of the competition of the workers for employment. It was based on the Malthusian theory of population.

Malthusian Theory of Population—Malthus was an English college professor who was opposed to certain radical proposals that were being advocated during the closing years of the eighteenth century. These proposals urged the establishment of an ideal or Utopian state of society involving the complete reorganization of conditions as they then existed so as to bring about a new era in which poverty, unemployment, wars, and similar objectionable features of life would be eliminated. Malthus was interested in combating these ideas, and in his efforts to show that such an ideal state of society could never be put into effect, he proposed his theory of population in 1798. He maintained that population was continually pressing upon food supply, that, in fact, population was tending to outstrip food supply and was held in check only by famine, disease, war, and moral restraint. The last-mentioned check to the growth of population signified that men refrained from marrying until they possessed an income sufficient to support a family upon a satisfactory basis. Malthus advanced the argument that if, in an ideal state of society, such as that advocated by the radicals of his time, there were no wars, famines, or unemployment, and if disease were curbed, population would expand at such a rapid rate as to make it impossible to provide humanity with a sufficient supply of food. This would be the case because there is a limit to the amount of foodstuffs that can be produced from land. With the increase of population unchecked, famine would result, with disease, war, and unemployment following in its wake. Thus, Malthus claimed that an ideal state of society was impossible of attainment.

The iron law of wages was based on the Malthusian theory in the following manner: It was claimed that if wages rose above the subsistence level, population would rapidly increase, because the workers would have no fear of lack of food. This increased population would lead to serious competition among the workers for jobs, forcing the wage down to the subsistence level. If, on the other hand, wages should fall below the subsistence level, population would decrease, because the workers, with such low incomes, would be unable to support their families. Death rates would increase; parents would have fewer children because of the fear of starvation; and the smaller population would result in a scarcity of laborers. With more jobs available than there were laborers, employers would have to bid higher for laborers, thus causing wages to rise to the subsistence level. Consequently, it was claimed, wages could not long vary from an amount required to provide a bare subsistence.

The iron law of wages has been used and still is used by groups of radicals to show that wages cannot be raised by means of trade union activity, legislation, or similar methods and that it is necessary, therefore, to overthrow our capitalistic state of society in order to improve the condition of the wage earning class.

Objections to the Malthusian Theory—The adherents of the Malthusian theory of population and of the iron law of wages could not foresee the surprising progress that would be made in subsequent years in improving agricultural and industrial processes. We are now able to produce so much food that we cannot market it. In fact, it has been estimated that food supply is increasing about twice as rapidly as population. The newer methods of agriculture have been able to increase the yield of the land, and the technique of the factory system has made possible the more advantageous use of the products of the soil by canning, preserving, and so forth. Wages also have risen as a result of certain factors later to be discussed. An increase in wages raises the plane of living of the people and tends to result in fewer children per family. If wages are so low as to jeopardize the prevailing plane of living, many men and women either will not marry or, if married, will not have children. Raising the plane of living tends to bring about increased prudence and more careful planning for the future.

From conditions as they exist today, it must not be deduced that Malthus was wrong in principle at the time he wrote, for he based his ideas upon the conditions in existence at that time. More efficient methods of production have thus far enabled the world to escape the consequences of overpopulation which Malthus predicted and have also made the iron law of wages untenable.

Wages Fund Theory—During the first quarter of the nineteenth century, the wage earners of England began to organize unions for the purpose of increasing wages, decreasing hours, and improving working conditions. Some time between 1820 and 1870, the subsistence theory of wages was displaced by the *wages fund theory,* which aimed to show that the wage earners could not increase their incomes as a result of trade union activities. It was declared that wages were paid out of capital before the employers had the opportunity of selling the products upon which the workers labored. In other words, the wages of labor were advanced by the employers before they had received any income from the products of their employees. It was claimed that wages depended upon the proportion existing between the number of wage earners and the amount of capital available in the industry. There was only a fixed amount of capital which could be used at any one time for the payment of wages. If the workers in one industry organized and secured an increase in their wages, there would be just that much less capital available for other workers, who would have to accept lower wages. The wage earning class, however, paid no attention to the arguments of those who upheld the wages fund theory but went on organizing their unions and making their demands for higher wages. In the long run they were successful, with the result that the wages fund theory was subsequently discarded.

Marginal Productivity Theory—During the middle of the nineteenth century, the socialists, led by Karl Marx and others, became very active in demanding a radical rearrangement of the economic organization of society. One of their demands was that inasmuch as labor created all exchange value it should get all that it produced. This argument struck at the very roots of the capitalistic system, and, to offset this claim, the marginal productivity theory was advanced. This theory endeavored to show, as pointed out in earlier pages, that labor and the other factors of production actually receive what each adds to the product of industry. There is no need to present the details of that theory again or the arguments that have been urged against it, for they have already been discussed at some length.

Standard of Living Theory—Another theory holds that the wage of the worker is determined by what is commonly called his *standard of living*. If the worker, feeling that he must have certain things to enable him to live as he desires, finds that his wages do not permit him to purchase these things, he will demand higher wages. Accordingly, employers cannot force wages down below the amount required by the workers to maintain their customary standard of living. It is claimed that the standard of living of Americans is very high and that consequently their wages are very high. On the other hand, the standard of living of the Chinese is very low, and consequently their wages are low. Is it not possible, however, to raise the rather embarrassing question of whether people live on a high level because their wages are high or whether they are paid high wages because they live on a high level?

The standard of living wage theory sounds well enough, but it is not applicable to conditions as they exist in the economic world. For example, if a bank fails and its president, accustomed to a salary of $50,000 a year, obtains employment as a bond salesman, he cannot command his previous salary. He cannot claim that his standard of living does not permit him to accept a salary of less than $50,000 a year. He will have to accept the salary ordinarily paid to bond salesmen unless perchance he is especially adept at selling bonds, in which case his salary will probably be a little higher than that customarily paid to similar employees. If a college lad becomes a ditch digger and goes to his boss with the plea that his standard of living requires a salary of about $2,000 a year, he will be unable to obtain that wage, owing to the fact that any number of workers can be hired at the customary lower wage.

Workers are paid the going wage for the job upon which they are engaged, and there are many factors involved in determining that going wage. These factors may be said to be embodied in the bargaining power of the employee, as contrasted with that of the employer. The plane of living or the customary level of living of the worker naturally has some influence on his bargaining power and makes its influence felt in the bargaining for wages.

Bargaining Theory of Wages—There are many other theories of wages, but we have space to consider only one more, which we shall call the *bargaining theory of wages*.

Wages are the prices paid for personal services—for the human element in production. They are fixed as the result of a bargaining process, in which those who have labor power to sell bargain with those who wish to purchase it. This bargaining process takes place between the wage earner and the salaried man, on the one hand, and the employer, on the other; between the professional man, on the one hand, and his clients, on the other. The process is not always as open as is the higgling that takes place between two horse traders, but it exists, nevertheless, and assumes various forms. The price paid for labor power is determined by the supply of it and the demand for it. Many economic factors have a direct bearing upon the demand for labor or labor power and the supply of it.

Demand for Labor—The demand for different kinds of labor power arises because there is a demand for products. Goods have to be produced and services have to be rendered to satisfy human wants. Labor power has to be employed in all productive activities.

The advent of the automobile, for example, created a demand for garage mechanics, for gasoline station attendants, for rubber workers, and so on. During the World War, the demand for a "bridge of ships across the Atlantic" created a demand for boiler makers, ship carpenters, and other ship workers. Moreover, every increase in consumption standards—in the general level of living of the people—results in an increase in the demand for laborers. Inasmuch as our workers constitute the majority of our population, they are entitled to receive wages sufficiently high to enable them to become effective consumers. If they cannot buy, there will be a decrease in the demand for the goods that have been produced.

Of late years a vigorous campaign for high wages has been carried on by many employers. They claim that with a high wage the worker can purchase more goods, that an increase in the amount of goods purchased leads to an increase in the production of goods, and that this in turn results in more profits for the business owner and more employment for laborers in general. A demand for goods, therefore, constitutes a demand for laborers. There are many influences that cause us to demand or to refrain from demanding goods. Advertising, the desire to imitate others, custom and tradition, the dictates of fashion, the general price level, and prosperity are only a few of the many factors that enter into the situation.

Another factor that affects the demand for laborers is the supply of natural resources and capital. The United States is bountifully supplied with both natural resources and capital and hence provides much more employment for its population than does Tibet, which is short of natural resources, or Russia, which up to the present has been short of capital.

The demand for labor power of particular kinds at a particular time is lessened by the introduction of machinery. A bookkeeping machine may throw some bank employees out of work. The linotype temporarily caused many printers to lose their jobs. During 1929 and 1930 much was said and written about "technological unemployment," which means the unemployment that is caused by the introduction of machinery or by the improvement of productive processes. However, many investigations have shown that although the introduction of machinery temporarily increases unemployment, ultimately it leads to the employment of a greater number of laborers. The use of the linotype, for example, so decreased the cost of printing that more printing was demanded and more workers were consequently employed. The working class has consistently opposed the introduction of machinery, yet machinery has made it possible for humanity to produce and to sell goods at low prices. Thus, the use of machinery has increased the demand for goods and has led to an increase in employment.

Supply of Labor—As has been noted in earlier pages, the supply of labor power of a nation is dependent both upon population and upon the productivity of the workers. Population is affected by a number of factors—the birth rate, the death rate, immigration, emigration, age, and sex. The number of workers available in any one community also depends to a certain extent upon the geographical mobility of labor. The productivity of the labor force is dependent upon the industrial technique, or the processes that are used, as well as upon the skill of the worker, his social status, and his consumption standard, or level of living. We consider our labor force in the United States as being much more productive than that of any other country, because our workers have a high standard of living, are generally fairly well educated, and enjoy many rights and privileges that foreign workers do not. The use of the latest kinds of machinery and of productive processes by big business also adds to the productivity of our laborers. In connection with this section of the chapter, it is advisable for the student to read again the material contained in Chapter VI relative to the influences affecting the supply of labor, or labor power.

Bargaining and the Rate of Wages—Those who have labor power to sell are forced to dispose of it to employers or to clients and patients. Let us first consider the case of the wage earner. What rate of wages can he obtain? Although he is desirous of being paid a high wage, what he actually receives will depend upon his bargaining power in dealing with his employer, either as an individual or as a member of a group of employees. If he has to face the vigorous competition of other workers, as is the case during a period of business depression, he may have to accept a low wage. If there is a scarcity of workers and opportunities for employment are plentiful, the wage earner has a much greater bargaining power and consequently should be able to exact a higher wage from his employer. If he has a rather high level of living, he will oppose any attempt on the part of the employer to pay him a wage that will force him to renounce that standard.

The lowest possible limit to wages is a bare physical subsistence, which, of course, varies with different individuals to a very considerable degree. The least that a man will work for is just enough to keep body and soul together.

It is extremely difficult, if not impossible, to estimate the upper limit to wages. Under our present capitalistic system, an employer hires laborers to work for him so that he can carry on a business enterprise which he hopes will yield him a profit. Wages are paid out of product. If the workers are very productive as a result of the use of machinery and the latest productive methods, the employer can pay higher wages than if the workers are less productive. In China, where most commodities are still made by hand, the employer does not receive sufficient income to pay high wages, because the workers do not produce enough to give him such an income. There is no means by which the product of a laborer or of a group of laborers can be definitely ascertained; hence, it is not possible to declare that the upper limit to wages is the amount that the laborers actually produce. If the laborers demand too high wages, it may mean that the employer will receive no profits. If still higher wages are demanded, rent or interest may have to be reduced or go unpaid. There have been many instances in which business enterprises have been forced into bankruptcy because of the continued demands of the workers for wages which the business could not afford to pay and continue in operation.

As a result of the persistent demand on the part of laborers for higher wages, employers are compelled to effect many economies in order that costs may be reduced. Only in this way can many of them keep from being forced into insolvency.

Basis of Bargaining—Generally, the individual worker is at a disadvantage in bargaining with the employer. It is more necessary that the worker work than that the employer hire him. Workers are usually in need, and they have a tendency to underbid each other when acting as individual bargainers. Consequently, the workers organize unions of their respective crafts or trades for the purpose of bargaining more effectively with their employers or with the employing group. In many cases, also, the employers of an industry form associations in order to bargain more effectively with the unions which represent their employees. Thus it is that individual bargaining by both employees and employers has largely been displaced by collective bargaining.

In some cases, the union rules and regulations relative to wage rates and other matters affect only one employer; in other cases, however, they affect all employers in one line of business in a state or district, or even in several states. The general result has been uniformity and standardization of wages and employment conditions to a considerable extent. In many industries the hours of work, the wage rates, and the conditions of employment are fully standardized, and no individual employer or employee is permitted to deviate from the standards. This standardization has tended to bring about the payment of a uniform rate of wages not only within one trade or craft but within many crafts. Thus we see that the policy of standardization in producing goods has had its effect in standardizing wages and working conditions to a considerable degree.

Customary and Legal Rates of Wages—In some of the unskilled trades, customary rates of wages frequently remain in effect over a long period of years. For example, before the World War unskilled day laborers received on an average $1.50 a day. These customary rates fluctuate but little, because of the lack of bargaining power on the part of the workers. In some cases wages are fixed by law, and to the uninitiated these cases may appear to be exceptions to the bargaining theory of wages. For example, the wages or salaries of practically all government officials are fixed by law, and the rates are such as to attract candidates for those offices. If politicians were unwilling to accept the salaries that are paid, we should have fewer candidates for office. Such a situation would give the remaining candidates a greater bargaining power, which might be strong enough to compel the lawmaking body to raise the salary scale. In some states the wages of women employed in certain industries are fixed by minimum wage boards. Arguments are presented before these boards by the representatives of both employers and employees, and the wage is set on the basis of the data presented by both sides. If the representatives of the women workers can present more convincing arguments than those of the employers—in other words if they have a greater bargaining power—it is possible for them to induce the board to give a higher rate of wages. The reverse is also true.

Salaries versus Wages—Salaries are less affected by changing economic conditions than are wages. While wages fluctuate to a considerable degree, salaries remain more or less fixed over a period of time. This is true largely because salaried employees are not organized for collective bargaining. They usually have to take what they can get, and what they can get depends for the most part upon their individual bargaining power. If a salaried man makes a request for a higher salary, he has no group of fellow workers to support him in his demand. The general level of money wages does not rise as rapidly as does the general level of retail prices, nor does it fall as rapidly. Salaries are even less responsive to changes in the price level. Although wages are frequently reduced in times of business depression, salaries are usually little affected.

Effect of Certain Conditions on Wages—What influence do the dangers of the job, its attractiveness, its regularity, the chances of success, and the requirements of training exert upon the wage rate? In many jobs that are attractive wages are high, while in others equally attractive wages are low. In comparison with the wage of a garbage collector, the salary of a bank president is high. The salaries of bank employees as a whole are low because the jobs are attractive and because there are many individuals who are eager for employment in banking institutions; moreover, bank employees are not organized to bargain collectively with their employers. Some dangerous trades pay high wages, while others pay low wages. Many positions that are "blind alley" jobs with no opportunities for advancement pay low wages, while others that open wide the door to promotion also pay low wages. In a few trades, the worker has to serve an apprenticeship term for the purpose of obtaining the required training and experience. Strangely enough, many crafts of this character pay a lower wage than do those in which no apprenticeship term is required.

Conditions such as those mentioned affect the wage rates of the workers only as they influence in one way or another the bargaining power of the laboring group. Supply and demand and the various factors that go to make up supply and demand still remain the most potent influences in determining wage rates.

Bargaining Power and Fees—In explaining what determines the fees of the professional man, we must again have recourse to the bargaining theory of wages. If a dentist, a lawyer, or a physician has built up an excellent reputation, he is able to charge higher fees for his services than if he has not built up such a reputation. The amount of money that he has spent on his education and training, the funds that are required to maintain his consumption standards, and the expense of running his office have nothing whatsoever to do with his ability to charge high fees. If he charges high fees, he does so because he has sufficient bargaining power through the reputation he has built up.

It is customary in some professions, especially the medical, for their members to organize local associations and to agree to charge certain uniform minimum rates for various services. If this were not the case, competition might result in the setting of lower fees by many physicians in the district to the detriment of the profession.

High Wages in the United States—Both money wages and real wages are much higher in the United States than in any other country. If such were not the case, we should not have an immigration problem, for foreigners would then prefer to remain at home. There are three reasons for our high wage level. First, the American workingman is exceedingly productive. This is due, as we have seen, to his racial characteristics, to his training, to his education, to the freedom and privileges which he enjoys, and to the tools, machinery, and business methods with which he works. Second, the United States has unsurpassed natural resources to serve as a basis for its productive activity. Third, business organization in our country has achieved unparalleled success. In no other country have business enterprises been so ready to discard the old and adopt the new methods of production. Nowhere else has the amount of capital expended in proportion to the number of laborers employed been so high as here. The widespread use of machinery has been one of the important factors in bringing about low unit cost of production. Business has been compelled to use machinery because of our high wage level, and the use of machinery in its turn has made a high wage level possible. Many employers appreciate the fact that with higher wages they are able to obtain a larger and a better product. Of course, it is not possible to state what is the maximum limit to the wages of the American workers, but so long as high wages result in low unit cost of production, just so long will goods be marketed at a premium and business remain profitable.

CHAPTER XV

Labor Problems

THOSE who depend upon the sale of their labor power for an income pursue various tactics in order to obtain a larger return. The group that is of the greatest interest to us in this connection is the wage earning class, as distinguished from the salaried and fee receiving classes. Whenever possible, the wage earners form organizations so as to bargain with their employers more effectively by means of collective action. These organizations are known as unions. In the beginning of the union movement in the United States, only the skilled wage earners were unionized, but about the year 1890 such unskilled laborers as dock workers, waiters, teamsters, and building construction workers began to form unions. At present, however, only about 20% of the wage earners of our country are members of unions. This low percentage is due to several reasons. First, unions can be readily organized only where wage earners are hired in large numbers. Second, it has always been difficult to induce women workers to unionize, largely for the reason that many of them work only for so-called "pin money," to keep busy at something outside the home, or to support themselves until they marry. Child workers are also unorganized. Third, in a number of communities, employers are so thoroughly organized into open shop associations that they are able to prevent the workers from forming unions.

Justification of Unions—The organization of labor was made necessary and inevitable by the conditions that arose out of the development of modern industry. In the days of handicraft production, the journeymen worked with the master and frequently lived in his home. The relationship between them was to a large extent personal in character. With the advent of the factory system, however, large numbers of employees were hired. Usually the employer was a corporation, and the relationship between employer and employee therefore became impersonal in character. One worker alone could not bargain effectively for higher wages or for improved working conditions. Collective effort was necessary.

Competition among the individual workers for employment was keen, and this competition interfered with their bargaining power. Among business enterprises, however, competition was frequently replaced by cooperation and combination. Even farmers organized cooperative associations. Following their example, laborers attempted to meet the evils of competition by effecting their own combinations or associations, and thus the union came into existence. The union aims to strengthen the bargaining power of its members by combined, united action in dealing with the employing class and thus to enable its members to obtain higher wages, shorter hours, and better working conditions. Much has been accomplished by this means.

Types of Unions—There are four general types of

unions. A *labor union* (using that term in its technical sense) is a combination of workers, regardless of the trade or industry in which they are employed. To illustrate, let us say that the blacksmiths, the machinists, the carpenters, the printers, and the stenographers in your town desire to form a union. Such an organization would contain workers employed in various industries and in various trades and would be designated as a labor union. This type of organization formed the basis on which the Knights of Labor, a national federation of unions, was organized in 1869; it has long since passed from the field of unionism.

A *trade union* is an association of workers who follow the same trade or craft but are employed in different industries. For example, in the case of a carpenters' union, there are only carpenters as members, but they may work on office buildings, on homes, in factories, in mines, and in shipyards. The trade union forms the basis of the American Federation of Labor, which was organized in 1881 as a national federation representing the organized workers of the United States and Canada. This proved to be a more effective type of organization than the Knights of Labor and in the course of time displaced it.

An *industrial union* is a combination of all the workers in one industry, regardless of the trades or crafts in which they are employed. Thus, the Amalgamated Clothing Workers of America, an industrial union, includes within its ranks all of those who are employed in the men's clothing industry, regardless of whether they are cutters, pants or coat workers, or buttonhole machine operators. The industrial union idea is championed by the Industrial Workers of the World, which was organized in 1905, but which has played an insignificant part in the affairs of organized labor since that time.

A *company union* is an organization of all the workers in the employ of one company or firm. For example, all of the employees of the International Harvester Company, regardless of what work they perform, have joined the company union of that concern. A company union is not affiliated with any other organization of workers. It is established by the employer primarily for the purpose of preventing any other form of labor organization from obtaining a following among his employees. It is more subservient to the employer than are other kinds of unions and is not so likely to cause him difficulty. There were 432 company unions in existence in 1926, comprising a total of 1,369,078 workers.

Affiliations of Organized Labor—The American Federation of Labor is a federation of most of the representative bodies of organized workers in the United States and Canada. For the year ending August 31, 1930, its affiliated organizations had an average paid-up or reported membership of 2,961,096. A workingman does not belong to the American Federation of Labor directly; he belongs to a local union which is affiliated with one of the national or international bodies of the American Federation of Labor or to a local or federal union which has no national or international organization but is affiliated directly with the American Federation of Labor.

Associations of union workers in the United States are grouped in such a way as to provide greater bargaining power and greater influence than any one association would have by itself. First of all, a union member belongs to his local union, which in its turn is affiliated with its national or international organization, except in cases in which it is affiliated directly with the American Federation of Labor. The local union is usually a member of a city federation of labor, or labor council. It may also belong to what is called a local trades council.

For example, the building trades council of a city is made up of all the local unions that are engaged in building construction work. In addition to building trades councils, there are printing trades councils, metal trades councils, and so on. The local union also commonly belongs to a state federation of labor, an organization which includes all local unions, trades councils, and city federations of labor within the state. All of these various kinds of councils that have been mentioned are also affiliated with the American Federation of Labor.

The American Federation of Labor does not control the affairs of the affiliated union organizations; it leaves practically all matters in the hands of the affiliates. It aims to promote better labor conditions, to secure the enactment of labor legislation, to influence voters, and to assist in the organization of the workers. It never declares or conducts strikes, nor does it make demands upon the employer, although it commonly gives assistance to those of its associated national or international unions that do so.

Demands of Organized Labor

Collective Bargaining—First of all, organized labor demands the right to engage in collective bargaining. It insists that if employers have the right to combine or to belong to their various associations for the purpose of eliminating competition, raising prices, restricting output, or combating the efforts of their workers, their employees are equally entitled to enjoy that right and privilege. When collective bargaining is engaged in between an association of employers and a union or a group of unions, the result takes the form of a trade agreement. Such an agreement may be drawn to last for a period of from one to five years, and it usually covers the most important matters relating to employment, such as wages, hours, apprenticeship regulations, and working conditions.

Wages—The second demand of organized labor is for higher wages. The worker is usually more interested in income than he is in hours of labor or conditions of employment. If given the opportunity, he will usually work for long hours and under unsatisfactory conditions in order to obtain a larger income. Investigation has shown that, as a rule, wages are higher in trades in which the workers are organized than in those in which they are not organized.

Hours—The third demand of organized labor is for shorter hours of employment. During the early days of the factory system, the hours of work were extremely long, in many cases amounting to fourteen or fifteen per day. Later, as a consequence of the demands of the unions, the hours were reduced to twelve and then to ten hours per day. Before the World War, the average working day in the United States was ten hours, although on the Pacific Coast, for many years, it had been only eight hours. The conditions that arose as a result of the World War brought about the general adoption of the eight-hour day. It was discovered that the pace set by machinery and the conditions under which the wage earners worked were such as to cause extreme fatigue and reduced output. An attempt was made in the early days of the war, both here and abroad, to increase production by lengthening the number of hours of labor. The results did not fulfil expectations. Hence, the eight-hour day became widely adopted and is now the generally accepted rule among the factory, the mine, and the store workers employed in our country.

In many industries, it has been found that the workers can produce as much in eight hours as in nine or ten. In other cases in which the eight-hour day has displaced the longer working period, production has not been maintained at the earlier rate. In still others, however, it has actually been increased. Today, in a number of plants, the workers are hired for eight hours but are given a fifteen minute rest period in the morning and another fifteen-minute rest period in the afternoon. The result has been an increased output over that of the full eight-hour day.

In the past, successful efforts have been made by trade unionists and others to reduce the length of the working day by the enactment of legal measures. Various state legislatures have passed laws requiring the eight-hour day in dangerous and unhealthful occupations, the eight-hour day for women workers in other than household, agricultural, and horticultural occupations, the eight-hour day for child workers, the ten-hour day for all factory workers (in Oregon and Mississippi only), and the shorter working day for the employees of transportation carriers. Such laws have been upheld by the courts. Congress has enacted legislation reducing the hours of the employees of interstate railroads. The right of state legislatures and of Congress to fix the hours of work for government employees has never been questioned.

The demands of organized labor have also made possible the five and one-half day week, with Saturday afternoon off. During recent years a campaign has been carried on for a five-day week and has been successful in many places. In 1929, approximately 500,000 workers in the United States were employed on a five-day week basis; about one-half of that number were engaged in the building trades. In most cases, wages have not been proportionately reduced. Some employers report the same amount of output, while others report that production has decreased. Some of the factors contributing to the inauguration of the five-day week have been the relatively high overhead cost of running a plant for only half a day on Saturday and the lowered efficiency of the employees during Saturday morning. Many employers have felt that it did not pay them to open up for only a half-day's work on Saturday and hence have not strenuously opposed the request of the workers for the five-day week, although some employers have objected or have refused to maintain the former weekly wage scale.

The Closed Union Shop—The demand of organized labor which has called forth the most bitter opposition from the employing class, as well as from the general public, is the demand for the closed union shop. Controversies over wages and hours can be compromised, but there is no compromise possible over the closed union shop issue. There is no half-way house. The closed union shop is a shop that is closed to wage earners who are not union members or who are unwilling to become union members. The non-union worker is frequently given employment in a closed union shop, but with the understanding that he is to apply for admission into the union within a short time after employment, usually within a month. If he does not do so, he must be discharged by the employer. At times, the closed union shop problem is aggravated by the existence of a closed union. A closed union is a labor organization which is restricted as to membership. Among the methods employed by this type of organization to limit its membership are the following: complete refusal to admit additional members, the imposition of extremely high initiation fees, and the requirement that an examination or test of ability be passed which is beyond the powers of even a first class journeyman.

The closed union shop is advocated by the union for various reasons. It is claimed that unless only union members are employed, the non-union men will be given the better jobs and in various other ways will be shown preference by the employer, for the purpose of bringing about the disruption of the union. The union claims that it can enforce its rules and regulations properly only when the closed union shop exists. Non-union men share in the higher wages and in the better working conditions for which the union men have fought and sacrificed, and accordingly, it is claimed, they should be compelled, if necessary, by means of the closed shop to join the union and thus to share in the expense and the sacrifice required to improve the working conditions of their class.

The opponents of the closed union shop, on the other hand, maintain that it interferes with a man's right to seek and to obtain employment. Why should a worker be compelled to carry a union card in order to get a job, any more than he should be required to carry a card of membership in the Masons or the Knights of Columbus? Many men do not wish to belong to a union. Therefore, why should they be forced to do so? The closed shop gives the union extensive control over the business of the employer, enabling it to tell him whom he shall hire or discharge, whether or not he shall raise or lower wages or pay more than the union scale to some of his more capable employees, whether or not he shall be permitted to introduce new methods of production or to install new machinery or to do various other things that he may consider to be necessary or advisable, and so on.

There is nothing illegal about the closed union shop, as such. If an employer wants to operate under the conditions that it imposes, legally he may do so. But the matter of whether or not workers legally may strike for the closed union shop, frequently involving the discharge of non-union workmen, is one on which the courts are divided. The courts of some states hold as being legal a strike which is designed to enforce the closed union shop. However, the courts of other states take the contrary view. The problem seems to depend to a considerable extent upon whether or not the act of the union would prevent a man from earning a living.

Restriction of Output—Organized labor has been guilty of restricting output, of "soldiering on the job," but so have all of us. Few of us accomplish all that we could if we were willing and eager to put forth our greatest effort. Business combinations, monopolies, and associations of employers, all are accustomed to restrict output to their own advantage. During the agricultural depression extending from 1920 to 1930, even government officials urged farmers to plant less grain and cotton and thus to restrict their output in order to raise the prices of their crops. Thus, restriction of output is a common practice in every field of our economic activity.

Unions restrict output in various ways. They oppose the introduction of machinery. They may require that a man operate only one machine, even though he could easily tend two or more. They limit the size of the paint brush, the number of bricks that may be laid in a day, the amount of roofing that may be placed in eight hours, the number of pieces of work that may be put out in a day, and so forth. By no means is it true, however, that all unions restrict output. The Amalgamated Clothing Workers Union of America is an outstanding example of an organization that is eager to do all within its power to increase the output of its members, and it has adopted some interesting practices in that regard.

Restriction of output is practised by the workers for three reasons: (1) to protect their health, (2) to wreak revenge upon the employer, and (3) to make the work last longer. It sometimes has happened that the employer has so speeded up the work that the employees have been forced to adopt a restrictive policy in order to protect their health and safety. Occasionally, an employer earns the ill will of his employees, and for the purpose of "getting even" with him, they "lie down on the job," thus increasing his costs of operation; at times they even go so far as to wreck his business. However, the justification of restriction of output usually takes the form of the "lump of work" argument. According to those who advance that argument, there is only so much work to be done, and if the output of the individual worker is restricted or curtailed, the job will be made to last longer, or more men will be given employment. The fallacy of this argument lies in the fact that the amount of work to be done is never fixed, except for a relatively short period of time. If costs of production are too greatly increased by restriction of output without an accompanying reduction of wages, the employer may be unable to obtain a price for his goods that will enable him to remain in business; thus restriction may bring about the failure of his enterprise and result in unemployment for his men.

Methods of Enforcing Demands

Strikes—The means that are employed by organized labor to enforce its demands are adapted to serve the particular object or end in view. Ordinarily, a strike is declared. A strike is a general quitting of work by employees, accompanied by an attempt on their part to prevent others from taking their jobs. If the workers merely quit and accept employment elsewhere, no strike has been called. The courts have upheld as being legal strikes that are declared for higher wages, shorter hours, or better working conditions, where the intent of the strikers is primarily to better their own condition. Strikes declared in a demand for the closed union shop, or out of sympathy for other workers who have been discharged, or in opposition to the use of non-union materials have been held by some courts to be legal and by others to be illegal.

Boycott—A boycott exists when the strikers refuse to trade with an employer or when they induce others not to trade with him. The courts have held that strikers legally may refuse to patronize their former employer, but similar action by others directed against the same employer or action directed against the transportation of, or work upon, material subject to the boycott is open to question.

Picketing—To enforce a strike or a boycott, strikers frequently have recourse to picketing. A picket is any one who is stationed in the vicinity of the entrance to an industrial plant where a strike or a boycott is in progress, for the purpose of preventing others from taking the places of the strikers or from patronizing the concern that is being boycotted. Some courts hold that all picketing is illegal, as necessarily involving intimidation, and that if a particular act is not intimidating, it does not come within the definition of picketing. The great majority of court decisions, however, hold that picketing of itself is not illegal.

Union Label—Organized labor also makes use of the union label to further its ends. Many unions have a label which they affix to their products in order to inform the customer that the products have been made under union labor conditions. The public is urged to purchase union label goods, in order that employers may be encouraged to give employment to union members.

Employers' Associations

Kinds of Employers' Associations—Employers also

have organized associations for the purpose of protecting their economic interests, not only against the unions but also against the public, the fundamental reason being their desire to retain or to increase their share of society's income. The objects of such associations naturally are economic in character.

In practically every large city, there is a local chamber of commerce, which is interested in developing home industries or in encouraging the establishment of additional business enterprises. Frequently, such organizations are anti-union in character. Sometimes there is a local association of merchants and manufacturers composed of all classes of employers who are active in opposing the demands of the organized working class; there are also local metal trades associations, shipowners' associations, and similar groups founded for the same purpose. Many lines of industry are nationally organized, such as, for example, the Stove Founders National Defense Association, the Steel Erectors Association, and the National Metal Trades Association. There is also the National Manufacturers Association, a body which brings together the employers of the country for the purpose of protection.

Yellow Dog Contracts—Some employers' organizations are interested primarily in the development of business relations and devote only a small portion of their time and money to labor matters. Others, however, are decidedly aggressive and antagonistic in their attitude toward the union movement. Associations of the aggressive type make use of all available means to maintain the open, or non-union, shop, a system which, since the World War, has been known as the "American Plan." An interesting development in connection with the opposition of employers to organized labor has been the adoption of the so-called "yellow dog contract." Upon accepting a job with a concern which uses it, the worker must sign a contract stating that he is not a member of a union and that he agrees not to become a member of a union as long as he remains in the employ of the concern. The courts will uphold the right of workmen to join a union in the absence of a contract to the contrary, but they are divided in their judgment as to the legality of a yellow dog contract.

Blacklist and Lockout—Employers at times have recourse to the blacklist and to the lockout. When an employer uses the lockout, he "goes on a strike" and closes the doors of his plant to his employees—he locks them out. This practice, however, is seldom resorted to by the employing class. When the blacklist is used, employers place the names of objectionable employees on a list, and this list is passed from one employer to another, making it difficult or impossible for the blacklisted person to obtain employment. The blacklist is looked upon with disfavor by the courts, but it is practically secure against judicial interference.

Proposals for Remedying Difficulties

Industrial Peace—The constant struggle of the

organized and unorganized workers against the employing class for more of the income of society and for better working conditions necessarily brings about a state of industrial unrest. Sometimes the situation becomes so serious that an industry or many industries are prostrated. Various proposals have been made from time to time in the hope that industrial peace might be secured and the interests of the employers and the employees and the public thereby conserved.

Conciliation—A method rather commonly used to prevent or to end a dispute is conciliation. By this means, the employer and the employee, usually through their representatives, come together voluntarily or are brought together by a local group of bankers, merchants, or other leading citizens to settle their difficulties without submitting the issues to an outside party for decision.

Arbitration—Another method frequently used to end a labor dispute is to submit the controversy to an arbitrator or to a board of arbitration. The decision is thus rendered by a third party. Frequently, the labor interests choose one representative, the employer chooses a second, and these two representatives choose a third person, an outsider. In this case, the decision, of course, is made by the third person, for on all issues submitted to the arbitration board the employer's representative naturally votes for the employer's side of the case, while the employees' representative votes for the demands of the employees. In some cases, the entire arbitration board is selected from a group of outsiders who have no economic interest in the dispute between the employer and his employees.

Arbitration may be either voluntary or compulsory. In the United States, with the exception of Kansas, there has been no compulsory arbitration. In 1920 Kansas passed a compulsory arbitration measure, prohibiting strikes in certain industries and requiring that all labor disputes therein be settled by a legally constituted arbitration court. In 1923, this measure was declared by the United States Supreme Court to be unconstitutional. Many of the Australian states and New Zealand have compulsory arbitration laws, which have proved fairly successful in preventing strikes and lockouts. In the United States, we have had frequent recourse to voluntary arbitration, and for the most part it has worked successfully. In all such cases, the parties to the arbitration proceedings have agreed to abide by the terms of the award handed down by the arbitration board selected in the manner we have outlined. The awards are not always lived up to, however, both employers and employees having at times been guilty of breach of faith in that regard.

Compulsory Investigations—For some years Canada has used a rather unique measure in the effort to prevent losses arising from industrial conflicts. This measure, which embodies the principle of compulsory investigation by a government board, was adopted in 1907. In a certain class of industries affected with a public interest—namely, public utilities and mines—it is now unlawful to change the terms of employment, to strike, or to declare a lockout without thirty days' notice, and the law further requires that if, within that time, an appeal is taken to the minister of labor, the terms of employment shall remain unchanged pending an investigation. After the investigation a change of terms, a strike, or a lockout is perfectly lawful. In 1925 the law was amended so as to limit the application of the act to interprovincial commerce. Reliance is placed upon the powerful influence of public opinion in bringing success to the side that deserves support. In 1915 Colorado passed a law similar in some respects to that of Canada.

Railroad Labor Board—The Transportation Act passed by Congress in 1920 provided for the creation of a railway labor board, clothed with power to arbitrate in a voluntary manner all labor disputes concerning an interstate railroad. The plan did not succeed, and in 1926 Congress passed the Railroad Labor Act. This act provides for a conference between the representatives of the railroads and the railroad unions as the first step in settling disputes. It also authorizes an appeal to be taken from the decisions of this conference to a board of mediation. Finally, the President of the United States may appoint an emergency arbitration board if he believes that immediate action is necessary in order to prevent the development of a serious situation on our interstate carriers.

Profit Sharing—Some ardent reformers have suggested profit sharing as a means of bringing about industrial peace. Under a scheme of profit sharing, the workers are paid the customary wages and also share in the profits of the enterprise. It is believed by some that this method encourages loyalty among the employees and creates goodwill between them and their employer, because of their interest in seeing that nothing is done to diminish the profits of the business.

Profit sharing, however, has proved to be a failure as a panacea for industrial unrest. Among the reasons for this failure the following may be listed: Employees feel that the profits of the company are not disclosed. Profit sharing payments are usually so small as to be disappointing. Such payments are gifts which can be granted or not, as the employer sees fit, and in amounts determined solely by him. Employees would much rather receive higher wages than wait until the end of the year for an unknown amount of the company's profits.

Employment Management—As a result of conditions growing out of our participation in the World War, many of the country's leading employers were induced to believe that a more efficient and more satisfactory method of handling their labor problems was possible. Out of that situation and belief there developed a much wider use of what is known as employment management, or personnel work. Employment management is based on the idea that labor is the most difficult factor of production to handle. It can make or break an enterprise. To handle labor problems intelligently requires skill and ability and the services of those who are trained for the task. Industry employs high priced men as production engineers, advertising experts, and purchasing agents, all skilled in their fields. Why should not an equally high priced, skilled person be employed to care for the labor needs of a business enterprise?

Many large organizations now have as a member of their executive staff an employment manager, who devotes all his time and thought to such problems. His rank is sometimes that of a vice president. It is necessary that he be a person of high character, who is able to command the confidence of both executives and employees. He must be familiar with all matters affecting the conditions of labor in the plant. He should possess a knowledge of accounting and of law, especially of labor law. His task is that of maintaining industrial peace for his company. He and his assistants frequently have the responsibility of hiring all workers other than the executives and of placing men on those jobs where they can do their best work. He and his staff must listen to all complaints regarding labor conditions, make adjustments, remove irritating causes of discontent, care for wage claims, and attempt to settle the numerous little difficulties that continually arise among the employees of any large concern. When an employment management office is properly organized and operated, the employees may be sure of reasonable treatment, and they will have cause for less dissatisfaction than under any other plan attempted so far.

The interest of the public in an effective and equitable

system of supervision of personnel is threefold. In the first place, a democracy is predicated upon the ability of the voters to secure information and to make proper decisions regarding those questions which they may be called upon to decide from time to time. According to the census of 1920, about 17,500,000 of our citizens are organizable workingmen. If this large group finds itself forced to accept a wage which does not provide the proper facilities for both mental and physical development—in other words, if the income which the members of the group secure is not adequate to provide a proper standard of living—not only the workers but also society in general must suffer. If the surroundings and conditions under which the workers live are such as to create in their minds a feeling of distrust and dissatisfaction, their mental state will be reflected not only in their work but in the votes which they cast. Therefore, if employment management can help to increase output and wages and, at the same time, can aid in bringing about a proper understanding between workers and executives in large corporations engaged in production, the interests of the public are advanced.

In the second place, for reasons already discussed, a proper system of personnel administration means, in almost every instance, an increase in the productive capacity of the plant. Multiplied by thousands of plants, the result is an increase in the total amount of economic goods available for distribution to the public. If overproduction on a large scale ever becomes general, society as a whole may benefit, for the necessary maximum production may then be attained by fewer hours of labor, and more time will be left for culture, education, and self-improvement on the part of the workers.

In the third place, in so far as employment management tends to bring about better relations between men and management, society profits by the reduction of industrial strife. While it must be recognized that the strike is the most effective weapon with which the laborer can support his demands, the fact remains that it is a two-edged weapon and has more than once cut the hands of those who have used it. It appears probable that in the future labor will have recourse to the strike less and less often and then only after discussion and reason have failed in an attempt to harmonize the difficulties arising between employers and employees. This tendency has been clearly apparent in many instances in which modern methods of dealing with labor have been adopted. In one instance a committee of workmen, after consultation and thorough discussion with the management regarding the profits of the organization, the stock of goods on hand, and the state of the market, returned to their fellow workmen and made clear their own opposition to a demand for an increase in wages—the very demand which they had been selected to present. When men and management can meet on common terms, with confidence in each other and with assurance of fairness and honesty growing out of past relations, strikes will be called only as a last resort.

Legislation

Labor Legislation—A vast amount of legislation has

been enacted for the purpose of improving the conditions under which men, women, and children labor. Such legislation has been brought about by the efforts of organized labor and of individuals who have been interested in the welfare of the working class and of society in general. The law in most states now forbids the employment of women at night, as well as in certain dangerous and unsanitary occupations during either day or night, and provides for their employment under conditions which will protect their health and morals. Frequently, children under certain ages are prohibited from working at night, from working in certain objectionable occupations, and from working more than a fixed number of hours per day.

There is no sane argument against the enactment of legislation for the purpose of protecting women and children workers. Any nation that attempts to increase its wealth and raise its economic status at the expense of the future of the race is not only inhuman but also blind to its own best interests.

Factory Acts—Factory acts contemplate the regulation of the physical conditions and surroundings of factories to the end that accidents and occupational diseases may be minimized. Factories should have proper fire escapes, and employees should be protected from dangerous machinery, dust, and unhealthy fumes. A majority of the states have passed laws regulating factory conditions. In many instances, however, the proper state inspection has been lacking. After all, such legislation is necessary only for those producers who disregard the fundamental conditions of good business standards.

A happy, contented labor force is the first need for high productivity. Modern factories have introduced lunch and rest rooms, athletic fields, and many improvements in environment. As a rule, laws are required only to protect laborers against the lack of vision of the unprogressive employer.

Minimum Wage Laws—In some lines of industry, where little skill is required and where the competition of employees seeking work is very bitter, wages quite commonly fall below the margin of decency. In the past, such a condition prevailed in many of the sweat shops of our larger cities and also in some of our factories and stores. Australia was the first country in the world to adopt minimum wage legislation. Following Australia's example, fifteen states of the United States and the District of Columbia adopted similar legislation, but their laws were confined to the fixation of minimum wages for women only, and then only in certain lines of employment which were subject to low wage conditions. Such legislation was deemed necessary on the grounds of social, moral and human consequences. In 1923, the United States Supreme Court declared the minimum wage law of the District of Columbia to be unconstitutional; in 1925 it extended that decision to cover the law of Arizona and, by implication, the laws of most of the other states. Some of the measures in other states, however, are still being enforced, because of the support voluntarily given by employers who feel that they, as well as their employees, have been benefited by such legislation.

Workmen's Compensation—The toll of human life taken and the suffering caused by industrial accidents are seldom sensed by those who are out of touch with the harsh facts of the industrial world. Every year from 25,000 to 30,000 workers are killed by accidents arising out of their employment, and from 2,000,000 to 3,000,000 are injured.

Under the provisions of the old common law, an employer was compelled to use only reasonable care in protecting his employees from disability or death arising out of industrial accidents or industrial disease in the regular performance of their duties. Naturally, it was not an easy task to define just what constituted reasonable protection. The injured employee, or his dependents if he were killed, had to sue the employer in order to obtain damages. In a suit for damages, it had to be shown that the employee had not by his own acts contributed to his injury, that the accident was not the fault of a fellow employee, and that the accident had not arisen out of those risks of the job which the worker had assumed. In short, it had to be shown that the accident had occurred as a consequence of more than ordinary negligence or carelessness on the part of the employer in providing a reasonably safe place in which to work. The damage suit of the employee might drag through the courts for years, attended by frequent appeals and great expense. If the worker won his suit for damages, a considerable proportion of the amount awarded, not infrequently ranging from 25% to 50%, went to his attorney as a fee. Both the employer and the employee, not to mention the public, suffered as a consequence of the abuses that arose out of this state of affairs, which was made possible and inevitable by the employers' liability laws of the time.

Gradually it became evident that the cost of the injury, illness, or death of workers arising out of their employment should be borne by the industry itself. In the course of time, therefore, what are known as workmen's compensation laws were passed by all but four states, and such laws have now been almost universally adopted by foreign countries. These laws make it unnecessary for a worker or his dependents to sue the employer in order to obtain damages for injuries, illness, or death "arising out of" and "during the course of" employment. They require that certain payments be made to the worker who is disabled by injury, or to his dependents if the worker is killed; such injury or death, however, must arise out of and during the course of the worker's employment. Most American workmen's compensation laws do not cover occupational diseases. Compensation for such diseases is provided for fully by only ten states and to a limited extent by six other states. Quite generally, workmen's compensation acts do not apply to those who are employed in agricultural, horticultural, or household occupations or to what are called casual laborers.

The rate of compensation which a worker receives while he is incapacitated varies with the different state laws, ranging from 50% to 66⅔% of the average weekly pay of the worker (within certain fixed minimum and maximum limits). Some states set an additional limit on the total amount of compensation payable. If the worker is killed, a prescribed percentage of his wages is paid to his dependents, again within certain fixed minimum and maximum limits. The employer usually protects himself by carrying insurance against labor risks, just as he does for fire, burglary, and similar emergencies. Such insurance is generally carried with an ordinary insurance company or with a state compensation insurance fund, although in some cases the employer may be allowed to carry the insurance himself by setting aside a reserve fund for that purpose, under the supervision of the government board that has the responsibility of enforcing the workmen's compensation act. Thus, the burden of compensation for injury, illness, and death from industrial causes rests with the employer, who, if he can do so, shifts the cost to the consumer by charging higher prices for his goods or services.

Workmen's compensation laws have greatly reduced industrial accidents as a cause of poverty among those seeking charity. By requiring payments for industrial injury, illness, and death, this legislation has stimulated the employer to take extensive precautions for the purpose of protecting the safety and the health of his workers.

CHAPTER XVI

Rent

WE have seen that those who sell personal services receive wages, salaries, or fees. We have also seen that those who obtain an income from the ownership of property receive it in the form of (1) rent, which is paid for the use of property leased or rented to others; (2) interest, which is paid for the use of funds (money or credit) loaned to others; or (3) profits, which belong to the owner of a business after its costs have been met. In this chapter we shall discuss the subject of rent.

Nature of Rent—In the course of our economic activities, we rent or lease from others such things as bare land, farms, houses, stores, office buildings, apartments, automobiles, tuxedos, dress suits, and bathing suits, all of which we use either for productive purposes or to satisfy our consumption needs. When property is rented or leased to us, we do not obtain title to it. We are merely given the privilege of using it for a definite or indefinite period of time. The property still belongs to the owner, who usually retains the right to take possession of it whenever he deems it advisable to do so in order to protect his pecuniary interests. After the property has served our purpose, we return it, not some other property like it, to the owner.

Rent versus Interest—The question may be raised

as to why we do not speak of renting or leasing money and credit instead of lending them at interest. We do not do so partly because of custom and partly because renting and loaning transactions are different in character. When we lease or rent property from others, we turn back the identical property to its owner. When we borrow money or credit at interest, we do not turn back the identical dollars of money or the same credit instruments that were loaned to us, although we do pay back the same number of dollars plus interest. Furthermore, money and credit do not depreciate or wear out while the borrowers are using them, although their value may change with the changing price level. On the other hand, property that is leased or rented usually wears out or depreciates to a certain extent.

Many economists have maintained that rent is paid only for the use of land. As we have already explained, this view is not in accord with the practices of the economic world. We are interested only in describing our present economic system and the practices concerned with it. We are not attempting to establish an ideal set of terms and definitions and to describe an ideal set of conditions to which our economic world ought to conform. There is no need of our claiming that rent ought to be paid only for the use of land, when in reality it is paid for the use of other things that are leased to us, as well as for land.

The contention that rent is paid only for the use of land forces a number of needless complications into the discussion of the problem of rent. It requires that a distinction be made between the returns that are received for land and those that are received for the improvements made on and in the land. If fertilizer is used, if drainage and irrigation ditches are dug, or if vineyards and orchards are planted, how is it then possible to distinguish between the sum that is paid for the use of the land as originally provided by nature and the sum that is paid for the use of the capital embodied in the improvements on and in the land? How much of the product is due to the land itself and how much to the improvements thereon? It is not possible to answer these questions, nor, from the standpoint of a discussion of the conditions and practices as they actually exist, is it necessary for us to do so. Rent is paid for a farm as a farm, not solely for the use of the gifts of nature embodied in the farm. The same situation exists in the case of city real estate for which rents are paid. If I erect an office building on my lot, I cannot divide the income which I receive into the part that arises from the use of the land and the part that arises from the money which I have put into the building. I charge a rental for the use of the building, and this rental is supposed to provide me with a return upon the money that I have invested in both the land and the building.

Why Rent Is Paid—Rent is paid because the owners of property that is rented or leased to others will not permit the use of their property unless payment is made for its use. It cannot be claimed that the owners are making sacrifices by permitting others to use their property, because all too frequently they themselves (the owners) cannot use it and do not wish to do so. In fact, the owners are usually eager to rent their property to others. Sometimes they receive their entire income in this way. As a general rule, the property depreciates during the period that it is rented, although occasionally in the case of farms or houses it is handed back to the owner in much better shape than when placed in the hands of the renters. At times it rises in value while in the possession of the renter. Rent is paid, therefore, merely because there is a demand for the property in question. Others want to use it, and to obtain the use of it they are compelled to pay rent to the owner.

Justification of Rent—Some writers claim that, inasmuch as land is not produced by man, the mere fact that he has the title or legal claim to it does not justify him in charging a rental. They claim that the act of obtaining title to land is not an act of production and that land, being a gift of nature, should belong to the members of society as a whole. Its use, therefore, should be controlled by society, through the government, for the benefit of all the citizens. They make no similar claim in the case of those things that are produced by man, including improvements made by him upon the land, because they hold that in such cases the returns are paid for man's productive activity.

The justification of rent is based upon our concept of private property. By permitting individuals to own property, we provide an incentive to effort, to economic progress. Many individuals desire to own land or other kinds of property in order either to use it or to rent it to others. If we were to deny them that privilege, we should remove one of the most important causes of the economic advance of mankind. Private ownership of property results in better utilization of its possibilities, for, as a rule, owners take better care of it than do those to whom it is leased.

Agricultural Rents—The people of the United States have been accustomed to believe that there is no problem of farm tenancy, or "absentee landlordism," in our country. It is therefore surprising to many to learn that, although in 1880 only 25.6% of our farms were operated by renters, or tenants, in 1925 this figure had risen to 38.6%. In some of the southern states over two-thirds of the farms are leased to tenants, and in many other sections of the country the extent of tenancy rises to as high as 50%. The renting of agricultural land, therefore, constitutes the basis of the income of a large group of property owners.

Advantages and Disadvantages of Tenancy—Farm tenancy arises out of certain economic conditions. Frequently the price of land and the cost of improvements are so high as to make ownership impossible to many people who would like to buy land. The tenant is not required to assume the risk of a decrease in farm values. He does not have to worry over meeting payments for land, taxes, or insurance. If he does not succeed in his farming operations in a community which specializes in one kind of crop, he can pack up and move to another community. His geographical mobility is increased because he owns no land.

Tenancy, however, is not conducive to the best interests of the district. It adds an element of instability. Tenants do not care to take an active part in the local political life, because many of them are only transient residents. Schools, churches, and other institutions seldom receive their support. A tenant tends to exploit the rented farm for all that it is worth and is not interested in keeping it in first class condition; frequently buildings and equipment are not repaired and orchards and vineyards are neglected.

Factors Affecting Agricultural Rent—What are the general factors affecting agricultural rent? They are five in number, and all of them have to do with the productivity of the farm. When we use the term "productivity" we must be careful to distinguish between its two meanings. The term may refer to the productivity of the farm (1) in terms of bushels of grain, bales of hay, tons of cotton, and crates of fruit or (2) in terms of the dollars and cents income obtained from the sale of the grain, hay, cotton, and fruit. We are concerned not only with productivity in terms of the physical units of farm products but also with productivity in terms of dollars and cents.

However, the farmer is interested in the receipt of a money income, and the money income in his case depends upon the size of his crops, the cost of producing them, and the prices that they sell for in the market.

The physical productivity of the farm depends, first, upon the fertility of the soil. In the case of two farms, the one that has the better or more fertile soil will rent for the larger sum, other things being equal.

Second, there is the matter of location, or the proximity of the farm to the market. If two farms are equally fertile, the one that has superior transportation facilities—in other words, the one that is so situated that its owner can transport his products to the market the more cheaply—will rent for the larger sum, other things being equal.

It should be noted that in each case we have used the phrase "other things being equal." This reservation is necessary because there are other factors besides fertility and location that enter into the amount of rent which will actually be paid, and we must allow for their influence in determining agricultural rents.

There are many tracts of land in the United States that are extremely fertile but are so far removed from the market or from cheap transportation that they are handicapped in competing with less fertile land which is more advantageously situated. The introduction of land and water transportation facilities, which bring in new land as a competitor, helps to reduce the rent of land in the older sections of the country and to raise the rent of land in the newer sections. New England experienced a decrease in land rental when railroads were constructed to connect the western plains of the United States with the Atlantic seaboard.

Third, the extent to which the land has been improved by buildings, drainage and irrigation ditches, fences, orchards, and vineyards—in short, by the investment of capital—will very materially affect the amount of rent that can be charged for a farm. An unimproved or partially improved farm will not rent for as much as one that has had extensive improvements made upon it.

The intensive cultivation of land requires more capital per acre than does extensive cultivation. It is interesting to note that the best grade of land (considering both fertility and location) can be cultivated intensively with greater profit than can land which is not so fertile nor so satisfactorily located. One also finds that there is a tendency for the farmer to cultivate the most fertile parts of his land more intensively than the less fertile parts.

Fourth, the acreage or size of the farm is still another factor that affects the amount of rent which it can command. Some farms are so small that it is impossible to use agricultural machinery upon them advantageously; hence they do not yield as large a money return as might be the case if they were part of a much larger acreage.

Fifth, the price paid for farm products is a most important factor in the rent situation. When the prices of farm products are high, people are eager to rent farms, because of the opportunity afforded to make satisfactory returns. Therefore, rents tend to rise when the prices of farm products are high and tend to fall when prices are low. During a period of high prices for farm products, such as that which existed during and immediately following the World War, farm rents and also farm values rose to amazingly high levels. With a decline in the price level, which began in 1920, both farm rentals and farm values decreased greatly. At present many farm owners are unable to rent their farms to others at any price, because of the impossibility of obtaining a large enough income from farm operations even to pay expenses. Thus it is evident that the prices of farm products very definitely affect rent. In Chapter XXI we shall discuss the question of whether or not rent in its turn affects prices.

In stating that rent is affected by prices we do not mean to imply that agricultural rent is adjusted annually or monthly as the prices of agricultural products change, for such is not the case. Farms are frequently leased with the understanding that the owner is to have one-third or one-half of the crop, regardless of the price level. In any such cases the rent of the owner, in terms of dollars, naturally is greater when prices are high than when they are low, but his proportion of the physical product of the farm remains the same, regardless of the price level. Sometimes the rent of a farm is fixed at a certain amount in dollars, the contract running for a definite period of years. In this case, the rent remains stationary during the life of the contract, regardless of price changes.

The changes in the price level and the introduction of new products are matters of great concern both to the farmer and to the tenant. In India, where for years the natives used a sugar cane product called gur for sweetening purposes, sugar is now being imported from Java in increasing quantities. As a result, the value, as well as the rent, of that portion of land in India which is suited to raising sugar cane for gur production has greatly decreased. During the World War the price of rice rose to very high levels. Land in the Sacramento River Valley in California which had previously been of little value and which had commanded a ridiculously low rent was found to be suitable for rice cultivation. Thereupon, both the value and the rental rate of this land greatly increased.

Urban Rents

Urban Rents—The most important general factor affecting urban or city rent is location. If you wish to rent a city lot upon which to erect an office structure, you will not concern yourself with the nature of the soil; you will not care whether the soil is sandy, rocky, or fertile. Location is the primary matter in which you are interested. Is the lot near the center of the metropolitan district? Is it accessible by adequate transportation facilities? Is it located where potential renters will prefer to have their offices? These are some of the questions that you will ask yourself before leasing or purchasing city land.

After you have erected your office building, certain other general factors will help determine the rent which you can charge for office space. What did your building cost? Is it up to date? Has it the latest and best equipment? Has it plenty of light and satisfactory elevator and janitor service? Are the office suites large or small? What accommodations or services other than the bare office are furnished the tenants? Does the rent include the use of electric light, water, and gas? These are a few of the questions that you will consider in determining the amount that you will charge for the rent of your office building.

Many of the same questions enter into a determination of the rent to be charged for a house or an apartment. The location of the building, the character of the accommodations offered, the capital invested, the number of rooms, and the extra services supplied to tenants will all be taken into consideration.

Extent of Urban Renters—It is seldom appreciated how many of our city dwellers are tenants or rent payers. In 1920, 54.4% of the families in the United States lived in rented homes. In New York City the number reached 87.3%, in New Orleans 76.9%, in Chicago 73%, in San Francisco 72.6%, and in Philadelphia 60.5%. The percentage of rent payers would be considerably greater were we to include single persons who have rooms in apartment houses or in hotels or in private homes, as well as all of the professional and business men who rent accommodations in buildings used for office purposes.

Great stress has been laid upon the importance of home ownership. With the passing of years an increasingly large number of families have become renters, for several reasons. Land values are high; houses are more costly than formerly; the ownership of real estate binds a worker to his community or his section of the city and makes it difficult for him to move elsewhere in search of employment. Many of our cities have grown to such great size that if a worker wishes to own a home, he has to purchase a site many miles removed from his place of employment. He feels that he cannot afford to spend the time, money, and effort involved in traveling to and from work. Apartment houses and hotels furnish such conveniences as steam heat, electrical refrigeration, and janitor service—conveniences which few homes can afford. Lack of home ownership, however, tends to lessen civic pride and frequently results in failure on the part of many to participate in the government of the community.

Other Rentals—In fixing rentals for automobiles, tuxedos, dress suits, and so forth, a larger sum is charged for the more expensive articles than for those which are less expensive. No other general factor enters into the situation, although the rate of rental usually depends upon the relative bargaining powers of the owner and the renter.

Fixation of Rents—We now come to the problem of how the rate of rental is actually fixed. Again we must fall back upon the bargaining theory and state that rent is determined by the relative bargaining powers of those who have property to rent and those who wish to rent it. The owner bargains for a high rent; the renter bargains for a low rent. The owner hopes to receive a large enough gross income so that, after providing for taxes, insurance, depreciation, obsolescence, and various other charges (depending upon what kind of property is being rented), he will have a net income sufficiently large to yield a fair percentage return upon his investment. This hope, needless to say, is by no means always realized.

Suppose I have grown wealthy from my farming operations and desire to retire and live in a nearby city. You wish to rent my farm. Unless there are others who actively bid against you, I am not in a good bargaining position, and thus I am not able to charge as high a rental for my farm as I might obtain under other circumstances.

If, on the other hand, I am not eager to rent my farm but you are anxious to obtain it, you will have to bid much higher for it than in the reverse situation. If there are several farms for rent in my community and if there are only a few persons who desire to rent them, rentals will naturally be lower than when the reverse situation exists. I shall endeavor to charge you sufficient rent to yield me a fair return upon the value of my property; whether or not I shall be able to obtain it will depend upon my bargaining power as compared with yours.

In the case of homes, hotel rooms, office and store buildings, and apartment houses, similar influences affect the actual determination of rents. If the city is overcrowded and home and office accommodations have not kept pace with the demands of the population, rents will be high, because of the greater bargaining power of the owners.

On the other hand, if it happens that the city has been overbuilt, rents will be low, because of the increased bargaining power of the renters. Frequently the center of a city moves blocks or miles away from where it was originally located. A decrease in demand for accommodations in the old district results, and rentals of buildings in that section of the city decline, because the owners have lost some of the bargaining power that was formerly theirs.

Buildings may become old fashioned; in that event, even though these structures have good locations, their owners will be unable to charge as high rents as will the owners of new buildings close by—not because it has cost the latter more to erect their buildings, but because tenants are willing to pay higher rents for new and up to date accommodations.

The owner of a structure of any kind hopes to obtain sufficient rent to yield a fair return upon his investment, but he is not always able to obtain it. Many office buildings fail to yield enough rent to pay the cost of operation, repairs, taxes, and insurance. During the post-war boom, from 1918 to 1920, many office buildings were erected at very great cost, because of the high prices and the high wage levels existing at that time. When the boom subsided in 1920, rents declined to points that were generally below the amount required to net a fair return upon the funds that had been invested in the buildings.

The same general principle that rent is fixed by bargaining power holds in the case of rent that is charged for automobiles, articles of clothing, and the like. Competition among the owners for customers may be strong, or there may be a decided lack of patronage; in either event the rent will tend to be low. If there is competition among the customers or if there is a general increase in demand, the charges will of necessity tend to rise.

Combinations among Rent Receivers—Just as wage earners combine for the purpose of obtaining an improved bargaining position, so we often find the owners of rental properties combining. Every city of any size has an office building owners' association, and many cities also have a similar organization among apartment house owners. These associations aim to protect the interests of their members against adverse tax and building legislation, undesirable tenants, and other elements that might possibly reduce the income of this group of property owners. Such associations have not infrequently been known to be active and influential either in raising rents or in resisting attempts to lower rents, in spite of an oversupply of rental properties.

Conclusion—We cannot at any time state exactly the amount that will be paid for rent, any more than we can state exactly the amount that will be paid for wages. Different rents may be paid for exactly the same kinds of property in the city or in the country, just as different wages may be paid for the same type of labor power in the same community or in communities that are widely separated.

Rent arises because some individuals have property (land, buildings, or automobiles, for example) which others are desirous of using. The owners can and do charge rent, which others are willing to pay in order to obtain the use of the property in question. Although there are a number of general factors that influence rent, the amount that will actually be paid depends upon the relative bargaining powers of the owner of the property and the person who desires to rent or to lease it from the owner.

CHAPTER XVII

Interest

INCOME as interest is paid for the use of funds loaned in the form of either money or credit. The rate of interest is expressed as a percentage of the sum loaned. Funds are usually loaned for a definite length of time. In the case of a demand or a call loan, however, the borrower may repay the funds before he is asked to do so, or the lender may order the loan repaid at any time and without previous notice to the borrower.

Nature of Interest—Many economists claim that interest is the return that is paid to the owners of capital for the use of their funds; in other words, the owners of capital receive interest. As we have seen, capital is used to purchase labor power, to buy or to rent land, and to buy or to rent capital goods—labor power and land and capital goods all being used for productive purposes. In short, capital consists of funds that are used in production. The owner of a farm who leases it to another receives rent, not interest, for the use of the capital that is represented by the value of his farm. He who owns a business enterprise hopes to make profits on the capital which he has invested in his business. The person who lends funds to others receives interest upon them, regardless of whether they are used for the purpose of producing goods or services or for consumption needs (as in the case of loans that are made for the purpose of enabling an individual to purchase a house or an automobile). We cannot therefore maintain that the owners of capital (the owners of funds used in production) are the only ones who receive interest. Otherwise we should have to maintain that bondholders, whose funds are used in production and who are paid interest on those funds, are the only ones who receive interest. If such were the case, the country's bondholders would be its only capitalists. As a matter of fact, the owners of capital (funds used for a productive purpose) may have it invested in a farm which they lease to others for rent, or they may have it invested in a business from which they receive profits, or they may have it invested in bonds or in other forms of credit instruments on which they receive interest.

Interest is paid for the use of loanable funds; it matters not for what purpose they are used. They may be employed in productive enterprises, as in the case of loans that are made by bondholders, banks, or individuals to various kinds of business enterprises. They may be used solely for consumption purposes, as in the case of loans made by banks, building and loan associations, pawnbrokers, and private individuals for the purchase of homes, automobiles, or washing machines or for the payment of doctors', lawyers', and grocers' bills.

Money versus Credit—Loanable funds may be advanced in the form of money or in the form of credit. Individuals, Morris Plan banks, pawnshops, and similar institutions lend money. Commercial banks and savings banks lend both money and credit, but for the most part credit. An individual who borrows from a bank usually asks that the loan be placed to his account—that it be added to his deposits—so that he may draw checks against it. As we have seen in Chapter XI, the bank does not set aside an amount of money equal to the loan but merely builds up credit to the extent of the loan by setting aside the required reserve and by keeping enough counter cash on hand to care for any checks that may have to be cashed in money over the counter.

Interest Rates—The first thing that a student must realize in delving into this field of economics is that there is no one interest rate. There are many interest rates, as a glance at any financial magazine will disclose. Interest rates vary for different types of loans, for different lengths of time, and for different borrowers. It will be sufficient at this point in our discussion merely to call attention to some of the more outstanding types of loans for which interest is charged or paid. Among those that may be mentioned are real estate loans, call loans, thirty-day, sixty-day, and ninety-day loans, corporation and government bonds, savings accounts, commercial accounts, accounts of correspondents, and loans based on various kinds of commercial paper. The rates on commercial paper are usually known as discount rates, although in reality they are interest rates since they represent a charge that is made for the use of loanable funds.

Discount versus Loan—To explain briefly the difference between an ordinary loan and a discount, let us say that I lend you $100 on your promissory note for one year at 6%. You have the use of $100 for one year and at the end of that time repay me $100 plus 6% interest, or a total of $106. If, instead of making a straight loan, I discount your promissory note, I deduct 6%, our agreed rate, in advance and hand you $94, which you use for one year. At the conclusion of the year, you pay me $100. In the case of the ordinary, or straight, loan you pay $6 interest for the use of $100, but in the case of the discount, you pay $6 for the use of $94.

Whenever a bank or any other party discounts a piece of commercial paper, it does not pay the face value of the paper to the person who presents it for discounting. It deducts the discount (interest) from the maturity value of the paper (the total amount that is to be paid when the paper matures) for the length of time that the paper still has to run. There are many different kinds of commercial paper, but the loan or discount practices and principles involved are the same as in the simple case given in the preceding paragraph.

Objections to Interest—For many centuries interest-taking was roundly condemned by the church and by the civil authorities. Lending money at interest under any circumstances was classed as usury, and usury was frowned upon by the Old and New Testaments. Money was considered to be barren. It was claimed that in and of itself money could not produce anything of value, although labor and land could. Much of the borrowing in olden times was in the nature of personal loans for consumption and not for production purposes. Various subterfuges were employed to evade the restrictions which the church and the law imposed upon interest-taking, one such subterfuge being the practice of lending the money free of charge but imposing a fine (really an interest rate) for the failure of the borrower to pay back the funds immediately.

With the growth of commerce and industry the need for funds increased, and as early as the fifteenth century the opposition to interest-taking began to wane. Changing economic and social conditions forced a revision in the teachings of the church and in the statutes of the state. The term usury, as at present employed, refers to interest rates that are in excess of the maximum fixed by law.

Interest-taking is still objected to by some groups of people. The radical groups maintain that, along with rent and profits, interest is used as a means of exploiting the working class, of robbing it of part of the value produced by labor. The socialists and certain other groups of radicals claim that labor produces all exchange value and that rent, interest, and profits are therefore taken out of the products of labor; hence they seek to abolish not only interest but also rent and profits.

How Interest Can Be Paid—In answering the question as to how the payment of interest is possible, we are concerned with the purpose for which funds are borrowed. First, if the funds are borrowed to pay for consumption goods or services, the answer is simple. People who borrow for this purpose are able to pay for the use of the borrowed funds because they obtain an income from other sources. They make no use of the funds for the purpose of obtaining the wherewithal to repay the principal plus the interest.

Second, there is the other group of borrowers which uses the funds for production purposes, and it is this group that employs by far the larger amount of our loanable money and credit. These borrowers are able to pay interest plus principal to the lenders, for the reason that their business enterprises are made more productive through the use of the borrowed funds than would be the case if they did not have the additional funds at their disposal. The additional product and the income received therefrom make interest payments possible.

Why Interest Must Be Paid—The question as to why interest must be paid is a far more complicated one, and in this connection there is considerable disagreement among the economists, who have provided us with many answers. In this brief text we can consider only the more important theories that have been advanced, practically all of which are concerned with the justification of interest payments. Most of them are based upon ethical reasoning, because of the fact that in olden times, as we have pointed out, interest-taking was objected to as being a sinful, unethical, and unjustifiable practice. A theory explaining why interest must be paid usually contributes a justification for its payment.

Abstinence Theory—Many writers claim that interest must be paid to those who accumulate loanable funds, as a compensation for their abstinence, for the effort required by their saving, or for the sacrifice involved in their waiting. If we used up all we produced, nothing would be saved for the future, and there would be no loanable funds available to meet the demands of borrowers. It is maintained that saving involves sacrifice or abstinence and that no one would save unless he were rewarded for his sacrifices by means of interest.

With many people, however, saving is a pleasure; it is more or less instinctive and involves no sacrifice. Especially is this true of the very wealthy, who cannot possibly use up all of their income in caring for their daily needs. Moreover, the commercial banks, which are the chief providers of loanable funds for the use of business enterprises, pay no interest to their depositors (except to correspondents and to the few depositors who maintain large balances), yet their deposits actually represent savings which are used in creating large funds of capital in the form of credit. Some people even rent safe deposit boxes in which to keep their savings.

Not all of our savings are amassed by individuals. In fact, some writers claim that individuals save only a relatively small part of the funds that are accumulated annually and are used for lending purposes. The greater proportion of savings, so it is stated, results from the policy of corporations in setting aside a portion of their earnings in surplus and reserve funds or in reinvesting their earnings in their business. Of course, the earnings of a corporation actually belong to the stockholders, but not all of the earnings are distributed in the form of dividends. A considerable portion is used to build up surplus and reserve funds. The surplus is reinvested in the business, while the reserve funds are used for emergencies or for special purposes. All large corporations, including insurance companies, set aside such sums out of earnings, in addition to paying dividends to their stockholders.

One of our well known statisticians has estimated that from 1910 to 1920 American corporations reinvested an average of over two billion dollars a year in their business. It is also estimated that from 20% to 50% of the profits of a corporate business are annually carried to surplus or to reserve funds, the amount depending primarily upon whether business is in a prosperous or a depressed condition. Henry Ford began the manufacture of automobiles with a capital of only $49,000, but in twenty years he had "plowed back" into the business nearly half a billion dollars' worth of earnings. These surplus or reserve funds and the earnings that are plowed back into the business are just as representative of savings as is your $100 in the savings bank. It causes no sacrifice or pain to corporations to set aside these sums. They represent what might be termed "painless saving."

Funds that have been inherited or have been received as gifts are loaned out at interest, but no sacrifice or abstinence has been required of the owners. Again, the greater part of the funds which banks lend to their borrowers does not represent savings on the part of the banks. Their depositors are the ones who have saved and have deposited their savings with the banks. The latter, in turn, lend these funds to others or use them to create credit which they lend to others. When banks create credit, they are not forced to save or to undergo any sacrifice or abstinence.

If one believes that interest rates are paid as compensation for sacrifice, abstinence, or saving, he must also accept the conclusion that the higher the interest rate, the greater the savings of the people. Various investigations made by bankers and others, however, have shown conclusively that raising or lowering the interest rate does not increase or decrease the amount of savings.

Time Preference Theory—Some writers state that interest must be paid because human beings want things in the present rather than in the future. "A bird in the hand is worth two in the bush." If I should offer to give you $100 either now or a year from now, unquestionably you would take it now—you would rather not wait for a year to elapse before receiving it. If I lend you $100, I must wait until you pay it back before I can use the money. I am sacrificing the use of the funds in the present; therefore, so it is claimed, I expect you to pay me interest as compensation for my waiting.

Another phase of this argument considers the matter from the standpoint of the borrower. He is eager to obtain the use of the funds in the present rather than in the future. He needs the funds now in order to purchase goods, to pay for labor power, or to buy a house or an automobile. The funds mean more to him in the present than they would if he were forced to wait for them until some future date. Therefore, in order to obtain the funds in the present, he is willing to pay interest for them.

Is there any justification for this theory? Usually I lend funds because I have no present or immediate use for them. If I actually need them, I will not lend them to others, regardless of the rate of interest offered. Banks are established primarily for the purpose of lending funds, but neither they nor any other lenders would part with their funds if they had use for such funds in the present for any purpose other than lending. They have no time preference.

What about the borrower? He needs the funds, others have them, and to get possession of them he is compelled to pay interest whether he wants to do so or not. He has to pay interest for the funds regardless of whether he agrees to pay the interest a year hence or ten years hence. It is merely a case of his having to pay to get the use of something that some other person possesses, just as is true in the case of those who make payments for the use of labor power and for the use of land, office buildings, and other kinds of property that others possess.

Risk Theory—Still another theory maintains that interest must be paid because of the risk that the lender has to face in making the loan. Let us see if there is any basis for such a theory. If I have a house and lot conservatively appraised at $20,000 and if I borrow $1,000 from the bank, giving a mortgage on my property as security for the loan, does the bank run any risk of not getting back its funds plus interest? It is more than amply protected under any circumstances and runs no risk of loss. Yet in spite of the fact that the risk element is absent, I have to pay interest for my loan. If the United States Treasury borrows $20,000,000 from the Federal Reserve Bank of New York for one day, as it frequently does, the latter charges the government a certain rate of interest for the loan. Is this charge made because the Federal Reserve Bank of New York fears that the United States Government will become bankrupt before the next day arrives? Of course not. While it is true that risks are assumed at times by the lenders of funds, such is not always the case, and a theory as to why interest must be paid should be applicable under all circumstances.

Some students may say that a low rate of interest is charged on a safe loan and a high rate of interest on a doubtful loan and that therefore risk actually does explain why interest must be paid. One who thinks clearly will see the error in such a statement. The factors or circumstances affecting interest rates are one thing; the explanation as to why interest must be paid is another. Later in the chapter we shall devote some space to a discussion of the factors that determine interest rates, and in that connection we shall consider the influence of risk.

Scarcity Theory—How can we explain satisfactorily why interest is paid? Interest is paid to the owners of loanable funds, because, as we have seen to be true in other cases, those owners have something which others want and for the use of which others are willing to pay. If no one had need of funds—in other words, if every one had all the funds he wished—no one would be willing to pay interest to any one else. Therefore, it is the scarcity of loanable funds that explains why interest must be paid.

Interest Rates—What determines how much must be paid for the use of funds? In other words, what factors determine interest rates? We have seen that we cannot explain the existence of interest on the basis of abstinence. Neither can we invoke this motive to explain the rate charged. In the first place, even if an individual really experiences abstinence or sacrifice, how does he know what such abstinence or sacrifice is worth? Then, too, while a rich man may save without sacrifice, you, a bank clerk, may have to go without lunch or without other necessities in order to save a few dollars a month. In spite of this evident difference between you and the rich man in the matter of sacrifice or abstinence, the savings bank will pay both of you exactly the same rate of interest.

What about the time preference theory as explaining the interest rate? You may need your money for lunches and for clothes now, not in the future. I may have no need for half my income, which I am happy to lend to others. Nevertheless, if you and I buy United States bonds, we receive the same rate of interest, regardless of the differences in our present need for the funds involved in the transaction.

Productivity and the Interest Rate—Can the marginal productivity theory help us solve this problem as to the factors that determine interest rates? The arguments for and against this theory have already been discussed and need not again be presented. It may be advisable, however, to outline an additional argument in so far as it connects the marginal productivity theory and the interest rate. It may be recalled that, according to the marginal productivity theory, the rate of interest is determined by the productivity of the marginal unit of capital. The marginal unit of capital is that unit which produces just enough to pay the interest necessary to obtain its use. Therefore, following the circular reasoning of this theory, interest equals marginal productivity and marginal productivity equals interest. We must remember, however, that interest is paid for the use of loanable funds. One dollar of money or credit loaned is exactly the same as any other dollar of money or credit loaned.

Let us say that some of the owners of loanable funds lend their funds to two railroad corporations by investing in the bonds of these two companies. The bonds of both yield 5% interest. Is the yield the same because the railroads are equally profitable—in other words, because the dollars invested in both of them are equally productive? Not at all. One railroad may be headed toward bankruptcy, while the other may be most successfully managed; yet the bonds in both cases yield the same rate of interest, regardless of the productivity of the funds which have been invested in the two railroads.

To take another example—suppose your bank lends me $5,000 at 6%, and I invest it in two different ventures. One proves to be very profitable, and the other suffers a loss; yet the rate of interest that I pay to your bank is 6% in each case. Suppose you borrow $100 from the bank to pay a doctor's bill. The $100 has produced nothing so far as you are concerned; it has been used solely for the purpose of satisfying a consumption need. These examples should make it clear that interest rates do not depend upon the productivity of capital, although, as we have stated, interest can be paid on funds used for production purposes because land and labor are more productive with capital than without it.

Bargaining Theory—Does risk affect the rate of interest? Yes, it does at times, but only because it affects the bargaining power of the parties concerned. Therefore, we come once more to the bargaining theory of the division of income. There are many factors that affect the bargaining powers of lenders and borrowers. We shall discuss but two of them—the supply of funds in the market and the demand for funds.

Supply of Funds—If there are many persons who possess funds or credit which they desire to lend to others, and if there are only a few who are willing to borrow, interest rates will tend to be low. During periods of business depression banks usually have a large supply of funds on hand, and interest rates tend to fall. It may be more difficult to obtain loans at such times, because banks usually are more cautious then and require greater security, but rates of interest tend to decrease during such periods. On May 8, 1931, for example, the discount rate of the Federal Reserve Bank of New York dropped from 2% to 1½%, and call money was abundant on Wall Street at about the same rate.

On the other hand, in boom times interest rates tend to rise, because the supply does not always keep pace with the demand. As a bank's loanable funds decrease in amount, the bank raises its interest and discount rates in order to make borrowing more expensive and therefore more difficult, and this act enables it to protect its credit position. However, high money rates are frequently one of the causes of a decline in business activity. In New York, during the orgy of stock speculation that lasted from 1927 to 1929, money rates rose to high levels, because of the increased demands of the market and because of the desire of the banks to guard against an unwise extension of credit. In 1930 and 1931, on the other hand, many savings banks decided to reduce the interest rates on savings. Funds were plentiful, and the savings banks could not continue to pay the customary rate of interest because of the lack of investment opportunities.

The character of the banking system of a country has always had a great influence on the supply of loanable funds. With the growth of confidence in our financial institutions, scattered funds have been deposited in banks, where they have been made available for loans. By means of our credit practices, banks can stretch one dollar of money into from $10 to $15 of credit, which they can use for loaning purposes. The widespread use of the check, as we have seen, aids in this extension. The establishment of the Federal Reserve System, with its centralization of the reserves of member banks and with the very great reduction which it brought about in the legal reserves of the latter, has helped to increase the supply of loanable funds.

Thrift campaigns, school savings accounts, and the large earnings of corporations are additional factors which affect the supply of loanable funds and tend to decrease the bargaining power of those who lend funds.

Demand for Funds—The demand for funds comes from many quarters. First of all there is the call that is made upon our financial resources by numerous business enterprises. Railroads, factories, stores, mines, and steamship companies, all make great demands upon our supply of loanable funds. Farmers require large sums each year to care for their needs. There are also those who wish to build homes, to pay current bills, or to engage in stock speculation. Then, too, we must not overlook the commercial and savings banks, the building and loan associations, and similar credit institutions. They cannot operate merely on the capital subscribed for their stock by their owners. The greater portion of the funds which they use for the purpose of extending loans to business enterprises and to individuals is obtained from their depositors. On the funds deposited, the credit institutions pay interest, although commercial banks usually pay interest only on very large accounts. In any case, the rate of interest paid to depositors is less than the rate charged by the credit institutions when they lend to others who desire funds.

The interest rate depends primarily upon the relative bargaining powers of the lender and the borrower as influenced by the supply of and the demand for funds. The reputation of the borrower affects his ability to get funds. One reason why the interest rate paid to depositors by savings banks is low is that the reputation of these banks for solvency gives them an advantageous bargaining position. On the other hand, savings bank depositors are usually individuals who cannot invest their small sums in any other manner, and therefore they have slight bargaining power.

The nature of the call loan, which may be paid or called in at any time, normally makes for a low interest rate, although in times of a stock market crash the call rate may rise to dizzy heights. A person will not pay a high rate for funds if he has to face the risk of having the loan called in unexpectedly; therefore he is in a good bargaining position. In the case of call loans the banker's position is weaker than that of the borrower, because the banker desires to place his funds in the kind of loan for which he can demand repayment whenever he desires to do so. During a stock market boom, call rates rise, because the bargaining positions of the lender and the borrower are then reversed.

If a borrower has an unsatisfactory reputation or is engaged in a very hazardous enterprise, he will have to pay a higher rate of interest for his funds than would otherwise be the case, because he is in a weaker bargaining position than is one who is conducting a conservative business enterprise. Companies that have a questionable dividend record have to pay more for funds than does the United States Government, which has never failed to pay the interest on its obligations and the principal when they were due.

Loans that run for short periods of time usually carry a higher rate of interest than those that run for long periods of time, the reason being that long time investors prefer to have the lower return and be freed from the bother of frequently reinvesting their funds.

Fluctuations in the price level affect interest rates. When prices rise, the cost of living and the general levels of wages and rent also rise. Those who receive their income in the form of interest payments on loanable funds inevitably feel the burden of rising costs, and they too demand a higher return. Whether or not they are able to obtain it depends upon their bargaining power. When prices fall, interest rates tend to decline.

Combinations among Lenders—Associations among interest receivers and among interest payers seldom exist. The borrowers themselves, as well as their needs, are so diverse in character that it is exceedingly difficult to form an association among them. The outstanding example of an association among lenders is found in the banking field. The banks in a community may belong to a local clearing house, which is an unincorporated association formed primarily for the purpose of facilitating the clearing of checks and the settlement of claims among its member banks. Frequently the clearing house association adopts rules regulating the rate of interest to be paid by its members on savings accounts and on commercial account balances.

CHAPTER XVIII

Profits

IN the preceding discussion we have seen that wages are paid to those who sell labor power or personal services, that rent is paid to those who lease or rent property of various kinds to others, and that interest is paid to those who lend funds (money or credit). What about profits? Briefly, we may say that profits are paid to those who are the owners of productive enterprises.

Gains—In addition to the receivers of wages, rent, interest, and profits, we might say that there is still another group, which obtains part of the wealth of society in a manner not thus far mentioned. That group consists of those who make gains (not profits) from the sale of certain kinds of property. If I purchase a city lot for $2,000 and sell it a year later for $3,000, I claim to have made $1,000 on the transaction. If I buy ten shares of bank stock for $100 a share and two years later sell them for $125 a share, I claim to have made $25 a share. The sums which I have obtained from such transactions are not considered as income, for they do not represent payments received for personal services or for the use of property. Neither are they considered as profits, for they do not arise out of the activities of a business enterprise. Hence we call them gains.

How Profits Are Possible—In the preceding chapters we questioned how it is possible for a business enterprise to pay wages, rent, and interest. We must now make the same inquiry as to profits. The answer is simple. Profits are earned because the business enterprise is able to produce goods and to sell them at a price higher than the cost of production (including marketing, for marketing is a phase of production), or because, as in the case of a store, it can buy and market goods at a cost lower than the price at which they are sold.

Profits as Compensation for Managerial Ability— It is quite commonly claimed that profits belong to the owners of a business enterprise as compensation for their managerial ability. This contention does not seem tenable. In the first place, as we have noted in Chapter V, whenever a person manages a business, he is rendering personal services; he is therefore a laborer, and what he is paid is wages, not profits.

In the second place, who is it that manages a business enterprise? When it is completely owned by one individual, he is the person who usually manages it, although at times he may hire for that purpose another person to whom he pays a wage or salary. The individual owner seldom sets aside out of the earnings of the business a certain sum as wages for himself. He usually counts as profits all of the income over and above what he has to pay out to others.

Partners also usually manage their own enterprise, although at times they, too, may employ a manager to whom a wage or salary is paid. In the case of many partnerships, where the partners are actively engaged in managing the business, the owners pay themselves a weekly or a monthly wage and count it as one of the expenses of the business. At the end of the year, when they close their books and figure their expenses and total income they divide the profits among themselves or put a portion of the profits back into the business.

In the case of a corporation, it is usually impossible for the owners (the stockholders) to act as managers or to display their managerial ability if they have any. The owners of a corporation are usually too numerous. The stockholders of a large corporation often are scattered over the civilized portions of the globe. Some of them may be old persons, feeble-minded individuals, or children and consequently have no ability to manage. Many of them may not even know in what kind of business their funds are invested. As we have seen in preceding pages, a corporation is managed by a board of directors, which is chosen by the stockholders (or at least by a portion of them). The board of directors, in turn, selects a general manager or a superintendent, by whom usually the foreman and other minor executives are appointed. The board of directors, the general manager, the superintendent, the foreman, and the sub-foreman are all engaged in managing the business of the corporation. Frequently the directors are paid directors' fees (wages) for their services in deciding the major policies of the corporation. The general manager, the superintendent, and the other minor executives also receive wages or salaries for their services. It should be clear, therefore, that the stockholders of a corporation (its owners) do not usually manage, and hence it cannot be said that they receive profits because of their managerial ability.

Profits as Compensation for Risk Taking—Some writers claim that profits rightfully belong to the owners of a business as compensation for taking the risks involved in a productive enterprise. Every business enterprise involves risk taking. However, there are others besides stockholders who engage in economic activities and take risks, but these persons do not receive profits. Those who rent or lease property run the risk of getting it back in a depreciated condition; those who labor run the risk of being injured or killed or of not receiving their wages; those who lend funds run the risk of not being paid interest or of not having their principal returned; and those who buy real estate or corporation securities in the hope of selling at a higher price run the risk of having to take losses on their ventures. Risk taking does not explain why wages, rent, interest, and gains are paid, nor does it explain why profits are paid. Wages, rent, and interest arise out of payments that are made by others in order to obtain the use of labor power that can be hired, property that can be leased, and funds that can be borrowed. Payments to the seller involving gains are made in order that title may be obtained to certain kinds of property that are desired by the purchaser. The same reasoning applies in the case of profits. The business enterprise has something to sell that we, the public, are willing to buy, and we buy it at a price that usually, although by no means always, enables the business to make a profit. We desire something that the business enterprise has, and in order to obtain it we have to pay a price for it, just as we do when we hire laborers, lease property, or borrow funds.

Risk Not a Cause of Profits—The owners of any business take the risk of suffering losses, but the mere fact that they have taken a risk does not account for either profits or losses. Two grocery stores may be established across the street from each other. Both operate in the same economic environment and take the same risks; yet one may fail and the other may succeed. Thus, it should be evident that there is no relationship between the risks that are taken and the profits that accrue to the owners of a business enterprise.

Social Approval of Profits and Gains—Why should we pay more for an article, quite frequently a great deal more, than it has cost to produce it? Why should we pay more for property or for corporation securities than the seller has paid for them? In other words, how can, and how does, society justify profits and gains? Let us first consider the case of the profit takers, the owners of a business enterprise.

Many kinds of commodities and services are needed by human beings to satisfy their wants. Factories, stores, mines, banks, railroads, farms, and various other kinds of business enterprises are necessary in order that goods may be produced and services may be rendered. Labor power, land, and capital goods have to be brought together to form productive units. In our present state of economic society, the government does not engage in very many lines of business activity. Consequently, it is left largely to individuals in most countries to organize and to operate the business enterprises of the nation. Individuals with funds at their disposal, therefore, use them to procure labor power, land, and capital goods and take the chance of making a profit or of suffering a loss. They are engaged usually in a legitimate activity, in a socially justifiable venture, and, under our present régime of private property, they are permitted to make all they can out of it. Society does not guarantee them a return, but it declares that if they can make a profit, they are entitled to it, because they are producing something that consumers want or need.

Individuals become owners of a business, partly because they prefer to be their own bosses or to be able to boss others and partly (possibly this is the more important reason) because they think they may be able to obtain a larger return from investing their funds in an enterprise than they would receive if they depended upon the possibility of getting an income from rent, wages, or interest.

The payment of gains to those who do not engage in a productive enterprise but make gains from the purchase and sale of certain kinds of property is justified by society on slightly different grounds from those outlined in the preceding paragraphs. In such cases gains arise from a person's having bought real estate, stocks, bonds, and so forth, and having sold them at a higher price than he paid for them. The increase in the price is frequently the result of no effort on the part of the owner and may not even be due to his foresight or ability. Society declares that in such cases gain taking is justified because society benefits from the right of its members to buy and to sell property so long as no socially unjustifiable conditions result. It is quite evident that many individuals would not invest their funds in land, buildings, and other kinds of property if they knew that they would be prohibited from making a gain through the sale of that property. Consequently, society would suffer from lack of thrift, ambition, and progressiveness on the part of its members. Many persons who purchase stocks buy in the hope that they may be able to make gains through an increase in the market price. If they were not permitted to make gains, they would not purchase stocks, and the growth and activity of industry would be handicapped for lack of funds.

As our society is at present organized, profits and gains are sanctioned in order that productive enterprises may continue and in order that the people may be induced to invest their funds in such enterprises. There are many radicals, however, who claim that profit taking can and should be abolished. This, they claim, would inaugurate a new type of economic society. Some of the arguments for and against their proposal will be discussed in Chapter XXII.

Profits Not Guaranteed—It is advisable to repeat that society does not guarantee that profits and gains will be paid. The owners of a business have a legal claim to profits only if profits are earned. The owners of property have a claim to gains only if they can make gains. Each group takes its chances of making profits or gains, as the case may be, or of suffering losses on its ventures. However, it should not be overlooked that society does lay down rigid rules and regulations which permit those who sell their labor power, rent their property, and loan their funds to enforce their claims to wages, rent, and interest, respectively, in the courts. Those who expect to make profits or gains enjoy no such privilege.

Who Receive Profits—Who receive the profits of a business enterprise? To whom do the profits belong? Profits go to the owners of the business. In the case of the individual proprietorship, the profits belong to the individual owner; in a partnership they belong to the partners; and in a corporation they belong to the stockholders. As has been previously stated, although all of the profits of a corporation belong to the stockholders, the stockholders, as a rule, do not receive all of the profits, because usually from 20% to 50% of the profits are set aside as surplus or are reinvested in the business. The remainder, after allowing for reserves, usually is turned over to the stockholders as dividends.

Profits as a Residual Share—Profits represent that portion of earnings which remains after costs of operation and other expenses have been paid. Costs consist of various items—rent, wages, interest, insurance, taxes, prices paid for supplies, machinery, advertising, and so on. Business firms do not all have to meet the same kinds of expenses. A newspaper distributor who hires ten boys to work for him in distributing a metropolitan newspaper in a country town does not have to pay rent or interest if he leases no property and borrows no money with which to carry on his business. If I am a drayman, I probably pay no rent for the part of the street where my truck stands while I wait for customers to appear, and I pay no interest if I borrow no funds with which to carry on my trucking business.

When a farmer owns his land and equipment, hires no laborers, and borrows no funds from others, he pays no wages, rent, or interest. He usually considers as his profits the total amount of money received for his crop less the expenditures that he has to make for seed, wire, boxes, gasoline, taxes, and interest. Many economists, however, claim that in such a case the farmer has figured his profits incorrectly. They state that he should set aside a certain amount of his income as wages for himself and for the members of his family who work on the farm, a certain amount as rent for the use of his own land, and a certain amount as interest for the use of that part of his own capital which he has invested in the farm. As a rule, however, the farmer does not do so. He is the owner of a business, and he counts as his profits all of the income over and above the sums that he has to pay out to others.

Again, let us say that a grocery store keeper owns his store, does his own clerking, and borrows no money. The same situation exists as in the case of the farmer. The independent groceryman probably does not pay himself rent, wages, or interest. He counts as profits his total income less expenses incurred for cost of groceries, string, bags, taxes, and so forth, which he has to pay out during the year. We make no claim that he is applying the highest principles of business practice. He may not be operating his enterprise as he should, but it must be remembered that in this text we are merely analyzing things as we find them at present in our business world.

Many corporations issue no bonds and borrow no money from banks; hence they pay no interest. Some economists, however, argue that even in such cases the corporations should figure the interest on the capital invested in their business and count it as a part of their costs, before arriving at the amount of their profits. Ideally this might be an acceptable practice to follow, but actually the owners of corporations would seldom think of doing so. In this connection, the question might be raised as to whether these economists would suggest that, before arriving at the amount of its profits, the corporation should figure interest on the actual amount of the capital invested in the business, or on the appraised value of the business, or on the amount of the capital stock the corporation has issued. These are three entirely different matters, as any banker can easily appreciate. Corporations are inclined to calculate their expenses for interest only upon the amount of the funds they have borrowed from banks, bondholders, and others.

Some economists also maintain that when a stockholder receives his dividends, he should set aside a certain portion as representing interest upon the amount of money that he has invested in the stock and should call the remainder profits. In other words, dividends, according to this group of economists, represent both interest and profits. To the stockholders, however, dividends usually represent profits and nothing else. It is true that dividends are paid on a percentage basis just as interest is and that the rate at which dividends are actually paid year after year frequently remains stationary, as does the interest rate on a long time loan. Moreover, stockholders sometimes assert that their dividends do not amount to as much as they would have received in interest had they invested their funds in bonds. But these facts do not change the nature of dividends as profits. It must also be remembered, as has been stated several times in the preceding pages, that, although all the profits of a corporation belong to the owners, or stockholders, the entire amount that has been earned is seldom distributed to the stockholders. The stockholders are entitled to all the profits and yet are paid only a certain percentage. On the other hand, those who lend funds to a corporation have a claim to a certain amount of interest, and the entire amount is paid to them if the corporation is in a solvent condition.

Factors Affecting Profits—Profits arise from the sale of goods at a price higher than the cost of producing and handling the goods. If a business concern is engaged in manufacturing and marketing a commodity, it must keep the cost below the price which it obtains for the product; otherwise, there will be no profits. If the selling price rises, greater profits may be earned, unless the cost of production also increases. An increase in profits minimizes the incentive to reduce the cost of production. But if the price of the goods declines and profits are reduced or completely eliminated, then the managers of a business become vitally interested in reducing costs and therefore endeavor to purchase supplies more cheaply, to introduce improved machinery, to devise more efficient methods of handling material, to cut down the cost of overhead, to close inefficient plants, to secure a reduction in transportation rates, and sometimes to reduce wages.

In meeting lower prices or increased costs of production, some business executives follow a policy that is radically different from that outlined in the preceding paragraph. The two matters in which a business executive is interested are the total cost per unit of product and the price of the commodity in the market. Consequently, an executive may attempt to reduce the cost of production by spending more money instead of less. He may raise wages, in order to obtain the most efficient workers in the community and thus have in his employ a contented group of employees, who are happy at their work and are eager to cooperate with their employer.

The economies of high wages are evident in many lines of production. Business executives know that high wages will increase the buying power of the workers and will therefore increase the demand for goods and make possible greater production and larger profits. In addition to increasing wages, executives may spend large sums in advertising, for the purpose of increasing their sales to the point where greater production at lower unit cost will be possible. They may establish branches at home and abroad or purchase the business of competitors. They may introduce new products or manufacture by-products. They may voluntarily cut prices so as to increase sales. An interesting instance of the effectiveness of cutting prices has lately arisen in California in connection with the displacement of manufactured gas by natural gas from the oil fields of that state. When the Pacific Gas and Electric Company of California introduced natural gas, the price was reduced to about 50% of what had been charged for manufactured gas, and the lower price caused a much greater amount to be consumed. Coal, wood, and oil fuel users installed gas furnaces, and the profits of the company in the long run were actually increased to a considerable extent.

Thus it sometimes happens that by spending more money, executives are able actually to lower their unit costs and thereby increase their profits. Each business enterprise presents an individual problem, however, and no general rule of procedure is applicable in all cases when it comes to solving the problem of reducing unit costs and obtaining greater profits. The policy which succeeds in one case will not necessarily succeed in another.

Some business enterprises are monopolistic in character and can control the prices of their products. However, as we shall note in Chapter XXI, high prices do not always yield the greatest profits to a monopoly. In fact, quite frequently a low price with a small profit on each sale yields far greater profits to a monopoly than a higher price with a smaller number of sales.

Another matter which may appear strange to the uninformed, but which must always be kept in mind, is that not all business enterprises can make greater profits by becoming larger in size. Some companies have become bankrupt by expanding too rapidly. Because of the operation of the law of diminishing productivity, costs may increase so rapidly as to bring about a decrease in profits or even to eliminate profits entirely. To illustrate this matter in a rather striking way, we may point out that it would not be profitable to establish a bank as large as the National City Bank of New York in a town of only 5,000 population, nor would it pay to increase the money invested in a peanut wagon from $200 to $20,000.

The element that looms largest as affecting profits is the difference between the unit cost and the price received from customers. But what are the factors that affect this difference? They are many, and we can discuss only a few of the most important.

Managerial Ability—A company with a capital stock of $100,000 is established in close proximity to another of exactly the same size. Both have the same wage scale, pay the same prices for supplies, and produce the same products; yet one company succeeds and the other fails. Why? It is because the ability of the executives—those who actually manage the business—is not the same in both cases. The successful enterprise has as its general manager an excellently trained individual, who is capable, farsighted, agreeable to work with, keen in handling business problems, alive to changing methods and changing business conditions, and capable of inspiring loyalty among his employees. The other enterprise has not been so fortunate in the selection of its chief executive, and the results are not so satisfactory. The earnings and consequently the profits of a concern thus depend in part upon the managerial ability of its executives, who, if they are employees (and they usually are), receive wages or salaries for their services.

Chance Gains—One of the outstanding leaders in the mail order field has publicly stated that 90% of success in business is the result of pure luck or chance. Chance gains do play an important part in the success of every enterprise, but it is doubtful if they are as significant a factor as this mail order executive claims.

Every business depends upon the patronage of the public, and the public is extremely fickle in its tastes and demands. In 1930 its fancy was captivated by the game of miniature golf. Millions of dollars were invested in the business, but in a few months the fad had passed. Through no fault of the owners or the managers of these golf courses, huge losses were sustained. The Prince of Wales stops at my hotel. Over night my hostelry becomes the popular place in town, although there are other hotels in the vicinity which are equally good or even better. A fire sweeps across a town, destroying business blocks and houses and wiping out fortunes. Immediately the prices of building materials rise, as do rents for offices and houses and the prices of foodstuffs, thus increasing the incomes of the fortunate ones. The Mediterranean fly devastates the citrus orchards in Florida and removes the Florida crop from the market. California orchardists are accordingly benefited. A drought lays waste the wheat fields of Russia or Argentina, and American wheat growers secure higher prices for their crops. Many other instances could be cited to show the great influence exerted by chance or luck in the realm of profits. However, it is not well for the business man to depend upon luck or chance; he should be so prepared as to be able to take advantage of opportunities when they arise.

By far the most important factor affecting chance gains is the so-called business cycle, with its ever recurring periods of high and low business activity in which the average business man is as a speck of sawdust swirling about in the rapids of a river. Periods of high business activity are characterized by active markets, large sales, and large profits. Periods of low business activity are characterized by sluggish markets, diminished sales, reduced profits, and failures. The business concern is unable to prevent depression or to retain prosperity. To the business owner depression spells chance losses, while prosperity spells chance gains. We shall discuss the business cycle more fully in the next chapter.

The Supply of Business Enterprises—The number of those who desire to become owners of enterprises is very great. This is especially true in the United

States. There is an old saying which runs thus: "If you want to get on, get in business for yourself." The large plums in the top of the tree are attractive. The romantic careers of "captains of industry" constitute an incentive to use one's savings, or those of others, to launch a business. It is easier, also, to start an enterprise of one's own than to enter any one of the older professions. In many states a man is required to pass a difficult bar examination before he can practise law; a physician can qualify only after a vast amount of preparation and must have a license to practise medicine; an educator must possess a teacher's certificate; and an engineer must spend years of study in order to master the technicalities of engineering. There are only a few limitations, however, placed upon a business career. In the case of railroads and public utilities, special permits may be required before duplication of equipment and plant is permitted. In the formation of corporations, the organizers must subscribe to the general requirements of state corporate law.

It might well be argued that it is too easy to start out in business. To correct this situation, legislatures have been importuned to limit the number of new enterprises, especially in merchandising. There is an economic disadvantage in the existence of too many small distributing units. An excessive number of furniture stores in a city of 300,000 means a small average turnover per store with resulting high prices to the public. Low grade business ability destroys legitimate profits and eventually passes the burden of production on to the community, because it is from the prices paid by the public for goods and services that business obtains the money with which to keep on operating. In every large city there are many more stores than are required to satisfy the demands of the public. If stores were fewer and were permitted to enjoy a larger trade, they could sell goods for lower prices. Although the public pays the cost of the existing duplication of enterprises, nevertheless there is a well defined tradition that men must be free to try out their business ability.

In some lines of business, the evolution of large scale enterprises has created a limitation on the establishment of competitive plants. The capital requirements in the steel industry, for example, practically prevent an individual or even a small corporation from starting out in that field. Business enterprises in the younger countries have frequently found it difficult to meet the competition of old established firms in other lands. Recognizing this condition, many countries have granted subsidies or passed protective tariff acts.

On the other hand, the vast accumulations of funds awaiting investment make it a relatively simple matter to "promote" a multitude of doubtful business undertakings. There would seem to be no dearth of schemes and plans eager to gather up the savings of such people as always have faith in the possibility of obtaining future profits.

Marginal Firms—Whenever a business enterprise is found to be making large profits, there is a tendency for other concerns to become established in the same field. Competition develops and prices fall, with a consequent decrease in profits. Some enterprises are forced to close their doors because they cannot meet the expenses of operation. Others may hang on for a few years, but, unless conditions within or without their business change, they too will ultimately be forced into bankruptcy. These are called the *submarginal firms.*

Other enterprises make expenses but are unable to make profits. As a rule, they remain in the field much longer than do those which cannot meet expenses. They are called the *marginal firms,* because they "just break even." Other enterprises are able to earn varying rates of profits. They are said to be above the margin, but conditions may change even in their case and force them down below the margin. No enterprise can always be certain of making profits for its owners.

Business at best is extremely hazardous and speculative in character. Some of the risks that enter into the success or failure of a business may be insured against—such as risks of fire, burglary, public liability, and industrial accidents. Other risks may be offset by certain kinds of speculative activity known technically as hedging. By means of hedging one risk is minimized by being set off against another, the additional risk being assumed for the purpose of "playing safe." However, there is no insurance that will guarantee the payment of profits, nor can the policies adopted by the business executive always assure profitable operation.

Extent of Risk in Business—The public, for the most part, fails to appreciate the extent of the risk faced by the owners of business. People hear only of large profits, stock dividends, and the accumulation of large surpluses, because only the events that are unusual find a place in the columns of our daily newspapers. Reports of deficits, of decreased earnings and dividends, and of bankruptcies are suppressed to a surprising degree. The public should be acquainted with the fact that by no means all business is profitable and that not all those who purchase land, buildings, or corporation securities make gains by doing so.

The extent of the annual losses by business owners in the United States is astounding. Each year more than 100,000 corporations, not to mention partnerships and individual proprietorships, have nothing left, after meeting the cost of operation, for the payment of dividends, or profits. In 1921, 52% of the corporations making income tax returns to the United States Treasury Department reported deficits. In 1927, 44% reported deficits. In periods of prosperity about 4% of all business concerns fail. In times of depression this percentage is more than doubled. Especially in the retail field is the rate of failure exceptionally high. It has been stated that over 90% of our mercantile firms fail sooner or later. One of the most careful investigations of "life expectancy" in the retail field was made in 1930, when the stores in Buffalo were studied by the Bureau of Business and Social Research of the University of Buffalo. The results showed that within five years after having been established 52% of the drug stores, 62% of the hardware stores, 75% of the shoe stores, and 85% of the grocery stores of that city had failed.

The rate of failure among banking institutions also is discouragingly high. Especially has this been true since the business depression of 1920. During the nine-year period from July 1, 1920, to June 30, 1929, about one-fifth of all the banks in the United States closed their doors, tying up deposits of approximately $1,500,000,000. In some sections of the country, more than half the banks failed, and in some agricultural districts all of them were placed in the hands of receivers.

Gains from Unearned Increment—Many of those who obtain a portion of the income of society do so from the sale of property. They purchase land, buildings, stocks, bonds, and so forth, and, without adding anything to the value of the property, they often sell it at a higher price, because of the demands of society for their possessions. For example, if you purchase a plot of ground in a rapidly growing community, or during dull times, and let it lie idle, its price usually rises without any effort on your part. This is due to the fact that other property owners come in and build homes or office structures near your property, or that economic conditions improve. What have you done to earn or to deserve the added value of your property? You have done nothing, yet that gain belongs to you.

Let us say that you purchase 1,000 shares of stock in the United States Steel Corporation. You may know nothing whatsoever about how to value a corporate security, and even if you did, it would not affect the situation in the least. Suppose the price of the stock rises. You have done nothing to make the company more profitable as a going concern, yet you are able to sell your stock at a higher price and pocket the gain.

These two instances are sufficient to show what is meant by gains arising out of the *unearned increment* of property values. The acts of others, not your own efforts, have increased the worth of your property. On the other hand, in countless instances owners of property have had to take heavy losses through no fault of their own. Such losses are called *unearned decrements*.

Regulation of Profits—During the Middle Ages there was much talk of "a just price" and the payment of a "fair return," the idea being that an individual should be allowed to charge only a fair or just price that would yield him a fair or just return. In some cases, the government did not hesitate to fix prices at what it deemed to be a fair figure. The idea still prevails among our citizens that something should be done to regulate profits by regulating prices. Some attempts were made during the World War to realize that ideal. During that uncertain period, the United States Government taxed what it called "excess profits" at a very heavy rate, the assumption being that there was a normal or fair return of profits which business enterprises should be permitted to earn. In addition, the government fixed the prices of some essential commodities in order to limit the profits of the producers. "Profiteering" was condemned in no uncertain terms by the public. The government also limited the amounts of raw materials that might be sold to the non-essential industries and by that means handicapped the owners of those industries in their profit making operations. Many business enterprises had to close their doors temporarily, while others were forced into bankruptcy.

During peace times the regulation of profits is effected by two different methods. First, the power to tax is used, both state and federal governments levying taxes upon the incomes of their citizens. Those who receive large incomes are taxed at a much higher rate than those who receive small incomes. This difference in taxation is not intended as a penalty for those who have earned large incomes, but rather as an effort to force each citizen to contribute to the support of the government, according to his ability. The result is a slight equalization of incomes among the people. Those who make gains from the unearned increment of land occasionally find that their gains are reduced by the action of the city, county, or state in levying heavier rates of taxation upon unimproved land than upon land that has been improved. This action of the government reduces the amount of the gain obtained from the sale of land held for speculative purposes.

The second method of regulating profits has to do with the fixation of the rates of public service corporations. At present, the Interstate Commerce Commission fixes the rates of interstate carriers, while state commissions exercise the same authority in regard to intrastate carriers. Railroads, street cars, gas and electric light companies, auto bus lines, and telephone and telegraph companies, all have their profits regulated by the government, which, through its various commissions, fixes the rates that may be charged for the services rendered. Just how far this latter method of regulating profits may be extended in the future and applied to the prices charged the public by other kinds of business enterprises cannot be surmised.

The Farmer as a Business Man—We must not overlook the farmer as a receiver of profits. He, too, has his problem of keeping down costs and of getting an adequate return for his products. His farm is as much a business enterprise as is a bank, a store, a factory, or a railroad. The average farmer lacks managerial ability. He is poorly trained for his task, which is one that really requires special preparation. He usually plants what others plant and cultivates his land as others do, regardless of peculiarities in his own situation. He lacks capital and, because of the nature of his business, often finds it difficult to obtain funds to farm efficiently.

The United States Government has been compelled, by force of circumstances, to supply the farmer with short term credit for the marketing of his crops. Such credit is made available through the Federal Intermediate Credit banks. The government also provides the farmer with long time credit (for from five to forty years) for the financing of his needs in purchasing and developing land, such credit being made available through the Federal Land banks. In 1929 Congress granted the Federal Farm Board an appropriation of $500,000,000 to spend in aiding the farmer to obtain adequate returns for his crops. This board has made loans, purchased farm products, and engaged in other kinds of activities in an attempt to keep the prices of farm products from declining to an excessively low level.

In the United States farmers for the most part constitute an unorganized group. It is exceedingly difficult to form cooperative organizations among them, in order to enable them to bargain more effectively for higher prices in the market. They are engaged in a highly competitive business, and each farmer strives more or less helplessly for his individual advantage. He can never tell when drought or pests will ruin his crops, or whether, if he has a good crop, a reasonable price will be obtained for it. Agriculture has not been placed on a sound business basis. Accurate accounts are seldom kept by the farmer, and this fact explains in part the confusion and inefficiency which exist in farming operations. When the usual type of business enterprise cannot earn profits, it dissolves or goes into bankruptcy. The farmer, however, does not follow any such procedure. He remains on his farm, usually until the mortgage is foreclosed, even though in the meantime he is not making enough money to pay expenses. The farmer is also handicapped because he cannot easily shift from some crops to others in order to meet changed economic conditions. For instance, it takes years to bring vineyards and orchards into bearing; they cannot be handled like crops of wheat, oats, or corn.

Of late years farmers have been increasingly affected by world conditions. Improved means of transportation have made the farmers of North America competitors of those in Asia, South America, and Europe. Through no fault of their own and in spite of the fact that they may be careful managers and may keep accurate accounts, the vagaries of the price level in the market may force many of them into bankruptcy or very close to it.

The Bank as a Business Enterprise—The bank is a slightly different kind of business enterprise from those which we have previously considered. The bank sells no such tangible commodities as soap, furniture, or clothing. It makes only a small portion of its income by buying and selling bonds and commercial paper. Its main concern is the lending of funds for a price, or interest. It obtains its funds from its stockholders (who subscribe to its capital stock), from its depositors, and from other financial institutions when it needs to borrow. These funds are used for the most part in creating credit. The bank loans money and credit to its customers or invests its funds in bonds, commercial paper, and so forth.

The profits of a bank depend to a certain extent upon business conditions. If business is brisk and the demand for funds is great, the bank receives more income than it does if business is depressed. Its profits are also affected by the competition of other banks, the rates of interest (which are determined primarily by the supply of and the demand for funds in the market), and by the ability of the bank's executives or managers to handle its affairs skilfully.

CHAPTER XIX

Business Cycles

THE most important influence in determining the returns received by those who obtain wages, rent, interest, profits, and gains is the condition of the business world. During periods of prosperity business for the most part is good, although even in the most active years numerous failures occur. Prosperous times mean that wage earners have no difficulty in finding employment; houses, apartments, and office and store buildings are rented to capacity; money and credit are loaned in large amounts; property values rise and sales of goods increase, resulting in larger gains and profits. When depression occurs, conditions are exactly reversed. It is more difficult for wage earners to find employment; houses and buildings go unrented; there is a lessened demand for loanable funds; lower prices and lower property values bring decreased profits and gains and frequently failures. At present the laborer and the property owner have no control over these alternating periods of good and bad times, known as business cycles. Every one is eager to have prosperity last forever, but the individual appears to be helpless under the circumstances.

Capitalism and the Business Cycle—As one writer has pointed out, the business cycle is like a cancer. We know what the cancer is and what its effects are, but we have not as yet learned the cause, the cure, or the means of prevention. Similarly, we know what the ups and downs of business are and what their effects are, but we know neither the causes of nor the cures for these alternating periods of depression and prosperity, although there have been suggested many remedies which, if intelligently applied, might aid in stabilizing business and in smoothing out the curve of the business cycle. Our economic society is so complex and changes so constantly and so rapidly that it is difficult for us to learn enough about it to be able to understand and to analyze some of its most important phases.

The business cycle is one of our unsolved problems. We do know, however, that the business cycle has been far more frequent since the widespread adoption of the methods of capitalistic production than previous to that time. It did not actually make an appearance until toward the close of the eighteenth century, although previously drought, famine, and wars caused failures in business and general suffering among the people. We also know that even today the more backward races, who live simply and who supply practically all of their personal needs through their own individual efforts, do not suffer from its effects. The business cycle, therefore, is a phenomenon of capitalism, of our present pecuniary system, where goods are made for sale and not for use and where the greater proportion of the people are dependent upon others for jobs and for markets for their products.

Nature of the Business Cycle—The ups and downs of the business world may be likened to the ups and downs of an ocean wave as it rolls in toward the shore. The ocean wave drops down into a trough, swells upward to the crest, breaks, and again goes down into a trough; it rises again, breaks, and then goes down into a trough. That is just what business has been doing since the latter part of the eighteenth century.

The outstanding or important ups and downs in business come at more or less irregular intervals. For many years past severe hard times have occurred at intervals of from seven to ten years. Without going back very far in our own business history, we may note that serious breaks in the condition of business occurred in 1873, 1884, 1893, 1907, 1914, 1920, and 1929. These important breaks are called *crises*. A crisis is usually followed by a period of depression or stagnation, during which business is "dead." The recovery from the depression may be either rapid or slow.

On every large wave of the ocean, there are smaller waves that also rise and fall as the large wave rushes in toward the shore. Similarly, in the business world, during every long period between crises there are shorter periods of prosperity and depression. These smaller fluctuations of business are known as the *business cycle*. The business cycle includes "one wave of rising and falling," while the intervals between crises often include two, and sometimes three, such waves. Between the crisis of 1920 and that of 1929, we had the less serious business recessions of 1924 and 1927.

A crisis is of major importance. The business cycle may occur once, twice, or even more frequently between crises. The depression suffered by the business world during a crisis is severe, while the depression suffered by the business world during the minor dips of the business cycle is usually much less so. That is why economists speak of major and minor depressions.

Panics—When the stock market crashes or some similar event occurs to shake the business world and bring things tumbling down around our heads, the phenomenon is known as a *panic*. It is marked by runs on banks and by the existence of great tension in the money market.

Seasonal Variations—Mention must also be made of the *seasonal variations* in business, which occur annually and which are influenced by holidays, the weather, and temperature. Retail business, for example, is usually very brisk at Christmas time and in the spring months but tends to fall off during the hot summer months. Seasonal variations can be forecast and their effects guarded against, because they come at regular intervals.

The Typical Business Cycle—The typical business cycle consists of just one wave. If we start with business in a depression, we find that it recovers sometimes rapidly, sometimes slowly, and rises to a point of feverish activity. Sooner or later the situation gets beyond control, something breaks, and a recession occurs. Business then drops into a depression. Every period of depression generates within itself certain elements which bring about prosperity, and every period of prosperity likewise generates within itself certain elements which bring about depression. Just what these elements are in each case, it is difficult, if not impossible, to state or to foresee. The existence of these swings in the condition of business is unquestioned. But each business cycle is unlike its predecessors. It may be of longer or of shorter duration. It may be generated by a set of circumstances completely different from that which produced its predecessors. Even after a most careful and detailed investigation and analysis, economists differ as to the causal factors involved in any particular business cycle. We know in general the factors that make for prosperity and those that make for depression, but we are not so sure of our ground when we come to applying these factors in explaining the vagaries of any particular business cycle.

Accident Theories—Many theories have been advanced as to the causes of these alternating periods of prosperity and depression. Some writers maintain that prosperity is the normal state of business and that a depression occurs more or less accidentally. Others claim that depression is the normal state and that prosperity occurs only as the result of some accidental occurrence.

Weather and the Cycle—Another group of writers declares that the business cycle is inevitable and that neither prosperity nor depression is the normal state of affairs. Some members of this group hold that the explanation of the business cycle rests upon certain physical phenomena. Jevons, an English economist, many years ago claimed that there was a close relationship between sunspots and the climatic conditions of the earth which periodically affected crop conditions and thus caused a business cycle of about ten years' duration, owing to the dependence of general business conditions upon agriculture. Professor H. L. Moore of Columbia University has proposed a theory to the effect that rainfall is subject to an eight-year cycle, because of certain movements of the planet Venus. Rainfall affects crops, and crops affect business. Both of these explanations, however, rest upon the assumption that the business cycle is of eight or ten years' duration. This is an erroneous assumption, for since 1885 the duration of the business cycle has, on the average, been only forty months. Again, the dependence of business upon the prosperous condition of agriculture is not particularly evident, especially at the present time. In the United States agriculture has been greatly depressed since 1920, yet during the period from 1921 to 1929 our country experienced a fair degree of prosperity, with some boom years.

Psychology and the Cycle—With most people who are untrained in the field of economics, the explanation of the business cycle which makes the greatest appeal is that based upon the state of mind of the business leaders—in other words, upon psychology. When every one is optimistic and confident about the future, it is said that prosperity smiles upon the business world. But when confidence is lacking, when people for any reason whatsoever become dubious as to the future, depression sets in. Most popular explanations, however, do not really explain. The mental attitude of the business leaders is dependent to a very great degree upon business conditions. Prosperity begets optimism; depression begets pessimism. It is true that as business begins to recover, optimism returns and assists in further recovery, and also that as business starts to decline, pessimism sets in and assists in making conditions worse. But all of us should recognize the fact that prosperity cannot be brought back by having the people sing "Cheer up, good times are coming," or by their continually repeating "Every day in every way, business is getting better and better." Business conditions are based upon something far more substantial than the influence of Old Man Psychology.

Politics and the Cycle—Closely allied with the psychological explanation is the popularly accepted theory that good and bad times are brought about by the party in power. It is claimed that if the wrong political party is elected to office, business leaders will fear the economic and political results and will curtail their activities, thus bringing about hard times. The business cycle, however, is no respecter of the political party that is in power; it goes its way, regardless of whether a republican or a democratic representative is in the White House. This fact is clearly evident from a glance at the past. The depression of 1873 occurred during the administration of Grant (a republican); that of 1884 and that of 1893, under Cleveland (a democrat); that of 1907, under Roosevelt (a republican); that of 1914, under Wilson (a democrat); that of 1920 and 1921, under Wilson and Harding (a democrat and a republican, respectively); those of 1924 and 1927 under Coolidge (a republican); and that of 1929 under Hoover (a republican). This brief summary should provide convincing proof that the business cycle plays no political favorites.

Economic Causes of the Business Cycle—Most of the outstanding students of the business cycle base their explanations of this phenomenon upon economic conditions or causes. There have been many theories advanced, but space can be devoted to presenting only a few that are considered to be the most outstanding in character.

Savings and the Cycle—Some economists claim that depression results from too much saving by the people and by business. If too much thrift is indulged in, savings accumulate in the banks. The fact that these savings are not spent for goods of various kinds constitutes a decrease in the demand for the products of industry. Production then decreases, unemployment becomes widespread, bankruptcies follow, and depression sets in. On the other hand, the opponents of this theory point out that increased savings by individuals and by business enterprises provide more abundant funds and that surplus funds tend to bring about a reduction in interest rates, making it possible for business to be carried on at lower costs and increasing productive activity. Those who have savings, it is pointed out, buy more freely than they otherwise would, knowing that they can fall back upon their savings in times of need. Savings, therefore, so it is claimed, really tend to result in more buying, rather than in less buying.

Overproduction and the Cycle—Another rather popular theory of the business cycle—almost as popular as the psychological and political theories—is that which finds the cause of the business cycle in overproduction. This theory maintains that when, for any reason whatsoever, production outruns consumption, factories have to close their doors, because they cannot find purchasers for their goods, farmers cannot sell their crops at prices that will cover costs, and unemployment, business failures, runs on banks, frozen credits, and all the miseries of the business depression follow in quick succession.

Some economists, however, claim that there can never be a general overproduction of goods and that the condition which is described as overproduction is really one of underconsumption. During hard times, when warehouses are filled with commodities of various sorts, people who want clothing, food, and other articles of consumption cannot make purchases because they have not the funds with which to buy. Some economists go a step farther and maintain that a condition of underconsumption is due to the fact that wage earners are not paid a wage sufficiently high to enable them to buy back the greater portion of the values which they have produced. This state of affairs results in the piling up of goods until employers are compelled to shut down their plants. This explanation was undoubtedly at the base of the campaign carried on during 1929, 1930, and 1931 to induce employers to maintain the existing wage scale of the workers, in order to enable them to purchase more goods than they could have done if wages had been reduced.

Mitchell's Theory of the Cycle—The most widely recognized authority in the field of the business cycle is Professor W. C. Mitchell of Columbia University, who has presented an explanation that is very comprehensive and detailed in character. It has been excellently summarized for the banking profession by the Commerce Monthly (June 1920 issue). This publication was formerly issued by the National Bank of Commerce of New York, which was merged with the Guaranty Trust Company of New York on May 6, 1929. The statement of the Commerce Monthly is so excellent that, with the permission of the Guaranty Trust Company, the following lengthy excerpt is herewith reprinted with a few modifications.

The Cycle—The description may start at any place in the business cycle, and the analysis will work around again through the cycle to the starting point. It is convenient to start with the close of the period of depression.

Conditions during a Depression—At the end of a period of depression we find the following situation: (1) Prices are low; (2) there have been drastic reductions in costs; (3) the margins of profits are narrow; (4) bank reserves are high; (5) conservative policies obtain as to borrowing, capitalization, and loans; (6)

stocks of goods on hand are moderate; (7) buying is cautious. In such a situation an expansion in the physical volume of production and sales takes place, often with prices still falling. During the period of depression, which is coming to a close, people have used up their stocks of clothing and shoes; they have reduced the volume of household furnishings, linen, china, and the like; factories have allowed equipment and stocks of raw materials to get as low as seems wise; and new buying is forced upon every one who is in a position to undertake it. Moreover, a growing volume of conservative business men and investors who had "sold out" on the crest of the preceding wave of prosperity have reached the conclusion that things have about reached bottom, and they are therefore disposed to invest or to start business again. There then comes a slow and cautious expansion in the physical volume of trade. Slow at first, this process is cumulative, and it gradually turns slow business into active business. The revival may start in a narrow field, but necessarily it spreads to other fields, because the active concerns will have more spending power, a condition which leads them to increase their buying from other enterprises. The active concerns, moreover, employ more labor, with a resultant increase in the spending power of laborers and in the demand for goods. Increased retail demand leads to increased demand on jobbers and wholesalers, who pass it on to manufacturers, who take on more laborers, who increase their retail buying. The quickening of industries reacts on the starting point, which in turn is quickened and gives renewed impetus to other fields.

Psychological Change—There comes, moreover, a psychological change. The "temper of business" is not a thing which is made by men as separate individuals. Rather, it is a social product. The man who finds business in his own line expanding becomes an optimist with regard to business at large. He talks with other men. They, even though they have not had increased orders for their own goods, begin to be influenced by his optimism. The process is partly rational and partly non-rational. The mere fact that men find their neighbors more cheerful influences them unconsciously, even in the face of facts. On the other hand, the man who has been delaying an increase in his own business activity may well find a valid ground for taking positive action if he finds increasing confidence among those about him. The temper of business, an intangible and a psychological thing, is, none the less, one of the most fundamental realities with which business men must reckon. No business man can run counter to a general feeling of despondency, even though he is sure that it is ill grounded, without incurring risk of loss. On the other hand, a business man may well find it worth while to "swim with the tide" of business optimism for a short time at least, even though he is sure that it is ill grounded. In the business world there are a few strong figures that can stand out against the prevalent optimism or pessimism, little influenced by it, and profit by running counter to it, but to do so requires a long purse, a clear head, and unusual courage.

Price Changes—The price level is often slowly falling when the revival begins, but the expansion of trade stops this, for when business men have plenty of orders they stand out for higher prices. Moreover, when prices start to rise, the expectation of higher prices makes buyers increasingly eager. The rise of prices, like the volume of trade, spreads rapidly through all fields. The advance in prices in one establishment puts pressure on some one else to recoup himself.

The rise of prices is uneven. Retail prices lag behind wholesale prices. Consumers' goods lag behind producers' goods. Finished products lag behind raw materials. Retail prices are influenced a good deal by custom. Moreover, the retailer's total costs do not increase as fast as the wholesale prices he has to pay. His overhead charges do not increase as fast as wholesale prices do, and even if he adds all the increases of the wholesale prices to the retail prices, the percentage increase in retail prices is not so great as the percentage increase in wholesale prices.

Unspecialized raw materials, like pig iron, tend to rise faster than finished products, like knives, because they respond more quickly to demand from many quarters, increasing demand not only for knives but also for steel rails, for wire fencing, for tin plate, and for many other things.

Wages often rise more promptly than wholesale prices, but in general the increase is much less. Wages are much more influenced by custom than are wholesale prices. Discount rates rise sometimes faster and sometimes more slowly than wholesale prices. Interest rates on long time loans move slowly in the early stages of the revival. The prices of stocks, especially common stocks, advance before the rise in wholesale prices and go much higher than wholesale prices.

The unequal rise in prices in the great majority of cases means a great increase in profits in the revival period, since most of the elements of cost rise more slowly than wholesale prices. Raw materials, and sometimes bank rates, rise faster than finished goods, but wages lag behind, while supplementary costs or overhead charges are commonly fixed by old agreements covering rentals on leases, salaries, and interest on bonds.

The increase of profits and the prevalence of optimism lead to a great increase in investment. This means more orders and higher prices for structural steel, other building materials, machinery, and so forth.

These factors are cumulative. The rise in prices at one point, increasing the incomes of those engaged in a given industry, increases their ability to buy, which stimulates others, and so on.

Why should not this process continue indefinitely? What is there to bring prosperity to a close? The answer is to be found in several facts.

Mistakes Made—For one thing, business mistakes are made. Heavy investments are made in enterprises which either fail to return profits altogether or else fail to return them on the scale expected. The crisis of 1873, for example, largely grew out of an overbuilding of transcontinental railroads, which ran so far in advance of the increase in population that they were unable even to earn interest on their bonds. In some measure, overextensions in particular lines occur in every period of prosperity, with the result that profits fail to materialize and even fixed charges fail to be earned. Business optimism tends to run beyond reasonable limits. Speculative imaginings take the place of careful calculation.

Costs Increase—In the second place, even though business plans be soundly laid at the beginning of a period of prosperity, taking into account the prices and costs that prevail at that time, the very prosperity itself may so alter the data on which the plans as to construction and other costs were made as to upset the plans and make it necessary for the enterprise to call a halt, take stock, and readjust. Finally, throughout the business field, as the period of prosperity goes on, there is a tendency for costs generally to rise at a very rapid rate.

During the early part of the prosperity period, supplementary costs, or overhead charges, tend to decline per unit of output until existing plants are fully employed. When, however, production necessitates an increase in plant, the overhead charges increase more rapidly than the output. Leases and other contracts expire, moreover, and have to be renewed at much higher rentals. Bond issues at low rates of interest mature, and, especially toward the end of the prosperity period, renewals can be made only at much higher rates. It regularly happens that strong corporations, toward the end of a boom, will defer the refunding of maturities and issue short term notes, expecting after a year or two to be able to refund them into long time issues at lower rates. The pressure on the capital market grows more and more intense as prosperity increases. Prosperity breeds extravagant consumption, and extravagant consumers save less for investment. Even those who regularly save for investment find it increasingly difficult to do so as the cost of living rises. The end of a period of prosperity is almost always characterized by high interest rates on investments and by a great scarcity of new money for long time investment.

Short term money rates and the rates on commercial paper rise, making it more expensive for the wholesaler to carry his inventories and for the manufacturer to carry his materials and the articles in process of being produced.

Labor in Prosperity—Other costs increase rapidly. Old plants and poorly located plants are brought into use as the better plants, which alone were worked in the period of depression, are fully utilized. The output of these old and poorly located plants is turned out at a higher cost. Labor cost rises perhaps most of all. This is due not only to the increase of wages: it is due partly to overtime work, which involves higher rates of payment and diminished productiveness of labor. Laborers cannot engage in overtime work week after week and month after month without reducing their efficiency. Employers, seeking to enlarge their labor force, are obliged to take on undesirable individuals who would not be employed in a depression period. Perhaps most important of all, shop discipline is relaxed in a prosperity period. Laborers who are sure that they can get a job across the street for the asking cannot be held to their tasks in a period of prosperity as they can in a period of depression. On this point both laborers and manufacturers seem agreed. Laborers complain of "speeding up" in a time of depression, and manufacturers complain of "loafing on the job" in a period of prosperity.

Managerial efficiency is lessened as the pressure of prosperity increases. Managers cannot watch the business so closely. Small wastes multiply and rush orders make for confusion. Moreover, the pressure which working on small margins involves is removed.

Decline in Profits—The very prosperity of most businesses imposes serious burdens on those types of enterprise which are least able to raise their prices or to increase their markets. Where prices are fixed by law or by public commissions, as in the case of municipal utilities or railways, a prolonged period of prosperity is likely to increase costs seriously at the expense of profits. Businesses tied up with long time contracts are similarly placed. Moreover, there are always lines in which recent construction has grown faster than the market. Maladjustments increase. High rates of interest not only check current demand for goods of various kinds but also make it difficult for speculators to hold them off the market.

Consequently, at the height of a period of prosperity, an important minority faces declining and vanishing profits. The decline of profits means the doubtful solvency of many outstanding credits. In such a situation it is only a question of time until readjustment and liquidation are forced. Creditors begin to get nervous. The very rise in interest rates tends to reduce the value of investment securities which have been used as the basis of collateral loans—a phenomenon well known in the bond market. The basis of all credit is, in the last analysis, earning power, and with the actual or prospective decline in the profits of a business, its creditors, whether banks or other businesses, tend to demand additional security or to insist on contraction of credit. When profits get shaky, creditors get still more nervous and force liquidation. A crisis comes. The liquidation extends over the whole field. If a debtor is pressed he is obliged to press his own debtors. The pressure may take the form of offering extra inducements for prompt settlement, as when a seller offers a buyer more than the customary 2% discount for cash. It may take many other forms. If one man succeeds in meeting the pressure upon himself, he does so at the expense of others whom he embarrasses. A sudden change takes place in the temper of business. For many business men the question of profit making gives place to the question of maintaining solvency. Business men quit pushing sales vigorously, especially when doubtful of the credit of buyers. There comes a rapid falling off in the volume of business. Even when few failures occur, the temper of business changes. Pessimism replaces optimism—sometimes almost over night.

Panic—If banks fail to pay their depositors on demand and if they contract loans (or fail to expand loans), a panic comes. This has happened in America a number of times, notably in 1893 and 1907. It did not happen in England, Germany, and France in those years because of the better organization of the banking systems of those countries. There is little chance of panic when depositors can get their money on demand and when solvent business men can borrow the amounts necessary to meet their pressing obligations.

If a panic comes, a great many plants are temporarily shut down. With the passing of the panic these plants are reopened, and there comes a short lived revival. This short lived revival is brought about chiefly by the desire to finish orders for delivery to solvent firms which do not desire to buy the goods but which are obliged, under their contracts, to take them. New orders do not follow, however, and a period of real depression sets in. In this period, consumers' demand falls off as labor is discharged and as profits fail to appear. Investors' demand for construction falls off most sharply of all. These tendencies are cumulative, just as the reverse tendencies in the period of prosperity are cumulative. The falling off of orders in one business reacts on the other businesses which sell to it. Prices fall. Wholesale prices fall faster than retail prices. Prices of raw materials fall faster than those of finished products. Wages do not fall so fast, but they fall. Common stocks fall faster and farther than anything else. High grade bonds, on the other hand, tend to rise as investors turn to the safest forms of investment and as the pressure on the capital market is relaxed. The depression lasts until liquidation is completed. Inefficient firms are weeded out. Costs go down. A reorganization of leases and of bond issues brings down rentals and other fixed charges. Interest falls. Bank rates decline. Bank reserves increase. Labor costs decrease. This is partly because wages decline, partly because overtime work ceases, partly because shop discipline improves, and partly because the least efficient laborers are unemployed.

Depression—We are thus brought back to the point at which we started, the point at which a revival is due. As the depression period continues, clothing, materials, structures, machinery, and so forth wear out. Population continues to grow, bargain sales of the equipment of defunct enterprises cease, and new things finally have to be bought. The men who have been waiting for "bottom" to be reached decide that the time for action has come. At low prices business begins to increase, and the cycle of prosperity, crisis, and depression starts again.

Banking Policy in a Crisis—When the banking and currency system is sound and elastic, it is almost always possible to prevent a crisis from degenerating into a panic. It is no part of the duty of the banks in a crisis period to force, by artificial methods, a continuance of waning prosperity. It is not their duty to provide funds for expansion of new enterprises at the high costs which the end of a prosperity period involves. It is not their duty to encourage customers to borrow for the expansion of established businesses. Banks will rather seek to persuade their strongest customers to curtail borrowings in the interests of the general situation and may even seek to persuade them to make loans to help relieve the situation. But banks will lend freely to enable solvent firms to meet their quick liabilities. It is their business to protect solvent firms but not to protect insolvent firms. It is their business to assist solvent firms to mobilize slow assets, but it is not their business to validate bad assets of insolvent firms. They may sometimes find it necessary to protect a firm which is largely but not wholly good for its liabilities, in order to prevent the throwing of its assets on a demoralized market, which would occasion severe losses to its solvent creditors. The banking community will be especially disposed to come to the rescue of temporarily embarrassed banks if such should appear.

Value of Depression—The significance of a crisis is that the business community pauses to take stock. The crisis is a time when weak spots are tested, when unsound policies are reversed. If a crisis and depression are to be followed by a period of soundly based prosperity, it is necessary that the cleansing be thorough and that really insolvent businesses be reorganized. The difference between a crisis and a panic is that in a panic solvent businesses may be pulled down and new weaknesses created. The banking community has done its full duty to the business community if it prevents a crisis from degenerating into a panic.

Federal Reserve System and Panics—The Federal Reserve System, under which Federal Reserve notes can be freely issued against the rediscount of commercial paper and under which the legal reserve ratio can be suspended in emergencies by the Federal Reserve Board, would seem to eliminate all danger that an actual shortage of hand-to-hand currency would embarrass our banks in crises in the future. Bank reserves, under the Federal Reserve System, consist of deposits with the Federal Reserve banks, which can be replenished by rediscount of commercial paper or paper secured by obligations of the United States Government at need; and hand-to-hand cash, which banks may pay out to depositors, can be increased at need by obtaining Federal Reserve notes through the same process. No currency and banking system can prevent the recurrence of crises in the sense of liquidation periods, or periods of readjustment, but we have strong grounds for confidence that under wise financial leadership our currency and banking system has made us panic proof.

Business Barometers—Business executives are interested in ascertaining the current condition of business and also in forecasting its possible future trend. There are available many indices of current business conditions, some of which apply to business in general throughout the country and some only to particular industries. The latter are very accurately compiled and have been of great assistance to business executives in enabling them to plan their activities in a very satisfactory manner. It is also possible to compile a satisfactory index showing the condition of related businesses. But no index has as yet been devised that can disclose the condition existing in all industries at any definite time, because all enterprises do not enjoy prosperity or suffer from depression simultaneously or to the same extent. In fact, it is quite possible to have one particular industry at relatively high activity, while at the same time the curve of general business activity may be relatively low.

Possibly of more concern as an aid in assisting executives to outline their future programs is the question of the trend of the business cycle. It is theoretically possible to forecast what conditions in the business world will be a month, a half-year, or a year hence. Various attempts in this direction have been made, but with no great degree of success. A number of forecasting bureaus sell their services to subscribers, and many executives place unwarranted confidence in them. Some of these services forecast conditions for the entire United States. This on its face is a questionable procedure, because conditions throughout the country are never uniform. California, for example, may be enjoying prosperity at the same time that Maine is suffering from depression. Some forecasting bureaus confine their efforts to prophesying the future of business in a district or in a small section of the country. The latter, theoretically, is the better plan of the two, but it has not brought us any more satisfactory results than has the attempt to forecast business conditions for the nation as a whole.

Business is so complex that it has not yet been reduced to a formula or to a set of index numbers. It is affected by local, national, and international conditions, by weather, plagues, insect pests, floods, wars, and numerous other matters that do not announce their coming in advance.

Future of the Business Cycle—Constructive efforts are being made, however, to minimize the effects of depression and to shorten its duration. Business executives now watch their markets, their costs, and the price level, as never before. They study conditions in their own field and in other fields as well. Big business has aided greatly in bringing about the curtailment of competition and the removal of many of its more serious results. It has made possible the accumulation of huge reserves or surpluses upon which to fall back in case of need and has thus reduced the possibility of failure. Most of the insolvencies among banking, industrial, and mercantile enterprises occur among the smaller concerns, which are handicapped by inadequate reserve funds.

The government also has assisted by making available much helpful information relative to business matters and business conditions. The publications of the Department of Commerce, the Federal Reserve Board, and other government bodies have been of great assistance to business executives in providing them with data concerning conditions in this country and in other countries. Colleges and universities, business and financial magazines, high grade metropolitan newspapers, and Federal Reserve banks are continually publishing the results of economic research and are thus enabling business executives to chart safer courses.

The reader is urged to take advantage of such publications and items in order to arrive at a better understanding of the problems that are involved in this study of the business cycle and the attempts that are being made to solve them.

Control of the Business Cycle—In discussing the possibility of controlling the business cycle, the Commerce Monthly of June 1920 makes the following comment which is both interesting and informative to students of economics:

The most important proposal that has yet been made for the mitigation of the extremes of the business cycle is that the various grades of government—federal, state, and municipal—together with large corporations like the railroads, should adopt a buying policy which would enable them to enter the market as much as possible in a period of depression and to withdraw from the market to a considerable extent at the height of a period of prosperity. A railroad, for example, which can so adjust its affairs as to increase its purchases of rails, freight cars, and the like in relatively dull times and to reduce its purchases of rails and freight cars when the strain of productive capacity is greatest, would itself profit by the process and would lessen the extremes of prosperity and depression for general business. This policy is sometimes difficult, since the credit of the railroads is apt to be better in prosperous than in dull times, but it is perfectly feasible for the various grades of government, and especially for the Federal Government, to work out far reaching plans covering a very substantial part of their buying.

As yet this policy has been very little applied by the governments. Some railroads have been able to do it. Government activity, however, has taken the form chiefly of emergency works in periods of depression, notably municipal woodyards and the like. These devices may relieve acute unemployment but do little to start a revival of business activity. It is better that the governments should make orderly plans stretching over a series of years and that they should make their expenditures through the ordinary channels of trade rather than through emergency organizations of their own.

We have already seen how sound bank policy can, and does, prevent crises from degenerating into panics. Banks can, and do, moreover, by careful scrutiny of credits, prevent the expansion of credit, both by themselves and by their customers, on the basis of unsound assets and limit the development of dangerous weak spots at all stages of the business cycle. The banks, which are in touch with all kinds of businesses and which consequently have information concerning general business conditions available to few merchants or manufacturers, can give advice and information of a valuable sort to customers. The steadying influence of contact with many diverse kinds of business makes the banker less optimistic than many of his customers in times of boom and more optimistic than many of his customers in times of strain, crisis, or depression. He exercises, therefore, a steadying influence on the temper of business, which tends to modify the extremes, both of enthusiasm and of gloom. It rarely happens that business is wholly bad or that it is wholly good. In the worst crisis and depression there is a large volume of ordinary business going on. At the time when business generally is most prosperous, there are always unsatisfactory elements in the situation. Business never goes wholly "to the dogs," and it is never free from some uncertainties and dangers.

Control by Business Executives—There has come, too, a general knowledge on the part of business men that there are variations in prosperity and that periods of reaction, crisis, and liquidation sooner or later may be anticipated. The older business men, who have lived through the troubled times of 1893 and 1907, are apt to recognize this more fully than the younger business men, to whom periods of trouble are matters of tradition. But there are few managers of important industries who are not on the lookout for various signs which indicate whether business is to wax or to wane and who do not in good times seek to make provision for the pressure of bad times.

Conclusion—In spite of all that has been done and all that has been suggested, it is too much to expect that our complicated economic world can be so organized or controlled as to abolish completely the business cycle. We may be able to eliminate some of its high peaks and some of its low valleys, but we can never hope, under the present economic system, to stabilize business upon a perfectly even plane. Some economists have expressed the opinion that it is possible so to arrange our economic activities that future business cycles may be made less pronounced both as to their intensity and as to their duration.

CHAPTER XX

Public Receipts and Expenditures

THE preceding chapters have dealt with the income and expenditures of individuals and business enterprises, or, in other words, with the field of private finance. Still another phase of economics remains to be considered, namely, that of public finance, which is concerned with the income and expenditures of the federal and state governments and their subdivisions.

The government, whether it be national, state, or city, is a form of business enterprise; and if it is a republican or a democratic form of government, theoretically it is controlled by its citizens, for the conservation and furtherance of whose interests it performs many different functions. It has to possess an income out of which to meet expenses. This income is obtained from many sources, such as, for example, taxes, bond issues, fines, gifts, the operation of certain kinds of business, and the sale of property (such as public lands). The expenditures which it makes are for education, the protection of person and property, sanitation, roads, waterways, the post office system, and so forth.

Public versus Private Enterprise—In carrying on its activities, the government follows ideals that differ greatly from those of private enterprises. It is concerned primarily, though not solely, with rendering non-material satisfactions to its people and with doing things for them that are of an intangible character and cannot be estimated in terms of money—such as securing and maintaining peace, independence, justice, intellectual development, public health, and, within certain limits, freedom of thought, speech, press, and action, all of which may be briefly summarized by the phrase "general welfare." It does not guarantee to its taxpayers that they will receive a definite amount of education, health, or protection in proportion to the taxes that they pay. When private business provides the public with goods and services at a price which it hopes will yield a profit, it is concerned primarily with its own welfare. It demands a definite payment for a definite amount of goods and services. It measures the value of its product in terms of money. The government is not interested in quick returns from the expenditure of its funds. It builds for future generations. Private business must play for quick returns on its investment, because its owners depend on its earnings for their money income. The citizens of a country generally do not in their turn depend directly on the expenditures of the government for their money incomes. Private business has to gauge its expenditures by its receipts, actual or expected, but the government decides what it wants to do and then arranges its revenue system to yield the desired income.

The Increase of Public Expenditures—The expenditures of the various subdivisions of the governmental structure have increased at a surprising rate during the past century, until today the aggregate is almost beyond human appreciation. This has been due, first, to war and militarism and, second, to an increased socialization of consumption. At present both the European countries and the United States represent huge war camps. President Hoover, in his first message to Congress in 1929, said, "While the remuneration paid to our soldiers and sailors is justly at a higher rate than that of any other country of the world, and while the cost of subsistence is higher, yet the total of our expenditure is in excess of those of the most highly militarized nations of the world." The extent to which the costs of past wars and of our present war machine dominate federal expenditures is disclosed by the following table:

TOTAL NET EXPENDITURES—1920

(Not including loans and trust funds)

Percentage Distribution of Expenditures

Primary Government Functions		3.9
Research, Education, Development		1.0
Public Works—New Construction		1.5
Army and Navy	23.7	
Pensions	5.8	
Interest	16.3	93.6
Debt Reduction	19.1	
Recent War Obligations	28.7	
Total		100.0

In 1920 expenditures for the primary functions of our Federal Government (the legislative, executive, and judicial branches) constituted but 3.9% of the total; research, education, and development 1%; and new public construction 1.5%. Over 93% of the expenditures of the Federal Government in that year was made for military purposes. Professor C. J. Bullock of Harvard University, in commenting upon this apportionment of federal expenditures, remarked, "Thus it appears that our Federal Government is, on the financial side, mainly a huge machine for collecting taxes in order to defray the direct and indirect costs of war." If it were possible to eliminate war and the preparations for war, the burden of taxation upon the people would be greatly decreased, and the things for which the government spends its income would be strangely different from what they have been in the past.

The increased socialization of consumption also has accounted in part for the growth of the expenditures of the Federal Government and especially of the expenditures of our states, cities, and school districts. Instead of depending on private enterprise, we look to the government to do an increasingly greater number of things for us. The Federal Government must aid in locating foreign markets for our goods. It must assist in marketing goods at home. It establishes and supports the Interstate Commerce Commission, the Federal Trade Commission, the Federal Farm Board, and scores of other commissions as aids to industry, agriculture, and other branches of business. It finances the United States Department of Labor for the welfare of the working class and the Department of Agriculture for the welfare of the farmers. Appropriations for roads and schools and for welfare work of various kinds are demanded and obtained from it.

State legislatures likewise are called upon to set aside huge sums of money for labor commissions, banking commissions, highway commissions, workmen's compensation boards, boxing commissions, housing and immigration commissions, and many similar regulatory bodies, as well as for state universities.

The Expenditures of Cities—The rapid increase in the expenditures of city governments has startled many observers in the field of public finance. Professor Everett Kimball has made the following statement:

"During the last half of the nineteenth century municipal expenditures increased with startling rapidity, and during the two decades of the twentieth century not only the aggregate grew large, but the rate of increase was higher. Thus, from 1860 to 1890 the population doubled and the estimated value of property increased fourfold, but the total state and local taxation was five times greater. Since 1900 the city expenditures have been growing nearly three times as fast as the urban population and faster even than the increased valuation of the municipal property, rapid and great as this has been.

"Between 1903 and 1919 the general departmental expenses of cities having a population of 30,000 more than doubled. The reasons for this are not hard to see. Obviously there was a general increase in wages and salaries. In the second place, the cities were continuing to grow in size at a phenomenally rapid rate. It becomes always more expensive to protect and to serve the inhabitants of a city when the population increases beyond a certain size. Finally, what was probably the most important and controlling factor in this rapidly growing rate of expenditure was the added demands for public service and improvements which were made upon the city. Better pavements, better lighting, purer water, and more efficient schools were all demanded and must be paid for. Not only were these improvements in kind demanded, but the cities were expected to enter new fields of municipal service. The result was startling. The cost of general government more than doubled between 1903 and 1919. The expenses of the fire department were almost twice as much. The cost of health conservation and the police department has increased more than threefold. The outlay for sanitation has more than doubled, as has the amount appropriated for charities, hospitals, and corrections. The cost of the city schools has increased from $80,000,000 to more than $216,000,000; the amount spent on recreation from $7,000,000 to more than $24,000,000; the amount on pensions and gratuities from $3,000,000 to $18,000,000, or more than four times as much as in 1903. In 1919 the cost per capita for the cities having a population of more than 30,000 was $21.75."

Theories of Expenditures for Public Good—The preceding discussion has pointed out that the different branches of the government have assumed a larger responsibility than ever before and have undertaken to render increasing service to the people. How far is this to continue? It is difficult to lay down definite rules limiting the extent to which governments are justified in expanding their functions. However, the three following principles of expenditure may be suggested:

1. All public expenditures must be for the good of society and not in the interests of any individual.

2. The state government should not take over enterprises for the public good if individual enterprises could and would accomplish the same end. The burden of proof should always rest upon the state government to show that in assuming responsibilities it is prepared to promote the greatest good of the greatest number and that private enterprise could not do this. It is difficult to prove such a contention, however, for governments are organized for political purposes rather than for business. Government enterprises, such as railroads, mines, and factories, have frequently been operated at a loss, even though the intention was to show a profit.

3. The fundamental object of the activity of the government is not to make money but to increase social welfare, although history records instances in which governments have produced revenue at the expense of the public good. The government may even be justified in carrying on activities at a loss provided social welfare is increased.

Sources of Government Income—The various branches of the government obtain the funds out of which to pay their expenses from two main sources: (1) from an issue of bonds or other forms of promises to pay and (2) from their revenues, that is, payments made to them by others. Sales of property (mostly public lands) have at no time provided an important source of revenue. During the first century of our country's existence, the income received therefrom amounted to less than 2½% of the total receipts of the National Government.

At times a government obtains a portion of its income from its power to issue money. During the Civil War, for example, the United States was short of funds, and in order to make the necessary payments it placed about $450,000,000 of irredeemable paper money (called greenbacks) in circulation. Originally there was no security whatsoever behind this large amount of greenbacks—nothing but the promise of the government to pay at some time or other. It was not until 1879 that the government was willing to redeem this paper money on demand in gold. At present the greenbacks are secured by gold to the extent of only about 45%, the remainder representing a gain to the government.

A similar situation exists in connection with the issue of silver half dollars, quarter dollars, and dimes. The United States Government pays them out to the public at their face value, yet they do not contain an amount of silver equal to their face value. With the price of silver what it was in February 1931, it was possible for the United States Mint to take about twenty cents worth of silver and mint it into two half dollars, or four quarters, or ten dimes, thus yielding the government a gain of approximately eighty cents on every dollar's worth of silver coins minted.

Bonds—The nation, state, city, county, and various political subdivisions of the government have constantly borrowed from the public through the sale of bonds, which usually run for fairly long periods of time.

Occasionally bonds have been issued without there being any date set for redemption or payment. Bonds are sold to obtain funds for the payment of old debts, to provide for war needs, to finance a construction program, and to do other things which it is thought cannot be accomplished advantageously by taxation.

Treasury Certificates—Frequently the National Government resorts to an issue of United States Treasury certificates of indebtedness in order to obtain funds in anticipation of the receipt of other income. Such securities are short term civil promissory notes or debentures running usually for a few months and are issued during both war and peace times. In times of special emergency, the certificates may run for longer periods than in normal times. Frequently treasury certificates are issued in series, so that certain numbers of them will come due on successive dates. In the United States during the World War, treasury certificates were sold in large quantities to the banks to be redeemed when the funds from the sale of liberty bonds had been received.

Tax Warrants—States, counties, school districts, political subdivisions, municipalities, and irrigation, drainage, and reclamation districts occasionally find that their expenses have temporarily outrun their income from taxation sources. In order to obtain the funds with which to meet current expenses while waiting for the tax money to materialize, they frequently resort to an issue of obligations called tax warrants.

Public Revenues

Classification of Public Revenues—Professor Seligman, in his Essays on Taxation, presents the following classification of public revenues:

Revenues
- Gratuitous .... Gifts
- Contractual ... Public Property and Industry ... Prices
- Compulsory
  - Eminent Domain .... Expropriation
  - Penal Power .... Fines and Penalties
  - Taxing Power .... Fees / Special Assessments / Taxes

Gratuitous Revenues—The gratuitous class of government revenues requires little comment, for modern governments receive very little revenue from gifts, although local governments sometimes receive gifts for hospitals, asylums for the blind, and so forth.

Contractual Revenues—Contractual revenues are received when the state owns property or carries on forms of industry. In such cases the state is the seller of land, goods, or services, for which it receives a price. This price is a special payment for a special commodity or service and is voluntarily paid by the purchaser.

Compulsory Revenues—The third class of revenues includes those payments which are made by the subjects of the state under compulsion. The right of eminent domain is still practised when a government wishes to acquire property for a public purpose. The most common example of the exercise of this right is found in the acquisition of land to be used as the right of way for lines of transportation, to be turned into public parks, to be employed in improving public health conditions.

The second class of compulsory revenues is that collected by the government by virtue of its penal power. For centuries rulers have increased their revenues by imposing fines and penalties upon those who break the law. The primary object is to punish the evil doer rather than to acquire revenue, but a considerable amount is received each year from this source.

The taxing power is by far the most important source of revenue for the state. Governments claim the right to tax their subjects. If the subject wishes to continue to reside or to carry on business within the boundaries of the state, he must contribute toward the support of the government.

The Benefit Theory of Taxation—According to the benefit theory of taxation, the individual is taxed, theoretically at least, in proportion to the benefit which he receives from the government. The large landholder pays more taxes than does the smaller landholder, because the government protects more property for him than for his less wealthy neighbor. While the benefit theory is no longer the chief justification for taxation, yet certain kinds of revenue are still collected on this basis. For example, when a new road is built, the owners of property along the road are assessed either for a part or for all of the cost, because they receive a benefit greater than others who do not live near the road.

Today the forms of property are so varied, the disparity of wealth and income so great, and the undertakings of the state so enormous that it is impossible to claim justice in taxation according to the benefit theory. A poor family which is unable to care for itself often costs the state much more than a rich family. A poor man with seven children, all of whom are educated in the public schools, is likely to cost the state more than a wealthy bachelor. According to the benefit theory, the poor man ought to contribute more revenue to the government than the rich man, but the poor man is not able to make any payment whatsoever.

The Ability to Pay Theory—The ability to pay theory of taxation holds that we should contribute to the government as we are able. The statesmen of leading nations do not hesitate to declare to the rich, "You are required to contribute more because you have more and are better able to contribute than are those who have less." Taxation according to ability introduces a social point of view. The benefit theory expresses a relationship between the state and the individual in which the taxpayer contributes to the government in proportion as the government serves him. The ability theory makes no pretense of conferring something on the taxpayer in return for his taxes; the taxpayer pays in proportion to his wealth for the welfare of society.

Different Forms of the Taxing Power—In modern states the taxing power is expressed in three different forms—fees, special assessments, and taxes. The distinction among these three forms of the taxing power is made on the basis of the degree of public purpose involved and the degree of special benefit assumed in requiring the citizen to make a contribution.

1. Fees. A fee is charged for a service which is undertaken by a government primarily for the public good, but which at the same time confers some special benefit upon the individual who makes the payment. A fee may cover all or a part of the cost, but it may not yield a profit; any charge above the cost constitutes a tax. For example, in maintaining an office for the registration of mortgages the government confers a service upon the general public, but when such registration occurs, it charges the individual who registers the mortgage a fee, because he is receiving a special benefit. Payment for a marriage license is in reality a fee, because it fulfils the conditions suggested above. Other forms of fees are payments for automobile licenses, charter fees for corporations, fees for business licenses, and court fees.

2. Special Assessments. Special assessments are limited to charges made by the state for the improvement of property, and as far as public purpose and special benefit are concerned, these assessments closely resemble the fee. The important difference between the two is that the special assessment involves a greater public purpose and less special benefit than the fee. Special assessments are levied when the government undertakes public improvements which render a great degree of social utility and at the same time confer some degree of special benefit. The building of roads, the laying of sewers, the paving of streets, and the laying of water

mains are usually paid for by levying special assessments on the property holders who are benefited. The levy made by the government is in proportion to the particular benefit that accrues to the owner of the property.

3. Taxes. A tax has no reference whatsoever to any special benefits conferred; it is levied upon the taxpayer to pay the costs of those services undertaken by the government in the common interest of all.

As we proceed from the discussion of the fee to that of the special assessment and the tax, the element of compulsion becomes more evident. The individual may avoid payment of a fee by refraining from calling upon the government to render him a service, although if he is to live the life of a normal citizen, he will find this rather difficult. He may avoid the payment of special assessments by refraining from owning property, but the fact remains that he cannot avoid paying taxes in one form or another, either direct or indirect, no matter where he may live. A tax, therefore, is more completely a compulsory contribution than is a fee or a special assessment. Not only is the element of compulsion greater, but the government makes no promise to render a special service in return.

The Importance of Taxation as a Source of Revenue—Taxation is the most important form of federal revenue. Taxes may be levied upon the individual or upon property, whether tangible or intangible, or upon the transfer of property. Taxes may be levied upon goods when they are produced, sold, or consumed.

Equality in Taxation—So far as possible, taxes should be levied with the idea of having the burden rest uniformly upon all citizens. It is impossible to have absolute equality, but by levying taxes in accordance with the ability to pay theory, the burden can be distributed in proportion to the wealth and income of the taxpayers. The problem of equality in taxation is made extremely difficult, because in many cases the tax, when once levied, is shifted to another party who actually pays it in the form of increased prices.

Universality in Taxation—Every citizen should be called upon to pay something to the state, no matter how poor he may be. This rule is especially applicable to a democracy. Men are interested in those enterprises in which they have something invested. The essence of democracy is that all the citizens shall be interested in the state. It is necessary, therefore, in perfecting a just and satisfactory system of taxation, to find some form of assessment which will fall upon all citizens but which will, at the same time, not increase the burden already resting upon the poor. In order to achieve this moral effect of having each citizen feel that he is a contributor toward the support of his government, the tax should be so levied that the taxpayer will be aware that he is bearing a share of the expenses of the government.

Direct taxes are more desirable for this purpose than indirect taxes. A *direct* tax is one that is imposed with the intention that the original taxpayer cannot pass it on to another person. An *indirect* tax is one that is levied with the assumption that it will be shifted to some person other than the one originally taxed. A poll tax, that is, a tax of a fixed amount levied upon each adult male, has been used in many countries to accomplish the purpose in question, for in this case every adult male is made to feel that he is contributing to the support of the government. An indirect tax on consumption goods frequently does not satisfy this requirement, because the tax is shifted and the consumer who buys the goods pays the tax in the form of higher prices without knowing that he is doing so.

The Principle of Elasticity of Taxes—A good tax system should be elastic, in that it should provide for a sudden expansion or contraction of its revenues. The government is often called upon to meet emergencies in times of war, of flood, of famine, or of epidemic. The tax system of a nation should be so constructed that revenues can be increased without greatly affecting the system itself. The revenue system should also lend itself to sudden contraction if necessary, for history has shown that it is as disastrous to have too much revenue as to have too little. When the United States Government has had more revenue than it needed, it has sometimes been led into expenditures which were unwise and unjustifiable. Before the adoption of the income tax law the Federal Government obtained its revenue from customs duties, internal revenue, sales of public lands, and other miscellaneous items, practically all of which were inelastic, in that they could not be regulated to meet the variations in annual expenditures. The income tax has increased the elasticity of the federal tax system, in that the revenues can be increased or decreased by adjusting the rates of taxation levied on the different classes of income.

The Rates of Taxation—Tax rates are proportional or progressive. If the rate is proportional, it does not change, whether the wealth or income of the taxpayer is large or small. Rich people would, of course, pay more than poor people if taxed according to a proportional rate. If A has an income of $100,000 and B an income of $1,000 and the tax rate is 5% of the income, then A would pay $5,000, while B would pay only $50. The rate has remained the same, although the amounts subject to taxation are different. This is an example of proportional taxation. Manifestly this form of taxation is inequitable, because A with an income of $100,000 can pay a tax of $5,000 much more easily than B with an income of $1,000 can pay even the smaller tax of $50.

On the other hand, progressive rates of taxation are disproportionate, since the rate of taxation is higher for the taxpayer who has much wealth or income than for one who has less. To refer again to the illustration of A and B, A with an income of $100,000 might be taxed at the rate of 10%, while B with an income of $1,000 might be taxed at the rate of 1%. This arrangement would probably prove to be more equitable than proportional taxation. Under progressive taxation the rate increases directly with increases in the taxable base. Practically all the civilized nations of the world now use progressive rates of taxation.

Single Tax versus Multiple Tax—Some writers have urged the advisability of levying a single tax, a tax on only one object, and the abolition of all other forms of taxation. A single tax on income, on the unearned increment of land, on land values, on houses, or on capital has been proposed at various times. The single tax has been opposed by eminent tax authorities on several grounds, but primarily because it would not meet the requirements of the government for revenue. The government at times has to resort to taxation for the purpose of encouraging or discouraging an industry. The power to tax is the power to destroy. In 1866 the Federal Government levied a 10% tax on state bank notes for the purpose of removing certain abuses in the economic world. A tax system should be capable of increasing or decreasing the revenues of the government to meet changing situations. Several of the single tax proposals fail to provide for such expansion and contraction in the amount of government revenues. In a democratic or a republican state every citizen should be forced to bear a portion of the burden of the government. A single tax would place the burden only on the few and would exempt the majority.

Because of the difficulties involved in each form of single tax, the multiple system of taxation is universally used. Among its many advantages are the following:

1. It is easier to reach all the subjects of a government, because, if one tax does not fall on a certain class of people, another tax will. This tends to increase not only the revenue of the state but also the feeling of responsibility of the people for the state.

2. It is much easier to obtain elasticity through the multiple system. At least one form of tax can be used to take up the slack; that is, its rates can be expanded or contracted as the situation demands.

3. The economic system of today is dynamic and not static. Changes are continually taking place either in the size of the industrial units, in their methods of organization, or in the forms in which their assets are held. Business and industry are ever growing more complex. It is impossible to cope with these changes and complexities of our modern economic life without the use of a number of different kinds of taxes.

4. Special assessments are still made on the basis of benefit. It would be unfortunate to have the element of benefit entirely lacking in our tax system. In the building of roads or in the paving of streets and in the use of water, gas, and electricity, it is fitting that the payments should be in accordance with the benefits received. According to the benefit theory, as long as any element of taxation remains, new taxes and assessments will have to be devised as improvements are carried out.

Sources of Federal Revenues

Federal Taxes—The Federal Government obtains its revenues from a variety of taxes. Customs duties, that is, taxes levied upon imports, have always occupied a prominent place in the tax system of our Federal Government. From the Civil War to the World War (1914), they made up a considerable part of its annual income. In 1918, however, they comprised less than

5% of its total tax receipts, but in 1924 they had risen to about 14% of the total. Internal revenue taxes include income taxes, inheritance taxes, and excise or consumption taxes. In 1929 the receipts of the government from internal revenue (income and profits tax and miscellaneous) were around 73% of the ordinary receipts of the United States Government.

Excise Taxes—Excise taxes are levied on (1) a producer or a seller, or (2) a commodity. In the first instance, if the person on whom the tax is levied does not pay, he is deprived of the right to produce or to sell his goods. The payment of this tax entitles the payor to a license. In the second case, all those who sell the article to be taxed must be listed. Usually the method of collecting the tax is by means of government stamps sold to producers or sellers. These stamps must be affixed to each unit of the commodity sold. The stamps are affixed in such a way that the goods cannot be opened without breaking the stamp.

The first form of the excise tax is not so important as the second. At times the object of issuing licenses is to regulate industry rather than to gain revenue. The amount of revenue obtained from licenses is relatively unimportant. Taxes levied on units of goods are really indirect taxes. The intention is that they shall be shifted to the consumer. It is usually true that the consumer bears the burden of excise taxes. Sometimes he bears more than the burden of the tax, because the producer or the seller often adds a sufficient amount to the price to reimburse himself for the trouble of having paid the tax in the beginning. Commodities on which the United States Government levies excise taxes are spirits, tobacco in various forms, fermented liquors, oleomargarine, and playing cards. In times of special emergency, as during a war, this ordinary list is usually increased. The taxable commodities on the excise list are regarded, socially speaking, as "doubtful benefits." The object in taxing these articles is both fiscal and sumptuary; that is, while the government receives a certain income therefrom, the public is to be discouraged from excessive use of these goods.

Federal Inheritance Taxes—Inheritance taxation is of ancient origin. Egypt is said to have levied a tax on succession some 2,000 years before Christ. The Romans raised money to pay their soldiers by levying taxes on property transfers by succession. During the Middle Ages, when feudalism flourished, the idea of levying a tax on the individual who succeeded to property was not unknown. The principles of inheritance taxation are now so firmly implanted in the minds of European statesmen that the justification of the tax is rarely discussed. No serious objections have been offered to the taxation of inheritances.

Different theories justifying the inheritance tax have been advanced. One line of opposition to the right of inheritance has become, in the minds of some, an argument for inheritance taxes, namely, the so-called opposition to the family theory of property. If there is no natural right by which the son may inherit the accumulations of his father, the heir can raise no objection to an inheritance tax. There is no natural right of inheritance, no matter how close the relationship may be, just as there is no natural right to private property itself. Hence, the argument against inheritance taxation which is based upon the family theory of property is not convincing.

Taxes on inheritance have sometimes been justified by reference to the benefit which the heir receives in being permitted by the state to inherit property. Another form of the benefit theory is that the state is a partner in the ownership of property, inasmuch as it protects and maintains the right of private ownership; when the partner dies the state naturally takes its share. The difficulty inherent in this argument is the inability to measure the extent to which the state is a partner in privately owned property.

The more modern theory of justification for inheritance taxes is ability to pay. An inheritance tax is essentially an income tax and can be justified on the same grounds. Inheritance creates taxpaying power of the heirs. If the inheritance is great, the rate of the tax should be high; if the inheritance is small, the rate should be low.

The Fiscal Advantages of an Inheritance Tax—The fiscal advantages of an inheritance tax are as follows:

1. An inheritance tax cannot be shifted.
2. The yield can be made elastic by increasing or decreasing the rates.
3. Where the political unit is large, the flow of in-

come tends to be regular. For this reason the federal inheritance tax yields a much more regular flow of revenue than a state inheritance tax, because the greater the number of people in the political unit who are subject to the tax, the more uniform and steady will be the revenue derived therefrom.

4. The cost of collection of the tax is negligible.

For some years a controversy was waged between the states and the Federal Government over the jurisdiction of each in connection with the taxation of inheritances. Finally in 1928 Congress passed a law permitting the inheritance taxes paid to the states to be credited on the federal inheritance tax up to about 80% of the total, the Federal Government collecting approximately 20%.

The Income Tax—In the serious business of earning a living, man puts forth his energies and invests his accumulations, and he realizes therefrom a flow of goods and services. To measure this flow a limited time is chosen, usually a year. The returns from a man's toil and investments are spoken of as contributing a certain amount per annum. Economic life is dynamic, not static, and the volume and rapidity of the flow of goods have a greater significance than the reservoir or fund (wealth) from which such flow takes place. Roughly speaking, the amount of this flow to any individual within a given year may be said to be his income.

Many argued points in income taxation turn on the distinction between gross and net income. In any business enterprise all that is received from any source during a definite term constitutes gross receipts. In case funds are received from a sale of goods or property, the cost of the goods or property is subtracted from the gross receipts in order to obtain the gross income. Under the Federal Income Tax Law, from gross income may be subtracted the expenses of the business; such expenses are wages, rentals, interest on certain forms of indebtedness, certain taxes (income taxes and special assessments may not be subtracted), losses and bad debts, and depreciation due to physical wear, tear, and obsolescence. The remainder is net income, the base upon which the income tax is levied.

It is obvious that these distinctions have more significance for those whose incomes are derived from business enterprises than for those whose incomes are derived from wages and salaries. Living expenses do not enter into the question of net income, for no deductions may be made for living expenses. To meet the requirement for an untaxed income sufficient to cover the bare necessities of life, personal exemptions are allowed. Therefore, from net income are subtracted personal exemptions in order to obtain the net taxable income. In actual procedure, however, personal exemptions are counted as a credit and are entered on the opposite side of the ledger to be subtracted from the net income.

Retention of the Income Tax—The income tax, while simple in principle, is an exceedingly complex tax, difficult to assess and difficult to collect. In the United States many objections have been raised against the income tax. It is said to invade the right of privacy. The Federal Government must develop a spy system in order to prevent tax evasion. Unless harsh and strong-arm methods are used, evasion is likely to occur on a large scale. In fact, it has been insisted that, as Gladstone said, an income tax produces a nation of liars, because the tax is likely to be evaded by all except the ignorant and the honest.

The advantages of the income tax as an important part of our federal system of taxation are so great and so well recognized by statesmen that it is safe to predict that such a tax will remain an important part of the system. The advantages claimed for the income tax are as follows:

1. It is the most equitable of all taxes in that it reaches the professional and other classes who have ample income. It is equitable also because it exempts the poor people and puts the burden of taxation on those who are best able to bear it. As to the wealthy, it is fair to them because it accommodates itself to the varying condition of the taxpayer. It is equitable to the small business man because it does not tax him heavily until his business is well under way. The tax seems to be fair to the storekeeper because there is no tax on goods in stock upon which a profit has not yet been realized.

2. A general income tax, because it cannot be shifted, does not produce changes in the prices of goods. It has already been indicated that the problem of shifting and incidence is the most difficult problem of taxation. In regard to the income tax, the Federal Govern-

ment may rest assured that the burden of the tax will stay where it was originally placed.

3. The income tax gives the needed degree of elasticity to the annual tax system.

Sources of State Revenues

Revenue from Taxes—The expenditures of the states have increased so rapidly of late that each state has endeavored to build up a revenue system to meet its own particular needs. The methods used in raising funds vary with the economic and human resources of the different states, but a large part of the revenue is raised by means of taxation.

Revenue from Sources Other than Taxes—Less than 20% of the total revenue receipts of states comes from sources other than taxes. These sources include:

1. The earnings of general departments (including fees for services rendered by the government, such as the issuance or filing of legal documents, the regulation of different trades, boiler inspection, and moving picture censorship)

2. Highway privileges, rents, and interest—for example, revenue receipts from public utility companies for privileges relative to docks, wharves, canals, and so forth, and for interest due the state on general and special funds

3. Subventions, or those grants made by the Federal Government for highways, education, and experiment stations

4. Donations, including gifts made by individuals for schools and hospitals

5. Special assessments, which are special charges to cover the outlays made by the state and usually relate to the building of parks and highways

6. The earnings of public service enterprises

7. Fines levied by the courts

8. Forfeits, including bonds forfeited because of non-fulfilment of contract

9. Escheats, which are derived from the sale of property the owner of which cannot be located.

Revenue of the States from Taxes—As almost 78% of the revenue of our states is derived from taxes, it is necessary to survey the most important of the taxes used by the various states. The first of these, and by far the most important as a source of revenue, is the general property tax.

General Property Tax—For the states as a whole the general property tax yields 45% of the receipts from taxation and 35% of all the revenue receipts of the states. The base of this tax is defined as "all property, real or personal, in the state not especially exempt." According to the Bureau of the Census, the general property tax includes "all direct taxes upon real property and taxes upon other property which are apportioned and levied by substantially the same methods employed in apportioning and levying taxes upon privately owned real property." As the student is doubtless aware, by real property, or realty, is meant real estate, and by personal property, or personalty, is meant privately owned property other than real estate. The only states which do not possess a general property tax are Pennsylvania and Delaware.

Exemptions under the General Property Tax—Exemptions under the general property tax may be classified as follows:

1. All public property, including greenbacks and federal bonds, is exempt from this tax.

2. The property of all charitable, religious, and benevolent institutions is exempt from the general property tax. In some states the property of fraternal and secret societies is free from the tax, on the ground that such institutions are charitable enterprises.

3. The property of all schools and colleges, of public libraries, and of literary and scientific societies is free from the tax, on the ground that these institutions are founded for educational purposes and not for profit.

4. The property of other institutions or associations which have been organized for social welfare is also free from taxation. In most states, this class includes volunteer fire companies, agricultural societies, and any other private organizations which are organized for social helpfulness and not for the making of profit.

5. In different states different exemptions are made for the purpose of favoring the poor, as well as for fiscal reasons. In some states the tools with which the workman earns his living are exempt; in some states a certain amount of cultivated land is free from the tax. As suggested before, there are two principles involved in

the exemptions of this group: (1) that the poor are unjustifiably burdened when they are forced to pay high taxes and (2) that the assessment and collection of taxes on small amounts of property often cost the state more than the return from the taxes.

The Method of Apportionment—The general procedure in the states is to have a valuation made of the realty and personalty in the different localities by local officials. A return is made to the state as to the total value of the real estate and personal property of the different counties and towns. The state estimates the amount of revenue to be raised from the general property tax. The rate of the tax, so far as the state is concerned, is determined on the basis of the ratio between the total valuation of all the property and the amount to be raised. On the basis of the property values sent in from the different local bodies, an apportionment is made to the local bodies of the amount that each is to raise for the state.

The Defects of the Property Tax—The defects of the property tax may be stated as follows:

1. Inequality as between local bodies. It will be seen at once from the foregoing discussion that, in order to have the tax operate with justice and equality, the evaluations made by the local officials in the different tax districts should be uniform. Unfortunately this is not the case. In some counties within a state the assessment has been known to be 100% of the fair cash value; in other counties it has been as low as 20%. Ap-

portioning the total amount to be raised on the basis of such unequal evaluations produces injustice and inequality.

2. Inequality as between different taxpayers in the same local body. The assessment of real and personal property within the different local units of government has not been uniform. Real estate has constantly borne more than its share, while personal property has in many cases borne very little of its share of the tax. For example, in the State of Connecticut, personal property as it was listed for taxation in 1915 constituted 16.3% of the total; the value of real estate constituted 83.7%. It goes without saying that the 16.3% of the total listed as personalty did not represent anything like the actual value of personal property. One reason for the escape of personal property from its just share of the tax is that it is more difficult to list and to evaluate than realty. Realty can never be hidden; it does not change in location; and it is easily listed.

3. Assessment incommensurate with ability to pay. A fundamental defect of the general property tax lies in the fact that its assessment is not according to ability to pay. The rates of assessment are proportional, not progressive. It is the opinion of experts that a proportional tax levied on property will press more heavily upon the small property owners than upon the large property owners. Furthermore, property is not a good base for taxation. There may be a great disparity between the value of property and the income from it at any one time. As has been shown previously, income is a very much better base for taxation than property.

4. A premium upon dishonesty. Commissions appointed in the states to inquire into the operation of the general property tax have been unanimous in their conclusions that the system is responsible for widespread demoralization. From this very brief discussion of the defects of the general property tax, one must draw the conclusion that it is the cause of injustice and dishonesty. Since these defects are so deep seated, it does not seem possible that they can be reached by remedies. Certain improvements have been made in cities, but no one claims that the city assessments are made with justice. The wisest solution seems to be for the states to look about for more equitable and ethical methods of raising revenue and, having found them, to abandon the general property tax.

State Inheritance Taxes—All but three states and the District of Columbia levy taxes on inheritances. As we have already indicated, in 1928 the Federal Government passed a law whereby in the future the inheritance taxes paid to the states might be credited up to 80% of the federal tax. Thus, the states now obtain about four-fifths of all the taxes arising from this source.

Corporation Taxes—As long as the people of the United States were eager to encourage the formation of corporations, the taxation which these organizations bore was light. At first the formation of corporations was encouraged by protective tariffs, special franchises, subsidies, and grants of land. As public opinion turned against large scale enterprise, corporations were regarded with less favor, and the states began to devise means of taxing them. Certain states were eager to have corporations establish themselves within their boundaries; other states looked with suspicion upon large corporations and were inclined to treat them somewhat harshly in the matter of taxation.

The taxation of corporations under the general property tax did not run smoothly. Local assessors were not able to evaluate the property of the corporations. Stocks and bonds usually escaped taxation altogether. Some assessors had methods of evaluation of corporate property which were different from those used by other local assessors. The problem was further complicated by the fact that much of the property of some corporations lay in different states. For example, in taxing railroads each state presumed to tax only property which lay within its boundaries; yet the value of railway property depends upon the earning power of the line as a whole, and practically all of the large railroad lines run through two or more states. Because of these considerations, the taxation of corporate property under the general property tax was not successful in the early stages. Since that time, considerable progress has been made in adjusting the taxes on corporate property. One method of taxing an interstate railroad is to assess its total value and to allocate to each state the proper percentage to cover the right of way and other physical property which lie within that state.

Franchise Taxes—A franchise tax is imposed on the

assumption that the corporation is receiving from the state some special privilege which enables it to earn more profits than enterprises not so favored. Such a tax is sometimes levied because the state has enabled the corporation to come into existence, sometimes because it permits the corporation to continue in business, and sometimes for other reasons.

Incorporation Fee—A franchise to come into existence is the right which the state gives to an organization to carry on business as an individual. A franchise tax paid for the right to come into existence is paid once and for all. It is properly called a fee and is known as the incorporation fee. In some states this fee is a flat sum for all corporations; in other states it varies directly with the capitalization. The income from incorporation fees is not a very important source of revenue.

Taxation of the Right to Exist—The difficulties in assessing taxes of this kind reside in the different classes of interests represented in the corporations. Shall the tax be levied upon the stockholders or upon the corporation alone? Shall the bondholders be taxed? Some corporations receive a considerable part of their capital from the sale of bonds. If taxes are to be levied according to the ability to pay theory, then income from the sale of bonds should be taken into account in those institutions in which the receipts from the sale of shares is considered a measure of ability. The states have answered these questions in different ways, and the results are highly complicated. The most popular plan of measuring corporate values has been to levy a tax on corporate stock.

Taxation of Public Utilities—Different states have used different methods in the taxing of public utilities. There are three possibilities. The tax may be levied on the value of the physical assets of the corporation, on gross earnings, or on net earnings. If the state should decide to choose the first method, that is, levying on the value of the physical assets, it would still be faced with other problems. In evaluating the properties of public utilities, shall the basis be the market value of the stocks, or the original expenditure in physical properties at the time when they were constructed, or the cost of reproducing the physical properties at the existing prices? There is an objection to each one of these methods of evaluating property.

1. It has been pointed out that the market value of stocks is not always a measure of ability to pay, because the market value is apt to depend upon the dividends which have been declared.

2. If the second method of evaluation—the original cost of the property less depreciation—is chosen, unfairness to the stockholders may result. If the public utility has not been prosperous and has not been able to earn profits, it should not be called upon to pay taxes according to its original expenditure. Furthermore, the value of the property may not be accurately measured by the original expenditure because of a change in the price level.

3. If the property is evaluated according to the cost of reproducing the physical assets, unfairness to the shareholders may result. If, at the time when the evaluation by this method was made, the price level was double what it was at the time when the original expenditures were incurred, the tax would be twice as great as it would be if the original cost were the basis of evaluation. The increase in the price level by 100% does not necessarily mean that the ability to pay taxes has been doubled.

The only adequate method for the evaluation of property is to base the estimates upon its earning power. Any form of measuring ability to pay by considering the properties as apart from the business as a "going concern" must prove inadequate.

Tax on Gross Earnings—In those states in which public utilities are taxed according to gross earnings, there are many willing to justify this method of taxation. There is no necessity for discussing the complications of evaluating the property where the tax is levied on gross earnings. Injustice is apt to exist, because there is a great diversity among corporations as to their ratios of expenses to earnings. In order to make this method just, it would be necessary to classify corporations according to the prevailing ratio of net earnings to gross earnings. If this is necessary, would it not be better to base the tax on net earnings rather than on gross earnings?

Tax on Net Earnings—A corporation tax based on

net earnings presents greater administrative difficulties than a tax based on gross earnings. Corporations use different methods of accounting and often observe different fiscal years. From an economic point of view, however, taxing net earnings appears to be the soundest method of levying the tax, because net earnings most accurately show the ability to pay. Taxes should be paid from net income, with exemptions for those corporations which are not able to show large net earnings. If the tax is levied on the value of the corporate property and this value is determined according to net earnings, then the practical result is the same as if the tax had been levied on net earnings. In both cases net earnings become the measure of the ability to pay taxes.

Necessary Reforms in Corporation Taxes—There is no reason for making changes in the corporation fees, except to bring about greater uniformity in the size of the fees and in the methods of assessment in different states. The fees for incorporation are relatively small and do not play an important part in deciding the location of corporations. One reform is greatly needed, however, to take the matter of the assessment of corporations out of the hands of local officials and entrust it to state officials. This would insure reasonable uniformity throughout any one state. Because a large corporation, whether or not a public utility, is essentially an interstate and not an intrastate enterprise, many students of corporate business have urged that all charters of incorporation be issued by the Federal Government. In so far as corporations are to be regulated, this centralization of charter issuance would bring about a greater degree of uniformity of accounting and would greatly simplify the collection of corporation taxes. The states would be sure to raise strenuous objections to this plan, because corporations are lucrative sources for obtaining revenue. However, compensation might be offered by the Federal Government. If corporation taxes were paid into the central treasury, the Federal Government might be willing to give up to the states certain taxes which it now collects. For example, if the Federal Government were to relinquish its right to collect inheritance taxes, the state rates on such taxes could be raised.

Taxation of Banks—During the Civil War the Federal Government placed restrictions upon the freedom of the states to tax national banks. These restrictions have reacted upon the taxation of banks of all classes. There is more uniformity in the method of taxing banks than there is in the method of taxing corporations in general. In 1864 Congress definitely stated that the states might levy taxes upon the shares of stock of national banks as the personal property of the owners. Although the legislatures of the states in which the banks are located have the right to determine the method of taxing the shares, they are subject to two restrictions: (1) Taxation must not be at a rate higher than that imposed upon other moneyed capital; (2) the shares owned by individuals living outside the state must be taxed at the place where the bank is located. The phrase "other moneyed capital," after many court decisions, has come to be restricted to that capital invested in the stocks of other commercial banks and trust companies and that money in private hands which is employed in a way similar to that in which bank capital is employed.

The general result of these restrictions has been to bring about uniformity both in the tax rate and in the methods of assessment. The law permits the state to require the banks to pay the tax on shares and to collect the amount of the tax from the stockholders. This is a form of collection at the source. The property of banks, with the exception of real estate, which is usually assessed by the local officials, is not taxed by the states. The methods of taxing bank shares may be divided into two classes, as follows:

1. In the majority of states the local officers levy a tax on the bank shares as a part of the general property tax. In this case the tax rate which applies is the local rate under the general property tax.

2. In some states the taxation, in both assessment and rate, has been made uniform throughout the entire state.

The inequality and confusion which arise in the taxing of banks are due mainly to the use of different methods in determining the value of the shares. Some states estimate the value of shares from previous sales. Sometimes the value of the shares is determined on the basis of the sum of the capital, surplus, and undivided profits. Certain reforms are necessary to bring about justice in taxation as among banks in the same state. Much of the difficulty would be avoided if uniformity of assessment by the local administrators could be worked out.

Taxation of Insurance Companies—Insurance companies are regarded by the public as a means of promoting the general security and welfare of the people. There is, therefore, a general feeling that insurance companies should not be taxed. On the other hand, the government bureau which supervises insurance companies within the state promotes the welfare of the public by so doing, and it is fitting that insurance companies should pay for the maintenance of the government insurance bureau. The usual method employed by the states is to levy a percentage tax on the gross premiums. Because of the similarity of method by which insurance companies carry on their business, no injustice follows the adoption of this measure.

Tax on Motor Vehicles—Of the total receipts in all the states from taxation, 8.3% is derived from taxes on motor vehicles. In 1919 the sum of $43,950,000 was obtained from such taxes. This huge sum was derived from license taxes on motor vehicles, including the receipts from permits to operate motor vehicles and the receipts from licenses or permits granted to the operators of such vehicles other than those granted to operators engaged in the business as chauffeurs.

Sources of Municipal Revenues

Municipal Revenues—Cities obtain their revenue

from a variety of sources. Of the revenue of 146 cities for 1919, 66% was obtained from the general property tax. As has been indicated in the discussion of the general property tax, the assessment of real estate and personal property is made by local officials. The common method of making up the rate on the basis of this assessment is to add the state rate to the local rate and to collect the taxes for both the state and the local body at the same time. Therefore, the general property tax is not only the most important state tax but also the most important tax for the maintenance of the city governments.

Taxes on the liquor traffic were formerly the source of about 6% of the total city revenue. By 1929, owing to prohibition laws, this had fallen to 2.8%. License taxes, other than license taxes on the liquor traffic, netted city governments about 1.5% of the total revenue. Other taxes of various forms brought in about 3.3%. In 1919 special assessments netted 5.6% of the total. This was a smaller percentage than usual. The average for the past seventeen years is about 8%. Special assessments cannot be considered as net revenue, because they are collected from the people by the city government in payment for some special service or benefit rendered.

Subventions, grants, gifts and donations, and pension assessments have been classified together by the Bureau of the Census. The income from this source has consistently comprised more than 4% of the total revenue. Donations and gifts are gratuitous contributions by corporations and individuals to the government for the purpose of establishing or maintaining hospitals, infirmaries, libraries, and kindred institutions. Pension assessments are amounts of money collected from public servants, such as firemen, policemen, teachers, and government employees, toward the maintenance of pension funds in the interest of those employees contributing.

Another important source of revenue to cities is the earnings of public service enterprises, which in 1919 made up 10.2% of the total revenue. The largest earnings in the 146 cities from public utilities came from the water supply systems, which netted $95,000,000 out of $127,000,000, the total earnings of public service enterprises. Next in importance are the electric light and power systems, which in 1919 showed earnings of $10,000,000.

Shifting and Incidence of Taxation—Not all taxes are borne by the persons upon whom they are levied. A tax is shifted when the burden is removed from the place where it was first laid. The incidence of the tax refers to the place where the burden finally remains. The common method of shifting the burden of the tax is by raising the price of the product by the amount of the tax, so that the purchaser, while he does not pay the tax, bears the burden of it. Sometimes the shifting occurs several times. For example, a tax is levied on a producer, who pays it and shifts it to the wholesaler; the latter raises the price of the goods by the amount or more than the amount of the tax when he sells to the retailer; the retailer in turn shifts the tax, if he can, to the consumer. The shifting of taxes greatly complicates the work of the administrators of the government, for if taxation is to be equitable and just, the officials must know where the incidence will finally be. Sometimes it is intended that the tax shall be shifted, as for example, when taxes are levied on consumable goods. In some cases the legislators and statesmen cannot be sure who will bear the ultimate burden of the tax. In many cases a tax may be only partially shifted, so that the payer bears a part and the purchaser a part. The problem of shifting and incidence is so complicated and difficult that it is impossible to treat the subject adequately in this volume.

Kinds of Taxes and Shifting—In discussing this subject, six general groups of taxes will be considered.

1. Customs duties. If import duties do not keep foreign goods out of a country, the prices of these goods are generally raised within the importing country. It is usually intended that the consumers shall bear at least a part of the burden of import tariffs.

2. Excise duties. Here again the intention is that the price of the goods which are taxed shall be raised by the amount of the duties.

3. Inheritance taxes. Inheritance taxes are not shifted. Sometimes a part of the inheritance tax is evaded by means of gifts before the death of the testator, but this does not constitute a shifting of the tax.

4. Income taxes. Taxes on income are seldom, if ever, shifted. An income is a surplus, and a tax on surplus is rarely shifted.

5. Taxes on property. Since the value of property usually depends on the income from the property, the

general effect of taxing a particular piece of property is to cause a decrease in its value in the hands of the owner. The tax has been capitalized and, as has been indicated previously, will not be shifted provided the tax falls evenly on all income-yielding property.

6. Poll taxes. A poll tax cannot be shifted unless it produces some change in the conditions of employment. If a poll tax were levied in one state and not in an adjoining state, laborers might migrate to the state where the poll tax was not levied. Because of a decrease in the supply of labor in the state where the tax applied, wages would rise. However, this would seem to be not so much a real shifting of the tax as it is an effect of the tax.

The Individual and Taxation—We have discussed the means by which the various branches of our government obtain their funds. The question as to how the individual is affected by the government's activities and policies in that regard remains to be considered.

In the first place, if the government were unable, because of lack of revenue, to perform its various functions, law and order could not be maintained, educational facilities would not be provided, business could not be carried on as it is at present, and the welfare of the people would not be conserved to the extent that is now possible. Government and government activities are prerequisite to the proper functioning of our economic world. Unless the government is able to function in a satisfactory manner, chaotic conditions are bound to result, and the people will suffer as they always do when their government and their economic life disintegrate.

In the second place, the income of the individual is directly affected by the taxes which have to be paid. If he pays the tax directly, his income is reduced and he has less with which to purchase those things he desires in order to satisfy his demands. At times taxes have been exceedingly oppressive and have reduced the condition of the people to one of extreme poverty. Especially was this true of past ages when rulers were excessive in their demands for revenue.

Indirect taxes increase the prices of commodities purchased by the individual and add to his cost of living, thus reducing the purchasing power of his income.

Taxes are one of the costs of production which have to be met out of the income of the business enterprise, thus reducing the amount of income ultimately paid to its owners. At times business enterprises have been forced into bankruptcy because the tax burden has so greatly increased their costs of operation as to make it impossible to continue in business.

The protective tariff has both aided and hindered the individual in his search for income. As a consumer he has, as a rule, been forced to pay the tariff, because, wherever possible, the tariff is added to the price of the protected article. As the receiver of income from a protected industry, the individual has been benefited because of the earnings made possible by the tariff either through its having enabled the industry to exist or through its having made possible higher prices on the protected product.

CHAPTER XXI

Value and Price

WE have seen that in our economic activities we are concerned with obtaining and spending an income in terms of money so as to be able to do the things and to buy the things that we desire. I may have the high ambition of becoming a politician, but it costs money to run for office. You may be charitably inclined, but it takes money to endow hospitals, orphanages, universities, and playgrounds. We may be interested in art, literature, and music, but it takes money to pursue our interests either as a profession or as an avocation. We desire to "keep up with the Joneses," and that requires an income. Only exceptionally do we find a man who, living the life of a hermit and having but slight need for money, is unconcerned with the struggle for a greater income.

Price Economy—Our society is a pecuniary society, interested primarily in obtaining an income in terms of money. It is dominated by what we call a "price economy." We work for wages, lease property for rent, loan funds for interest, and own a business in the hope of obtaining profits. Wages, rent, interest, and profits are paid in money (with, of course, a few exceptions). Wages constitute the price paid for labor power; rent is the price paid for the use of certain kinds of property; and interest is the price paid for loanable funds. One might also say that profits represent the price which society (the people) has to pay the owners of business in order to induce them to assume the risks that as owners they must face. Unless there were a chance of receiving profits, no one would be willing to put his funds into a business enterprise.

In studying profits, however, we must consider the element of price from another angle. Profits consist of the difference between the *cost* of the article or of the service rendered and the *price* or return that is obtained for it. Profit seekers, therefore, are vitally concerned with the prices paid by consumers in the market; but so also are the receivers of wages, rent, and interest. If the latter group must pay high prices for the things that they purchase, their incomes will command a smaller amount of goods. If prices are low, those incomes will command a larger amount of goods. When prices in general rise, they tend to pull wages, rent, and interest to higher levels, and when prices fall, they tend to pull wages, rent, and interest to lower levels.

Thus, our entire economic structure resembles a gigantic spider web. If we touch one part of it, many other parts are affected. That is the reason why it is so difficult even for economists to understand completely how our economic system functions. It also explains why it is impossible for them to foretell just what effect upon the entire structure any slight change or modification may produce.

Problem of Prices—We have discussed wages, rent, interest, and profits as the prices that are paid to our various economic classes, and we have mentioned many of the factors that enter into their determination. It remains for us to consider the elements that determine the prices paid for the host of things that people buy with their incomes, not only the prices of articles such as farm crops and factory products, but also those paid for property and for the services of railroads, steamships, public utilities, and similar enterprises.

Demand and Supply—We buy things (that is, we pay a price for them) because we want them. We might like to have airplanes, yachts, and Rolls Royces, but we cannot afford to buy them. We have the desire, but we have not the ability to pay. The mere wish for a thing, consequently, can have no effect upon its price. It is only when we have the desire to buy and the means with which to pay that we become a factor or an influence in the market place. We then exercise what is known as *effective demand*.

On the other side of the market are those who have possession of articles which they desire to sell for a price. Of course, there are a few persons who decline to sell certain things, such as family heirlooms, regardless of the price that may be offered. In our discussion, however, we are concerned only with those goods that are offered for sale at a price. Thus, on the one hand we have the demanders, or buyers, and on the other we have the suppliers, or sellers.

The Market—The market is any place where a buyer and a seller come together for the purpose of making an exchange. The exchange may not take place, because the two parties may be unable to agree on the price; a market, nevertheless, has been constituted by their coming together with the intention of making an exchange. Such a market is simple and unorganized, with no fixed rules of trading. Other markets are much more complicated, with several buyers and sellers, the exact number unknown, who lack, however, both formal organization and full information relative to general conditions. Then, too, we have stock exchanges, cotton and coffee exchanges, boards of trade, and the like, which are formal affairs, with a fixed number of buyers and sellers who possess a considerable amount but not all of the information relative to market conditions.

Some markets are local in character; others are national and international. A student of economics, accordingly, must understand that the factors determining price and the institutions through which they function are extremely complex. In this chapter we can treat only their most outstanding characteristics.

Scarcity and Prices—An article cannot be sold for a price unless some one wants it. You and I do not want the same things. I may want many books; you may have no desire for books and hence will not buy them. You may want ice skates, for which I have no need and will give nothing. We pay only for those things that exist in quantities insufficient to supply all human wants, or economic goods—those goods which are relatively scarce. We do not pay for air in the open field, for rain, or for sunshine. We will not always pay for things merely because they are scarce, however. You may have a photograph of your grandfather, the only copy in existence, which you are unwilling to sell for any amount of money. I am unwilling to give you five cents for it, even though it is scarce, because I am not interested in obtaining the picture. However, if it were a picture of a famous character, such as Washington, Hamilton, or Lincoln, I might be willing to purchase it. Many things that are plentifully supplied to the market, such as nuts, bolts, screws, wheat, and similar products, command a price. It can thus be seen that the degree of scarcity is not the sole element determining price, although it is an important factor in price fixation.

Things are not worth a price unless others desire to purchase them. To command a price, they must satisfy human wants. However, not all the things that satisfy human wants are able to command a price, even though people must have them in order to live. As has been already observed, we pay nothing for air, rain, or sunshine, even though our very existence depends upon them. It is interesting to note that we pay but a small sum for food, without which we cannot live, and that we pay large sums for diamonds, jewelry, paintings, and so forth—things which are not at all necessary to life. Necessities usually command a low price, luxuries a high price. This is because necessities are provided in greater abundance than luxuries and because those who purchase luxuries have more money to spend than do those who are obliged to confine their purchases to necessities.

Factors Affecting Demand—Let us analyze a little more fully the factors affecting demand. Upon what does the intensity of demand depend? It is necessary in this connection to review briefly what was said in Chapter IV about the things that affect the consumption ideals of an individual. We cannot exist without food, clothing, and shelter. A few comforts make life easier. We want to exist on the plane that is customary for our group. Many of the things that we buy are purchased solely because we desire to imitate others.

Law of Diminishing Utility—The foregoing statements apply to the demand for things in general. What about our individual demand for a particular thing, say a glass of water? If you have come in from a long walk and are extremely thirsty, the first glass of water that you drink means much to you. It has great utility or want satisfying power. If you had to pay for it, you might be willing to give fifteen cents for a glass. The second glass means a little less, and the third glass possesses an even smaller amount of utility. Possibly you have no desire for a fourth glass of water. Thus, the more water you drink, the less each glass means to you, even though, if you were buying it, you might have to pay five cents for each glassful. The utility per glass of water decreases as your desire for it is increasingly satisfied. This, as you may remember, is the law of diminishing utility, which applies to all things.

To cite another example, take the photograph of your grandfather, which was previously mentioned. You might refuse to part with it for less than $5,000, yet I might be unwilling to give you even one cent for it. The photograph means nothing to me. Your personal or subjective valuation is different from mine. Take still another example; suppose that you and I attend an auction sale of art treasures. A picture by Rembrandt is put up before the group, and you bid $250,000. I, on the other hand, not caring for the paintings of the old masters, refuse to bid anything for it. Thus, all of us have our own personal valuations (subjective valuations), which vary greatly from individual to individual.

Supply—On the other side of the market, opposite the demanders, we have those who are willing to sell, and they too have their own personal, or subjective, valuations. They know at what they value their goods, and at what price they desire to sell. They know the lowest price that they will take, which, of course, is less than the price that they would like to get. Their subjective valuations are determined by their expenses of production, by their urgency to get funds with which to meet their obligations, by the possible supply of goods in the market, by the competition of other suppliers for the trade of the purchasers, by the eagerness of the public to buy, and by many other considerations.

Fixation of Price—The suppliers and the demanders meet in the market and the price is fixed as a result of their bargaining power, that of the one being played off against that of the other. There is no level at which prices must be fixed or at which they will ordinarily be fixed. Prices fluctuate in the market to a considerable degree. There is no formula or diagram which will disclose at just what point prices will be fixed, although, of course, we have many theories and diagrams which purport to do so.

Value versus Price—At this point it is well for us to explain the difference between *value* and *price,* two terms which are commonly confused in the minds of most individuals. If you were to make a detailed and thoroughgoing study of value, you would discover that there are many different kinds; but for our purposes in this elementary text we shall confine ourselves to defining only *use value* and *exchange value.*

Use value is the valuation that the individual places on a commodity, namely, subjective value. Use value depends on what the thing is worth to the individual personally. *Exchange value is what a commodity will exchange for in terms of other commodities.* For example, how many shoes is a coat worth? How many marbles is a knife worth? How many cigarettes is a cigar worth? Exchange value, then, is measured by comparing goods with other goods. However, when we measure the exchange value of goods in terms of money and say that a coat is worth $5 and a pair of shoes is worth $8, then we have what we call price. *Price, therefore, is exchange value expressed in terms of money.*

Intrinsic Value—In discussing value, it is well to call the attention of the student to the fact that there is no such thing as intrinsic value. A thing is not priced merely because it exists. It is worth something because some one wants it. A bathing suit has no real value at the North Pole, regardless of how much it cost to produce it. A radio broadcasting station has no value to the native of the African jungle. Things have to be wanted before they can possess value, and the amount of worth or value which they represent in the market place is measured by their command over other articles. Usually, as we have stated earlier, we measure the value of things in money, or, as we say, in prices. We seldom resort to measuring their value in terms of things other than money.

Effect of Price on Demand—Although we have said that price is determined in the market as a result of the bargaining power of the suppliers and the demanders, there are still other matters that must be taken into consideration. We have made our answer too simple. We have overlooked the effect of price itself on the demand of the demanders and on the supply of the suppliers. Few persons stop to think of the great influence of price on supply and demand.

If the price of an article is too high, fewer people, as a rule, will be willing to purchase it. This is usually the case, although there are exceptions to such a general statement. For example, in the stock market the public is eager to buy when prices are high. When the stock market has gone to pieces and excellent bargains can be obtained for low prices, the public refuses to buy. At times, also, the customer in a store will not buy an article if the price is low. Many merchants realize that fact and accordingly mark up their prices to higher levels. One of the large department stores in New York City secured a shipment of very fine reproductions of famous paintings from a French dealer. Because the owners of the store had purchased the lot at a ridiculously low figure, they decided to sell them at a very low price. The customers, however, looked at them, noted the low price, and refused to purchase, whereupon the manager of the art department raised the price considerably, and in an exceptionally short time had sold all of the pictures.

Inelastic and Elastic Demand—There are certain kinds of commodities which cannot be sold in increased quantities even when the price is reduced; take, for example, salt. Would your mother buy pounds and pounds more of salt if the price were reduced to one cent for two pounds? What about spices, bread, flour, and many similar commodities? This kind of demand is known as *inelastic demand,* because it varies little, if any, with price changes. On the other hand, there are many goods which people will purchase in greatly increased quantities if the price is reduced. This kind of demand is known as *elastic demand*. Merchants realize the importance of elastic and inelastic demand as affecting sales and proceed accordingly in pricing their goods. This is the reason why it is not always wise to declare that a merchant should lower his prices if he wishes to sell more to the public, thereby obtaining a larger turnover of his stock.

The reason why the demand for different commodities varies in its degree of elasticity will be seen from the following rules governing the elasticity of demand:

1. The demand for luxuries is more elastic than the demand for necessities.

2. The demand of the poor is more elastic and responsive to changes in price than the demand of the rich.

3. The demand for those commodities the use of which has become habitual is inelastic. One reason why governments levy taxes on tobacco is that the consumption will not greatly decrease because of the increase in price due to the taxes, and thus the governments are assured of considerable revenue.

4. The demand for those commodities which have substitutes is more elastic than the demand for those goods which have none.

5. Commodities which have many uses have a more elastic demand than commodities which have only a few uses.

If we apply these rules to the commodities mentioned as having elastic or inelastic demand, it is evident why the demand is either responsive or unresponsive to changes in price. The demand for bread is inelastic because bread is regarded as a necessity. The demand for eggs is elastic because they are not an absolute necessity and, furthermore, may be used in many different ways in the preparation of food. The demand for matches is inelastic, both because they are necessary and because there is no cheap substitute for them. The demand for moving picture theatre tickets on the part of the poor or the moderately well to do is far less elastic than it was formerly, because the workingman of today has come to look upon the movies as one of his necessities. The demand for tobacco, as we have said, is inelastic because its use is habitual to many people.

Effect of Price on Supply—The supply side of the market is also affected by price. If the price is high and if the commodity can be produced in large quantities, a greater supply will come into the market. New enterprises will engage in production, and old enterprises will, if possible, increase their output. On the other hand, if the price falls to too low a level and there is a greatly lessened opportunity to make profits, many firms will drop out of the market or will turn their attention to producing other commodities for which there is a better price available. Of course, there are some goods that cannot be reproduced. We call these *non-reproducible goods*. Typical of this group are the paintings and sculptures of the old masters, Stradivarius violins, and manuscripts and letters of famous people. The price of these articles cannot affect the quantity produced, although as the price rises, a larger number of such articles already in existence will come into the market and will be offered for sale. The price of non-reproducible articles depends upon the bargaining power of the parties concerned.

Price of Land—Land also is a non-reproducible good. Its quantity is fixed and so is its location. The price of land illustrates some interesting phases of the price fixing processes. In the first place, land has a price because of human desires When there is more than enough land to supply the needs of the people, no price will be paid for it. As population increases, however, it presses upon the supply of land, the demand becomes greater, and land becomes more valuable. The greater the pressure of population, the greater will be the demand for land and hence the higher the price. In the second place, as has already been stated, location and fertility are two important factors affecting the price of farm lands. Fertility has no effect on the price of city lands, however, location being all-important.

As the price of land rises, it is impossible to produce more of it. Two things, however, can be done to meet the increased demand. First, the use to which land has been put can be changed. In this way it is possible to meet the demand for additional acreage to devote to certain crops or to use for other purposes. For example, as the price of cotton rises, land devoted to grazing can be turned into cotton land As the population of a city increases, farm land can be turned into city lots. Second, while the actual location of land cannot be changed, easier and more efficient ways of getting to the land can be and are introduced. The development of transportation facilities has changed the relative location of land in response to the demands of the people. As the price of city land rises beyond the point at which people can afford to buy it for home sites, rapid means of interurban transportation open up outlying districts and bring into the market an additional supply of land for home building purposes.

The price of land does not depend upon the cost of producing it, for man does not produce land. He improves it in various ways, but land itself is a gift of nature. The owner of a piece of land may allow it to lie idle and yet discover that over a period of years it has doubled in value. This is known as the unearned increment of land, as we have pointed out, because the value of the land has been increased by the efforts of society and not by those of its owner.

Price and Cost of Production—Many writers maintain that the price of an article is determined by its cost of production, because the seller cannot afford to part with his product for less than it has cost him to produce it. In the first place, we have seen that the price of land is not so determined. In the second place, the prices of stocks and bonds are not so determined, for it costs but little to make the paper used for stocks and bonds and to pay the expenses of engraving. Furthermore, it cannot be argued that stocks and bonds are valued on the basis of what it has cost to produce the business enterprise, the ownership of which is represented by stocks and the indebtedness of which is represented by bonds. The cost of producing or reproducing a plant is at any one period of time, say during a day, a fixed sum; yet the price of the stocks and bonds of the company which owns that plant will vary greatly in the market during a day's time. Individuals normally purchase stocks only because it is anticipated that in the future they will entitle the holders to dividends or to gains resulting from their sale for higher prices. Sometimes they are high priced because various parties are striving for control of the issuing corporation and are willing for that reason to pay exorbitant prices, which cannot be justified on the basis of anticipated dividends or anticipated gains from the sale of the stocks in the future.

What about the price of any ordinary commodity? Is the price of wheat fixed by its cost of production? Immediately, many will say, "Why, of course it is. If the farmer cannot get a price for his wheat that will return to him what he has spent in producing it, he will not sell it, or he will stop producing it." The question, however, is by no means so easily answered. Many farmers, especially since 1920, have been unable to make any money on their wheat crops. In fact, a large number have suffered heavy losses. They have been unable to get a price sufficiently large to cover their costs of production. If prices were actually fixed by costs of production, then all producers would at least make their costs and thus break even. Consequently, we should have no failures in any line of business. Yet the fact is that we continually have thousands of farmers and firms forced into insolvency every year because they cannot get a price for their goods that equals their cost of production.

Many industries produce a large number of commodities. Most farmers raise several different crops; practically all mercantile firms carry different kinds of goods on their shelves. Our industrial executives, farmers, and storekeepers may lose on some articles and gain on others. They may even lose regularly on some particular kind of article but make enough on others to yield a profit for the business as a whole. For example, bankers may lose on small checking accounts and also on small loans, but they usually make up for such losses by handling larger accounts and by making larger loans. The ideal is to make a profit on the business as a going concern, regardless of the prices that may be charged for certain individual items produced or handled.

Continually, certain enterprises are being forced to the wall because they cannot sell their goods at a price that will enable them to meet their expenses. This decreases the number of producers and at times tends to raise prices, but even so there are always a number of enterprises in the field that do not make expenses (the submarginal firms) and also many that just break even (the marginal firms). The former do not cover costs, yet they have to sell their goods at the market price. Firms in both groups may remain in the field month after month and sometimes year after year, hoping that prices will rise or that they themselves may be able to reduce their costs of operation to the point where they can make a profit. Prices and costs are constantly changing. Firms that are above the margin one year may find themselves below it the next, yet no firm in a competitive field can absolutely fix the price of its products at cost of production plus a profit.

Rent and Prices—In discussing this subject, we come in contact with a commonly accepted idea which continues to play an important part in all arguments relating to price fixation, namely, that rent, being one of the costs of production, enters into the determination of price. In other words, an enterprise that pays a high rent has to charge a high price, and one that pays a low rent is able to and will charge a low price. Many individuals believe this statement to be true because they have noted that some stores in large cities pay high rents and charge high prices and also because they have read advertisements of this sort: "Trade upstairs and save $10, because we pay low rents." People are accustomed to believe what they read in print and seldom question what appears in their local newspapers.

Let us say that you are a farmer residing in a section of the state where you are able to rent land at $10 an acre, while I, who live nearer the city or who have hired more fertile land, am compelled to pay $20 an acre for my farm land. Let us say that both of us raise the same grade of wheat. When our wheat gets into the market, does yours carry a placard which reads, "This wheat has been raised on low rent land; therefore I will take a low price for it"? and is mine labeled with a sign which reads, "This wheat has been raised on high rent land; therefore it is high priced wheat"? Of course not. Your wheat and mine sell at the same price in the same market, regardless of the amount of rent that you and I have paid for our land. I may not be able to make a profit on my wheat because of my high costs of production, but my wheat sells for the same price as yours; likewise, even with your lower costs of production, you may not be able to sell your wheat at a profit. The price of our wheat is fixed in the market by the play of the forces of supply and demand, and not by the amount of rent we pay.

Does rent affect the price that will be charged by merchants to their customers? Can you buy at a lower price in a small store in a small country town or in a large store in a large city? Which pays the lower rent? Naturally, the small store in the small town; yet that store may charge higher prices. Take two stores in the same city. Which charges the higher price, the large department store located in the high rent area of town or the small store situated on the outskirts of town and paying a low rent? The answer is obvious.

High prices are charged by some stores that pay high rents because they are able to get high prices from their customers. If such stores have their rents reduced, they will not of necessity lower their prices.

What about upstairs stores and basement stores that advertise low prices because of low rents? Would you walk upstairs or go down into the basement if you received no advantage by doing so? You have to be induced to trade in such places, and low price is the inducement that is offered. Prices are not low because of low rents. In fact, quite frequently you will find a certain quality of goods sold in two stores at the same price even though one of the stores pays a high rent and one pays a low rent.

Many of the goods which we purchase today have their prices fixed by the producers. Can you purchase a Victor radio at a lower price in a low rent store than in a high rent store? Can you buy a Ford car in your home town at a lower price in an outlying, low rent auto dealer's show room than at a high rent show room located nearer the center of town? Again, what about the goods sold by chain stores? Can you purchase goods at Woolworth's, for example, at a lower price in one of that firm's low rent stores than in one of its high rent stores? Rent does not enter into the price of the articles that you purchase in five and ten cent stores or in any other chain stores.

There are some cases, however, where rent does enter into price. In many instances where prices are fixed by public authority, as is the case with railroad rates, the rates of public utilities, and so forth, costs of production are taken into consideration by the rate-fixing body, and rent is one of the costs of production. Again, where a business enterprise has the power to fix its prices, as in the case of some monopolies, an effort will be made to fix prices at a level that will pay costs of production plus a profit. Both of these exceptions to the general rule that rent does not affect price will be considered more fully in the later sections of this chapter.

Prices, Wages, Rent, and Interest—If prices are determined by cost of production, as is claimed by some writers, then an increase in wages, rent, and interest rates ought to raise prices, while a decrease in wages, rent, and interest rates ought to lower them. In other words, the cost of production theory of prices requires acceptance of the idea that wages, rent, and interest are active factors and that prices are passive ones. Oddly enough, however, as we study the economic world, we find that prices rise first and that wages, rent, and interest rates trail along behind on the way up. We also find that prices fall first, and that wages, rent, and interest rates trail along behind on the way down. This is due partly to the fact that as prices rise, those who receive wages, rent, and interest find that they cannot live as satisfactorily on their incomes as they did previously, when prices were lower, and they therefore insist upon a higher return for their services and for their property. They also have a much better bargaining power when prices rise, because those who are receiving the higher prices can better afford to pay a higher return. Wages, rent, and interest rates resist the pressure of falling prices to a certain extent, because their receivers, in order to retain their advantageous position, use various means at their disposal to bargain with those who purchase their labor power or who use their property. We find that wages, rent, and interest rates sometimes rise although prices are falling, and that prices sometimes rise although wages, rent, and interest rates are falling.

Joint Costs—Another point that seriously invalidates the cost of production theory of prices is the fact that many commodities are produced under conditions of joint costs. The act of producing some one thing may bring forth other quite distinct commodities. A farmer raises cattle; from the cattle come meat, hides, and various other products. When in the production of a principal commodity other products are created, the latter are called by-products. It is sometimes difficult to know just which is the main product and which is the secondary product, or by-product. A farmer raises sheep and markets both wool and mutton. A company produces coke and at the same time has gas for sale. The meat products of the great slaughter houses may not return a profit as great as that coming from lard and fertilizers. When the farmer raises sheep, his labor produces at least two things, mutton and wool, and there is no possible way of determining how much the wool cost as distinct from how much the mutton cost. This is the essential thing to note, and this is a problem of joint costs. One can only say that the wool and the mutton combined should bring enough in the market to cover the total cost of raising the sheep plus a reasonable profit. Where the costs are joint, it is impossible to determine a price which will make each of the commodities pay its share. The business that involves joint productivity has an economic advantage, because of the fact that low prices from one of the commodities may be offset by a strong market for the other.

Customary Prices—Very few persons realize how easy it is for the price of a certain article to become customary or fixed in the minds of the consuming public, changing only as the result of some unusual development in the economic world. Take, for example, the price of haircuts; it remained at twenty-five cents for many years, whether times were good or bad, whether the general price level was rising or falling, and whether the local population was increasing or decreasing. The public grew accustomed to thinking of haircuts in terms of a quarter of a dollar. The World War, however, changed this situation, as it did many others. The general price level rose rapidly; barbers found that they could not live on the income received from the old prices, and they consequently increased the price of a haircut to fifty cents and later to sixty-five cents, where it still remains, even though the general price level since 1920 has very greatly declined. The public has now become reconciled to paying sixty-five cents for a haircut, and that price has therefore become the customary charge. Street car fares were formerly only five cents, whether many or only a few rode on the cars and whether times were good or bad. Again, during the World War the rising price level increased costs of operation. This, with other conditions, made it possible for the street car companies to ask for the right to increase the fares, and the request in most cases was granted. Street car fares still remain at the higher level even though conditions have greatly changed in later years. The new rates, therefore, have now become the customary rates.

Customary prices may be changed by the bargaining power of the parties concerned, just as may other prices. If, for example, competition develops among the barbers, or if the public expresses unwillingness to continue paying sixty-five cents for a haircut, the price will then be modified. We shall see in the next section how the bargaining power of the public and of the operating companies affects the rates of railroads, telephone and telegraph companies, and similar concerns, the rates of which are fixed and determined by various government commissions.

Public Authority—The determination of prices by public authority is no new phenomenon in the economic life of the people. One does not have to go back very far in history to find certain prices being fixed either by law or by the edict of the ruler. During the Middle Ages it was customary for the government to fix the price of ale, bread, and various other articles of general consumption. With the dissolution of the mercantile system and the introduction of capitalism, accompanied, as it was, by the philosophy of *laissez faire* (freedom of competition), the old regulations were removed, and prices, wages, rent, and interest were left free to be fixed by the forces of supply and demand.

During the past thirty years, however, the pendulum has swung back again, and we now find ourselves living in a state of society in which there is a considerable amount of price fixing by government authority. Railroad, telephone, telegraph, motor bus, gas, electricity, pipe line, and street car rates are fixed in practically all the states of the Union by government commissions. For interstate traffic, rates are determined by the Interstate Commerce Commission. It is not possible to predict precisely to what extent the determination of prices by public authority will develop in the future. During the World War the United States Government fixed the prices of wheat and various other commodities for the purpose of conserving the interests of the country while at war. During that period the principle of "cost plus profit" was used in a number of instances. In other cases, however, the government followed the policy of fixing prices at "bulk line costs," the ideal being to fix the price of an article at a level that would enable the bulk of the producers, about 80%, to make a profit on their sales.

In fixing the rates of public service corporations, the various government commissions concern themselves primarily with costs of operation, the policy being so to fix the rate as to enable the companies to earn an amount which will defray costs and yield an average profit, usually about 6%, which rate appears to be rather commonly accepted as a fair return upon such types of enterprises. The Transportation Act of 1920 fixed that percentage as the basis to be used by the Interstate Commerce Commission in determining the rates of interstate carriers.

The rate fixing public commissions sit as courts and listen to the arguments of representatives of the company desiring to maintain the existing rates or to raise the rates, as well as to the arguments of representatives of the parties who are opposed to increased rates or who are demanding lower rates. Witnesses are examined, oral and written arguments are made, political and personal influence is used, and the decision is rendered in favor of that side which possesses the greater bargaining power. At times the decision may appear to be eminently unfair to the defeated side, and appeals are made to the courts, where again the two parties concerned fight the case out with all the strength of their respective bargaining powers.

Monopoly Prices—Thus far our discussion has been concerned primarily with the determination of prices in the competitive market. We have still to consider monopoly prices and the influences that affect them.

The difference between the monopolist and the individual who is engaged in a competitive business is that the monopolist has the power to limit the supply of his product placed in the market, while the owner of the competitive enterprise has no such control over the supply that enters the market. The supply of a competitive commodity is determined solely by the wishes of the various competitors. In the case of both monopolistic and competitive enterprises, the main object is to obtain the greatest net return on the business as a whole. The slogan of the competitive enterprise is "Big sales and a small profit on each sale," for it is hoped that this policy will yield the greatest net return. The monopolist, however, may have the opportunity of making the greatest net return either by large sales or by small sales, depending entirely on the situation with which he is faced and the character of the product which he has for sale.

The policy of the monopolist is to fix the price as nearly as possible at the point, not where he will make the greatest percentage of profit on each article sold, but where he will make the greatest net profit on all of the articles which he sells. If he fixes the price too high, he may be able to sell but a small amount of the commodity and obtain only a small net profit. If he fixes the price too low, he may make only a small profit on each sale and, even though he makes many more sales, may not obtain as great a net profit as he would have done had he fixed his price at a somewhat higher level. Of course, a monopolist cannot actually know at what price he will secure the greatest net return, for his costs vary from day to day and the demand for his goods likewise varies continually. He will, however, watch the situation carefully and, as well as he can, fix his price at that point which, over a period of time, will yield him the maximum net return.

Many who are unacquainted with the problems of monopoly and monopoly price maintain that monopoly price is exorbitantly high. This is by no means always the case. The monopolist, like the individual engaged in a competitive business, is concerned with the forces of supply and demand. There are certain limitations on the price which the monopolist can charge for his commodity. First, he cannot control the demand, and he dares not fix his price immoderately high lest the demand fall off to such an extent that his net profits will be reduced. Second, the monopolist who wishes to maintain his advantage must always remember that, if his price is very high, there is always the possibility that others may enter the field and compete with him. Although at any one particular time there may be no active competition, the monopolist must always take into account potential competition which may become active. Third, the monopolist usually tries to avoid arousing unfavorable public opinion with regard to himself and his goods. If the great body of consumers gets the impression that the price of the monopolized commodity is so high as to be exorbitant, there is danger of antagonism toward the business. Fourth, since in the United States legislation has been adopted limiting the scope and freedom of big business in striving for monopoly profits, monopolists have learned to fear further legislation which might reduce the advantages they enjoy as monopolists. The legislation enacted against monopolistic privileges in the past has related to prices, the marketing of goods, methods of advertising, and railroad rate discrimination.

Certain other elements enter into the situation which are frequently ignored by the uninitiated public. These may be briefly stated as (1) the nature of the demand for the commodity (whether elastic or inelastic) and (2) the nature of the industry (whether one of increasing or decreasing costs). The significance of these matters will be evident after a study of the four situations in which a monopolist may be placed.

1. Elastic demand and decreasing cost. Here the monopolist is selling a commodity the demand for which is elastic. He can greatly increase the quantity demand for his commodity by a small reduction in price. On the supply side, the monopolist is producing under decreasing costs; that is, the greater the quantity produced, the less the unit cost of production. Both of these forces working together make it profitable for the monopolist to produce large amounts of goods and to sell them at low prices. The elasticity of the demand for a monopolized commodity brings about an increase in the gross income from the sale of the goods, because the gross income equals the total quantity sold multiplied by the price of each unit of the commodity. Because the demand is elastic, a very small reduction in price will mean a great increase in the quantity de-

manded. Therefore, it will be profitable for the monopolist to lower his price to gain the advantages of a large quantity sale. In addition to the elasticity of demand, there is also the added inducement of diminishing costs, which would make it profitable for the monopolist to produce and sell a large quantity of goods for the sake of a low per unit cost.

2. Inelastic demand and increasing cost. Here the forces are the reverse of those just mentioned. The quantity demand does not greatly increase with low prices, nor does it greatly decrease with high prices. The greater the supply produced, the greater will be the cost for each unit. For these reasons the monopolist will obtain a greater net revenue by selling a comparatively small quantity at a high price than by selling a large quantity at a low price. Agricultural produce has for the most part an inelastic demand and is produced under increasing costs. In a general way the same may be said of coal and other mineral products. If the monopolist were able to monopolize these necessities of life, the social loss would be very great. Fortunately, however, the sources of supply of these commodities are so scattered that it is extremely difficult to gain a monopoly of them, even for a short period of time.

3. Elastic demand and increasing cost. As we have already seen, elasticity of demand for a commodity tends to increase the quantity put upon the market and so to lower the price of each unit. Increasing costs make it profitable to limit the supply and sell at a high price. In a situation of elastic demand and increasing

cost the two forces are counterbalancing each other in such a manner that, generally speaking, the monopolist will probably produce a moderate amount and sell it at a moderate price.

4. Inelastic demand and decreasing cost. Here again the two forces counterbalance each other, for inelasticity of demand is the factor which limits production, and a decrease in cost tends to bring about an increase in quantity production. If the two forces mentioned are equally balanced, the monopolist will produce a moderate amount and will sell at a moderate cost.

Summary and Conclusions on Price Determination—Prices for commodities may be established (1) by monopoly, (2) by competition, and (3) by the government or by other public authority.

The reasonableness of monopoly prices depends on the wisdom of the management of the monopolized product, on an analysis of the nature of the demand, on the cost of the supply, and on the responsiveness to public opinion. Intelligent monopoly may mean low prices if the economy of mass production is large and especially if costs decrease as the output is increased. One of the greatest dangers of a monopoly is to be found in inefficient management, largely the result of a lack of competition. In other words, an unfair price may result from an unreasonable increase in the cost of production.

Monopoly prices may obtain even where there is no official agreement as to policy. The coal dealers of a city may follow the quotations of one large dealer. In some lines of business the different competitive units await the opening prices of some old, well established company. Such instances may not constitute a compact, monopolistic price control, but, temporarily at least, there is an implied or a passive understanding.

Competitive prices result from the free play of demand and supply. When merchants and manufacturers quote prices, such quotations represent an analysis of market conditions and of the practice of competitors. Many conditions other than direct competition may enter into these prices. Selecting ten widely scattered stores in a large city, one would find considerable variation in price, even for staple commodities. Differences in the class of shoppers patronizing the store, in the nature of the service, in the extent of display, and in the amount of advertising contribute toward the creation of price differences. It must also be recognized that many business men are ignorant of their costs of merchandising, or even of their costs of production, and this condition allows considerable scope for price variation. It is also true that no two merchants or distributors produce or distribute products at the same cost. In the long run, however, general competitive prices must approximate one another. As we have seen, the degree to which demand and supply reach equilibrium depends upon the standardization of the commodities, the nature of the market, and the completeness of competition.

In practically every country there will be found some government effort to fix prices and rates. In the

United States thus far this policy has been extended only to public service corporations. The future may see a noticeable development along this line in other fields of economic activity. It is a very short step from the determination of rates for public service corporations to the determination of prices for some or many of the most necessary articles of ordinary consumption.

Class Price—One of the most interesting phenomena in connection with the subject of prices is what is known as class price. The consuming public represents a series of layers of demanders, arranged primarily on the basis of income. Producers realize that there are these various classes of demanders in the market and that not all of them will be appealed to by the same article at the same price. For example, not all members of the traveling public are content to carry their lunches with them or to ride in day coaches. Consequently, the railroads supply different classes of service to appeal to the pocketbooks of the different groups. They provide private coaches, special fare trains, fast trains, slow trains, compartments, upper berths, lower berths, day coaches, observation coaches, diners, all day lunch cars, and so forth. By this diversification each group of the traveling public is encouraged to use the services of the railroad. The manufacturer of automobiles produces a low priced car, a medium priced car, and a high priced car, so that the various income groups may be induced to purchase automobiles priced within their reach. The manufacturer of soap knows that many will refuse to purchase a soap that is not scented or a soap that is not put up in a box. Consequently, he places on the market unscented soap, scented soap, soap not in boxes, soap in ordinary boxes, and soap in fancy boxes. Some housewives are unwilling to purchase a cheap baking powder, regardless of its excellence. Others will purchase only a cheap baking powder. At times, in order to take advantage of the vagaries of the consuming public, which usually knows little and cares less about what it buys, the manufacturer may place the same product on the market under different names and at different prices.

Thus it is that by taking into consideration the demands of the various layers of income groups, producers are able to extend their markets and to obtain greater profits.

The General Price Level—Thus far we have considered only individual prices or the prices of individual commodities and the factors that affect them. There is another problem, however, that is even more difficult, not only to solve but also to understand. This problem concerns the influences that determine the *general price level*. We ordinarily think of the prices of only a few commodities. We seldom stop to consider the average prices of all commodities, or what is known as the general price level. Of course, we can never obtain any figures or data showing what is actually happening to all prices, because there are literally millions of prices in the market. In discussing this matter of prices we must again recall to our minds the fact that wages, rent, and interest, railroad rates, telephone rates, and the like are just as much a part of the general price level as is the price of wheat, clothing, and food.

Because of the complexity of the situation, it is impossible for us to obtain information concerning all of the prices in the market place, but we are able to obtain abundant data relative to the prices of hundreds of articles which are of general importance. We can take these prices and arrange them in tables of various sorts and can ascertain therefrom whether prices in general are rising or falling. When the general level of prices is rising, some prices will be falling, others will be remaining stationary, and still others will be rising very rapidly. It is the average or general price level that we are interested in. When prices rise, the cost of living increases, and when they fall, the cost of living decreases.

In the course of our history as a nation we have had some peaks of very high prices and some valleys of very low prices. The chart on page 500 graphically discloses what our experiences have been in that regard. Our problem is to explain these great variations in the general price level of our country. In passing, it is interesting to note that these great swings in our general price level have been roughly paralleled by those of other capitalistic countries, such as England, France, and Germany.

Quantity Theory of Money—Of the numerous explanations that have been offered for the variations in the general price level, the one that has been most widely accepted by economists is known as the *quantity theory of money*. Although this theory is a rather complicated one and should be presented in a very detailed manner, we have space in this volume only for a brief and general explanation of its more important aspects. Briefly, the quantity theory of money is based on the idea that the fluctuations in the general price level are due to the changing value of money.

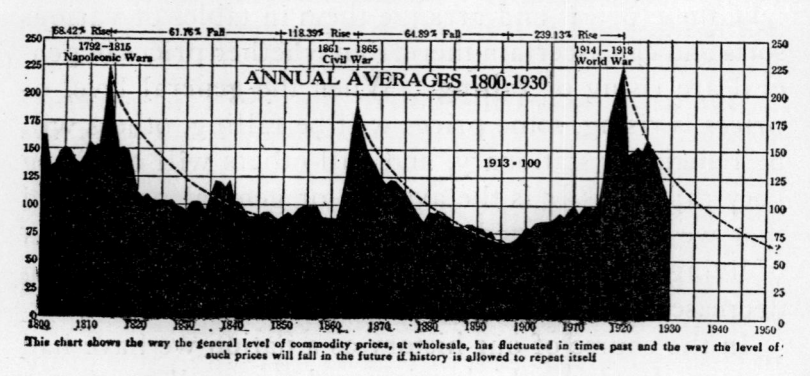

GENERAL LEVEL OF WHOLESALE PRICES IN THE UNITED STATES FROM 1800 TO 1930*

What is the value of money? We have noted in earlier pages that money is valued only because of what it will buy. Our gold dollar remains the same in weight and in size from year to year. Yet what it buys today will be more or less than what it will buy tomorrow. As the price level goes up the dollar will buy less, and as the price level goes down the dollar will buy more. There is no way of measuring the value of the dollar except by what it will buy. If anything

---
*Chart prepared by the Stable Money Association.

happens to make the dollar cheaper, it will not be worth as much as it was before. It will not buy as much as it did before. Consequently, with the dollar being measured in terms of what it will buy, if it becomes cheaper its lowered value will be shown by the tendency of prices to rise. Conversely, if anything happens to make the dollar more valuable, it will be worth more; being worth more, it will therefore buy more than it did before, and that means that the general price level will fall.

But what makes the dollar rise and fall in value? When we speak of the dollar in connection with the quantity theory of money, we mean all kinds of dollars that are actually used to buy things—metallic dollars, paper money dollars, and dollars in the forms of checks, drafts, and other negotiable instruments that are used to make purchases. Furthermore, it is only the dollars in circulation that have any effect upon the value of the dollar. The funds that are stored away and are not in circulation, not being used to buy things, can have no more effect upon the value of the dollar than the uncaught fish in the sea can have upon the value of the fish that are for sale in the market. Most people forget that dollars are things that are demanded by the public, just as are other commodities. The demand of the public for dollars varies considerably from time to time. Most people also forget that the supply of dollars likewise varies greatly from time to time. Not infrequently we have in circulation more dollars than are required to meet the demands of the people, and at other times we have fewer than are required. Dollars, therefore, are subject to the forces of supply and demand just as are all of the other things that people desire and use, and the forces of supply and demand affect the value of dollars just as they affect the value of the other things.

The quantity theory of money holds that if something happens to increase or to decrease the supply of or the demand for dollars, their value will be affected and prices will be adjusted to meet that changed value, for it must be always kept in mind that the value of the dollar is expressed in terms of what the dollar will buy, and in no other terms.

Supply of Dollars—What affects the supply of dollars? Two important matters must be considered: (1) the actual number of dollars in circulation and (2) the velocity or rapidity with which these dollars pass from hand to hand. In estimating the quantity of dollars in circulation, we first of all must take into consideration the various kinds of money that are put into circulation by the government and by the banks of the country—both our metallic money and our paper money. But, as has been noted earlier, such kinds of money are employed to make but from 5% to 10% of our purchases. The other source of our supply of dollars is our credit machinery, primarily our banks. Banks create credit and enable us to use checks, drafts, and other kinds of negotiable instruments just as we use metallic and paper money dollars, and it is these credit dollars that are employed to take care of about 90% to 95% of our purchases. Anything, therefore, which enables banks to create more credit dollars is bound to affect the quantity of dollars in circulation. From the Institute course entitled Money and Banking you will learn what the various factors are which influence the amount of bank credit available in a country. We cannot discuss that matter here.

What is meant by the velocity or rapidity of circulation of our dollars? If during last year I carried a $10 gold piece in my pocket and finally spent it on the last day of the year for groceries, that coin was used to make but $10 worth of purchases during the year. On the other hand, if, as soon as I had obtained that $10 gold piece I had spent it for groceries and the grocer had on the same day used it to pay his wholesaler and the wholesaler had used it to pay his laborers, then in one day's time that $10 gold piece would have actually performed the work of $30 of money. In the first case cited, the $10 gold piece had a very slight velocity of circulation; in the second case, the rate of circulation was much greater. A great deal of our money passes quickly from hand to hand and makes many purchases, doing the work of a much larger quantity of dollars. Checks are usually used two or three or four times before being cashed at the bank upon which they have been drawn, thus doing the work that otherwise would have required the use of a much larger number of dollars. Obviously, then, the number of times dollars are used in a year greatly affects the total number of dollars in circulation during that period.

Demand for Dollars—We must also consider the

demand for dollars and the forces which produce that demand. Our people must have various kinds of dollars with which to carry on their business activities and to make their daily purchases. If the demand for these dollars is great and if the dollars do not come into circulation in sufficiently large quantities to meet that demand, their value must rise. If, on the other hand, more dollars come into the market than are required to meet the popular demand, their value will fall. The rising value of the dollar affects prices and causes them to fall, and the decreasing value of the dollar affects prices and causes them to rise.

Application of the Quantity Theory—If space permitted, we could show how economists have explained the rise and fall in the general price level of the United States by means of the quantity theory of money. We have room for but one brief statement regarding the application of this theory to the changing price level of our country. Let us take the period following the Civil War. Prices fell from the very high level of 1865 to the very low level of 1896. Meanwhile, American industry was expanding at an amazing rate. The West was being opened up; railroads were being constructed, farms developed, factories built, and mines dug. The number of dollars available, however, by no means increased at the rate demanded by the expansion of business and the needs of the people. Dollars, consequently, became relatively scarce. They increased in value, and prices accordingly fell. Then gold was discovered in Alaska and in the Rand district of South Africa. Some of it got into circulation as gold coins and gold certificates. Much more of it went into the banks, where it was used to create dollars in the form of credit. These dollars got into circulation; in fact, more of them were put into the market than were actually required. Prices did not remain the same, as they would have done had just the right amount of dollars been placed in circulation; instead, prices began to rise. From 1896 to 1913 they rose more than 33 1/3%.

Other prominent swings in the general price level could be similarly explained if space permitted. Further discussion of the quantity theory, however, must be postponed to the course in Money and Banking.

Stabilization of the Price Level—Great variations in the general price level have a marked effect upon our different economic classes. Rising prices always give a more optimistic tone to business, and falling prices exert the reverse influence. Producers always prefer a rising price level, because this leads to higher prices for goods and usually to greater profits. Consumers prefer a falling price level, because it enables them to buy more for their money. Debtors benefit from rising prices. For example, if they are farmers, they can sell their crops for higher prices and thus pay off their debts more easily. Creditors benefit from falling prices, because when their money is paid back by their debtors it will purchase more goods. In general, however, business prefers a stable price level, because this enables the executives to plan their future operations with greater certainty.

The marked rise in the general price level in the period from 1914 to 1920 and its rapid decline during 1920 and 1921 have provoked discussions as to the advisability of adopting some plan whereby prices in general might be prevented from fluctuating as widely as they have done in the past. Many proposals have been made, some of them extremely fantastic. Thus far, however, but one plan has been partially tried out, and the results obtained have been only moderately satisfactory. Only a few lines can be devoted to outlining the general features of this plan.

We have seen that our credit dollars in the form of checks, drafts, and other negotiable instruments form by far the greater proportion of all of the dollars in circulation—in fact, about 90% to 95%. If it is deemed advisable to try to control the number of dollars in circulation for the purpose of stabilizing the general price level, efforts should be concentrated upon controlling the amount of credit dollars in circulation. The Federal Reserve banks are the most important and powerful elements in the credit structure of our country. By means of their statistical bureaus they keep a constant check on prices, business activities, the demand for credit, the supply of dollars available, and a host of similar matters. They are also enabled to increase or to decrease the amount of credit in the market by lending to member banks, by discounting commercial paper for them, and by engaging in what are known as open market operations. When the Federal Reserve banks engage in open market operations, they go into the market and buy or sell United States bonds or United States certificates of indebtedness (short time loans of the national government) and commercial paper of various kinds, primarily bank acceptances. If there appears to be a shortage of credit or of dollars available, the Federal Reserve banks purchase the above mentioned obligations, usually from banks or from stock and bond houses. This procedure places in the hands of the sellers more dollars, which can be used to satisfy the demands of business for more funds. If, on the other hand, there appears to be too large a number of dollars in circulation, if there is too much credit available, then the Federal Reserve banks go into the market and sell the securities and commercial paper, thus withdrawing some of the surplus dollars from the market.

The method described was employed in the period from 1921 to 1929 and worked fairly satisfactorily, the general price level fluctuating within rather narrow limits. Since July 1929, however, although the Federal Reserve banks have placed what really amounts to an oversupply of credit or dollars in the market through their open market operations and although they have greatly lowered their discount rates (to the lowest point in their history), prices have steadily declined. This fact shows how difficult it is for any method, no matter how convincing it is on paper, to be effective in stabilizing the price level, especially during abnormal times.

One objection to the proposal that the general price level should be stabilized is based upon the fact that the general price level is a composite of the prices of many different groups of commodities. We have prices of imported goods, of exported goods, of farm products, of manufactured products, of products of the mine, and of products of the forest. How is it possible to effect any stabilization of the general price level that will stabilize the prices of all of these various groups of commodities? For example, if for any reason, farm products began to rise, then by some means or other the prices of manufactured products would have to be forced down so as to keep the general price level stationary. No scheme has thus far been devised that could successfully stabilize the price level of each of these various groups of commodities.

There are other objections to the suggestion that the general price level should be stabilized, but these will be more fully considered in the Institute course in Money and Banking.

CHAPTER XXII

Suggested Methods of Reform

THUS far we have been concerned with the attempt to obtain an understanding of the philosophy, principles, institutions, and methods of capitalism. In this concluding chapter we shall consider some of the suggestions that have been made for the improvement of our economic scheme of things.

It would be difficult to find a person who is thoroughly satisfied with things as they exist today. The spirit of discontent has always characterized the human race. Not being satisfied to "let well enough alone," it has ever continued to demand more things, different things, and better economic, social, and political conditions. Our economic life and our economic institutions have always been in a state of flux, or change. This has been due to the fact that in every situation there develop certain forces which make changes inevitable. Some of these developments are planned by the leaders of the people; others are not.

Groups Advocating a Change—Those who suggest modifications of the present economic arrangements may be divided into two groups: (1) those who desire to retain the essence of capitalism, that is, private ownership of property, but who wish to modify it in certain minor points; and (2) those who are of the opinion that capitalism has outlived its usefulness and should be supplanted by another and a radically different kind of economic society. The first group consists of those who are known as *social reformers;* the second, of those who are known as *radicals* or *revolutionists.* The term revolutionist, as applied to those who desire a complete change in our economic order, does not imply that the individuals so characterized wish to resort to violence or armed revolt to accomplish their ends. With the exception of the violent anarchists, of whom there are practically none at present, the means that the revolutionists propose to employ in attaining the overthrow of capitalism are either political or economic in character.

Social Reformers—The social reformer is desirous of retaining the outstanding institutions of capitalism, especially that of private ownership, but wishes to modify or to change them somewhat in order that some of the present defects or abuses may be removed. He is interested in advocating labor and factory legislation, so as to eliminate the evils of child and woman labor, shorten the hours of work, improve working conditions, and provide for safety of employment and for compensation in case of the injury or death of the worker. He urges the adoption of various economic and political reforms which will give the employed class more economic, social, and political rights, improve the standards of business practices, remove graft from political life, and bring efficiency into government activities—in short, create upon this earth a better life for the great majority of the people by removing the weaknesses of capitalism.

The social reformer admits that all is not well with our economic, social, and political institutions. He agrees with the radicals that changes ought to be effected for the purpose of improving the condition of the people as a whole, but he parts company with them when it comes to suggesting the means proposed for bringing about the desired conditions. He is of the opinion that capitalism is still strong and virile in character and that it provides mankind with many opportunities and with more freedom of action than any other state of society would provide. He maintains that the abolition of capitalism would be not only undesirable but actually disastrous so far as the interests of the people in general are concerned. His ideal, therefore, is to modify capitalism by patching up its weak spots, at the same time retaining its more outstanding features.

Radicals—Radicals refuse to listen to what they call the "mild" suggestions of the social reformers. They claim that capitalism cannot be modified so as to insure increased happiness and greater economic well-being for the people and that consequently it should be thrust aside and replaced by another and more desirable state of society. They are not content to patch up its weak spots; they wish to abolish it completely. In passing, it is advisable to point out that the radicals wish not to destroy capital but merely to change the character of its ownership. It is now privately owned. They wish to place its ownership in the hands of the public or in the hands of the workers who are employed in the individual industries. As we have noted in earlier pages, public ownership would involve government ownership, socialism, or guild socialism, while worker ownership would involve cooperation, syndicalism, collectivist anarchism, or communism.

The Indictment of Capitalism—The outstanding criticisms which the radicals direct against the capitalist régime and the manner in which it functions may be briefly summarized as follows:

1. Capitalism is wasteful of natural and human resources. It is not concerned over the facts that annually thousands of workers are killed and millions are injured in the course of industry and that the nation's supplies of oil, lumber, coal and other gifts of nature are exploited wastefully, with no thought of the future. Business is business, and the ideal in mind is to make profits regardless of the present or future welfare of the people.

2. Capitalism results in continued strife. First, there is the never ending struggle between labor and capital, which results in great economic losses and distress. Second, there is the never ending struggle between one business enterprise and another for markets, for customers, and for profits.

3. Capitalism causes waste of effort and waste of productive resources. Many more enterprises are established than are necessary to supply the needs of the public. Duplication of railroads, stores, manufacturing plants, oil wells, and other enterprises makes for a waste of capital, capital goods, land, and labor power.

4. Capitalism is responsible for overproduction, un-

employment, poverty, inequality, the concentration of wealth, adulteration, "cheap and shoddy goods," commercial dishonesty, crime, slums, sweat-shops, lack of opportunity for the masses, and injustice in the courts.

Groups of Radicals—There are various kinds of radicals advocating many varieties of proposals. It is possible, however, to classify the most important groups broadly as follows: socialists (Utopian, Christian, Fabian, state, guild, scientific, Marxian), single taxers, anarchists, syndicalists, and communists. Only the briefest discussion of the ideas of these various groups can be presented in the following pages.

Utopian Socialists—The Utopian socialists are those radicals who have devised some "perfect plan" in accordance with which society should be organized. They draw up their various plans with the greatest detail and describe just how people are to live and to work in the ideal future state. They fail, however, to appreciate the fact that society is continually evolving and changing from one stage into another and that it can never be consciously molded to fit into any particular scheme or plan; furthermore, because society is of an evolutionary, continually changing character, even though it could be forced into a certain ideal set of arrangements, it would not long remain there but would in time pass on to something else.

The Utopians claim that if only a majority of mankind could be induced to believe in their ideal plan, it could be put into effect in just the same manner as the plans of an architect for an office building are worked out in wood and stone. The Utopians do not appeal to any particular class of people but to all classes. They have at times attempted to put their plans into effect by establishing what are called "communities," or "cooperative colonies," the idea being that when men see that the ideal scheme works out satisfactorily on a small scale, they will be willing to adopt it nationally or even internationally. Edward Bellamy's books entitled Looking Backward and Equality, published in 1888 and 1897, respectively, excellently expressed the aspirations of the Utopian socialist, as did that interesting book called Utopia, written by Sir Thomas More in 1516.

Christian Socialists—The Christian socialists may be divided into two groups. One group believes that an ideal state of society could be brought about if the doctrines of the church were universally adopted. These people maintain that if all of us followed the teachings of the golden rule, our industrial and social evils would soon pass away. The second group consists of those who maintain that the ideals of Christianity can be realized only under a régime of socialism. They find in the teachings of Jesus Christ the basis for a belief in scientific or Marxian socialism.

Fabian Socialists—The Fabian socialists are a small group of individuals who are members of the Fabian Society of London, organized in 1884. This society at one time had within its ranks many of the prominent men and women of England. The Fabians believe that the abolition of capitalism should be brought about gradually. They advocate government and municipal ownership of the tools of production as a step toward the attainment of their ideal. They are decidedly opportunistic in their demands, insisting upon using the means nearest at hand to modify capitalism so as to bring about its ultimate dissolution. The Fabians have exerted a powerful influence on the socialist movement in England but have had slight, if any, effect upon the socialist movement in other countries.

State Socialists—The advocates of state socialism believe that the functions of the state should be expanded into fields occupied at present by the individual. They prefer to work through the present state for the purpose of accomplishing such economic and social changes as government ownership, government irrigation, reclamation and forestry projects, social insurance, factory legislation, and similar reform measures.

The demands of the state socialists are objected to by those who are more radical in their views on the ground that, under government ownership, the members of the working class would be exploited by a bureaucratic government instead of by the capitalists. They fear that the ideal sought would result in a military landlord and a police state, which would not be favorable to the ideals of democracy. Under government ownership, as it is at present in effect, the workers have no control over their wages, hours, or conditions of employment. In the United States, government employees are not permitted to organize into unions for the purpose of increasing their bargaining power. If a strike were declared against the government by the employees of the post office, it would be deemed an act of treason. The more radical groups oppose the demands of the state socialists on the ground that if these demands were attained, they would prevent the establishment of a state of society controlled by a democratically organized working class.

Guild Socialists—The guild socialists advocate a rather unique sort of arrangement, in accordance with the terms of which the government is to own the industries and the industries are to be operated and managed by the guilds or associations of the workers employed therein. For example, the government would own the railroads but would turn their management and operation over to the guild of railroad workers. The different groups of railroad employees, through their organizations, would elect representatives to serve on committees and councils, and through the committees and councils they would completely control and manage the railroad activities of the country. The guild socialists have been confined almost solely to England, where the principles of the movement were widely discussed during and immediately following the World War. At present, however, the agitation is practically non-existent.

Scientific or Marxian Socialists—The principles which underlie the most important and most active phase of the socialist movement are based upon the writings of an outstanding German economist of the nineteenth century, Karl Marx. The essence of the ideas, advocated by the Marxian socialists is found in a small pamphlet, the Communist Manifesto, published in 1848 and written by Karl Marx and Friedrich Engels. These ideas were later amplified by Marx in his monumental work of three volumes, entitled Capital. Marx and his associates essayed to place the philosophy of socialism upon a scientific basis. They attempted to explain the origin of capitalistic society, to analyze and account for its dominant characteristics, and to present an interpretation of its future. The fundamental thesis of scientific socialism is that the great mass of the people, the working class, is exploited under the capitalistic régime by the employers and that the only means by which the economic and social freedom of the workers can be attained is through the activities of a united and class-conscious working class imbued with the ideals of socialism. The Marxian socialist movement, therefore, makes its appeal primarily to the working class, although there are others in all walks of life who have become advocates of the socialist ideals.

In analyzing the present capitalistic society, the Marxian socialists find that it contains within itself certain germs or conditions which they claim will inevitably lead to its downfall and its replacement by socialism. Briefly reviewing the tenets of the Marxian socialist, we find that, first of all, it is claimed that society has consistently passed from one stage into another. Society, so it is stated, was at first in an era of barbarism, next in one of slavery, and then in a period of feudalism, which in turn gradually evolved into the present state of capitalism. Inasmuch as society has always progressed from one stage to another, they maintain that capitalism in its turn will be discarded and that the next era will be that of socialism.

In addition to this description of the evolutionary development of society, the socialists propound the materialistic conception of history, with its accompanying doctrine of the class struggle. The Marxians maintain that the history of all society has been a history of class struggles—the slave against the master, the serf against the lord, and the employee against the employer. They claim that history can be interpreted only in this manner. They point out that throughout the past the workingman has continually improved his industrial, social, and political position, passing from the status of a slave into that of a serf, and then into that of a free workingman with the right to vote, to hold office, to organize unions, and to engage in various kinds of activities that were denied him previously. They declare that as the working class has struggled upward it has pushed aside other classes. The slave-owning class, the feudal lord class, the merchant class, the farmer class—all in their turn have been relegated to the background, until today the workers find themselves faced merely by the employing class. The employers are few in number; the workers are many. The struggle between these two groups, so it is stated, will be short-lived if the workers will only appreciate their strength and become imbued with the idea that their interests can best be served by the introduction of a socialist régime. The Marxian socialists, therefore, urge the workers of the world to unite under the banner of socialism and to vote for socialist party candidates, by that means paving the way for the introduction of a socialistic state of society.

The Marxian socialists base much of their propaganda on what is known as the Marxian labor theory of value. Marx claimed that the value of an article was determined by the amount of socially necessary labor power embodied in it. This theory is a slight modification of that which was earlier proposed by Ricardo, an outstanding English banker-economist, who held that the quantity of labor involved in producing an article determined its value. Marx, after advancing his labor theory of value, proceeded to show that labor creates all exchange value (not all wealth) but that the laborer does not receive in the form of wages an amount equal to the value which he creates. Thus a surplus value remains out of which are paid rent, interest, and profits to landlords, capitalists, and business owners, respectively, who constitute the exploiting class. The Marxian socialists maintain that, inasmuch as labor creates all exchange value, it should receive all of this value and that those who are paid rent, interest, and profits are mere robbers, who themselves produce nothing but take their income from the products of the workers.

Upon this theory of surplus value is based the Marxian or socialist explanation of crises. Inasmuch as the workers receive but a small share of their products, it is impossible for them to purchase an amount of goods in excess of their wages. The employer cannot use up all of the surplus products and consequently has to go in search of markets and customers. The workers of other countries, however, who likewise constitute a majority of the purchasing public, are also exploited by their employers and cannot purchase all that they produce. The result is that in time the surplus products of capitalistic industry accumulate. The employer has to close his plant because he cannot market his goods. A depression occurs, banks fail, unemployment is prevalent, poverty results, and all the miseries of a business depression follow in quick succession.

Accompanying this explanation of crises is an argument which, like many others advanced by the socialists, is used to support the contention that the socialist régime is inevitable. It is claimed that, with the increased productivity of the workers through the introduction of machinery and more efficient methods of production, industry will pile up surplus values at an increasingly rapid rate and thus bring about more frequent disruptions in our business life.

Capitalism, in its desire to create foreign markets, civilizes backward peoples, imbues them with the desire for cheap, machine made goods, and causes them in turn to establish capitalistic industries. Strangely enough, the capitalists of the more advanced nations assist in various ways in the establishment of industries in backward countries and by doing so destroy the markets which they have built up for their own goods. These backward countries in time become economically self-sufficient and begin to search for foreign markets. This leads to an increased competition between them and the older capitalistic countries and brings about more frequent periods of overproduction and depression. The so-called business cycle thus becomes shorter in duration, and business finds itself in a state of continued depression with millions of workers unemployed. Discontent then arises; the workers become class-conscious, accept the doctrines of socialism, vote to overthrow the capitalistic régime, and thus bring in a socialistically organized state of society.

The theory of surplus value is also used by the socialists as showing that the increased concentration of industry is inevitable. They maintain that, with employers receiving profits for which they have no need in satisfying their wants for food, clothing, and so forth, there arises the problem of the reinvestment of those profits. The profits are accordingly used to purchase or to establish other industries. There thus arise monopolies and combinations, which yield increased dividends, which in turn also have to be invested. This brings about further concentration, until finally the outstanding industries of the country fall into the ownership of a very few people. These owners of the nation's business enterprises then become so powerful that the government can no longer satisfactorily control or regulate their affairs. The condition of the working class becomes increasingly deplorable, and the people come to feel that in order to protect their economic interests something must be done. They then turn to socialism as a means of salvation and through the use of the ballot overthrow the capitalistic order and bring in collective ownership and operation of the industries of the nation.

Characteristics of a Socialist State—The Marxian socialists see in the present capitalistic system many tendencies which they claim will inevitably bring about a socialistic régime. They desire to assist in hastening the attainment of their ideal by educating the people to an appreciation of the defects of our present state of society and by outlining in a general way the conditions which they expect to see established under socialism. The Marxian socialists, although talking of the overthrow of capitalism, of their demands for revolutionary socialism, and of other fearsome matters, do not propose to employ force or violence to attain their end. They believe in government, in the state, and in the use of the ballot and educational means to secure their ends.

The Marxian socialists refuse to describe in detail the outstanding features of their proposed state of society. They advocate collective ownership and operation of the more important productive enterprises. They claim that, inasmuch as in the political field we have adopted the principles of democracy, it is advisable that we apply similar principles in the industrial field. Thus, the ideal state of society championed by the socialists is often characterized as an industrial democracy.

The principles of socialism have never been put into effect. The institution that today most closely approximates the ideals which the socialists seek to have realized is our public school system. The public grammar and high schools are owned by the city or school district; they are supported by public taxation and are usually managed by a board of education elected by the voters of the district. It is thought that a similar plan might meet the demands of the socialists for the democratic ownership and management of the industries of the nation. The socialist government would own all or practically all of the productive enterprises of the country. Administrative bureaus, elected by the people, would have complete charge of their operation. These bureaus would be subject to the will of the people through the exercise of the power of initiative, referendum, and recall. Under socialism the private ownership of small stores, farms, shoe repair establishments, and so forth might be permitted.

Nobody can tell definitely just what the details of the system would be. The socialists maintain that, unlike the Utopians, they are not interested in creating a future state of society in accordance with the details of a prearranged plan; that all that they are interested in accomplishing is the abolition of capitalism and the substitution of collective ownership and operation of the tools of production. They are willing to let the details of the new society be taken care of as each new situation arises.

It should be pointed out that the advocates of Marxian socialism have no desire to pay all workers the same wage or even to pay them in accordance with their needs, as practically all of the Utopians and many of the communists would do. Socialism stands only for collective ownership of productive enterprises, not for collective ownership of income and its equal distribution.

Socialist Methods of Obtaining Possession—Naturally the question arises as to how the socialist government is to obtain possession of the productive enterprises of the country. Four methods have been suggested: (1) to purchase them outright, (2) to provide their present owners with life pensions, (3) to build enterprises to compete with them, and (4) to confiscate them. There is no agreement among the socialists as to which of the proposed methods should be employed.

Single Taxers—The advocates of the single tax locate the source of all the ills of the present economic society in the private ownership of the unearned increment of land. The single taxers believe that man should have free access to land, a gift of nature. Land has value only because of the presence of society. The value of land increases through the demand of the people. Land is purchased and held in many cases for speculation, the owner being desirous of selling it for more than it cost him. If one buys a plot of ground in a rapidly growing community and lets it lie idle, it increases in value through no effort of the owner.

The single taxer maintains that this unearned increment belongs to society and should be taken from the owner by means of a tax. All other taxes should be abolished, and only the single tax absorbing all of the unearned increment of land should be levied. By this means the holding of land for speculation would be made unprofitable and would therefore cease. The people would have freer access to the land, because, if the owner could not obtain the unearned increment, he would be forced either to improve the land himself or to transfer it to others. The taxing of the unearned increment of land would open up much land to the public. People would leave the city to engage in agricultural activities. This would cause wages to rise and the conditions of the working class to improve. The single taxers see in their proposal a panacea for all of the ills of present-day society.

Many objections are raised against the single tax. It is claimed that it is unfair to tax the owners of land and to relieve all others from taxation. The single tax would not be elastic, as has been pointed out in earlier pages. It would not provide sufficient funds to care for the needs of the government for additional income in emergencies or at other times. The desire of many to own land would be destroyed if they were denied the right to profit from the unearned increment; thus the single tax would strike at the roots of the present concept of private property.

The single taxers were far more numerous in the United States during the last two decades of the nineteenth century than they have been since that time, largely because of the influence of their outstanding leader, Henry George, the author of Progress and Poverty, a volume which has been called the "bible" of this group of propagandists.

Anarchists—There are very few anarchists who desire to attain their goal by resorting to violence. Practically all of them depend upon education and propaganda to obtain adherents to their belief.

Anarchists refuse to recognize authority; therefore they are opposed to the state, to participation in political movements, and to the church. They believe that man is endowed with certain natural, inalienable rights and that, because those rights are derived from nature, the state and the church have no authority to place restrictions and regulations upon man as to how he should exercise them.

There are two general groups of anarchists: (1) the individualists and (2) the communists or collectivists. The individualist anarchist is a thoroughgoing believer in the principle of freedom of competition. He declares that no restrictions of any kind should prevent the forcing of the weak to the wall. The race should be to the swift, the battle to the strong. If it is possible for one man to obtain control of all the industries of a country, he should be free to do so. Thus the individualist anarchist is an advocate of the philosophy of the superman.

The communist or collectivist anarchist differs from the individualist anarchist in regard to the proposed ideal state of society. The collectivist anarchist, like the Utopian socialist, advocates a future state of society based upon communist or cooperative groups. Those who work on a railroad should own and operate it; those who work in a store should own and manage it. The collectivist anarchist, in short, is an advocate of the ideal of voluntary cooperation carried to its logical extreme. He sees in the present cooperative marketing societies, cooperative creameries, cooperative stores, and similar enterprises the germ of his ideal society. He merely urges the expansion of such activities until all of the productive enterprises are organized upon the cooperative basis.

Syndicalists—The syndicalist believes in a rather interesting combination of radical proposals. He maintains that all the workers should unite into industrial unions, all the workers of an industry belonging to a union of that industry. The syndicalist takes from the socialist the principle of class struggle, maintaining that the worker has nothing in common with the members of any other class. The worker should not engage in political activity, because other classes vote. He should have nothing to do with the church, because the church is not a working class institution. Thus the syndicalist follows the anarchist in his opposition to state and church. The syndicalist's ideal of future society is taken from the collectivist anarchist and embodies the proposal that the workingmen in an industry should own and operate it upon a cooperative basis.

To bring about the destruction of capitalism, the syndicalist, not believing in the state, refuses to use the ballot and demands that only economic measures be employed. He suggests that the strike be resorted to for the purpose of wearing down the employing class; he considers the industrial union a much more effective weapon for that purpose than the trade union. Strikes should be called as frequently as possible for the purpose of breaking down the resistance of the capitalists. The general strike should also be resorted to, involving all of the workers of the country, who would by common agreement lay down their tools on a certain day and thus bring about chaos in industry until such a time as their demands were granted.

The syndicalist also advocates the use of *sabotage,* which calls for the use of all possible tactics that can bring economic loss to the employer. Soldiering on the job, restricting output, misdirecting packages, wrecking machinery, and disobeying orders are a few of the many forms of *sabotage* which it is hoped by the syndicalists will be used by the workers to disorganize capitalistic industry and force its owners to turn their enterprises over to the workers' industrial unions. The unions will then proceed to own and manage the enterprises of the country. The syndicalist movement has never obtained a strong foothold in the United States, although for a time it was active and influential as a force in the French labor movement.

Communists—The communists of today comprise the adherents of the announced doctrines of the bolshevists of Russia. The bolshevists profess to be advocates of Marxian socialism, but the connection is repudiated by many Marxians. The latter claim that Russia has not passed through the capitalistic stage which Marx maintained would precede socialism.

The situation in Russia has been controlled by a dictatorship of the proletariat, involving a thoroughly autocratic government, which obtained its power and authority as the result of a bloody revolution in 1917. The Russian experiment has gone through several stages. Originally the plan involved the complete nationalization of both land and capital, with the government controlling all phases of production and distribution. Private property in consumption and production goods was abolished. Only those who labored were to receive incomes. The original plan proved to be impracticable, however, and as a consequence certain concessions were made in the nature of a compromise with capitalism.

Since 1920 the economic life of Russia has experienced many interesting developments. The government, while retaining the ownership of the more important industries, now permits private ownership of small enterprises. The most important concession has been to permit the peasants to own their land, although the government itself is engaged in several large agricultural projects. The soviet government has also leased certain industries to private parties on the basis of royalties or rentals. At present the group in control in Russia is striving to complete a five-year program by means of which it is hoped that the government industries will be placed upon a productive basis similar to that enjoyed by the more progressive capitalistic countries. Huge sums of money are being spent to build factories, to construct railroads, and to bring about the industrialization of the country along modern lines.

Objections Offered to Radical Programs—The criticisms of capitalistic society advanced by the radicals have had the effect of calling to the attention of the public the necessity of certain reform measures. As a result, much has already been accomplished in improving economic conditions. However, much still remains to be done, as undoubtedly will always be the case, for life in its various aspects will never be ideal. Very few radicals give thought to the objections that have been offered to their proposals. They are content to condemn the present order and make converts to their beliefs, but not to consider seriously the practicability of the schemes which they advocate. This criticism can also be truthfully directed against any group that proposes to change our economic society.

Strength of Capitalism—Serious objections can be and have been raised not only to the theories of the radicals but also to their proposals of an ideal state of society. In the first place, they unquestionably underrate the strength of the present capitalistic order. Capitalism is only about 150 years old. During the comparatively short period of its existence, however, it has furnished mankind with a huge supply of various kinds of goods, which have done much to raise the level of living of the masses. Economically the working class is better off today that at any time in its history. Conditions as yet are not perfect and many abuses still persist, but we must give credit for improvement, because credit is due. Hours of work are shorter, conditions of employment are better, many of the evils of child and woman labor have been abolished, and the lot of the worker in many other respects has been greatly improved over what it was in the past.

The founders of the radical movements which have

been briefly described in this chapter predicted the downfall of capitalism as due to occur in their time. However, their prophecies have not been fulfilled. On the contrary, to all intents and purposes capitalism has continued to gain strength with the passing of time, although it has been considerably modified in character. It has expanded its control over an increasing number of countries and has swept aside every form of opposition.

During the last half of the nineteenth century, the radical movement was much stronger than it is at present. This was largely because the economic abuses were much greater in number and more serious in extent. Government ownership, especially of the railroads, coal mines, and telegraph and telephone systems, was very generally demanded. Today the demand for government ownership is seldom heard, except in connection with the campaign being waged for the public ownership of electric power enterprises. During the last decade of the nineteenth century and the first decade of the twentieth century, the single tax and socialist movements were also extremely active. Henry George, the leader of the single taxers, campaigned for the mayoralty of New York City. It was claimed at the time that he was elected but was "counted out" by the corrupt politicians. The socialists were successful in electing mayors and councilmen in various cities, representatives to state legislatures, and even members of Congress.

As a result of the conditions which existed during and immediately following the World War, the situation became greatly changed. Prosperity, high wages, steady employment, increased living comforts, improved working conditions, and the enactment of needed labor and factory legislation, all played their part in allaying much of the discontent which existed among the masses. To a surpising degree employers became more enlightened as to their responsibilities in safeguarding the interests both of their employees and of the public in general. For the first time, they appeared to appreciate the fact that labor is one of the most important elements in the economic life of the country, that it can easily "make or break" an enterprise, and that greater profits are to be had by working with labor than by working against it. Progressive employers led the way, and many others trailed along in the procession.

The attitude of business executives toward the public has also been modified to a marked degree. After the war they began to realize that it paid in terms of dollars and cents to work with the public, to serve its interests. The word "service" became the widely adopted slogan of business. Although greatly overdone at times and worn threadbare and frequently used merely as a catchword with no intention of living up to its implications, the slogan became the ideal of many companies. Whereas previously almost any sort of disreputable practice had been engaged in for the purpose of extracting money from the consumer, business now began to set its house in order, to advertise truthfully, to "stand behind" its products, and to conduct its affairs upon a much higher ethical plane. This change of attitude helped create a kindlier feeling on the part of the public toward business in general. Instead of "the public be damned," the ideal became "the public be served," because by serving the public greater financial returns could be obtained than by ignoring its interests.

Then, too, the old ideal of freedom of competition has been gradually abandoned, combinations, monopolies, and cooperation taking its place. Big business can afford to do much more for its employees and for the public than can small competitive enterprises. It has more funds; it has a more impregnable position; it has "bigger" and more farsighted executives. The changes in business policies have made possible a change in the attitude of the workers and of the public toward capitalism.

Coincident with these developments came a movement which no one had foreseen—the involvement of the general public and of the workers themselves in the capitalistic order. The radicals had consistently maintained that with the growth of capitalism would come the increasing concentration of the ownership of industry in the hands of a few people, who would "grind the faces of the poor" and oppress the workers to such a degree that the discontent of the latter would find an outlet only in their determination to overthrow capitalism and to substitute another form of society which would better conserve the interests of the masses. With the growth in size of industries, however, a few executives conceived the idea of selling the stock of their companies to employees and to the public. The movement began slowly at first but gathered momentum and adherents with the passing of time. Especially active in this connection were the larger industries and the public service corporations. Both groups succeeded in placing large blocks of their stock in the hands of those who had never before been stockholders in a corporation.

With the World War came the general subscription of the citizens to liberty and victory bonds. These people constituted a new investing class. When the war was over and some of the bond issues were paid, many of the citizens, having tasted the fruits of investment, became interested in the stock market. During 1927, 1928, and 1929 millions of them went into the market to speculate. They experienced the sensation of being capitalists, of being part owners in the business enterprises of the nation. They became more and more capitalistically-minded. The stock market crash of October and November 1929 caused heavy losses; but nevertheless it appears probable that the public will again be back in the market at the earliest signs of its recovery.

Instalment buying produced a similar effect. It enabled the working class to enjoy such comforts of life as automobiles, vacuum cleaners, and radios, as well as scores of other articles which previously had been the luxuries of the few. It raised their level of living and made them increasingly conservative. Union rules were openly violated by union members, and labor organizations found themselves unable to hold their membership or to prevent defections from their ranks, because the workers were eager to work overtime and on Saturday afternoons and Sundays, in order to get the money with which to meet their instalment payments. The workingmen could see no reason for joining the unions when their wages were kept at high levels by the action of the employers, who to a considerable degree had accepted the philosophy of high wages.

The working class, which had always been the recruiting ground for radicalism, thus turned a deaf ear to the arguments and appeals of those who desired the overthrow of capitalism. Only here and there, in small numbers, were to be found those who campaigned under the slogan, "Workers of the world unite! You have nothing to lose but your chains, and you have a world to gain."

Then came the depression of 1929 to 1931, with unemployment, misery, and discontent in its wake. The radicals renewed their campaign for the abolition of capitalism, the agitation being carried on for the most part under the leadership of the communist party of the United States, the members of which urged the adoption of the soviet ideals of Russia. Discontent always makes for radicalism; but the American people, having tasted of the fruits of a reformed and changed capitalism, have thus far refused to waver in their advocacy of conservative ideals. Business leaders, awakened to the disastrous effects of depression and unemployment, have become vitally concerned with the problem of stabilizing industry so as to avoid the possibility of a similar situation in the future. Whether or not they will be able to do so, the future alone will tell. Upon the continued contentment of the masses depends the continued existence of capitalism.

Efficiency and Radical Programs—Another objection that has been raised to the proposed radical programs is concerned with the matter of efficiency. At the basis of practically all schemes advocated by those who wish to supplant capitalism with some sort of ideal society lies the principle of industrial democracy. Inasmuch as democratic principles form the foundation of our political life, it is proposed that the economic life of the future should be grounded upon the application of similar principles. Enterprises, it is claimed, should not only be democratically owned but should also be democratically managed; in other words, the workers should have the right to dictate as to who shall direct production in the ideal state.

To any one acquainted with the results of democracy in politics the suggestion makes no appeal. We seldom induce the best men to run for office. When one of two opposing candidates is a politician, a hand shaker, and a popular figure, and the other is a skilled, well trained, efficient citizen but not a vote-getter, we generally elect the former. We vote, not for efficiency, but for popularity, and the popular candidate is seldom the person who is fitted to produce the best results. Nevertheless, in spite of the possible inefficiency of those who are in control, it appears that government is able to exist and to function, even though in a more or less unsatisfactory manner. Industry, however, is much more sensitive than government. It requires skilled direction. The citizens can live, at times with a fair degree of comfort, even when their government is corrupt; but the citizens cannot satisfy their economic desires if industry breaks down, as it frequently does even under the management of the skilled and trained executives of capitalism. No claim is made that all of our business executives are as skilled as they should be, but it must be admitted that they are forced to produce dividends for the owners of enterprises and that such results require the expenditure of their best efforts.

In an ideal state, with the masses voting for industrial managers, industrial commissions, and so forth, who would probably be selected—the trained, efficient person or the vote-getting politician? We know from our experience in politics that the public is a fickle employer. An officer who has served efficiently and well is frequently permitted to serve but one term. Industry cannot be operated with a constantly shifting staff of executives.

It is claimed by the radicals that the people will elect only the best men to office, because they will be interested in securing results from the administration of their industries. They do not do so today, however, in connection with getting results from political office holders. Why should they suddenly change in their psychological make-up and become vitally interested in the selection of the right kind of industrial leader? They are apathetic in fulfilling their political duties at present. What would get them interested in voting for the best men to carry on their socialized industries?

Some years ago it was claimed that if the voters were given the opportunity of nominating candidates for political office, they would nominate only the very highest grade of men. The direct primary was accordingly introduced. It still remains to be proved that this plan has brought about any better results than those obtained under the caucus method of nomination. It costs money to run for a political office. If the leaders of the socialized industries were chosen in the same manner, they would have to be known to the voters and accordingly would have to spend money for campaign purposes. It is questionable whether the best and most efficient men would become candidates and, if nominated, would be elected.

The Question of Size—The socialists look forward to having all of the industries of the nation owned and operated by the collectivist state. This would result in the complete concentration of ownership and management. Would not such a condition of affairs encounter the law of diminishing returns? Even in capitalistic industry, business executives are compelled to regulate the size of their plant or industry. The combinations and monopolies of today are small in comparison with those that would exist if all of the enterprises of the nation were consolidated in the manner proposed by the socialists. Could such large business enterprises be managed efficiently? If increased costs of operation reflected the law of diminishing returns, would not prices have to be increased?

Initiative—The matter of personal initiative also has to be considered. Will an executive work as hard for the public as he will for himself or for a group of owners who are constantly checking the results which he obtains? Will a public officer blaze new trails, devise new schemes, or initiate new enterprises, as does one who controls a private business? Who is to suggest that fashions be changed, that models of automobiles and machinery be brought up to date, that new processes be introduced? The worker dislikes to change his methods. He opposes the introduction of new machinery even though it has no effect upon his employment. Who would decide these and similar matters in the state of society proposed by the radicals? If all such matters were to be submitted to popular vote, the masses might be compelled to spend more time in voting than in producing goods to satisfy their wants.

Index

	PAGE
Ability to Pay Theory	434
Ad Valorem Duties	169
Advertising	156
Agriculture	
Land	112
Rent	343
Resources	113
Anarchists	525
Arbitration	327
Banks	398
Credit	251
Kinds of	253
Taxation of	459
Bargaining	
Collective	316
Theory of Wages	300
Barometers	417
Barter	243
Blacklist	326
Boycott	323
Business	138, 193, 216, 388
Barometers	417
Cycles	399
Capital	73, 95, 203
Depreciation of	136
Goods	96, 135
Obsolescence of	136
Ownership	105
Returns on	138
Sources of	99
Use of	102
versus Wealth	100

	PAGE
Capitalism	399
Indictment of	512
Modified	37
Strength of	530
Clayton Anti-Trust Act	242
Combinations	51, 215, 227
Compensation	374
Compulsory Investigations	328
Compulsory Revenues	432
Conciliation	327
Conservation of Labor Power	135
Conspiracy	231
Consumption	27, 69, 78, 80
and Capital	73
and Distribution	73
Control of	84
Defined	71
Goods	58
Government Aids in	86
Kinds of	78
Standards	80
Cooperative Markets	157
Corporation	103, 196, 207, 235
Taxes	453
Costs	146
Bulk Line	489
Joint	486
of Production	480
plus Profit	489
Credit	356
Bank	251
Basis of	250
Evolution of	249
Institutions	249
Cycles	399

	PAGE
Demand	469
Effect of Price on	475
Elastic	476
for Dollars	503
Inelastic	476
Depreciation	
of Capital Goods	136
of Labor	137
Diminishing	
Productivity	140, 225
Utility	77, 472
Distribution	29, 70, 266, 286
Division of Labor	122, 126
Geographical	123
Industrial	123
Occupational	122
Technical	122
Territorial	123
Dollars	
Demand for	503
Supply of	502
Duties	
Ad Valorem	169
Import	169
Specific	169
Earnings, Taxation of	457
Economics	15, 21, 24
Consumption	27
Differences of Opinion	25
Distribution	29
Divisions of	27
Exchange	28
Fundamental Concepts	55
Government in	44
Motives of	55

	PAGE
Economics—*Continued*	
Production	28
Reading	34
Social Science	21
Stages of	35
Employers	41
Associations	324
Employment	219
Exchanges	158
Management	330
Entrepreneur	97, 193
Excess Profits	394
Excise Taxes	442
Factor's Agreement	240
Factors of Production	92
Factory Acts	334
Federal Taxes	441
Federal Trade Commission Act	242
Foreign Exchange	243, 255
Foreign Trade	159, 255
Franchise Taxes	455
Goods	56, 61
Consumption	58
Economic	57
Free	57
Human	58
Non-Human	58
Production	58
Government	31, 44, 86, 245
Holding Companies	233
Import Duties	169
Income	14, 31, 62, 258
and Production	106
Classes of	259, 278
Division of	277

544   Index

                                                                                                PAGE

Income—*Continued*
- Gross 65
- Levels 85
- Money 66
- Net 65
- Personal 67
- Real 66
- Sources of 64
- Taxes 445

Industrial Unions 313
Industry, Localization of 123
Inheritance Taxes 443, 453
Insurance Companies, Taxation of 461
Interest 339, 355, 485
- Nature of 355
- Rates 357, 366

Interlocking Directorates 235
Interstate Commerce Commission 52
Labor 94, 107, 115, 218, 289, 311
- Arbitration 327
- Collective Bargaining 316
- Compulsory Investigations 328
- Conciliation 327
- Conservation of 135
- Demand for 300
- Depreciation of 137
- Division of 122
- Employment Management 330
- Factory Acts 334
- Importance of 116
- Industrial Peace 326
- Legislation 333
- Minimum Wage Laws 335
- Mobility of 133
- Obsolescence of 137

	PAGE
Labor—*Continued*	
Organized	314
Power	109
Productivity of	121
Profit sharing	329
Railroad Board	329
Social Status of	133
Supply of	118, 125, 126, 302
Use of	218
Workmen's Compensation	336
See also Unions	
Laissez Faire	46, 241
Land	107, 111
Agricultural	112
Price of	478
Lockout	326
Malthusian Theory	294
Management	386
Employment	330
Scientific	130
Marginal Firms	390
Marginal Productivity Theory	279, 298
Markets	90, 124, 149, 469
Agents of	151
Cooperative	157
Definition of	150
Necessity for	151
Produce	157
Stock	158, 213
Minimum Wage Laws	335
Money	243, 356
Functions of	246
Government Control of	245
Income	66
Paper	246

PAGE

Money—*Continued*
   Primitive 244
   Quantity Theory of 499
Monopoly 51, 215, 237
   Prices 490
Motor Vehicles, Taxation of 461
Municipal Taxes 461
Net Earnings, Taxation of 457
Obsolescence
   of Capital Goods 136
   of Labor 137
Organized Labor 314
Output, Restriction of 321
Overcapitalization 203
Overproduction 407
Panics 402
Partnership 103, 194
Picketing 324
Pools 230
Price 467
   Competitive 496
   Customary 487
   Determination 495
   Economy 467
   Fixation of 473
   General Level 498
   Monopoly 490
   of Land 478
   Problem of 468
   Scarcity and 470
   Stabilization of 505
Private
   Business 54
   Property 50
   Wealth 60

	PAGE
Produce Markets	157
Production	28, 87
and Income	106
Cost of	480
Factors of	92, 107, 111, 118
Goods	58
Large Scale	42, 215
Nature of	87
Roundabout	89
Productivity	366
Constant	142
Law of Diminishing	140, 225
Marginal, Theory of	279, 298
Profit	39, 373
Cost plus	489
Sharing	329
Profiteering	394
Property Taxes	449
Protective Tariff	169, 239
Public	
Authority	489
Consumption Monopoly	238
Expenditures	423
Policy	241
Receipts	423
Utility Taxation	456
Wealth	60
Railroad Labor Board	329
Rates	
Birth	118
Death	118
of Taxation	439
Railroad	184
Raw Materials	39, 124, 222
Reform	509

	PAGE
Regulation	
of Profits	394
of Railroads	187
Rent	339, 482, 485
Restraint of Trade	230
Restriction of Output	321
Revenue	
Assessments	435
Classification of	432
Compulsory	432
Contractual	432
Fees	435
Gratuitous	432
Public	432
Taxes	436
Rule of Reason	235
Sabotage	528
Savings	406
Scarcity	365, 470
Scientific Management	130
Sherman Anti-Trust Act	233
Single Tax	440, 524
Social	
Control	46
Phenomena	16
Rights	48
Science	21
Status of Labor	133
Waste	83
Wealth	61
Socialists	
Christian	514
Fabian	514
Guild	516
Marxian	516

	PAGE
Socialists—*Continued*	
Scientific	516
State	515
Utopian	513
Stabilization of Price Level	505
Standardization	43, 121
Standards	
Ethical	65
of Business	80
of Living	298
State Taxes	448
Stock	
Kinds of	199
Markets	158, 213
Ownership	198
Watered	206
Strikes	323
Supply	469, 473
of Dollars	502
of Labor	125
of Labor Power	118
Tariffs	168, 239
Protective	169
Taxation	
Ability to Pay Theory	434
Apportionment	451
Benefit Theory	433
Compulsory Revenues	432
Contractual Revenues	432
Corporation	453
Direct	437
Elasticity of	438
Equality in	437
Excise	442
Federal	441

PAGE

Taxation—*Continued*
  Fees 435
  Franchise 455
  General Property 449
  Gratuitous Revenues 432
  Gross Earnings 457
  Incidence 463
  Income 445
  Incorporation 455
  Indirect 437
  Inheritance 443, 453
  Multiple 440
  Municipal 461
  Net Earnings 457
  of Banks 459
  of Insurance Companies 461
  of Motor Vehicles 461
  Poll 438
  Public Utilities 456
  Rates of 439
  Shifting of 463
  Single 440
  Sources of 441
  Special Assessments 435
  State 448
Taxes 436, 448
Theory
  Ability to Pay 434
  Abstinence 360
  Accident 403
  Bargaining 300, 368
  Benefit 433
  Malthusian 294
  Mitchell's 408
  of Marginal Productivity 279, 298

INDEX

	PAGE
Theory—*Continued*	
of Standard of Living	298
of Wages	293
Quantity	499
Risk	364
Scarcity	365
Subsistence	293
Time Preference	363
Trade	
Domestic	151
Foreign	159
Restraint of	230
Unions	313
Transportation	177
Act of 1920	189
Railroad	**178**
Water	191
Treasury Certificates	431
Trusts	
Trustee	231
Voting	232
Unions	
Arbitration	327
Blacklist	326
Boycott	323
Closed Shop	319
Collective Bargaining	316
Compulsory Investigations	328
Conciliation	327
Hours	317
Industrial	313
Industrial Peace	326
Justification of	312
Label of	324
Labor	313

PAGE

Unions—*Continued*
   Lockout 326
   Picketing 324
   Railroad Labor Board 329
   Restriction of Output 321
   Strikes 323
   Trade 313
   Types of 312
   Wages 316
   Yellow Dog Contracts 325
Utility 56
   Diminishing 77, 472
Value 467, 474
   Intrinsic 474
Voting Trusts 232
Wages 289, 485
   Bargaining Theory of 300
   Customary 306
   Iron Law of 294
   Legal Rates of 306
   Rate of 303
   Theories of 293
Water Transportation 191
Watered Stock 206
Wealth 13, 59, 67
   Distribution of 257
   Private 60
   Public 60
   Social 61
   versus Capital 100
Wholesaler 151
Workmen's Compensation 336
Yellow Dog Contracts 325